The Embodied Word

ReFormations

MEDIEVAL AND EARLY MODERN

Series Editors:

David Aers, Sarah Beckwith, and James Simpson

NANCY BRADLEY WARREN

The Embodied Word

Female Spiritualities, Contested Orthodoxies,
and English Religious Cultures, 1350–1700

University of Notre Dame Press
Notre Dame, Indiana

Manufactured in the United States of America

Library of Congress Cataloging-in-Publication Data

Warren, Nancy Bradley.
  The embodied Word : female spiritualities, contested orthodoxies, and English
religious cultures, 1350–1700 / Nancy Bradley Warren.
      p.   cm. — (ReFormations, medieval and early modern)
  Includes bibliographical references (p.   ) and index.
  ISBN-13: 978-0-268-04420-6 (pbk. : alk. paper)
  ISBN-10: 0-268-04420-1 (pbk. : alk. paper)
  1. Christian women—Religious life—England—History.   2. Spirituality—
England—History.   3. England—Church history.   4. Christian women—
Religious life—Europe—History.   5. Spirituality—Europe—History.
6. Europe—Church history.   7. Women authors, English—Religious life—
Europe—History.   8. Christian literature—Women authors—History and
criticism.   9. Human body—Religious aspects—Christianity—History.   I. Title.
  BR747.W37   2010
  274.1'05082—dc22
                                                            2010024341

∞ *The paper in this book meets the guidelines for permanence and
durability of the Committee on Production Guidelines for Book Longevity
of the Council on Library Resources.*

For Norm Jones

Contents

Acknowledgments

THIS IS A BOOK THAT IN MANY RESPECTS CENTERS ON COMMUNITIES, and it has been my pleasure to be part of many supportive and nurturing communities in the process of writing it. I want to begin by thanking the two communities to whom I owe, in so many ways, the most: Florida State University and the National Humanities Center. I am grateful to the Council on Research and Creativity at Florida State University for a Planning Grant, an Arts and Humanities Program Enhancement Grant, and a grant from the Committee on Faculty Research for summer salary support. These grants enabled me to conduct the necessary archival research for this book. The National Humanities Center gave me a fellowship during the 2007–8 academic year that enabled me to complete much of the writing of this book. One of the true highlights of my professional life thus far, the fellowship provided not only material support for the writing of the book but also extraordinary intellectual enrichment. I thus want to extend a special thank-you to all the members of the 2007–8 class of fellows for your useful questions, wonderful conversations, and warm collegiality. Additionally, I want to thank all of the staff of the National Humanities Center for their friendship and kindness. Having a fellow deliver her second child on the first day of her fellowship, as I did, did not faze them at all!

Parts of chapters 2 and 3 appeared previously in an essay entitled "Life Writings in Middle English: Incarnational (Auto)biography," in *Twenty-First Century Approaches to Literature: Middle English*, ed. Paul Strohm (Oxford: Oxford University Press, 2007); this material appears here by permission of Oxford University Press. Part of the material in chapter 2 was previously published in "Tudor Religious Cultures in Practice: The Piety and Politics of Grace Mildmay and Her Circle," *Literature Compass* 3.4 (2006): 1011–1043. I am grateful to Wiley Blackwell for permission to reprint this material. Brief excerpts from chapters 2 and 3 are included in an essay (which focuses largely on the writings of Katherine Parr) entitled "Women's Religious Writing and Reformation" in the forthcoming volume *The History of British Women's Writing, 1500–1610*, ed. Jennifer Summit and Caroline Bicks (Palgrave, 2011).

I have had the privilege of participating in several other communities as I wrote this book, and their members have also done much to aid its development. I am grateful to the Renaissance Reading Group at Florida State University for insightful observations on drafts of several chapters. Leigh Edwards, Meegan Kennedy, and Candace Ward are my writing group comrades, and they have patiently worked with me through multiple drafts of several parts of this book. To Ralph Berry and Kathleen Yancey, excellent department chairs both, and to my colleagues in the English and Religion departments at Florida State University, my sincere thanks for providing such a collegial environment in which to work. A special thanks to the interdisciplinary medievalist gang at Florida State (Charlie Brewer, Rick Emmerson, Paula Gerson, David Johnson, Lynn Jones, Elaine Treharne, Rob Romanchuk, and Lori Walters, as well as all the graduate student members of our medieval reading group/ methodology seminar), for your scholarly expertise and your lively fellowship. *The Embodied Word* is specifically a book about religious communities, and I would be remiss if I did not thank my "evencristen," to use Julian of Norwich's term, of Old First Church in Tallahassee and Chapel of the Cross in Chapel Hill, North Carolina; members of both congregations provided love and support for me and my family in joyful as well as in difficult times, and for this I will always be grateful.

There are also many individuals who deserve particular thanks—indeed, far too many to name here, but please know that all of you have my sincere appreciation. I must begin by expressing my profound gratitude to Norm Jones, to whom this book is dedicated; if Norm had not introduced me to the writings of Grace Mildmay, and if he had not been so supremely willing to help a medievalist negotiate the initially foreign landscape of early modern Protestantism, this book would never have existed. To David Aers, Sarah Beckwith, and James Simpson, editors of this series, thanks for your faith in this project, for your keen intellects that have helped me improve it, and for your friendship, strong enough even to permit scholarly and theological disagreement! To Barbara Hanrahan, thanks for a steady hand on the editorial helm and for your good humor. To David Wallace, thank you for your own extraordinary work on female spirituality and historical periodization, which has done so much to inform my thinking, and for your seemingly boundless generosity both intellectual and personal. To Paul Strohm, to whom my intellectual debts go back the farthest and perhaps run the deepest, thanks as always for believing in my work and for asking me just the right questions to help me say what you know that I know, even when I don't know that I know it.

Finally, I must thank the members of my most intimate community, my family. To my parents, I thank you for raising me to appreciate communities of all sorts and for teaching me how best to be part of them. To Bill, with whom, in all the best senses, I am privileged to live in a relationship to which the phrase "I am you" applies, my thanks for understanding—me, the book, and everything else. And finally to my children: thanks to Drew, whose kindness, strength, and perseverance inspire me; and to Michael, whose sunny happiness fills me with joy and who every day reminds me that the "God of surprises" is good.

Introduction

From Corpse to Corpus

IN 1716, THE ENGLISH CARMELITE NUNS OF ANTWERP, NEEDING A LARGER crypt for burials, hired laborers, who took down "an entire side of the vault, in which eleven or twelve religious had been buried." One of these was Margaret Wake (in religion Mother Mary Margaret of the Angels), who "had been buried thirty-eight years and two months" and for whom the community "had a great veneration." The nuns thus ordered the workmen "not to disorder the bones, when they came to that grave, till some of the religious had viewed them." In the presence of three or four nuns, Mary Margaret of the Angels's coffin was opened, and "the Community was much surprised to find the body perfectly entire, fleshy, and formed."[1] Thomas Hunter, the Jesuit author of the account of these events, provides a detailed description, declaring that the body "appears of a brownish complexion, but full of flesh, which like a liveing body yields to any impression made upon it, and rises again of it self when it is pressed: ye joints flexible, you find a little moisture when you touch ye flesh . . . and this very frequently breaths out an odoriferous balsamick sent . . . [which] has sometimes filled ye whole roome."[2] The nuns called in various medical men and clerics, who arrived at the opinion that the body was indeed miraculously preserved and thus "the body of a saint."[3]

The prioress in 1716 was Mary Birbeck (in religion Mary Frances of St. Theresa), and the discovery inspired her to inaugurate a systematic program of writing the lives of the Antwerp nuns from the house's foundation in 1619 onwards.[4] In the account of Mary Frances of St. Theresa's own life, we are told:

> It pleased his divine goodness to discover in her time [as Prioress] the hidden treasure of the incorrupt body of our Venerable Mother Mary Margarett of the Angels [Margaret Wake] in the year 1716, and allso the remainder of that of Sister Anne of St Bartholme the year 1718, as it is related in what is said of her. She also procured ye writing the lifes of Mother Mary Xaveria and Mother Mary Margarett, the first by Reverend Father Thomas Hunter, the 2d by the Reverend Father Percy Plowden . . . she took pains her self to transcribe all the memoires for this, as she allso did when they were finished by the aforesaid authours.[5]

That the prioress would react to the discovery of a nun's miraculously preserved corpse by producing a corpus of writings consisting of nuns' spiritual biographies befits the corporeally focused piety characteristic of the Antwerp Carmelites. In this monastic community, "spiritual and somatic experience" frequently "converged."[6] For instance, in a characteristic incident Catherine Burton (in religion the aforementioned Mother Mary Xaveria) recounts having "our Blessed Savior . . . realy present in my breast in ye Blessed Sacrament."[7]

Mary Xaveria's Eucharistic experience not only unites the nun with Christ but also joins her with numerous medieval holy women who had such mystical experiences at communion, prompting us to consider the significance of past holy lives for these nuns. The production of a collection of life writings is a particularly apt response to the miraculous discovery of 1716, since the Antwerp Carmelites frequently turned to the *vitae* of earlier holy women to authorize their own lives. St. Teresa, an important figure for the Antwerp Carmelites, formed a key link in a chain of relationships through which the past underwrote, and was animated in, the present. Not only was she the order's founder, but she also herself "drew on the earlier example of Catherine of Siena."[8]

The roles of texts, and especially life writings, in shaping the Carmelite nuns' lives transcended those of authorizing particular forms of spirituality by providing examples of recognized female holiness, or even of enabling *imitatio*. Textual accounts of past holy lives played quite literally formative roles in the nuns' own lives. Mary Birbeck's "Life," written as part of the ongoing program she began, elucidates a specifically textual dimension of the Carmelites' understanding of identity. It indicates that in her youth she had "yet never a thought of becoming religious on the contrary seemed on occasions quite averss to it." She was inspired to become a nun, however, by reading the life of St. Teresa of Avila:

> She thought it allmost impossible for her to save her soul if engaged in the world and, being allways a great lover of reading and looking into all books she met with, was once in ye chamber of a priest, tumbling over his little liberary and he, perceiving it, chid her for disordering his books, but bid her chuse any one and he would lend it her most willingly. Upon which she was put to a stand, and viewing them all she fixed upon one that was placed very high which had a guilt back, without knowing what it was. The priest told her she had made an excellent choice, for it was the life of the great St Teresa, upon which they had some discourse of the wonderfull saint and Holy Order &c. She read it severall times over, and every time was more and more delighted with it, till at last she was so effectually confirmed in ye thoughts of ye dangers of the world and the security of a religious life, and so inspired with desire of being of her Holy Order that she immediately begged the same Father to procure her admittance here, which he did.[9]

This scene in which reading the life of St. Teresa catalyzes Mary Birbeck's vocation demonstrates that texts provide a vehicle through which others' lives can be re-embodied, brought to life again in the reader's life.

A saint's earthly lived life made into a *vita* becomes for Mary Birbeck a *forma vitae.* That is, reading the life of St. Teresa causes a change in Mary Birbeck's very selfhood and subsequently in the form of her life when she is professed, conforming her life to another text, that of the Carmelite monastic rule. Her reincarnation of St. Teresa's *vita* is marked by the change in her name to Mary Frances of St. Theresa; her religious name marks the merging of her identity with that of the saint whose "Life" prompted her vocation. Mary Birbeck's own "Life" in turn offers itself to others as, perhaps, a formative text for their own lives, a text that can be reincarnated by future readers.

The textually mediated connection between St. Teresa and Mary Birbeck illustrates that just as the corporeal and the spiritual are not readily separable in the Antwerp Carmel, so too boundaries between selves and others both past and present are permeable. The textually forged, open-bordered forms of subjectivity characteristic of the Antwerp Carmelites make putting forth the community's history as a collection of individual nuns' lives especially appropriate. The individual and the communal are both fully present in these women's lived and textual lives, and the one is always informed by the other. The Carmelite nuns' life writings reveal a "sense of 'a social self lodged within a network of others.'" For these women religious, the self is both "reiterative" and "relational."[10] Appropriately, the "Lives" produced in the Antwerp Carmel blend first- and third-person accounts, as we see in the "Life of Mary Xaveria," which combines Mary Xaveria's autobiographical writings with Thomas Hunter's presentation of her life.

The embodied and textual lives of the Antwerp Carmelites create meaning not only in their monastic community but also in larger cultural contexts from the local to the international. Father Hunter indicates that following the discovery, the physicians who examined the corpse and other eyewitnesses could not refrain from spreading the news, and the existence of the incorrupt body at the nunnery was "immediately published all over the town." Crowds gathered at the Carmel, to the extent that, "[o]nce or twice, at the opening of the gate upon some necessary occasions," the throngs "surprised the religious and rushed in in great numbers, in so much that they were several times obliged to call soldiers from the citadel to guard the inclosure."[11] The news traveled further still, and the "concourse of people who came even from the neighbouring towns was so great, that the nuns could not for some days open their gate upon any account." With access barred, those gathered sent in "such numbers of beads, medals, pictures, linens, &c., to be touched that it was sufficient employment for one or two religious for many days to comply with their request in touching the body and bringing them back."[12] This scene highlights the extraordinary spiritual power attributed to holy bodies, power that could be transmuted to and through other individual and communal bodies via the circulation of material objects.

The town folk of Antwerp and neighboring cities were not the only ones to take an interest in the discovery at the nunnery. High-ranking government officials too became involved: "The Governor, Prince d'Escula, led the guard twice himself, and being permitted to see the body, he cast himself at her feet, kissing them with tenderness and many tears, blessing Almighty God that he had lived to see such a precious treasure in his Government. The next day he sent the Princess, his spouse, who was also wonderfully moved with devotion and piety, and in token of her respect she took the ring off her own finger and desired the director of the monastery to put it on the finger of the holy body, where it yet remains."[13] The participation of the prince and princess draws our attention to the ever-present political potency of holy bodies. Their involvement attests to their faith in the spiritual benefits available from the miraculously preserved corpse and to their devotion to the religious foundation. Their public acts of veneration also suggest, at least potentially, their sympathy with (perhaps even support for) the nuns' ongoing program of opposition to the English Protestant state.[14]

Both the English Carmelite house at Antwerp and the English Carmelite nunnery at Lierre were quite knowledgeable about, and intimately involved in, English politics in the seventeenth and early eighteenth centuries. Thanks to Queen Henrietta Maria's Catholicism, the Royalist faction was considered to be sympathetic to that faith and to the return of monastic communities to Britain. Not surprisingly, "The Carmelites at various times gave shelter to 'distressed cavaliers' . . . , and the religious appear to have been well aware of the intricate politics of the court in exile during the English Civil War."[15] The Royalist and pro-Catholic causes were of interest not only to the nuns, who in the "Carmelite papers . . . represent themselves as true patriots, praying for the 'poor distressed country of England,'" but also to the Catholic powers of the Habsburg Netherlands.[16] Mary Margaret of the Angels's miraculously preserved body might well have seemed to the nuns and their supporters to be a symbolic validation of their political position. The miracle was ripe for use in making the case for the divine approval of a re-Catholicized Britain, and the holy body's symbolic value could be enhanced and multiplied through textual representation. Complex relationships of past and present again obtain. The past in a sense lived in the present in the incorrupt body of Mary Margaret of the Angels; her preserved corpse metonymically stood in for the preservation of the English Catholic cause. Her body thus at once represented the ongoing existence of the Catholic realm of the past and acted as a catalyst for action to re-form (and reform) that body politic in the present.

The fact that Father Hunter reminds his audience of the precise date of Mary Margaret of the Angels's death "thirty-eight years and two months ago"—that is, 1678—seems politically significant. The year 1678 was that of the so-called "Popish Plot," and several of the Antwerp Carmelites, as well as their fellow English Carmelites at Lierre, had family members who fled England in the persecutions that ensued following the revelation of the plot.[17] That Mary Margaret of the Angels died in that year but, as the discovery of her preserved body suggests, still endured in 1716 not only implies divine favor but symbolically suggests the endurance of the Catholic cause as well. Such a positive sign bestowed on the English Carmelite nunnery and on the Catholic cause was probably particularly welcome in light of the state of political affairs in 1716. The previous year had witnessed the failure of James Stuart ("James III" or "The Old Pretender") to seize the throne through military force and to restore a Catholic monarchy, and many members of the exiled convents in the Low Countries had strong alliances with the Jacobites. The discovery of the miraculously preserved body could thus provide hope to the Catholic cause at a difficult juncture.

I begin with a fairly extended consideration of this series of events because they foreground precisely the tight, complex relationships among bodies and texts, pasts and presents, selves and others, that run through the writings and devotional practices of the women both Catholic and Protestant considered in this book. The miraculous discovery of 1716, and the textual production connected with it, provide us, quite literally, with a corpus of life writings of holy women founded upon a holy woman's incorrupt corpse. Both the corpse and the textual corpus it engenders bear witness to the very bodily nature of the spirituality of the English Carmelite nuns. They highlight the centrality of gendered, holy bodies for and in the history of the monastic community as well as of the English body politic. The events of 1716 manifest a set of foundational concepts that cast long shadows simultaneously forward and backward through medieval and early modern religious cultures Catholic and Protestant, orthodox and heterodox. These concepts are incarnational piety, incarnational epistemology, incarnational textuality, and incarnational politics, and through the subsequent chapters they constitute the bones giving form to the corpus of this book.

By *incarnational piety,* I mean devotional practices and forms of spirituality focused on embodied interactions with holy bodies, especially those of Christ and the Virgin Mary—as when Mary Xaveria has "our Blessed Savior realy present" in her breast when she receives the Eucharist. *Incarnational epistemology* refers to processes of knowledge production and acquisition grounded in corporeal, sensual, and affective experiences—as when the Antwerp nuns and clerics come to know Mary Margaret of the Angels's sanctity through sight, touch, and smell. In *incarnational textuality,* porous boundaries obtain between embodied writers and readers and the textual corpus, as we see in the Carmelite life-writing project sparked by the discovery of the incorrupt body and in the way in which the *vita* of St. Teresa becomes a *forma vitae* for Mary Birbeck. Finally, I use the term *incarnational politics* to describe visions and revisions of bodies politic shaped or legitimated by holy bodies, and particularly by the sufferings of holy bodies.

I also begin with the 1716 events at the Antwerp Carmel precisely because they fall at the very end of the period under consideration in this study; indeed, they fall just beyond the terminus date given in the book's subtitle. Beginning just beyond the imagined end point of the study highlights that this book is, quite deliberately, not organized according to a strict chronological trajectory from medieval to early modern. Though the first chapter concentrates at length on medieval texts and the final chapter concentrates extensively on early modern writings, the book's arguments do not assume a teleological progression from earlier to later, or from Catholic to Protestant. Indeed, quite the reverse is true, and one central aim of this book is to explore dialogic relationships between pasts and presents, to explore continuities and changes in concert.

Accounts of English religious culture have historically tended to organize themselves so that Catholicism and Protestantism, the medieval and the early modern, are mutually exclusive "others."[18] Each religion, each period, is often defined in large part by not being what the other is, or by being what the other is not; each embraces absolute, and opposed, categories of orthodoxy and heterodoxy. Furthermore, in each period a particular type of relationship between the individual and God is purportedly central to orthodox religious practice—an institutionally mediated relationship in the case of medieval Roman Catholicism, a personal and independent one in the case of early modern Protestantism. There is certainly some truth in this well-established way of seeing the religious landscape. However, this paradigm has its roots in the polemic generated by early modern religious strife, and its continued survival is to a large extent grounded in equally polemical disciplinary and scholarly conflicts. At the heart of this project is a desire to reconsider the binaries of medieval and early modern, Catholic and Protestant, domestic and foreign, orthodox and heterodox, that have obscured important aspects of English religious cultures. The phrase "contested orthodoxies" in this book's title thus refers as much to our contemporary academic orthodoxies concerning historical periodization and disciplinary organization as it does to confessional controversies in the medieval and early modern periods.

I also quite deliberately began my explorations of *English* religious cultures with events taking place beyond England's shores to complicate the national borders that so often, and so problematically, separate studies of "English" and "Continental" women's textual and devotional cultures. "Englishness" itself is a category whose nature and definition this project revisits. Thus, throughout this book, in examining English religious cultures, I spend a great deal of time with women who were not English by birth or who, though of English origin, spent much of their lives across the English Channel, as did the members of the Antwerp Carmel.

I open, furthermore, with this very late early modern case because the modes of piety and subjectivity operating among the Antwerp Carmelite nuns call into question a particularly troublesome, though long established, way of demarcating the categories of the medieval and the early modern. The lives and "Lives" of these eighteenth-century nuns are explicitly as well as implicitly sutured to medieval holy women's lives. The Carmelites exhibit forms of selfhood and modes of knowledge acquisition dependent on complexly continuous relations of past and present, interior and exterior, self and others. These early modern nuns force one to reconsider interpretive paradigms in which the early modern period is defined by a conceptualization of history that sharply divides past from present and by an awareness of subjectivity predicated on separations of interior from exterior, of self from others. In contrast, the medieval period, understood in such interpretive paradigms as the "other" against which the early modern is identified, is marked by a notion of temporality that precludes historical awareness and a notion of subjectivity that excludes interiority.[19] For example, to set up medieval forms of identity as a foil to the emergent Renaissance subject, Jonathan Dollimore argues, quoting Walter Ullmann, that in the Middle Ages "what mattered was . . . not the individual but society, the corpus of all individuals."[20]

As the case of the Antwerp Carmelites begins to show, and as I will explore at length in subsequent chapters, there is a sense in which scholars who espouse such views speak part of the truth, but, crucially, only part. As we shall see in the writings of such figures as Julian of Norwich, St. Birgitta of Sweden, Margery Kempe, and St. Catherine of Siena, in medieval female spirituality the "corpus of all individuals" does matter intensely, though not to the exclusion of individuality and certainly not in a way that allows us to presume that "the struggle for self-knowledge might legitimately be said to have its roots in protestantism and Renaissance humanism."[21] On the contrary, texts associated with all of these medieval women are fundamentally predicated on individual experience and the struggle for self-knowledge. As Rachel Fulton and Bruce Holsinger argue in their introduction to *History in the Comic Mode: Medieval Communities and the Matter of Person,* "[W]hile certain types of individualism, subjectivity, self-consciousness, and so on are undeniably perceptible in medieval culture, just as crucial to our understanding of these types must be the processes, institutions, associations, and roles that enable their emergence."[22]

Additionally, in some respects clear chronological separations between past and present do indeed break down in medieval forms of devotion. This breakdown, though, neither precludes nor excludes an awareness of history and historicity. Brigittine texts, St. Catherine's writings, *The Book of Margery Kempe,* and Julian's *Showings* combine a transcendence of history with a profound awareness of their own historical moments as well as of their, and their society's, own developments through historical time.

As the lives and "Lives" of the Carmelite nuns with whom this introduction opens have already shown, furthermore, the "corpus of all individuals" continues to matter intensely in the early modern period. One might readily repurpose Fulton and Holsinger's argument cited above by simply replacing "medieval culture" with "early modern culture." The English Benedictine nuns of Cambrai, Paris, Ghent, and Dunkirk considered in subsequent chapters will provide further evidence of this persistence of the communal.[23] Aemilia Lanyer's poetry, Grace Mildmay's meditations, and Anna Trapnel's prophecies and life writings, analyzed in chapters 1, 2, and 4 respectively, also reveal that the ongoing importance of the "corpus of all individuals" does not obtain only for early modern Catholic women who might be perceived as doggedly holding on to tattered remnants of a so-called "Age of Faith"![24]

Similarly, as the life writings of the Antwerp Carmelites have already demonstrated, something like the "undifferentiated temporality" so frequently assigned to medieval religious culture continues to exist in, and to inform relations of past and present in, the early modern period. Past and present are not always fully or readily separable in the early modern period, any more than are self and others, or body and spirit. To put it simply, in both medieval and early modern women's religious writings from diverse confessional origins, individuals and communities, bodies both personal and corporate as well as both past and present, matter together.[25] In the writings of the medieval and early modern women that I analyze, there is clear evidence of interiority and individuality; in both periods, however, these exist in dynamic, mutually constitutive interactions with corporeal bodies and corporate communities.

In the first chapter, entitled "The Incarnational and the International: St. Birgitta of Sweden, St. Catherine of Siena, Julian of Norwich, and Aemilia Lanyer," I explicate the modes of incarnationality running through this study to show how they enable us to build bridges between pasts and presents, selves and others. I turn initially in this chapter to the early part of the period under consideration in this book, the later fourteenth and early fifteenth centuries. I analyze the articulations of the incarnational paradigms that shape the events of 1716 in the lives and writings of three very important figures in later medieval English religious culture: St. Birgitta of Sweden, St. Catherine of Siena, and Julian of Norwich. These medieval holy women have, as later chapters demonstrate, important early modern afterlives. Additionally, as their appellations indicate, two of these three figures are not of English origin, one being a Swedish noblewoman and the other the daughter of an Italian dyer. Their significant roles in English religious cultures throughout the period of study further illuminate the profoundly international aspects of these cultures, even, perhaps especially, at moments when England struggled to craft a political identity separating itself from such Continental power centers as France, Spain, and Rome.

Because in the eighteenth century the English Carmelites of Antwerp still turned to texts, figures, and devotional practices drawn from medieval female spirituality in crafting their monastic identity, the resonances between their engagements with incarnational paradigms and those found in the fourteenth- and fifteenth-century holy women do not jar our expectations. In the final part of the first chapter, however, I turn to the early modern poet Aemilia Lanyer's *Salve Deus Rex Judaeorum* to explore medieval incarnational legacies in a Protestant context where our expectations have not been conditioned to lead us to look for them. Lanyer, who lived in the temporal interval separating the medieval holy women discussed in the first sections of chapter 1 from the Carmelite nuns with whom the introduction begins, further exemplifies the internationality and confessional complexity of the English cultures under consideration. Her father, Baptist Bassano, an Italian immigrant to England, is described in his will as a "native of Venice," and his family may have converted to Christianity from Judaism.[26] Her mother, Margaret Johnson, an Englishwoman who was Baptist's common-law wife, had connections with families (especially the Vaughan family) that had ties to the strongly reformist branch of the English Church.

Though Lanyer's *Salve Deus* is generically different from the life writings, accounts of mystical experience, and letters produced by the medieval women writers considered in the first chapter, it in fact shares much with those works in its subject matter, philosophical underpinnings, and textual operations. The important place of incarnationality in various forms in Lanyer's poetry initiates a series of explorations of continuities across confessional and temporal boundaries. These continuities have revisionary power not only for their own sociohistorical moments in which they reshape social relations among selves and others but also for our contemporary moment as they prompt us to rethink analytical categories and scholarly practices that are the ideological scripts for our own critical and professional cultures.

In the second chapter, I trace the early modern legacies of Julian of Norwich as I continue to revise some established views of English religious cultures Catholic and Protestant, medieval and early modern. Entitled "Medieval Legacies and Female Spiritualities across the 'Great Divide': Julian of Norwich, Grace Mildmay, and the English Benedictine Nuns of Cambrai and Paris," chapter 2 consists of a comparative exploration of the texts and devotional practices of Julian of Norwich, seventeenth-century English Benedictine nuns living in Cambrai and Paris, and a Protestant gentry woman named Grace Mildmay (b. 1552,

d. 1620). At its heart lies a desire to grasp what remains constant, as well as what changes, in the ways in which these women experience and theorize relationships between humans and God. At the same time, my aim is to shed light on the ways in which individual experiences of the divine, especially gendered, bodily experiences expressed textually, signify for others both personally and sociohistorically.

I turn first to the English Benedictine nunneries established in Cambrai and Paris after the Dissolution of the Monasteries. Women religious in these communities read and copied Julian's *Showings*; indeed, these communities played a vital role in the survival of Julian's texts. Margaret Gascoigne's writings provide representative examples of Julian's importance in this branch of English religious culture. In her and her religious sisters' engagements with Julian's texts, and in their own devotional and textual practices that were so strongly influenced by medieval female spirituality, affect and politics interpenetrate. Suffering human bodies, the textual corpus, and the corporate bodies of monastic communities intersect.

That early modern English Catholic women exiled from a Protestant England and devoted to the preservation of the "old religion" should form attachments to a woman whose writings and modes of spirituality embody "the medieval" is not terribly surprising, although the sustained importance of medieval female spirituality in the post-Reformation period is a little-studied cultural phenomenon. More surprising are the strong affinities between Julian's *Showings* and the nearly one thousand manuscript pages of meditations and spiritual autobiography written by Grace Mildmay. In the second part of chapter 2 I turn to a comparative exploration of Julian of Norwich's and Grace Mildmay's texts read alongside those of Margaret Gascoigne to examine the significances of medieval affective and contemplative piety for a woman belonging to a religious tradition that is so often understood as defining itself in opposition to such forms of devotion. Here too important continuities exist in the ways in which bodies, especially suffering bodies, and words shape each other, and shape communities, across a confessional as well as a temporal divide. Here too a political component to textual and corporeal negotiations of past and present exists, since Grace Mildmay's engagement with the spirituality of the past informs her visions of the constitution of the body that is the church and her attitudes toward the body that is the English nation.

The English Benedictine communities of Cambrai and Paris demonstrate that shaping an English body politic could take place beyond the confines of English shores. In chapter 3, entitled "Embodying the 'Old Religion' and Transforming the Body Politic: The Brigittines of Syon, Luisa de Carvajal y Mendoza, and Exiled Women Religious during the English Civil War," I build a clearer case than has yet been made for the profound importance of Spain as a nation and of women as spiritual subjects in forging distinctive forms of early modern Englishness strongly aligned with medieval religious culture. Like the Benedictine nuns of Cambrai and Paris and the Carmelites of Antwerp, members of the English Brigittine community of Syon, who following the Dissolution fled first to the Low Countries, then to Rouen, and finally to Spanish-controlled Lisbon, participated in simultaneous enterprises of spiritual conservation and oppositional nationalism. These nuns too formed bonds with a figure from the medieval past who had overlapping spiritual and political significance. For the Brigittine nuns in exile, the figure and writings of St. Birgitta of Sweden filled a role similar to that played by Julian of Norwich for the English Benedictines, or St. Teresa for the English Carmelites of Antwerp. The early modern Brigittines interpreted their experience of exile through the lens of the saint's *imitatio Christi* and the persecution she underwent in her career as a prophetic channel for God's Word.

The Brigittines of Syon and their English Catholic supporters in exile likewise formed connections with a Spanish woman engaged in her own embodiment of the "old religion," Luisa de Carvajal y Mendoza. Luisa played a vital, though largely overlooked, role in promulgating an oppositional model of English Catholic identity in the seventeenth century. She had a strong commitment to the Jesuit English Mission and, through her Jesuit connections, was closely connected to the "Syon circle" on the Continent. She traveled to England to aid English Catholics in 1605, the fraught year of the Gunpowder Plot that stirred up so much anti-Catholic sentiment in England. While in England, she founded a quasi-monastic order called the Society of the Sovereign Virgin Mary, Our Lady, the foundational texts for which demonstrate, I argue, significant Brigittine resonances.

The cases of the Syon nuns and of Luisa de Carvajal y Mendoza suggest that women not only aided in preserving English Catholicism in domestic settings, as many scholars have argued, but also took on more public and explicitly political roles—even, paradoxically, when they did confine themselves within domestic or monastic enclosures. In the final section of chapter 3, I look ahead to the years of the English Civil War and Protectorate, the historical environment for one of the central figures of chapter 4, to consider the ongoing, intersecting participation of Spain and English female monastic communities in oppositional English Catholic affairs. The chapter thus closes with a consideration of the roles played by the textual and devotional activities of the English Benedictine nuns of Ghent and Dunkirk in Royalist politics in the middle of the seventeenth century.

An overarching theme found in the writings of the eighteenth-century Carmelites of Antwerp, the fourteenth-century anchoress Julian of Norwich, the Tudor gentry woman Grace Mildmay, and the early modern nuns of Syon is that the autobiographical is both theological and political. In understanding the theological and political significance of the autobiographical, the body is, furthermore, central. Accordingly, the fourth chapter, entitled "Women's Life Writing, Women's Bodies, and the Gendered Politics of Faith: Margery Kempe, Anna Trapnel, and Elizabeth Cary," undertakes a dialogic, comparative analysis of these three women's (auto)biographical writings.[27] The fundamental place of the body in these women's piety, texts, and sociopolitical activities calls into view further continuities across temporal and confessional boundaries.

At first glance, Margery Kempe, Anna Trapnel, and Elizabeth Cary seem a disparate group indeed. Respectively, they are a fifteenth-century mystic, a seventeenth-century Baptist and Fifth Monarchist, and a seventeenth-century Catholic convert and author who became the subject of a biography written by one of her daughters, who was a nun in the English Benedictine community at Cambrai. Yet in spite of their different faiths and the divergent political situations in which they practiced their faiths, these women, separated by more than two hundred years and by the upheaval of the Reformation, conceived of their relationships with Christ in similarly personal yet political terms. Their relationships to the divine as gendered, embodied subjects are central to their spiritual lives as well as to their social lives within their communities. In crafting and representing their lives, they all use a multivalenced "body language." By this term I mean their bodily gestures and practices that signify so powerfully in their times and in their texts; I also refer to their language both written and oral that is so inseparably, and at time troublingly, linked to their female bodies. My readings of *The Book of Margery Kempe,* Anna Trapnel's *The Cry of a Stone* and *Anna Trapnel's Report and Plea,* and *The Life of Lady Falkland* highlight how all of these women turn texts into life even as they turn life into texts.[28] Strikingly, in the process these women, who themselves destabilize the boundaries between orthodoxy and heterodoxy, enact nearly identical self-authorizing strategies in publicizing their experiences of the divine both performatively and textually.

The final chapter, entitled "The Embodied Presence of the Past: Medieval History, Female Spirituality, and Traumatic Textuality, 1570–1700," addresses the politico-cultural uses of medieval history and medieval female spirituality in texts written by men in the service of competing orthodoxies. I treat works that present cases of exemplary feminine piety as well as texts that invoke feminine piety for purposes of stigmatization. In this chapter, figures from previous chapters return, and Spain once again makes its presence felt in English religious cultures. St. Catherine of Siena plays an important role, and St. Birgitta of Sweden functions as a sort of touchstone. I examine the nature and significance of St. Birgitta's appearance in sixteenth- and seventeenth-century texts both Catholic and Protestant that circulated at key moments of political uncertainty, including the furor surrounding the 1570 papal bull *Regnans in excelsis,* the succession crisis of the closing years of Elizabeth I's reign, the controversy in the 1620s surrounding the proposed "Spanish Marriage" of the Prince of Wales and the Infanta Maria, and the tumult occasioned by the deposition and execution of Charles I.

In relation to the bull *Regnans in excelsis,* I consider John Foxe's *Acts and Monuments,* a text that I see in some ways as the most Catholic of Protestant polemical works. I concentrate particularly on the edition published in 1570, an edition in which Foxe greatly enhances the role of the persecuting Catholic Church. In this version, particular medieval female saints (including St. Birgitta and St. Catherine of Siena), the genre of medieval hagiography, and Spain all feature importantly. In this case incarnational piety and politics serve to demonize the Catholic Church and the realm of Spain—in part by strongly connecting the two to each other—as foils for a Protestant England led by the Virgin Queen. The material is, however, slippery. It becomes all too easy to imagine the Virgin Queen to whom the edition is dedicated becoming, at the hands of Philip of Spain (or another Catholic prince inspired by the papal bull), a virgin martyr not unlike those of the medieval hagiography that the representations of Protestant martyrs do so much to evoke even as Foxe asserts his rejection of Catholic saints and their "Lives."

For recusant Catholics, and particularly for members and supporters of the highly politically involved community of English Brigittines in exile on the Continent, St. Birgitta serves as a figure of *true* English religion in a false Protestant age. As such, she becomes a nexus around which spiritual and nationalistic agendas coalesce, as the Jesuit Robert Parsons's *A Conference About the Next Succession to the Crowne of England* (1594) reveals. In Protestant texts, St. Birgitta's role is even more complex. Though Foxe recuperates her for the Protestant cause in the 1570 *Acts and Monuments*, using the critiques of papal corruption in her revelations to support his antipapal stance, in many Protestant writings she serves as a negative exemplar of "popish superstition," as in William Guild's *Anti-Christ pointed and painted out* (1655). I argue that she is singled out so frequently for this role in part because of her gender, since pejoratively feminizing the Catholic past is a common strategy in Protestant polemic, and in part because she did become so strongly associated with England during the fourteenth and fifteenth centuries. As a female saint who married and had children, she also is invoked by such writers as Thomas Goad in *The Friers Chronicle, or The Trve Legend of Priests and Monkes Lives* (1623) to make a case for the merely feigned chastity of nuns and the tainted, feminized nature of the Catholic Church as the "Whore of Rome" or "Whore of Babylon."

A particularly interesting appearance of St. Birgitta occurs in William Pomfret's *The Life of the Right Honourable and Religious Lady Christian*

Late Countess of Devonshire (1685). Christian Cavendish, significantly the dedicatee of Goad's *Friers Chronicle,* is described as living a religious life that puts that of St. Birgitta to shame. But as the author negotiates the political complexities of Christian's commitment to the Royalist cause in conjunction with her anti-Catholicism, the line separating Christian Cavendish from the medieval, Catholic spirituality embodied by St. Birgitta blurs. Indeed, in Pomfret's *Life* Christian ends up looking a great deal like the very saint from whom he takes such pains to distinguish her. The *Life of Christian Cavendish* thus strikingly reveals the ways in which the figure of St. Birgitta, and other dimensions of the medieval, Catholic, English past, can take on lives of their own in early modern texts and politics.

Chapter One

The Incarnational and the International

St. Birgitta of Sweden, St. Catherine of Siena,
Julian of Norwich, and Aemilia Lanyer

BODIES, BOOKS, AND BORDERS

In the miraculous events that transpired at the Antwerp Carmel in
1716, and in the texts produced as a result, we see the operations of incarnational piety, epistemology, textuality, and politics bringing into
focus some problems with such binary categories as medieval and early
modern, domestic and foreign. This chapter adds Catholic and Protestant to that list of problematic binaries as I examine the spiritual, philosophical, and historical meanings of incarnational paradigms in English religious cultures. I turn first in this chapter to a set of influential
women from the beginning of the period under consideration in this
book, women whose devotional practices, texts, and sociopolitical engagements are profoundly infused with the incarnational: St. Birgitta of
Sweden, St. Catherine of Siena, and Julian of Norwich. In the final section of this chapter, I examine the workings of incarnational paradigms

in the seventeenth-century Protestant poet Aemilia Lanyer's *Salve Deus Rex Judaeorum.* Lanyer's work dramatizes complex relationships between the medieval and the early modern as well as the Catholic and the Protestant, not to mention the domestic and the foreign, given her half-English, half-Italian heritage.

Reading these medieval and early modern women's texts in conversation with each other reveals that across both temporal and confessional divides, incarnational paradigms shape the ways in which women conceive of relationships among gendered selves, God, and human others. Indeed, it is through incarnational paradigms that such relationships are socially formed, historically categorized, and textually mediated. These shared qualities demonstrate that the "otherness" of medieval Catholicism and early modern Protestantism is only partial and provisional, not absolute. I have no desire to embrace an extreme revisionist position and claim that nothing really changed at the Reformation, and I have even less desire to embrace an essentialist position concerning the unchanging nature of woman or of female religious experience. However, the landscape of English religious cultures looks rather different when it is viewed through a gendered lens, and in this chapter I outline the contours of a new map of that landscape, a map to which subsequent chapters will add considerable detail.

St. Birgitta of Sweden, St. Catherine of Siena, and Julian of Norwich initially suggest themselves for joint consideration because they are closely contemporary holy women who produced substantial bodies of written work, much of it grounded in experiences of divine revelation. St. Birgitta's textual output includes not only the vast corpus of her *Revelations* but also a monastic rule and the lessons for the daily offices of the Brigittine nuns. St. Catherine is equally famous for her learned *Dialogue* and for her hundreds of letters addressed to popes, kings, nuns, and common people. Julian of Norwich produced both a Short Text and a Long Text of her *Showings.* All three of these women, therefore, had to extensively negotiate the complex processes involved in transforming embodied experiences of God, and especially of the incarnate Christ, into texts. Throughout these negotiations, their lives and texts illustrate the richly interpenetrating natures of words and bodies both divine and human. Furthermore, these figures and their texts played influential roles in English religious cultures not only in the holy women's own time but also well into the early modern period.

In connecting St. Birgitta, St. Catherine, and Julian of Norwich, my aim is not to prove the influence of one person or text upon another person or text. I do, however, want to sketch some connections among figures, places, and channels of textual transmission linking these three holy women, because such connections help establish the international complexity of English religious and textual cultures. They also illuminate the far-reaching scope of the political spheres both ecclesiastical and secular in which medieval and early modern female spiritualities are so intimately imbricated.[1]

St. Birgitta and St. Catherine have important links to each other in Italy, where Birgitta spent much of her life following her widowhood and the inauguration of her visionary career, as well as in England. After Birgitta's death in Rome in 1373, Pope Gregory XI sent her confessor Alphonso of Jaén to Catherine of Siena. Members of Catherine's *famiglia* were subsequently involved in translating Birgitta's *Revelations* into Sienese Italian.[2] Both saints were passionately committed to the cause of the Roman papacy; St. Catherine was in fact envisioned as a successor to St. Birgitta in supporting this cause.[3] The two saints appear together in a fresco, painted in 1368, in Santa Maria Novella's Spanish Chapel in Rome, an image designed to proclaim support for the Roman papacy and the Holy Roman Empire.[4]

Both St. Catherine's and St. Birgitta's involvements in ecclesiastical politics intersect with embroilments in secular conflicts. St. Catherine actively participated in contentious Italian civic affairs, matters never too far removed from papal politics, and English people too engaged in this strife, as the example of the mercenary John Hawkwood—a recipient of correspondence from St. Catherine—indicates.[5] In St. Birgitta's revelations, a topic of serious concern is the Hundred Years' War between England and France, a struggle that also overlaps with the papal schism, since England not surprisingly supported Rome (as St. Catherine may have encouraged English monarchs to do) while France took the side of the Avignon papacy.[6] Indeed, St. Birgitta's revelations concerning the right of the English king to the French throne helped make her an English "patron saint," and her revelation concerning the resolution of the conflict through marriage was known in England in the fourteenth century and continued to circulate, being brought to prominence at strategic moments, into the sixteenth century.[7]

The presence and prestige of St. Birgitta's and St. Catherine's writings in England expanded in the fifteenth century, and the holy women's texts often circulated in tandem.[8] Henry V founded the Brigittine house of Syon in 1415, and the nunnery quickly became the wealthiest and one of the most politically influential nunneries in England. Syon was known for its vibrant textual culture, and this religious community was the initial audience for the Middle English version of Catherine's *Dialogo*, entitled *The Orcherd of Syon. The Orcherd* found much wider circulation when Wynkyn de Worde printed it in 1519; he also printed a translation of the Life of St. Catherine of Siena that William Caxton likely prepared for publication.[9] This translation of St. Catherine's *vita* was probably made by Thomas Gascoigne, Chancellor of Oxford, who was also the author of the Latin text of St. Birgitta's life, which he then translated into Middle English for the Syon nuns. As was the case with Brigittine texts, St. Catherine's writings had an established place in the libraries of the politically influential in fifteenth-century England. For instance, "Among the 'holy matter' that Cecily duchess of York had read to her during dinner was the work of 'St. Kateryn of Sena.'"[10]

The English religious Adam Easton and William Flete play key roles connecting St. Birgitta and St. Catherine to each other and to England; they also bring Julian of Norwich into the picture. Though Julian as an anchoress might seem aloof from the sorts of social involvements that fill the lives and writings of St. Birgitta and St. Catherine, she is part of the same international, politically involved network. Furthermore, as I will argue at length in chapter 2, her *Showings* too has strongly political implications, especially for the English women religious who read and preserved her writings in their monastic foundations on the Continent.

Adam Easton was an English Benedictine educated and professed at Norwich Cathedral. He became cardinal priest of Santa Cecilia in Trastevere, perhaps as early as 1381. He was involved in examining the orthodoxy of Birgitta's writings in 1382–83, and he wrote a key defense of her for her canonization process. Julia Bolton Holloway indicates that he knew Catherine as well as Birgitta, and though we cannot know whether, as some have suggested, Easton influenced Julian of Norwich by introducing her to the writings of Continental holy women, we do know, at the least, that when he died in Rome in 1397 he left his extensive library of some 228 books to Norwich Cathedral Priory.[11]

William Flete was born about 1320 in southeast Lincolnshire, where he was educated and professed as Augustinian. Prior to leaving England for Italy, Flete was, as Aubrey Gwynn has noted, ideally placed geographically to be inculcated with ideas of the great figures of fourteenth-century English spirituality.[12] It is entirely possible that he may have passed on these ideas to St. Catherine, a possibility that prompts us to acknowledge that the circulation of cultural paradigms need not be understood as flowing only from the Continent to England. For instance, Benedict Hackett, who dates Flete's first meeting with St. Catherine to 1368 rather than 1374, emphasizes Flete's influence on Catherine as a theological advisor.[13] In Italy Flete lived in a hermitage at Lecceto, and he became a prominent member of Catherine's *famiglia;* shortly before her death, Catherine named Flete as the director of her *famiglia.*[14] Flete provides another potential link connecting St. Catherine and Julian of Norwich, since his letters to English Augustinians, including some discussing Catherine, circulated widely among houses of his order, and there was an Augustinian foundation adjacent to Julian's anchorhold. It would be quite fitting if Julian of Norwich did come to know of St. Catherine through Flete's letters, since, as I will discuss shortly, St. Catherine's own letters do so much to create an international community centered on incarnational spirituality.[15]

The nexus of personal and textual connections linking St. Birgitta, St. Catherine of Siena, and Julian of Norwich illustrates the wide reach of devotional practices and texts manifesting, as I shall show, the intersecting set of incarnational paradigms that I set out in the introduction. *Salve Deus Rex Judaeorum,* the only known poetic work of Aemilia Lanyer, demonstrates that the reach of these incarnational paradigms so prevalent in later medieval Catholic religious culture extends into early modern Protestant culture as well. Aemilia Lanyer published *Salve Deus Rex Judaeorum* in 1611, the same year that the King James Bible appeared. Though clearly different in genre from the mystical texts of St. Birgitta, St. Catherine of Siena, and Julian of Norwich, *Salve Deus Rex Judaeorum* shares a great deal with the earlier women's writings. Lanyer's title, alluding to the scene of Christ's crucifixion, signals the text's involvement with incarnational piety. In explicating this title, Lanyer signals that her poetry may not be all that ontologically different from medieval women's mystical texts, since it too originates in some respects in an experience of divine revelation. Lanyer writes:

> Gentle Reader, if thou desire to be resolved, why I give this Title, *Salve Deus Rex Judaeorum*, know for certaine; that it was delivered unto me in sleepe many yeares before I had any intent to write in this maner, and was quite out of my memory, untill I had written the Passion of Christ, when immediately it came into my remembrance, what I had dreamed long before; and thinking it a significant token, that I was appointed to performe this Worke, I gave the very same words I received in sleepe as the fittest Title I could devise for this Booke.[16]

This passage, which closes the *Salve Deus,* not only emphasizes the centrality of incarnational piety to the work but also calls our attention to the presence of incarnational epistemological and textual systems, the functions of which I will analyze in the final section of this chapter. The experience of writing about Christ's passion leads Lanyer to an understanding of the title revealed in her earlier prophetic dream, and the two together give her self-knowledge of her divine call, her authorization to write, and her mandate to "performe this Work." As I shall also explore in the final section of this chapter, Lanyer's *Salve Deus Rex Judaeorum,* which creates a textual female community in its inclusion of numerous dedicatory poems addressed to women and which is, as the concluding poem, "The Description of Cooke-ham," makes clear, in some way connected with Lanyer's experiences with a community of women, embraces a version of incarnational politics in which female bodies both individual and collective are central.[17]

Incarnational Piety: Producing, Consuming, and Uniting with the Body of Christ

The *Myroure of Oure Ladye* consists of a Middle English translation of the Brigittine lessons and divine service accompanied by an explication of them for the Syon nuns. This text, so important to the creation of Syon's monastic culture, recounts the scene of the lessons' origin in a revelation to St. Birgitta by an angel. In this dramatic episode, incarnational piety, epistemology, and textuality operate together. The account emphasizes the bodies of St. Birgitta as recipient and inscriber, and the angel as a re-later, of divine words. The bodily presence of Christ in the sacrament also features prominently. The *Myroure* author indicates that St. Birgitta had a chamber adjoining the Church of St. Laurence in Rome "& a wyndo to the hye auter, wherby she myght se the body of chryste eche day."[18] He continues:

> In the chambre saint Birgit eche day aftyr she had saide her houres, & her prayers, she made her redy to wryte with pen, & ynke, & paper or parchemyn so abydyng the angell of god, and when he came he stode by her syde right vp moste honestly. hauynge all way hys face with reuerence berynge and beholdynge towarde the aulter where the body of chryst was hyd and closed in a box as the maner ys. And so stondynge he endyted the sayde legende dystynctly and in order, in the moderly tongue of saynte Brygytte, and she full deuoutly wrote yt eche day of the Aungels mouthe. (19)

In the presence of Christ's body created by the priestly words of institution, St. Birgitta participates in a scene reminiscent of both the Annunciation and the Nativity. Through her bodily labor of inscription on the parchment she makes the divine Word spoken by the angel into a corpus written in her mother tongue. Textual labor, material labor, sacramental labor, and maternal labor overlap. Words and bodies participate in a recursive reproductive cycle in which the creation of a text whose subject is the Incarnation (a text meant to be brought repeatedly to life through the nuns' divine service) is itself brought to life as St. Birgitta reincarnates the Virgin Mary's act of translating the divine Logos into the "mother tongue" of human flesh.[19]

The central roles of bodies in the origins of the divine service that shapes Brigittine monastic life make abundantly clear the profoundly incarnational character of Brigittine monastic culture. Incarnational piety—devotion centered on the human bodies of Christ and the Virgin Mary, and particularly on the events of the Nativity and the Passion—is at the heart of Brigittine identity.[20] Sustained, dual emphasis on Mary's and Christ's bodies is appropriate to an order called the "Order of St. Saviour" and "ordeyned," as the Middle English *Rewyll of Seynt Sauioure* states, by Christ "pryncipaly to the worship of his holy moder."[21] As the author of the *Myroure* reminds the nuns, their divine service is designed especially to thank the Virgin Mary for her role in Christ's incarnation: "And for all your seruice ys of oure blessed Lady; therfore yt ys good that ye entende specyally therin, her praysyng and worship, and that god be thanked and praysed for all the gyftes, & benefytes that he hathe gyuen to her & by her to all mankynde" (61). In performing their divine service, the Brigittine nuns accordingly participate each week in the range of processes that enabled the enfleshing of the divine Logos, from Mary's own conception, birth, and life through Christ's nativity.[22] For example, the elaboration of the third lesson at Thursday matins treats Christ's corporeal existence and Mary's role in taking on a human body: "In thys lesson ye are enformed of foure thynges. First of the meruelous incarnacyon of oure lorde Iesu cryste. . . . The second thynge . . . ys to thanke and to love oure lorde Iesu cryste for hys incarnacyon and oure redempcyon. The thyrde thynge ys of hys meruelous entre in to the vyrgyns wombe and of hys longe abydynge therein. and of his meruelous goynge thense. The forthe ys that all folke shulde ioy of hys holy incarnacion and pray our lady . . . to brynge them to endelesse lyfe" (*Myroure*, 228–29). The translation of the lesson continues by explaining that Christ gave "hym selfe to the vyrgyns bowels by all her body. fourmyng to hymselfe most honestly a body of man of the flesshe & blowde of the onely vyrgyn" (230).

Brigittine divine service also concentrates the nuns' attention on Christ's corporeal experiences, particularly on the Passion. The Friday services all deal in some way with Christ's passion. The explication of the hymn from Friday lauds provides a particularly detailed account of the physical torments of the Crucifixion. The *Myroure* author states, "In the second verse of this hympne. We named xiiii poyntes of oure lords passion" (252), which are "spyttynges scourges. A spere, thretenynges. repreues. the crosse. betynges, naylles. thornes. dethe. woundes. galle. bondes. swellynge of flesshe" (252). The author clarifies in precise, graphic, even clinical, detail the last of these points. He writes, "For as ye may se when a man ys wounded. bothe sydes of the wounde swellyth and ryseth vp hyer then other partyes aboute yt. And when a man ys buffetted. or bette. the skynne, and the flesshe aryseth and swellyth. so dyd the holy flesshe and body of oure lorde Iesu criste when he was bounde and scourged. and buffetted and wounded" (252).

Incarnational piety is by no means idiosyncratic to Brigittine spirituality. Indeed, as has long been noted, Marian devotion and concentrated attention to Christ's nativity and passion, often combined with intense Eucharistic piety, are fundamental features of the affective spirituality so characteristic of later medieval female holy women. Not surprisingly, these devotional emphases make frequent appearances in the writings of Julian of Norwich and St. Catherine of Siena (though their devotional practices tend to exhibit somewhat less attention to the Virgin Mary in comparison to the strongly Marian orientation of Brigittine piety). To provide just one of numerous potential examples from the Long Text of the *Showings*, Julian, who longs for a "bodily sight" of Christ's passion, describes a mystical experience of Christ's suffering in great physical detail:

> I saw the bodily sight lasting of the plenteous bleding of the hede. The gret droppes of blode felle downe fro under the garlonde like pelottes, seeming as it had comen oute of the veines. And in coming oute they were browne rede, for the blode was full thicke. And in the spreding abrode they were bright rede. And whan it came at the browes, ther they vanished. And notwithstanding the bleding continued tille many thinges were sene and understonded, nevertheless the fairhede and the livelyhede continued in the same bewty and liveliness. . . . This shewing was quick and lively, and hidous and dredfulle, and swete and lovely.[23]

In Catherine of Siena's *Dialogue,* arguably the most important and most theologically sophisticated of her writings, a vitally important image is that of Christ as the bridge that joins God and humanity.[24] Christ as bridge makes connections between humankind and God possible and also makes the text of the *Dialogue* possible. In the Middle English *Orchard of Syon* (the version of the *Dialogue* made for the Brigittine nuns of Syon), God tells St. Catherine: "But firste I wil that thou loke the brigge of my sone, and that thou biholde the greetnes of that brigge which streccheth fro the heiȝt of heuene down to the erthe."[25] The bridge is explicitly figured as being composed of Christ's suffering body; God says that the stones and walls of the bridge were not laid "tofore my sones passyoun." After the Passion, though, "the stoones weren sett and leyd upon the body of myn holy sone, he made up the wal of stoones, and medlid it the chalk, and foorgide and foormede it with his precious blood."[26] Further, God explicates the body/bridge as having three stairs corresponding to three spiritual stages: first, Christ's feet; second, his side; and third, his mouth.

I want to stress that my concern with incarnational piety does not rest simply with the fact that St. Birgitta, St. Catherine, and Julian of Norwich are intensely devoted to the bodies of Christ and Mary. Nor does it lie with the well-established fact that these women's devotion often manifests itself in markedly corporeal ways. Rather, as what follows in this chapter and subsequent chapters will demonstrate, my interests are in the ways in which incarnational piety is put into practice in women's lives both private and public, and in the implications of such practices for women's texts and sociohistorical engagements.

INCARNATIONAL EPISTEMOLOGY: FEELING, BEING, AND KNOWING SELF AND OTHER

As we have seen in the lives and "Lives" of the English Carmelites of Antwerp, incarnational piety is complexly entwined with distinctively corporeal modes of coming to know the self and the divine. At the heart of Brigittine texts, St. Catherine's writings, and Julian of Norwich's *Showings* we similarly find multifaceted, though ultimately unified, quests for knowledge of self and God, and these epistemological journeys depend heavily upon the body. Frederick Bauerschmidt's assessment that in Julian's *Showings* seeing and knowing are "intensely somatic," that perception and knowledge of God and of oneself cannot be restricted "within the domain of consciousness," applies equally well to St. Catherine's writings as to Brigittine texts.[27] To take up the philosopher Stanley Cavell's claim in his work on Wittgenstein's *Philosophical Investigations,* in these women's spiritualities and their textual manifestations, "The human body is the best picture of the human soul. . . . The body is the field of expression of the soul. The body is *of* the soul; it is the soul's."[28] The spiritual truth that was written in the body of Christ, the Word made flesh, is made manifest in and through bodies that feel: in the bodies of the holy women and, as we shall see, also in the bodies of those who read their texts and, in reading, come to embody those texts themselves in their own lived experiences. In other words, as corollaries to their incarnational piety, St. Birgitta, St. Catherine, and Julian all exhibit commitments to incarnational epistemology.

For St. Catherine of Siena, her "journey towards God was also a journey into herself. In the journey towards God, which brought her at the same time to the depths of her own being, Catherine became more and more united with God and more and more unified within herself."[29] Catherine's statement in a letter to Madonna Jacoma is revealing; she instructs the recent widow, "[F]ind your pleasure in prayer, where you will come to a better knowledge of both yourself and God" (T264, 2:483). Similarly, in a letter to Raymond of Capua, she speaks to him of "the Lamb slain and abandoned on the cross," telling him to attend "the school of the Word . . . because it is there true teaching is found." She then directs him, "Look at yourselves, for in him you will find yourselves, and in yourselves, him" (T226, 2:5).

St. Catherine's directive to focus on the "Lamb slain and abandoned on the cross" in order to gain knowledge of the self and of God through the "school of the Word" reveals that self-knowledge and knowledge of God fundamentally depend on embodied experiences of suffering, emotion, and love. Caroline Walker Bynum points out that "hateful as body may have been to Catherine, it was *body* that she saw as uniting us to the body of God."[30] In a letter to Monna Giovanna di Capo and a woman simply called Francesca, Catherine aligns embodiment, self-knowledge, and knowledge of God to the extent that she posits the Incarnation itself *as* an epistemological event, a catalyst for the production of knowledge. Speaking of the need to hate what God hates, she says: "And this hatred— where can we get it? Only from knowledge of ourselves, from recognizing that we are not. This is what banishes all pride and infuses true humility. This knowledge lets us discover the light and the generosity of God's goodness and boundless charity, which is not hidden from us. It was, of course, hidden to our coarseness until the Word, God's only-begotten son, became incarnate. But once he had chosen to be our brother, clothing himself in the coarseness of our humanity, it was revealed to us" (T108, 3:22). Catherine posits that we know God only through knowing ourselves and that we can achieve such knowledge only through Christ, because Christ took on human, embodied form. Knowledge requires embodiment.[31]

Some scholars have argued against the importance of the bodily in Catherine's writings: for instance, Mary Zimmer claims that the *Dialogue* is not a work of affective piety, thus distancing Catherine's text from this corporeally focused tradition.[32] I would argue, though, that the *Dialogue* is very much a work of affective piety in precisely the same sense that Julian's *Showings* and Brigittine texts are works of affective piety. That is, all suggest the inseparability of affect, especially affect in its most bodily manifestations, and knowledge of the divine. Zimmer, referencing Suzanne Noffke, states that the significance of Christ's body for Catherine is not "its ability to stimulate emotional response, but rather . . . its ability to figure complicated theological concepts."[33] This argument poses a false dichotomy; Catherine's writings makes clear, as do Brigittine texts and Julian's *Showings,* that emotional responses grounded in embodied experience are inextricably bound up with complex theological concepts.

As I have already suggested, *The Myroure of Oure Ladye* is a text in large part about Mary's and Christ's bodies, and it is a text by nature made to be embodied by the nuns in performing the divine service.[34] The *Myroure* reveals that in the epistemological system underwriting the Brigittine divine service, seamless interactions of body, mind, and spirit obtain; feeling and knowing integrate with each other. Elizabeth Psakis Armstrong argues that the *Myroure*'s author would not embrace the idea that the nuns should "kee[p] mind and heart in separate boxes."[35] In Brigittine spirituality, bodies are not, to appropriate another of Cavell's formulations, veils or things that "come between [one's] mind and the other"; rather, bodies are crucial means to knowledge of self and others, including the divine Other.[36] Appropriately, this text so central to the formation of Brigittine nuns' individual and communal identities stresses at the beginning the role of the body in performing the words of the divine service. At the same time it emphasizes the importance of harmony between bodily and intellectual effort. In the first prologue the author writes, "And thus from Sonday tyll Saterday, dayly, wekely, and yerely; ye ar occupyed with youre tongues in oure Ladyes seruyce, wherfore ye ought to take hede, that your myndes be as besy and contynually occupyed aboute the same things by inwarde vnderstondynge and deuocyon" (*Myroure*, 5–6). Interior and exterior, minds and tongues, should work together to serve Our Lady and, in so doing, to reincarnate Christ's incarnation in the nuns' present time through the divine service.

When instructing the nuns in how properly to perform their divine service, the author of the *Myroure* further describes a process uniting body, mind, and heart. Complementing the joint attention given in the service itself to the interactions of the corporeal, the emotional, the spiritual, and the intellectual, he writes: "For ryght as bodely meate is not ryght profytable, but yf yt be wel chewyd in the mouthe & swolued in the stomacke; so thys holy seruyce, but yf yt be well chowed in the mynde, & sauerly felte in the harte, yt fedyth not the soulle sufycyently. & therfore sayth saynt Bernarde that yt profyteth but lytel, to syng only with the voyce, or to say only with the mouthe, wythout entendaunce of the harte" (40). This framing of divine service as food to be consumed by the mind and felt in the heart as it is performed by lips and voice recalls the monastic concept of *lectio divina* as *ruminatio*.[37] This passage also resonates with the scene in which the angel reveals the nuns' lessons to St. Birgitta; this scene, as we have noted, emphasizes the presence of Christ's Eucharistic body, a body that is food to be incorporated into the recipient's body for spiritual nourishment, even as the act of consumption incorporates the communicant into Christ's body.

A distinctive addition to the daily round of monastic offices enhances the Brigittine order's emphasis on embodiment as fundamental to intellectual and spiritual life. The Brigittine nuns are instructed by their rule to "haue in the monastery a beer & a grave to be contynually in your syghte. The beer in mynde of dethe & the graue in mynde of the laste dome. when all bodyes shall aryse out of theyre graues" (*Myroure*, 142; see also *Rewyll*, 66v–67r). Each day after terce, the community is to gather at this grave to sing the *De profundis*. As they do so, the abbess is instructed to "castyth oute a lytel erthe with tow fyngers. for then the soulle and body that are vnderstonded by the two fyngers and are sondered here by dethe. shall then be knytte a geyne togyther euerlastyngely" (*Myroure*, 142). A ritual centering on the body's fate in death and resurrection involves the abbess's performing bodily action to catalyze understanding of the spiritual realities of salvation. The collect that follows this ceremony too foregrounds bodies—those of the Virgin Mary, the incarnate Christ, and the nuns themselves—making clear the roles of those bodies in salvation history as well as in individuals' salvation:

> Lorde, holy fadir, þat keptist the body which þoue toke to thi sonne
> of the virgyn marie vnhurt in the grave and reysidyst it vncorrupt,
> we beseche þe: kepe oure bodies clene & vndefoyled in thyn holy
> seruice, & dresse so oure weyes in this tyme, þat whan þe grete
> deedful day of dome comyth, oure bodies more be reysid vp among
> thy seyntys. & oure soules ioye with the euerlastyngly & deserue to
> be felaschippid with thy chosyn. In the name of the fadir & of the
> sonne and of þe sonne & of the holi gost. Amen. (*Rewyll*, 66v–67r)

As do Catherine's writings and Brigittine texts, Julian's *Showings* posits that knowledge of self and God are coextensive. She says, "It longeth to us to have thre manner of knowyng. The furst is that we know oure lorde god. The seconde is that we know oureselfe, what we ar by him in kinde and grace. The thyrde is that we know mekely what oureselfe is anemptes our sinne and anemptes oure febilnes" (349). Indeed, she emphasizes the inseparability of the very existences of self and God, saying: "For oure soule is so depe grounded in God, and so endlessly tresored, that we may not come to the knowing thereof tille we have furst knowing of God, which is the maker to whome it is oned. But notwith-stonding, I saw that we have kindly of fulhed to desyer wisely and truly to know oure owne soule, wherby we be lerned to seke it ther it is, and that is into God. And thus by the gracious leding of the holy gost, we shall know them both in one" (301).[38]

The opening of Julian of Norwich's *Showings* reveals her profound reliance on embodiment as a crucial means to knowledge of self and God. Julian "did not think, with Augustine, that 'no pure truth can be expected from sensation,' nor did she think, with Occam, that univer-sals or concepts exist only in the mind."[39] The *Showings* originates, as is well known, with a series of revelations that Julian experienced in 1373. When she was precisely thirty years and six months of age, Julian, who desired to have both bodily illness and an in-depth awareness of Christ's passion comparable to that of the eyewitness Mary Magdalene, suffered from a near-fatal episode of disease. During her sickness, Julian con-centrated her attention on a crucifix, and, she says, at what she perceived to be the point of death, "[S]odenly all my paine was taken from me and I was as hole . . . as ever I was befor" (133). She was initially unhappy not to have been "delivred of this world" but was subsequently moved anew to desire that "my bodie might be fulfilled with mind and feeling of his blessed passion. . . . For I would that his paines were my paines" (133). This desire catalyzes a revelation of "the red bloud" that "trekile[s] downe from under the garlande, hote and freshely, plentuously and lively, right as it was in the time that the garland of thornes was pressed on his blessed head" (135). As Nicholas Watson states, "Far from going beyond her sight of Christ's body in its pain and glory as she ascends to God in rapt contemplation, Julian's revelation, at her own insistence, brings her back and back to that body, which remains for ever the medium through which the whole pattern of the divine plan is understood."[40] As it is for St. Cath-erine, for Julian the incarnation is itself an epistemological event; Christ's body is the source of knowledge, and her own body is the means by which that knowledge is acquired.

In the incarnational epistemological systems evident in the writings of St. Birgitta, St. Catherine, and Julian of Norwich, the inner and the outer are, as in a Wittgensteinian framework, not readily separable from or opposable to each other.[41] As P. M. S. Hacker writes in his commentary on Wittgenstein's thought, "What we so misleadingly call 'the inner' *infuses* the outer. Indeed, we could not even describe the outer save in the rich terminology of the inner."[42] Julian of Norwich's sophisticated conceptions of substance and sensuality admirably illustrate the complicated relationship of inner and outer—or, one might say, of soul (or mind) and body. Substance and sensuality do *not* refer to soul (or mind) and body respectively; nor do they differentiate the categories of divine and human. Julian articulates that substance and sensuality, which are properties of the soul, involve the soul and the body alike, even as they involve both God and fallen humanity. Julian writes, "For I saw full sekerly that oure substance is in God. And also I saw that in oure sensuality God is. For at the same point that oure soule is made sensual, in the same point is the citte of God, ordained to him fro without beginning; in which citte he cometh and never shall remeve it. For God is never out of the soule, in which he shalle wonne blissefully without end" (299).[43]

Incarnational piety and incarnational epistemology participate in the empathetic hermeneutic tradition described by Karl Morrison. This hermeneutic tradition does not depend on the stark separation of intellect and emotion required by empiricism but rather interprets understanding as "affective, imitative, progressive, and assimilative."[44] The empathetic hermeneutic tradition is characterized by the signature phrase "I am you," and in incarnational piety and incarnational epistemology, just as interior and exterior exist in complexly interpenetrative relationships, so too do self and other. As Morrison observes, the sentence "I am you" gestures "toward an inward communion beyond the external bonds of association in society, and beyond dialogue between 'I' and 'you' as separate persons. It points toward an identity beyond relationship, a common human identity that enhances the separate identities of individual persons."[45] The "I" of St. Birgitta's, St. Catherine's, and Julian of Norwich's texts is hence an "I" that is individual but simultaneously is—or strives to be—not *only* individual. It is an "I" constituted not simply in opposition to others but with reference to others. This open-bordered, outward-reaching "I" resonates with a paradigm that Cavell develops in part 4 of *The Claim of Reason*, a paradigm that has been called "intersubjectivity." Intersubjectivity "emphasize[s] the role of the other in the journey toward the realization of one's future self."[46]

Intersubjectivity permeates Julian of Norwich's *Showings*. When the suffering caused by Julian's illness is miraculously taken from her, it becomes clear that her relationship with Christ goes beyond imitation to become an intersubjective relationship. Following her miraculous recovery, Julian meditates upon her revelation of Christ's bleeding body, of his disfigured flesh, and says, "And in alle this time of Cristes presens, I felte no paine, *but for Cristes paines*" (183; emphasis added). The desire that she expresses in the opening of the *Showings* that "his paines" would be, as she says, "my paines" is fulfilled. Julian feels in her body Christ's very pain—not simply pain *like* his, not pain experienced in imitation of his, but the identical pain he suffered.[47] Julian's intersubjective relationship with Christ makes clear that for Julian, the divine and the human experience each other in recursive, reiterative mutual engagements. Julian's meditations on substance and sensuality are again instructive. Emphasizing that substance is shared by created humanity and the Trinitarian God in which the incarnate Son is incorporated, Julian writes:

> And I sawe no difference between God and oure substance, but as it were all God. And yet my understanding toke that oure substance is in God: that is to sey, that God is God and oure substance is a creature in God. For the almighty truth of the trinite is oure fader, for he made us and kepeth us in him. And the depe wisdome of the trinite is our moder, in whom we are all beclosed. And the hye goodnesse of the trinite is our lord, and in him we are beclosed and he in us. We are beclosed in the fader, and we are beclosed in the son, and we are beclosed in the holy gost. And the fader is beclosed in us, the son is beclosed in us, and the holy gost is beclosed in us: all mighty, alle wisdom, and alle goodnesse; one God, one lorde. (297)

The reciprocal enclosures (we are in the Father, Son, and Holy Ghost even as the Father, Son, and Holy Ghost are enclosed in us) highlight the ways in which interior and exterior as well as self and other blend, intersect, and inform each other.

Significantly, one of the most important words in Julian of Norwich's *Showings* is *kinde,* a word that in Middle English encompasses a complex variety of meanings, several of which Julian draws upon simultaneously. For instance, in writing of Mary's suffering with Christ at Christ's crucifixion, Julian says, "For in this I saw a substance of kinde love, continued by grace, that his creatures have to him, which kinde love was most fulsomly shewde in his swete mother" (185). She continues, bringing herself and all humanity into the equation: "Here saw I a gret oning betwene Crist and us, to my understonding. For when he was in paine, we ware in paine, and alle creatures that might suffer paine suffered with him. . . . For it longeth kindly to ther properte to know him for ther lorde, in whom alle ther vertuse stondeth" (185). *Kinde* for Julian refers to bodily existence (including bodily suffering), affect (including the valences of love, compassion, and mercy that the adjective *kind* carries in modern English), and nature (human, divine, and that of the created world). It also relates to knowledge acquisition as a process in which embodied selves and others both human and divine jointly participate. Julian, like her near contemporary the great poet and theologian William Langland, privileges what Langland calls "kinde knowing."[48] "Kinde knowing" is an epistemological mode that depends on feeling, loving, suffering, all of which one experiences in one's own body but all of which are at the same time inextricably bound up with others' bodily experiences of the same phenomena (including the experiences of the wounded, and hence literally open-bordered, body of Christ). "Kinde knowing" is thus crucial to intersubjectivity and is precisely the form of knowledge upon which the empathetic hermeneutic tradition is founded.

The opening passage of St. Catherine's *Dialogue* includes a striking self-portrait that provides a snapshot of processes like those that enable Julian to have Christ's very pains, processes by which "kinde knowing" makes possible the empathetic, intersubjective identity evoked by the statement "I am you." She writes: "A soul . . . has for some time exercised herself in virtue and has become accustomed to dwelling in the cell of self-knowledge in order to know better God's goodness toward her, since knowledge follows love. . . . [T]here is no way she can so savor and be enlightened by this truth as in continual humble prayer. . . . For by such prayer the soul is united with God, following in the footsteps of Christ crucified, and through desire and affection and the union of love he makes of her another himself."[49] The experience of coming to know herself ("dwelling in the cell of self-knowledge") and the embodied experience of imitating Christ ("following in the footsteps of Christ crucified") lead St. Catherine to a union with Christ in which she becomes "another himself."

In a letter to Raymond of Capua, Catherine articulates at some length the overlapping affective, embodied experiences and epistemological operations that make possible self-knowledge and the knowledge of God, even as she brings one's relationship with one's neighbors into the picture. She says:

> But I'm sure that if you are bound and set ablaze in the gentle Jesus, all the devils of hell with all their cunning will never be able to tear you away from so sweet a union. . . . I don't want you ever to stop throwing wood on the fire of holy desire—I mean the wood of self-knowledge. This is the wood that feeds the fire of divine charity, the charity that is gained by knowing God's boundless charity. Then we become one with our neighbors as well, and the more fuel we put on the fire (I mean the wood of self-knowledge), the more intense grows the heat of our love for Christ and for our neighbors. Stay his, then, within self-knowledge, and don't be caught outside yourselves. (T219, 2:90−91)

Union with Christ ignites the fire of holy desire, which is fed by self-knowledge. Self-knowledge in turn increases one's knowledge of God, especially of God's endless love. Knowing divine charity leads to union with one's neighbors, and the whole set of intersecting relationships (rather like Julian's multiple, mutual enclosures) exist in a continuous, self-perpetuating cycle.

A similar dynamic relying upon multiple mergings of identities enabled by shared, embodied experiences plays a constitutive role in

establishing subject positions in the Brigittine *Myroure of Oure Ladye.*
The *Myroure*'s numerous descriptions of Christ's passion and Mary's
compassion illustrate the place of intersubjective relations in knowledge acquisition. The third lesson at Friday matins, for example, "tel-
lyth of the sorowes that our lady suffered in tyme of the passyon of her
holy sonne our lorde Iesu Criste" (247). The explication of the lesson
emphasizes the ways in which Christ and the Virgin Mary alike undergo
interconnected bodily suffering with which the nuns identify through
their divine service:

> And when the mother se the sonne scorned with the crowne of
> thornes. and hys face made redde of the blode. and hys chekes
> rody of great buffettes. she wayled in most heuy sorowe & then
> for gretnesse of sorowe. her chekes waxed pale. *Sanguine quippe,*
> And water of innumerable teres ranne out of the vyrgyns eyne.
> when the blode of her sonne in hys scourgynge. flowed outte by all
> hys body. *Videns deinde,* And farthermore when the mother se her
> sonne cruelly spredde on the crosse. she began to fayle in all the
> myghtes of her body. *Audiens vero,* And herynge the sownde of the
> hamers when the handes and fete of her sonne were thryrled with
> nayles of yron. then all the vyrgyns wyttes faylynge. the gretnesse
> of sorowe threw her downe on the erthe as deade. (248–49)

As the passage details the Virgin Mary's embodied participation in
Christ's suffering, we see her body responding to what his undergoes.
The blood drains from her cheeks as she sees the blood running from
the wounds inflicted by the crown of thorns; tears flow from her eyes as
Christ's blood flows when he is scourged; her bodily strength deserts her
at the sight of Christ's body spread on the cross; and the sound of the
nails driven into his hands and feet causes her wits to fail and her body to
fall to the earth as in death. As the nuns repeatedly perform, week after
week, the divine service, this passage creates an extended dynamic of reiteration and of expanded intersubjectivity in which the nuns' experiences blend with the joined suffering of Christ and the Virgin Mary. The
hymn for Friday matins further delineates the extent to which Christ's

and Mary's suffering is a mutual experience, also calling attention to the Brigittine nuns' own reanimation of the sacred events:

> *Reflectis mundi,* Leue we all vanytyes & playes and vayne ioyes of the worlds. and haue we often in mynde in oure hartes the tormentes of the vyrgyns sonne. . . . *Pensemus matris,* Thynke we on the moste sharpe thornes of sorowe of the mothers tremelyng harte. whyle she se the body of her sonne suffer so manyfolde paynes. . . . *Auxit dolores,* The sorrowe of the mother. encresed the sorowes of the sonne. & the mothers sorowe was encresed by the reproues & paynes that her son suffered. *Sic nostra corda,* O Iesu thy passyon mote so perce thorugh oure hartes. & thy trew loue mote euer dwelle in us. (239–40)

Christ's passion pierces the nuns' hearts much as Julian of Norwich has Christ's very pains. As these portions of the Brigittine divine service illustrate, in Brigittine spirituality, individuals live and relive the lives of others past and present.

INCARNATIONAL TEXTUALITY: LIVING WORDS AND TEXTUAL BODIES

In incarnational epistemological systems, individual experiences of the divine do not, as we have seen, involve hard distinctions between interior and exterior, mind and body, or self and other. Individual experiences of God, even mystical experiences, therefore are not at all unrepresentable to others or, for that matter, unrepeatable by others.[50] For St. Birgitta, St. Catherine, and Julian, embodied knowledge can—indeed, even *must*—be conveyed in language for others to know and experience for themselves. Julian declares, "And thus I saw him and sought him, and I had him and wanted him" (159), and she further pronounces that such experience of God ought to be a central element of "our comen working in this life" (159). The word *comen* here carries two important meanings. It signifies "common" in the sense of a everyday or typical experience; Watkins and Jenkins gloss the line, "This is and ought to be our usual way of being" (158). At the same time, it signifies "common" in the sense of shared experience. As Julian succinctly puts it, "For alle this sight was shewde in generalle. . . . Alle that I say of me I meene in the person of alle my evencristen" (151–52).[51] Incarnational epistemology gives rise to, and makes itself available to others (*all* others, not only those with mystical capabilities) through, incarnational paradigms of textuality in which the borders between human and textual bodies are every bit as permeable as those between selves and others or those between the corporeal and the spiritual.

In later medieval religious writing, both the processes by which the Logos becomes flesh and the events of Christ's passion are often described as textual operations. As Eric Jager observes, "Scholastic accounts" frequently refer to God the Father making Christ the Word incarnate "by 'writing' with the 'pen' of the Holy Spirit in Mary's womb (*visceribus*),"[52] and St. Catherine writes on more than one occasion of the Crucifixion as an act of inscription, using language that resonates with the Middle English traditions of the "charter of Christ." In a letter to Sano di Marco di Mazzacorno, for instance, she says that Jesus

> assumed responsibility for us, paid our debt, and then tore up the bond. . . . And when was that paid? When he gave up his life on the wood of the most holy cross to give us back the life of grace we had lost. . . . That bond was written on nothing less than lambskin, the skin of the spotless Lamb. He inscribed us on himself and then tore up the lambskin! So let our souls find strength in knowing that the parchment our bond was written on has been torn up, and our opponent and adversary can never again demand to have us back. (T69, 1:66–67)

Representing Christ's incarnation and passion as acts of inscription reminds readers of the Logos that fully permeates Christ's human flesh. These representations also, though, suggest an understanding of texts that takes seriously their corporeal materiality, their inescapable connections with bodies. For much of the period under consideration, at least some texts are written on animal flesh that, once prepared to receive writing, resembles human skin, as St. Catherine's references to the lambskin reminds us (a reference that also reminds us that the creation of a text required the sacrifice of a life). Indeed, as my colleague Anne Coldiron has observed, preparing vellum to receive inscription involves steps that echo acts by which martyrs were tortured: stretching, scraping, pricking, and so on. And the act of writing consists of scoring that flesh with a sharp instrument, a process laborious for the scribe and, again, suggestive of the infliction of pain.[53]

One of Catherine's letters to Raymond of Capua, written in 1377, admirably illustrates the tight bonds between texts and bodies that undergird a sense of texts as incarnate, of the text as a corpus in a very literal sense of the term. St. Catherine tells of her miraculous experience of learning to write through divine aid and also includes the four petitions that become the basis for her *Dialogue.* Her description of learning to write links the embodied experience of the divine with "the physical aspect of writing and . . . the union of body and mind it entails."[54] St. Catherine says: "This letter and another I sent you I've written with my own hand on the Isola della Rocca, with so many sighs and tears that I couldn't see even when I was seeing. . . . He [God] provided for my refreshment by giving me the ability to write—a consolation I've never known because of my ignorance—so that when I come down from the heights I might have a little something to vent my heart, lest it burst" (T272, 2:505). In this letter Catherine also adopts her usual form of address ("I Caterina, servant and slave of the servants of Jesus Christ, am writing to you in his precious blood"). F. Thomas Luongo, noting this phrase, observes the importance of bodies—Christ's and Catherine's—in her miraculously enabled textual production. He argues that Catherine "has found writing as a way to 'vent my heart,' suggesting that the blood with which she writes her letters is now her own, mingled with Christ's, evoking also the famous episode in Raymond of Capua's *Legenda* in which Catherine exchanges her heart with Christ's. Her ability to write, indeed, the very stuff with which she writes, emerges from her interior experience of ecstatic union with God."[55]

St. Catherine's letter, like the lessons revealed to St. Birgitta by the angel in the presence of the consecrated Host, comes from the lived experience of a female body, has a connection to the body of Christ, and has a corporeal materiality of its own. In the late medieval religious culture inhabited by St. Birgitta, St. Catherine, and Julian of Norwich, bodies produce texts, and texts are themselves in some respects living bodies.

One of St. Birgitta's revelations contains an emblematic image of incarnational textuality, presenting both the idea of the embodied, living text and another important characteristic of incarnational textuality, a sense of a textual performative imperative. Birgitta says, "I saw a book in the same pulpit, shining like very bright gold. . . . The writing in this book was not written in ink; each word in the book was alive and spoke itself, as if a man would say to do this or that and it would be done then with the speaking of the word."[56] The book lives, and it makes things happen; the text causes what it says to be done. Another facet of this textual performative imperative is that incarnational texts seek their own reinscription in other bodies and reincarnation in other lives, as we see operating in the concatenation of embodied experiences and textual encounters joining St. Teresa and Mary Frances of St. Theresa. Ongoing oscillation characterizes the boundaries demarcating the body of the woman writer through which she comes to know Christ, the body of Christ himself, and the textual corpus that represents the writer's individual, embodied experiences. In its presentation of embodied experience, the textual corpus provides an opening into another's body, a means to embody another's experience. To apply Catherine's image of the incarnate Christ as a bridge, one might also say that the corpus of the text too is a bridge. Incarnational texts catalyze intersubjective relations and enable readers, through knowing another's embodied experiences textually, to participate in those experiences. To borrow Julian's language, readers come to be "ooned" with Christ and with the "I" of the text; one might equally say, returning to St. Catherine's formulation, that they themselves become "another himself" or "another herself."

A letter of St. Catherine's to Daniella da Orvieto presents a version of just such a paradigm through which an individual's experience becomes an embodied text that transforms lived lives. Catherine represents Christ's corporeal suffering as an act of textual production that creates a rule for Christians to follow. Christians then make the rule come to life by performing it in their own acts of suffering that will bring them to oneness with God. Christ's incarnation is, in short, inscription that demands embodied action. Catherine states:

> We must go God's way, suffering innocently even to the point of death in order to snatch souls from the devils' hands. For this is the way and the rule eternal Truth has given you. He wrote it upon his own body in letters so large that no one, no matter how dull-witted, has an excuse for not reading it. And he wrote it not with ink, but with his own blood. You can see clearly the illuminated initials of this book, and how large they are. All of them show the eternal Father's truth, the indescribable love with which we were created. (T316, 3:329–30)

Not only is the rule of eternal Truth an incarnational text in that it consists of Christ's inscribed, suffering body, but Catherine's letter too is an incarnational text in that it seeks the reiteration of Catherine's own knowledge of and experiences of Christ in the life of the reader.

This letter of St. Catherine's recalls the process through which Julian's embodied knowledge of Christ becomes the textual corpus of her *Showings*. This text records the very bodily processes of coming to know "oure lords mening" (379), which, famously, is love.[57] Christ's bodily experiences, the yoking of suffering and love, that Julian comes to know in her body are knowable to others through her textual corpus, which must in its own turn be incorporated and made to live again by a reader. Julian envisions such a concatenation of embodied experience, textual representation, and repeated embodied experience with concise precision at the beginning of the final chapter of the *Showings*, when she declares, "This boke is begonne by Goddes gifte and his grace, but it is not yet performed, as to my sight" (379).[58] To redirect the astute assessment Sarah Beckwith makes of Shakespeare's theater, one might say that the *Showings* too is occupied with "the persistence of its historical concerns in the incarnation of performance" (275). Her book is part of an ongoing process; it will achieve completion only as the knowledge that it presents is embodied in other bodies and enacted in other lives.[59]

INCARNATIONAL POLITICS: BODIES POLITIC
AND THE BODY OF CHRIST

The questions of doing and becoming upon which incarnational textuality insists point to this textual paradigm's larger sociopolitical implications. Indeed, a profound awareness of the communality of individual experiences of God combined with an awareness of performative textual
imperatives shapes St. Birgitta's, St. Catherine's, and Julian of Norwich's
interventions in and (re)visions of sociopolitical systems.[60] In a fascinating study of Julian of Norwich and autobiography, Christopher Abbott has
argued that "in Julian's case, the personal and the theological are best
taken together."[61] I agree with this assessment; indeed, as should already
be evident, I believe that Abbott's claim has significance far beyond Julian's writings. Following Frederick Bauerschmidt, who argues for the
importance in Julian's *Showings* of "the mystical body politic of Christ," I
would add the category of "the political" to the theological as something
that should be considered with the personal: to vary the classic feminist
claim, the personal is both political and theological. Incarnational piety,
incarnational epistemology, and incarnational textuality not only inform
each other but also underwrite as a corollary an incarnational political vision with implications both ecclesiastical and secular.

St. Catherine's political involvement, particularly as we know it
through her letters, provides an ideal illustration of the ways in which
incarnational political vision is grounded in and developed through incarnational piety, epistemology, and textuality. Thus, because in chapters 2 and 3 I explore at length the ways in which Julian's *Showings* and
Brigittine texts participate in incarnational political visions, I will use
Catherine as my central example here. In taking Catherine as an illustrative case in this section, I want to emphasize that I am not adopting
the position of some scholars who claim that St. Catherine's mysticism
is quite different from that of other later medieval female mystics, including St. Birgitta and Julian of Norwich. Karen Scott, for instance, sees
Catherine's mysticism as having an "exceptionally social dimension,"
and in contrasting Catherine of Siena and Julian of Norwich, Anna Maria
Reynolds argues that Catherine's spirituality is active whereas Julian's is

contemplative. Reynolds claims that "there is a dynamic quality in the Italian mystic that differentiates her completely from the English recluse."[62] Julian's commitment to the performance of her text, a performance taken up enthusiastically by the Benedictine nuns of Cambrai and Paris, however, calls this claim into question. Her *Showings* bears witness to embodied human experience in history and, simultaneously, issues a call to action, seeking re-embodiment in the lives of its readers through human history.[63] So, on the contrary, I do not see the social dimension of St. Catherine's mysticism or the active quality of her spirituality as exceptional at all. Rather, I see them as constitutive of all of the forms of female spirituality I investigate in this book.

The sociopolitical ramifications of Catherine's understanding of the endlessly permeable boundaries among self, others, and God manifest themselves in a section of the *Dialogue* that takes as its starting point the scriptural image of the laborers in the vineyard. In the *Orchard,* God tells Catherine that she, and we, are laborers hired to work "in the vyneȝard of holy chirche," yet at the same time each person labors in the vineyard of the individual soul. The two vineyards are, in the end, joined, as are the labors: "Thynke wel and haue in mynde that alle resonable creaturis haue her owne vyneȝeerd by hemsilf, which is ooned to her neiȝbore without ony othir mene; that is to seye, oon so ioyned with anothir that no man may do good to hymsilf, ne harme, but that he most ȝeelde the same to his neiȝbore. Of ȝou alle, that is to seye, of al the hool cristen religyoun, a general vyneȝeerd is gaderid togyderis, whiche ȝe alle ben knytt togyders in the vyneȝeerd of the goostly body of holy chirche."[64] Such passages make clear that, as Noffke indicates, Catherine's "mysticism very early became one with her life of service and concern for others and for the Church."[65]

Capua's *Legenda maior* emphasizes St. Catherine's devotional focus on Christ's body, foregrounding her Eucharistic devotion, her mystical marriage with Christ, and her reception of the stigmata.[66] As Scott points out, this is the account of St. Catherine's life "that became authoritative."[67] Scott, like some other recent scholars, explores the ways in which Catherine's version of her own life, which prominently features her political engagements, differs from Raymond's presentation of Catherine's more conventionally "feminine" spirituality. Significantly, however, Catherine's embodied piety and her devotion to the incarnate Christ are not separated from her accounts of her political and textual activities in her own writings. In fact, her incarnational piety is the foundation of her textual production and her active, very public participation in political affairs.

If Christ's crucified body is for St. Catherine a bridge, it is also a doorway through which she enters both Christ himself and the public sphere. The mystical experience that serves for St. Catherine as a stirring call to action opening the way to public participation in civic strife and ecclesiastical reform consists of an intimate union with Christ's wounded body. She writes:

> The fire of holy desire was growing within me as I gazed. And I saw the people, Christians and unbelievers, entering the side of Christ crucified. In desire and impelled by love I walked through their midst and entered with them into Christ gentle Jesus. And with me were my father Saint Dominic, the beloved John, and all my children. Then he placed the cross on my shoulder and put the olive branch in my hand, as if he wanted me (and so he told me) to carry it to the Christians and unbelievers alike. And he said to me: "Tell them, 'I am bringing you news of great joy!'" (T219, 2:92)

It is through just such active, sociopolitical dimensions of women's incarnational piety, epistemology, and textuality that we may begin to see why identification with Christ's passion is not necessarily a form of victimization or an acceptance of passivity, criticisms that David Aers has forcefully directed toward the work of Caroline Walker Bynum (among others) on medieval women's *imitatio Christi*.[68] In sharing an embodied experience of the incarnate Christ, these women create a communal body that transcends past and present and looks outward toward others and toward the future. Experiencing Christ's, and others', sufferings through textual encounters with them informs theological and political visions (or, better, revisions) committed to *performance* and to action rather than to stasis or passivity.

Protestant Incarnational Poetics: Aemilia Lanyer's *Salve Deus Rex Judaeorum*

Aemilia Lanyer's *Salve Deus Rex Judaeorum* (1611) opens with a dedicatory poem to Queen Anne of Denmark. This poem appropriately not only introduces the larger work's central subject—Christ's passion—but also signals the importance of incarnational epistemology and incarnational textuality to Lanyer's poetic project. From Christ's body, Lanyer accesses spiritual and textual authority.[69] Her poetic corpus recounting Christ's passion becomes Christ's body as Eucharistic food. Lanyer writes:

> For here I have prepar'd my Paschal Lambe,
> The figure of that living Sacrifice;
> Who dying, all th'Infernall powres orecame,
> That we with him t'Eternitie might rise:
> This pretious Passeover feed upon, O Queene.
>   (85–89)

The prophetic dream that provides Lanyer with the work's title emerges, in retrospect, as a moment of vocation, granting her overlapping poetic and sacerdotal powers that combine with the maternal, Marian mantle Lanyer wears as a woman who reincarnates Christ, who bears (in multiple senses) the Word.[70]

In directing Queen Anne to access Christ and his redemptive power by feeding upon the text, Lanyer underlines the corporeal aspects of textual encounters and of knowledge acquisition. Simultaneously, she suggests the text's capacity to enable union with God. She says:

> My weake distempred braine and feeble spirits,
> Which all unlearned have adventur'd, thus
> To write of Christ, and his sacred merits,
> Desiring that this Booke Her hands may kisse:
> And though I be unworthy of that grace,
> Yet let her blessed thoghts this book imbrace.
>   (139–44)

Staging the act of reading as kissing and embracing points toward the place in Lanyer's poetry of the affective, embodied epistemological para-digms we have already observed in the medieval women's writings in the first sections of this chapter. The affective, embodied aspects of Queen Anne's engagement with Lanyer's book that is Christ are in fact so pro-found that the scene of reading becomes a scene of sensual, quasi-nuptial union between the queen and Christ.

In "To the Ladie Lucie, Countess of Bedford," Lanyer again posits that reading her text enables a nuptial union with Christ. Lanyer here equates her poetry both with the incarnate Christ, who himself is a text to be read, and with scripture, the reading of which will lead to union with God. She first, like St. Catherine of Siena, interprets Christ's passion as an act of inscription. Lanyer describes Christ's wounded body as a legible document presenting the truth of salvation: "Loe here he comes all stucke with pale deaths arrows: / In whose most pretious wounds your soule may reade / Salvation, while he (dying Lord) doth bleed" (12–14). She then aligns her poem with the Ark of the Covenant, the receptacle of God's Word, as she imagines the countess's relationship with Christ as a lover:

> You whose cleare Judgement farre exceeds my skil,
> Vouchsafe to entertaine this dying lover,
> The Ocean of true grace, whose streames doe fill
> All those with Joy, that can his love recover;
> About this blessed Arke bright Angels hover.
>
> (15–19)

The countess's textual encounter with the divine Word present in Lan-yer's poetry ultimately leads to an embodied union with Christ "sweetly seated" in her "brest" (21).

In her poem addressing Susan Bertie, Dowager Countess of Kent, Lanyer even more explicitly presents her vision of the text as a vehicle for nuptial union with Christ. She repeats the Eucharistic language of her poem to Queen Anne, inviting the countess "to grace this holy feast, and me" (6). She then offers her poem as a means for the countess to join with Christ, adding to her own sacerdotal role and to the text's sac-ramental capacity. Not only does Lanyer textually celebrate the Eucharist in offering her poem to her female readers, but she also textually performs a marriage. Lanyer writes:

> Receive your Love whom you have sought so farre,
> Which heere presents himselfe within your view;
> Behold this bright and all directing Starre,
> Light of your Soule that doth all grace renew:
> And in his humble paths since you do tread,
> Take this faire Bridegroome in your soules pure bed.
>
> (37–42)

The dedicatory poems connecting a reader's engagement with Lanyer's text and that reader's nuptial union with Christ emphasize that the textual encounter is an embodied epistemological experience, even as these poems show texts to be a means of transcending the divide between exterior and interior as well as that between self and others. Another dedicatory poem, "The Authors Dreame to the Ladie Marie, the countesse Dowager of Pembrooke," further reveals the centrality of incarnational epistemology and incarnational textuality in Lanyer's poetic project. The poem to Mary Sidney Herbert is framed as a dream vision and describes Lanyer's search for "a Lady whom Minerva chose, / To live with her in height of all respect" (3–4). The poem begins with Lanyer's reliance on "the eie of Reason" (6), a formulation suggesting that even this most traditionally disembodied and intellectual of faculties has a corporeal dimension. Once in the dream vision, Lanyer witnesses a debate between Art and Nature, and the ladies who judge the debate rely on even more explicitly incarnational epistemological processes. They make what Woods describes as "judgments based on sensual pleasure, on a knowledge derived from the experience of beauty."[71] Lanyer writes that the ladies go to the sacred spring where Art and Nature contend for sovereignty:

> Judging with pleasure their delightfull case;
> Whose ravisht sences made them quickely know,
> T'would be offensive either to displace.
>
> (81–82, 85–89)

The emphasis on nature, and the attention to the senses as the means of acquiring knowledge, suggest that Lanyer, like the medieval holy women considered previously in this chapter, privileges a method of understanding that might be labeled "kinde knowing."

"The Authors Dreame" connects this privileged incarnational mode of epistemology, which it strongly genders feminine, to a woman's production of sacred text. Incarnational epistemology and incarnational textuality thus function in tandem. Lanyer writes that the aforementioned ladies "Those holy Sonnets . . . did all agree, / With this most lovely Lady [i.e., Mary Sidney Herbert] here to sing" (121–22). Lanyer's account insists upon the performance's bodily origins, expressing hope that the song may be carried to angels' ears by "her noble breasts sweet harmony" (123). The ladies' song also inaugurates further textual production. She continues:

> While saints like Swans about this silver brook
> Should *Hallalu-iah* sing continually,
> Writing her praises in th'eternall booke
> Of endlesse honour, true fames memorie.
>   (125–28)

King David first produced "those rare sweet songs" (117), which are reproduced in the poetry Mary Sidney Herbert writes, and which are in Lanyer's poem in turn sung by the ladies in concert with the countess; as a result of their song, the countess's praise is inscribed in the divine, eternal book of endless honor and true fame, where she will live forever. This entire concatenation manifests a textual dynamic of reincarnation, of linked relations of textual performance, embodiment, and reinscription reminiscent of the ones established in St. Catherine's letters and in Julian of Norwich's *Showings*.

This scene in "The Authors Dreame" also demonstrates Lanyer's interest throughout *Salve Deus Rex Judaeorum* in female communities, calling attention to Lanyer's strongly gendered approach to incarnational politics.[72] Lanyer returns frequently in her dedicatory poems to the identity of the bride of Christ that she offers to Queen Anne and

Susan Bertie, adding layers to it as she mobilizes it to support the creation of, and to argue for the significance of, female communities. For instance, she often specifically casts her female readers as the wise virgins of Matthew 25:1–13. In the poem "To all the vertuous ladies in generall," Lanyer instructs her readers:

> Put on your wedding garments every one,
> The Bridegroome stayes to entertaine you all;
> Let Virtue be your guide, for she alone
> Can leade you right that you can never fall;
> And make no stay for feare he should be gone:
> But fill your Lamps with oyle of burning zeale,
> That to your Faith he may his Truthe reveale.
>   (8–14)

Lanyer turns again to the parable of the wise virgins in her poem addressed to Anne Clifford, expanding further the significance of this identity for the creation of female community. Using the first-person plural, she presents herself and her readers as brides of Christ united with Christ and with each other:

> One sparke of grace sufficient is to fill
> Our Lampes with oyle, ready when he doth call
> To enter with the Bridegroome to the feast,
> Where he that is the greatest may be least.
>   (13–16)[73]

Marriage to Christ here seems inflected by a paradigm of monastic profession, as Lanyer joins herself, the female dedicatees of the poem, and the poem's female audience more broadly construed, in a nunnery-like community of brides of Christ.

Notably, Lanyer suggests that the very sort of quasi-monastic, idealized female community that she imagines in the poem to Anne Clifford initially led her to the devotion to Christ she expresses in *Salve Deus*. The final poem in *Salve Deus Rex Judaeorum* is entitled "The Description of Cooke-ham." Cookeham was the royal country house estate "occupied by the Countess of Cumberland at some periods during her estrangement from her husband in the years before his death in 1605, and perhaps just after."[74] Lanyer "spent some time before 1609" at Cookeham with Margaret, Countess of Cumberland, and her daughter Anne Clifford.[75] In the opening lines of this concluding poem, Layer writes:

> Farewell (sweet *Cooke-ham*) where I first obtain'd
> Grace from that Grace where perfit Grace remain'd;
> And where the Muses gave their full consent,
> I should have powre the virtuous to content:
> Where princely Palace will'd me to indite,
> The sacred Storie of the Soules delight.
>
> (1–6)[76]

Lanyer owes both her spiritual conversion (a sort of rebirth) and her birth as a poet to women. Incarnation, redemption, and textual production originate from female community, and the result is a text that works to incarnate Christ, perform redemption, and create more female communities.

Though Achsah Guibbory does not see Lanyer's position that marriage to Christ trumps earthly marriage as being indicative of Roman Catholic or promonastic views, I would argue that there are many affinities between Lanyer's poems and medieval Catholic devotion, including female monastic devotion.[77] It is not at all out of the question that Lanyer may have had some sympathies for the "old religion." Even Guibbory, though she does not see Catholic leanings in Lanyer's views on marriage, concedes that "certain aspects of her poem (particularly the attention to the Virgin Mary . . .) make the label 'Protestant' problematic."[78] Furthermore, it is worth noting that two of Lanyer's dedicatees "had Roman Catholic connections"—that is, Queen Anne, who "may even have converted," and Arabella Stuart.[79]

Whatever Lanyer's religious sympathies, *Salve Deus Rex Judaeorum* exhibits significant continuities with Roman Catholic texts. Strikingly, Lanyer's Christ is the Christ of medieval affective devotion and also of many Catholic Counter-Reformation writers.[80] Her description of Christ on the cross could be taken straight from Julian of Norwich's *Showings*, from St. Catherine of Siena's writings, or from the Brigittine divine service. She writes:

> His joynts dis-joynted, and his legges hang downe,
> His alabaster breast, his bloody side,
> His members torne, and on his head a Crowne
> Of sharpest Thorns, to satisfie for pride:
> Anguish and Paine doe all his Sences drowne,
> While they his holy garments do divide:
> His bowells drie, his heart full fraught with griefe,
> Crying to him that yeelds him no reliefe.
>
> (1161–68)

For Lanyer, as for many medieval female mystics, Christ's suffering flesh is female flesh that, in Bynum's memorable phrase, "bleeds and feeds," giving new life through corporeal suffering. Lanyer's representation of a feminine Christ highlights a significant distinction between her version of the Passion and that found in nearly contemporaneous male-authored Calvinist versions. As Deborah Shuger argues, these male-authored texts exhibit strong anxiety about the concept of Christ's femaleness and struggle to negotiate "questions about his manhood" that Christ's suffering raises.[81]

Throughout Lanyer's account of Christ's passion, she builds upon this bodily connection between women and Christ, seeking to revise women's places in religious and textual traditions through explorations of the value both spiritual and cultural of the female body. Lanyer's *Salve Deus* emphasizes the roles of women, and especially of women's bodies, in human history and, as do Brigittine texts, in salvation history. In the prose epistle "To the Vertuous Reader" that closes the sequence of dedicatory poems at the beginning of *Salve Deus Rex Judaeorum*, Lanyer clearly states her aim to "make knowne to the world, that all women deserve not to be blamed" (48). Emphasizing the fundamental importance of the female body, she sets out to refute men who, "forgetting they were borne of women, nourished of women, and that if it were not by the means of women, they would be quite extinguished out of the world, doe like Vipers deface the wombes wherein they were bred" (48). In this epistle, she briefly mentions the accomplishments of biblical women often cited as exemplars of female virtue (for instance, Deborah, Esther, Judith, Susanna) before turning to the roles of women in the life of Christ. Lanyer then presents a summary of what Guibbory aptly calls "the gospel according to Aemilia."[82] Lanyer writes:

> As also in respect it pleased our Lord and Saviour Jesus Christ, without assistance of man, beeing free from originall and all other sinnes, from the time of his conception to the houre of his death, to be begotten of a woman, borne of a woman, nourished of a woman, obedient to a woman; and that he healed woman, pardoned women, comforted women: yea, even when he was in his greatest agonie and bloodie sweat, going to be crucified, and also in the last houre of his death, tooke care to dispose of a woman: after his resurrection, appeared first to a woman, sent a woman to declare his most glorious resurrection to the rest of his Disciples. (49–50)

In her progress through the events leading up to Christ's death on the cross, Lanyer pauses at the moment of Pilate's judgment of Christ to introduce the figure of Pilate's wife. With this introduction, Lanyer's version of the Passion again departs sharply from male-authored Calvinist versions in which, as Shuger argues, "women . . . disappear."[83] Pilate's wife delivers what is perhaps the most famous section of the *Salve Deus*, "Eve's Apologie," in which she decries men's injustice to women, injustice that resonates with that perpetuated upon Christ.[84] "Eve's Apologie" presents a version of St. Catherine's intersubjective relationship with Christ in which St. Catherine becomes "another himself"; the Christ of *Salve Deus Rex Judaeorum* is, in effect, "another herself" of all suffering women (or, one could say, all suffering women reincarnate Christ's pain). The indictment of Christ's persecutors in "Eve's Apologie" serves to recuperate the figure of Eve and, at the same time, to recuperate female-oriented experiential knowledge as well as the roles of affect and emotion in knowledge acquisition. The "Apologie" first assigns greater culpability for the fall to Adam (778–79) and then argues that men's sins against Christ far surpass Eve's sin. Addressing Christ's persecutors, Lanyer writes:

> Her sinne was small, to what you doe commit;
> All mortall sinnes that doe for vengeance crie,
> Are not to be compared unto it:
> If many worlds would altogether trie,
> By all their sinnes the wrath of God to get;
> This sinne of yours, surmounts them all as farre
> As doth the Sunne, another little starre.
>
> (817–24)

Unlike the men who betray and kill Christ out of "malice" (816), Lanyer's Eve errs simply "for knowledge sake" (797), and her "fault was onely too much love" (801).

Lanyer's revision of the story of Adam and Eve does more than rehabilitate experiential knowledge (Eve eats the apple "for knowledge sake" because knowing requires corporeal experience) and gendered affectivity (she errs as a result of "too much love"). Her version of this story has profound implications for gendering sociocultural positions of power writ large. In other words, her incarnational piety here is profoundly political. Even as Lanyer aligns Eve and all women with Christ as the victims of men's unjustified malice, she at the same time reminds men again of the value—indeed, the necessity—of women's maternal labor for men's existence. Quite basically, she reiterates the point she has already made forcefully in "To the Vertuous Reader": all men come from women's bodies. Lanyer does not associate the suffering of the female body in childbirth with the curse of Eve. On the contrary, she reinterprets this quintessentially female pain, transforming Eve's "curse" that so often justifies male authority over, and persecution of, women. Lanyer construes maternal suffering not as a punishment or as a mark of female inferiority but instead as a powerful life-giving force that should forestall against, rather than prompt, male persecution. Again addressing Christ's tormenters and, simultaneously, all who persecute women, she says:

Then let us have our Libertie againe,
And challendge to your selves no Sov'raigntie;
You came not in the world without our paine,
Make that a barre against your crueltie;
Your fault beeing greater, why should you disdaine
Our beeing your equals, free from tyranny?

(825–30)

Naomi Miller argues that Lanyer "asserts that men . . . owe not only their bodily lives . . . but also their very knowledge to the first mother: 'Yet Men will boast of knowledge, which [Adam] tooke / From Eves faire hand, as from a learned Booke' (*Salve Deus* ll. 827, 807–808)." The implication is "what comes from the hand of a woman—indeed, the Mother of us all—may not only be compared to a learned book, but may even prove a source for learned books."[85] In Lanyer's view, the very conditions for textual production and knowledge transmission depend on the female body. Textual production, and knowledge production more generally, are valuable women's work every bit as much as maternal reproduction is. All texts, even (perhaps especially) the most sacred ones, owe their existence, as does Christ incarnate, as do all men, to the female body. In textual culture too, therefore, women ought to have their liberty and to be men's equals.

Significantly, when Lanyer praises Mary for her maternal labor in making the divine Word flesh, she adopts the language of textile production, language that is, not coincidentally, etymologically related to textual production. Lanyer describes Christ being born as "Giving his snow-white Weed for ours in change / Our mortall garment in a skarlet Die, / Too base a roabe for Immortalitie" (lines 1110–12). She then states:

Most happy news, that ever yet was brought
When Poverty and Riches met together,
The wealth of Heaven, in our fraile clothing wrought
Salvation by his happy coming hither.

(1113–16)

This choice of language exalts textile work, a strongly gendered form of work associated, like the pain of childbirth, with Eve's punishment (recall the traditional rhyme beginning "When Adam delved, and Eve span . . ."). Lanyer thus reiterates the connections that she forges in her revisions of the story of Adam and Eve between textual production and human reproduction, both of which are vitally important female work.

Lanyer continues the association of women and Christ as partners in suffering beyond "Eve's Apologie." She devotes considerable attention to female compassion at the Crucifixion itself. Lanyer describes the "teares . . . sighes . . . cries" (996) of the daughters of Jerusalem and incorporates sixteen stanzas (1009–36) treating the Virgin Mary's maternal pain. Here again we find a marked difference from male-authored Calvinist Passion narratives in which the "Blessed Virgin is rarely mentioned."[86] These stanzas resonate with the Brigittine lessons that detail the intersubjective relationship of Christ and the Virgin Mary and devote such attention to calibrating their mutual suffering. Lanyer laments:

> His Woefull Mother wayting on her sonne,
> All comfortlesse in depth of sorow drowned;
> Her griefes extreame, although but new begun,
> To see his bleeding body oft she swounes;
> How could shee choose but thinke her selfe undone,
> He dying, with whose glory shee was crowned?
>
> . . . .
>
> Her teares did wash away his pretious blood,
> That sinners might not tread it under feet.
>
> (1009–14, 1017–18)

Lanyer moves beyond Christ's passion to treat his resurrection as well. After recounting Mary Magdalene and the other Mary's discovery of Christ's empty tomb, Lanyer integrates an extended meditation on the risen Christ. In presenting this Christ, Lanyer plays upon the mechanisms of affective desire and physical pleasure, encouraging her female readers to sensual, even sexual, union with him.[87] Returning to the figure of Christ as the Bridegroom, she upholds Christ as the epitome of masculine beauty. Lanyer also, as many critics have observed, feminizes him through her use of traditional language from the Canticles and from the sonnet tradition, language that typically describes the beloved lady. Indeed, this section of the work is captioned "A briefe description of his beautie upon the Canticles." Proceeding blazon fashion, she lingers over minute details of Christ's loveliness:

> This is that Bridegroome that appears so faire,
> So sweet, so lovely in his Spouses sight,
> That unto Snowe we may his face compare,
> His cheekes like skarlet, and his eyes so bright
> As purest Doves that in the rivers are,
> Washed with milke, to give the more delight;
> His head is likened to the finest gold,
> His curled lockes so beauteous to behold;
>
> Blacke as a Raven in her blackest hew;
> His lips like skarlet threeds, yet much more sweet
> Than is the sweetest hony dropping dew.
>
> (1305–15)

Not only in his suffering and death, but also in his resurrected glory, Lanyer's Christ is profoundly embodied and strongly aligned with women. Lanyer's Christ is in fact doubly "with" women. He exists simultaneously as a feminized figure in community with suffering, life-giving woman-kind and as a male lover or spouse with whom women unite in a nuptial relationship.

Immediately upon completing her portrait of the resurrected Christ's beautiful body, Lanyer turns to the Countess of Cumberland and indicates that the textual corpus of Christ she has created by writing his body is now inscribed in, and incarnate within, the countess's body. She writes:

> Therefore (good Madame) in your heart I leave
> His perfect picture, where it still shall stand,
> Deeply engraved in that holy shrine,

Environed with Love and Thoughts divine.
There may you see him as a God in glory,
And as a man in miserable case;
There may you read his true and perfect storie,
His bleeding body there you may embrace,
And kisse his dying cheekes with tears of sorrow,
With joyfull griefe, you may intreat for grace.

                                    (1325–34)

Through divine inspiration, Lanyer creates a text of the divine Word become flesh, and, through reading that text, the countess herself becomes a text inscribed with the divine Word, even as her body and Christ's body become one. Significantly, here too incarnational piety, epistemology, and textuality contain a performative imperative. Lanyer directs the countess that she should bring "all your prayers, and your almes-deeds" to "stop his cruell wounds that bleeds" (1335–36). The stanza thus ends with a call to social action on the countess's part, action interpreted as an interaction with Christ's wounded body.

Chapter Two

Medieval Legacies and Female Spiritualities across the "Great Divide"

Julian of Norwich, Grace Mildmay, and the
English Benedictine Nuns of Cambrai and Paris

MEMORY, WORDS, AND THE "FRAGILE, SLIPPERY DREAM"
OF THE PAST

In an essay on the Chinese Manchu prince Yihuan's poetry about the destruction of the Summer Palace by British and French troops in 1860, Vera Schwarz elegantly declares that "[p]recisely because the past is a fragile, slippery dream, it can hardly be contained by something as exacting as words."[1] In this chapter, I consider the ways in which words can, and cannot, contain the fragile dream of the remembered past, especially interactions with the divine experienced in the past. I am also interested in what beyond words is necessary in the constitution of memory as well as in the constitution of dynamic relations of past and present that exceed memory. Particularly, I am interested in the bodies that are

necessary: bodies of writers and readers that translate fleshly experience into words and words into enfleshed experience once more. Or, to
put it another way, my focus is on the shifting and intersecting lines demarcating embodied writers and readers, the divine Logos, and a textual corpus.

As we have seen in the previous chapter, Julian of Norwich's *Showings*, along with Brigittine texts and St. Catherine of Siena's writings,
summons us to rethink how we understand relationships of bodies and
texts, selves and others. Such revisions in turn can help us to reinterpret
our ways of understanding religious categories and historical periods.
This chapter proceeds by first considering the place of Julian's *Showings*
specifically, and the place of forms of devotion strongly associated with
medieval female piety more generally, in the spirituality of the English
Benedictine nuns who formed communities in Cambrai and Paris in the
seventeenth century, communities that played a vital role in preserving
the texts of the *Showings*.[2] Julian's writings and other medieval texts act
as vectors for carrying the past into the present, giving past lives new
life in the embodied experiences of individual nuns as well as in the collective experiences of the corporate body of the monastic community.

That there would also be strong affinities between Julian's *Showings*, the medieval devotional traditions that text characterizes, and the
writings produced in communities of nuns who did so much to preserve
the *Showings* is readily comprehensible, though the place of medieval
texts and medieval female spirituality in early modern monasticism is
still relatively little studied. That similar affinities would emerge in the
nearly one thousand manuscript pages of meditations and spiritual autobiography written by Grace Mildmay, a Protestant gentry woman who
lived from 1552 to 1620, is perhaps more surprising, though the example
of Aemilia Lanyer considered in the first chapter suggests it should not
be so. In the second part of this chapter I thus turn to a comparative exploration of resonances among Julian of Norwich's *Showings*, Grace Mildmay's writings, and texts associated with the English Benedictines of
Cambrai and Paris. Grace Mildmay's meditations and spiritual autobiography illuminate the influential legacies of medieval affective and contemplative piety in a religious tradition that is often understood as de-

fining itself in opposition to such forms of devotion.[3] As we shall see, particularly important continuities emerge in the ways in which bodies, especially suffering bodies, and words shape each other and shape communities. The medieval past becomes not merely the other against which Protestant faith is defined but instead something incorporated into Grace Mildmay's Protestant spirituality.

On an overarching level, at the heart of this chapter lies a desire to begin to grasp what remains constant, as well as what changes, in the ways in which medieval and early modern women both Catholic and Protestant experience and theorize relationships between humans and God. My endeavor is to elucidate how such human/divine relations exist within, transform, and at times transcend history. At the same time, my aim is to shed light on the ways in which individual experiences of the divine, especially gendered, bodily experiences expressed textually, signify for others both personally and sociohistorically.

Porous Bodies and the (Re)Incarnate Word: The English Benedictine Nuns of Cambrai and Paris

The English Carmelites of Antwerp who feature in the introduction are part of a large network of English monastic communities residing on the Continent after the Dissolution. In addition to the Antwerp Carmel, there were English Carmelite and Franciscan foundations established in France and the Low Countries, and the English Brigittines of Syon lived at various locations on the Continent, ending up, as I discuss in the next chapter, in Spanish-controlled Lisbon. There were also several English Benedictine nunneries across the Channel, including the two on which I will focus in this chapter. The vibrant devotional and textual cultures that characterize the Antwerp Carmel have counterparts in these other English nunneries in exile.

The Abbey of Our Lady of Consolation was established at Cambrai in 1620 when nine women came over from England. Of these women, Helen More (in religion Dame Gertrude) was "considered the chief foundress, the pecuniary means having been mainly furnished by her father

Mr. Cresacre More."[4] Among these nine was also the first abbess, Catherine Gascoigne; her younger sister Margaret was admitted in 1628. A daughter house, Our Lady of Good Hope Priory, was founded in Paris in 1651.[5] When Augustine Baker took over the spiritual direction of the English Benedictine nuns of Cambrai in 1624, he sought to better train the nuns in contemplative prayer through which the nuns could, like Julian of Norwich, come to know and unite with God. Gertrude More, echoing Julian's emphasis on divine love, describes their distinctive mode of devotional life as "the way of love," and Baker significantly terms it the "unitive way," calling to mind Julian's descriptions of "oneing."[6] Dame Christina Brent, who was professed in 1629 and held the offices of abbess, prioress, and cellarer, writes of Baker's method, "The religious contented themselves to call it Father Baker's way, whereas they might better have called it the Mystic Way (or the Way of Affection)."[7]

Baker came to Cambrai because the nuns objected to the methods of spiritual training brought by the English Benedictine nuns who were sent from the Brussels foundation to help establish the community, methods that had a strongly Jesuit orientation. Conflicts about Jesuit influence in early modern English nunneries were common. As Claire Walker observes, "No discussion of the English convents' spirituality is possible without reference to the Society of Jesus, which constituted either the devotional orthodoxy or the 'other' against which alternative approaches were measured."[8] Baker's role at Cambrai was from the beginning controversial. "Officially termed 'a tabler,'" Baker occupied a position that "was somewhat exceptional. Neither chaplain nor ordinary confessor, he was sent for the express purpose of training the young community in the principles of a true monastic and contemplative life by means of private instructions, public conferences, and the confessional." Baker was initially well received, but opinion soon turned against him; nuns with the exception of Catherine Gascoigne objected to his methods, and Gertrude More "championed the opposition."[9] However, all, including Gertrude More, were eventually won over by Baker's approach, and Gertrude would become Baker's staunchest defender.

MS Mazarine 1062 from the library of Good Hope Priory, a text that Placid Spearitt identifies as being Augustine Baker's, makes abundantly clear the primacy of, as well as the interconnections of, divine love, corporeality, and union with God in the Benedictine nuns' spirituality.[10] The second item in the manuscript is identified as "Explication de différents passages de l'Evangile"; with its extended attention to the Nativity and Passion sequences, this text recalls such works of later medieval affective piety as Nicholas Love's *Mirror*. In the passage leading up to his account of the Nativity, Baker compares the religious and the secular life, outlining the obligations and benefits of religion. Here he neatly aligns the contemplative life and the experience of divine love, saying: "But in the desert, the desert is the only place, the place alone wher God speaketh. Who therefore desyrs to heare his sweete voice and Enjoy his Gratious presence now at his Nativitye yea relyse themselves to the Dessert the only Meanes absolutely Necessarye. . . . Love, devine Love is the desert. And who doth not willingly endure the Austerityes of Love which giveth Even the sourest sauce a sweet Relish" (27r).[11] Baker continues his discussion of the contemplative life by emphasizing the importance of the body as the locus both of contemplation and of the experience of divine love, something signaled by his use of the sensory language of taste in the passage above. He admonishes, "You say you have not commoditye of place. I say which of you cannot relyve yourselves into your owne Hart and there melt away in sweet feelings of Love with God. This is the <u>Desert</u> and easy to be found" (27r).[12] Divine love is experienced in the heart, which features as an interior space within the body into which the self enters. The self, once in the heart and in the presence of divine love, engages in a sensual response involving affective and embodied dimensions.

The section of the "Explication" devoted to Christ's passion highlights the extent to which the devotional practices that Baker encourages the nuns to adopt yoke the corporeal and the intellectual, additionally illustrating the characteristically reiterative dynamic through which past becomes present.[13] The introduction to a detailed account of Christ's bodily pain instructs the reader that "[w]ee must doe both. Loke with the Eye of the Bodye and consider with the Eye of the Mynd. Sorrow sure would be considered New then because as the Quality of the Sorrow is, accordingly it would be considered" (49v). The commentary further advises the readers, "[C]onsider his sufferings and so begin first with the . . . paynes of his Bodye his wounds and his stripes or Eye will soon tell us noe place was left in his Bodye where he might be smitten and was not" (50v). Baker's instructions here, not coincidentally I would argue, resonate with Julian of Norwich's complex relations of bodily and spiritual sight as well as with her intense attention to Christ's bodily suffering, both in the material crucifix upon which she concentrates her attention during her illness and in her mystical experiences.

In instructing the nuns in the "way of love" or the "unitive way," Baker stresses not only the vital role of the body but also the central place of texts. Baker foregrounds the interactions of affect and intellect in nuns' textual engagements when he suggests that a nun needing an aid to contemplation read "a verse or sentence in a Booke . . . to see whether his [sic] affection will be moved by it."[14] In Baker's directions to the nuns regarding how to read, he emphasizes, furthermore, that texts are to be performatively embodied and incorporated into lived lives. He says the nuns should read "with a serious resolution of putting in practice whatsoeuer you read that shall be good and proper for you. . . . [Y]ou must saie to yourself: This or that thing that I readde in this booke is a good and proper Instruction for me, and I will putt it in execution."[15]

The books toward which Baker directs the nuns to find the necessary "good and proper instruction" include the classics of English mystical and devotional writing from the fourteenth and fifteenth centuries.[16] In 1629 he wrote to the antiquarian Robert Cotton from Cambrai asking "on behalf of the English Benedictine nuns there, for the gift or loan of English manuscripts or printed books 'containing contemplation, Saints lives or other devotions.'"[17] Baker continues, "Hampole's works . . . are proper for them. I wish I had Hilton's *Scala Perfectionis* in Latin; it would help the understanding of the English."[18] He thus encouraged the nuns' serious engagement with modes of spirituality drawn from the English Middle Ages.[19]

Julian's *Showings* appropriately formed a mainstay of the nuns' library; one copy is recorded in the catalog of the Paris house as "Colections outt of Holy Mother Juilan" and another as "The Reuelations of Sainte Julian" (MS Mazarine 4058, 31v and 206v respectively). The catalog also includes entries for "St Bridgets Reuelations" (206v), Walter

Hilton's *Scale of Perfection* ("The School of Contemplation otherwise called ye old scal of Perfection New Clothed 2 seueral Books ye one is ye 1st and ye other ye second part composed by Father Walter Hilton a Cathusian *[sic]* Monk" [219v]), *The Cloud of Unknowing* ("The Cloude of which we have 2 with the Exposition which F Baker made upon it" [31r]), and William Flete's *Remedies against Temptations* ("A Booke called Remedies in all Temptations and this consisteth of 2 Partes both bound together" [206v]).[20]

I want to emphasize that in focusing on the roles played by medieval texts and forms of medieval spirituality in the monastic communities of Cambrai and Paris I do not mean to perpetuate "the assumption that Catholicism was always rooted in the past, looking backward," something against which Frances Dolan rightly warns in her study of early modern Catholic women's biographies.[21] My point is that for these nuns the past forms a vibrant part of their lives in their contemporary moment. Much as self and other are not simply opposites in Julian's spirituality, past and present too do not exist as a simple binary either for Julian or for the English Benedictine nuns. As Julian says of her *Showings*, medieval female spirituality is for the English Benedictines something begun but remaining still to be performed. Past lives (Julian's, Christ's, those of other holy women and religious sisters) and the texts that record them are not artifacts to be preserved as if under glass; rather, in these nuns' spiritual and textual practices, such lives are part of an ongoing process of individual and communal becoming that reaches forward as well as backward.

Indeed, in their practice of the "way of love" or "unitive way," the English nuns of Cambrai and Paris demonstrate, as they engage with works of medieval spirituality, and especially with Julian's *Showings*, just the sort of performative processes of textual incorporation and embodiment that Julian envisions in the final chapter of the Long Text of the *Showings* and that Baker recommends in his instructions. Julian's engagement with "interlocking problems of identity, faith, religious authority, and writing" becomes part of the nuns' negotiation of these same issues.[22] Frederick Bauerschmidt claims that in reading Julian's *Showings* he is "trying to read the text that Julian herself read, the text of

Christ's crucified body that she describes."[23] The Benedictine nuns do precisely this, reading Christ's body in others' bodies both corporeal and textual. In turn the women religious come to embody the experiences of others (Christ, Julian, each other) individually, corporately, and in their textual productions. To borrow Julian's language, the English nuns in exile simultaneously engage, through acts of textual production and consumption, in "oneing" with Julian, with Christ, and with their "evynn cristene."

Texts associated with Margaret Gascoigne illuminate the fluid, dynamic relationships of past, present, and future, as well as of self and others, that characterize the English Benedictine nuns' profoundly embodied, profoundly textual spirituality. *The Life and Death of Dame Margaret Gascoigne*, written by Augustine Baker after Gascoigne's death in 1637, provides considerable detail about her devotional practices.[24] Margaret Gascoigne's "contemplative anthology," *Devotions*, which contains excerpts from Julian's *Showings*, also survives and reveals much about her spirituality as well as about her textual practices.[25] In such works, and in the uses to which they and others like them were put in the monastic communities of Cambrai and Paris, affect and knowledge, theology and epistemology, interpenetrate.

In his *Life and Death of Dame Margaret Gascoigne*, Baker frequently calls attention to the importance of the body in experiencing divine love and in undertaking contemplation leading toward union with God. Turning to the familiar association of Mary and Martha with the contemplative and active lives, and aligning Margaret Gascoigne with the former, he writes:

> And it is the sentence of St Hildegardis, that the loue of God doth not dwell in robust or strong bodies. I saie, that yet such bodie as our Dame had, and infirme as it was, serued her in all sufficiencie towards the office of Marie during her whole time and to her last gaspe, when parted from the bodie she cessed not (as we maie wth good reason esteeme) from contemplation, / but continued the same in the succeeding estate, according to that promise of our Saviour to Marie, and in her to all contemplators and contemplatisers:

That *the beste parte chosen* and prosecuted by them in this life *should not* ende with it, or be *taken awaie from her,* but should in the future be continued for all eternite. (55, emphasis in original)[26]

Margaret also repeatedly interprets her own embodied experiences, especially her experiences of suffering, as integral to the process of coming to know God. She writes, for instance, "Surely, my God, thou dost not cause or permitt these things to be, to the end they should be a meane, lett, or impediment betweene my soule & thee, but rather yt they may be as helps, occasions, & meanes for vniting my soule more strongly & firmly vnto thee" (*Devotions,* 58). Her body is thus clearly not, to return to Stanley Cavell's formulation, a veil that comes between her and God, but rather the very locus where, and the means by which, God may be most fully and securely known.[27]

Margaret's "contemplative anthology" dramatizes the permeability of bodies and subjectivities, opening with a passage in which her selfhood merges with the body of the crucified Christ. Addressing Christ in the first chapter, she says, "Vse me therefore as the instrument, & take such satisfaction from me as I am able to performe; & for what my pouerty cannot afford, I humbly offer thin owne most sacred merits, beggin[g] that they may satisfie & supply whatsoeuer is wanting in me; & therefore wth a strong confidence in thy mercyes & merits, I leaue myselfe in thy most sacred wounds, hoping there to obteine whatsoeuer is necessarie for me, & wanting in me" (*Devotions,* 32). Margaret later includes a fragment of Julian's text intermingled with her own meditations in which her embodied experience of the Word made flesh joins with Julian's. She begins by quoting and identifying Julian. She writes, "Thou has saide, (O L:) [that is, Oh Lord], to a deare child of thine, 'Let me alone, my deare-worthy childe, intende (or attend) to me, I am enough to thee; reioyce in thy sauiour & saluation': *(This was spoken to Julian ye ankress of Norwich, as appeareth by ye booke of her Reuelations)*" (*Devotions,* 61). Margaret continues by aligning herself with Julian; her relationship with Christ is in effect a reincarnation of Julian's. Margaret says, "This, O *Lorde,* I reade & thinke on with great ioy, & cannot but take it as spoken also to me" (*Devotions,* 61).

That Margaret perceives her own experience to be contiguous with Julian's, even to *be* Julian's, emerges more clearly still when the focus explicitly turns to the body and its pains.[28] Margaret repeats Christ's words to Julian, "[I]ntend to me," and then links these words with Julian's experience of bodily sickness. After invoking Julian's experience of suffering and divine love, Margaret immediately repeats another excerpt of Christ's words to Julian, "I am enough to thee," in the context of her own suffering. She says, "[T]hese thy most delicious words, *I am inough to thee,* is soe great a ioy to my hart, that all the afflictions, yt are, or (as I hope) euer shall fall vpon me . . . doe & shall cause me to receiue from ym so much comfort, solace, & encouragment, as that I hope by thy grace they shall be most dearly welcome vnto me" (*Devotions,* 61–62).

Margaret Gascoigne's devotional writings reveal a complex process of subject formation as she interacts with Julian's text.[29] Much as the Antwerp Carmelites exhibit a "sense of 'a social self lodged within a network of others,'" of "reiterative" and "relational" selfhood, so too Julian's experiences and her text are implicated in Margaret's constitution as a contemplative.[30] Furthermore, the inverse is also in a sense true—Margaret, as one of Julian's "evynn cristene," is implicated in, and has always been implicated in, Julian's constitutive spiritual experiences and their textual expressions. And both are implicated in Christ's experiences of suffering. As Christopher Abbott observes, "One crucial effect of Julian's rigorously pursued emphasis on the incarnation, and on all this implies for humanity as a whole and for the individual, is to create certain intellectual and imaginative conditions in which a *theological* interpretation of contingent personal experience might credibly be made. It creates, that is, the conditions for *shareable religious autobiography.*"[31]

One might say that Julian and Margaret do just this—theologically interpret contingent personal experience and share a religious autobiography, an autobiography that is in some sense the biography of Christ.[32] Indeed, they do so to such an extent that, according to Augustine Baker, in dying Margaret reiterates the experience that Julian had on what she believed would be her deathbed, fixing her gaze upon the crucifix. In *The Life and Death of Dame Margaret Gascoigne* Baker says that in Margaret's last moments, she

caused one, that was most conuersant and familiar with her, to place
(written at and vnderneath the Crucifixe, that remained there before
her, and which she regarded with her eyes during her sicknes and
till her death) thes holie wordes that had sometimes ben spoken by
God to the holie virgin Julian the clustress of Norwich, as appeareth
by the old manuscript booke of her *Reuelations,* and with the which
wordes our Dame had euer formerlie ben much delighted: "Intende
(or attende) to me; I am inough for thee; reioice in me thy Sauiour,
and in thy saluation." Those wordes (I saie) remained before her
eyes beneath the Crucifixe till her death. (66)

The corpus of Christ on the crucifix and the textual corpus that is the
token of Julian's own embodied experience of oneness with Christ join
in Margaret's deathbed contemplation as she becomes one with Julian
and Christ simultaneously, reliving their shared pain.

Another way of viewing the multidimensional bonds of identification among Christ, Julian, and Margaret is as a solution to the dilemma
Cavell posits in working through what he calls "Wittgenstein's attempts
to realize the fantasy of a private language."[33] Cavell considers the case
of one who writes an "S" in his diary to mark the occurrence of a particular sensation; the question at stake is whether another person could have
that sensation and use the same token to express it. Cavell arrives at the
idea that one cannot deny either the sensation or the method of expression to another.[34] I would suggest that the *Showings* illustrates Cavell's
conclusion; it provide us with virtually the opposite of private experience and private language, as in turn do Margaret Gascoigne's text and
others associated with the exiled English Benedictines of Cambrai and
Paris. The *Showings* is itself the token of Christ's/Julian's pains. Margaret Gascoigne's contemplative writings reveal that through reading the
textual tokens of Julian's/Christ's sensations, and through writing them
herself, she *uses* Julian's textual token and simultaneously *experiences*
Julian's/Christ's sensation. Reading Julian's token, experiencing Julian's/
Christ's sensation, and recounting her own experience by reinscribing
Julian's token (which is never really just Julian's) in her own text become
for Margaret a virtually seamless whole.

Baker's discussions of Margaret's devotional writings in his *Life and Death of Dame Margaret Gascoigne* also emphasize the continuous relationship between her textual tokens and her interior experiences. He posits that her interior is accessible through her writings, something that makes her life not simply able to be described to others but also available to be experienced by others. He states that "we finde for her interior by her owne writings" (63), and, in speaking of her "puritie in soule supernaturallie wrought by grace" (64), he underlines the privileged aspect of texts as a means to know that which concerns the soul, even, perhaps paradoxically, texts not intended to be read. He says: "the which [i.e., her purity in soul] her writings do shew to haue ben in her, as much as writings (and those writings neuer intended by her to comme to the view of mortall man) can shew in such a case; and shew much more they can, (they being her soules immediate treatie with God concerning her conscience), then can or could anie the meere externe carriadge of her or of anie other, or can other ordinarie externe tokens proceeding from them" (64). Baker goes on to express his hope that Margaret Gascoigne's experiences, her edifying life and death, "will be taken accordingly" by "the residue of the convent" to aid "their owne further progresse in vertuousnes and preparation towards the like happie or happier death" (65).

Given such an understanding of the experiential openness to others of individual experiences expressed textually, it seems telling that Margaret's writings do not always make clear where the words of one person began and those of another end. For instance, though Margaret does explicitly identify Julian in the passage including the excerpt from the *Showings* discussed previously, she frequently uses Julian's language without identification or attribution. In chapter 17, Margaret writes, for example, "Is that most indulgent heart of his become more hard to thee, then to any other? Surely I will neuer admitt any such conceipt into my minde, but will always conclude, that Thou, my God, art enough to mee" (*Devotions*, 44; underlined in original). The underlined words in this passage come from chapter 36 of the Long Text of the *Showings*, but here, as in the many other instances where the same words appear in Margaret's devotional writings, Julian is not mentioned at all. Similarly, Mar-

garet repeatedly employs without attribution Julian's frequent Trinitarian formulation—which Julian in turn derives from St. Augustine—of
power, wisdom, and goodness (see, for instance, chapter 15 of *Devotions*).

The catalog for the library at Our Lady of Good Hope Priory (MS
Mazarine 4058) contains numerous descriptions of devotional texts like
Margaret Gascoigne's written by the nuns; they are typically called simply
"collections" or "collection books." We find, for instance, under the catalog entries for the letter C, "Eight Collection Bookes of the Verie *Reverend* Mother Clementia Cary who was the beginere or Foundrisse of our
Monistarie of our Bl*essed* Lady of Good Hope. fower and part of the fift
are of her owne hand writting" (32r), as well as entries for "Little Bookes
of Colections" including "the relation which the V*ery* R*ev*ere*nd* M*other*
Cathirin Gascoigin 2d Lady Abbisse of Cambray made of her praier" and
the "collections of R*everend* Dame Madelene Cary" (32r). Additional entries include those for "a little book of Dame Mary Watsons Collections"
(32r); "2 Books of S*i*ster Mary Temple's coll*ections*" (32r); " 2 Books of of
[sic] R. M. Bridgit's More's *[sic]* Collections" (32r); "a Book of S*i*ster Scholastica Hodson's Coll*ections*" (32r); "a Book of S*i*ster Placida Quyno's
Coll*ections*" (32r); and "a Book of Dame Eugenia's Houghton's *[sic]* Col-
lections" (32r). Elsewhere a reviser of the catalog has added under the
letter D "Dame Margaret Gascoigne Deuotions 3B" (45r; "3B" indicates
three copies of the text) and "S*i*ster Placida Quyno's deoutions 1 B" (45r).
Furthermore, under E there is an entry for "A Booke intituled of Spirituall Emblemes. 3 coppies one bound by its selfe and the other 2 with collections; by R*everend* Mary Wattison and S*i*ster Mary Tempest" (60r).[35]
That these collections are identified by the sisters' names emphasizes
the importance of the personal in them; indeed, they contain, like Margaret Gascoigne's text, nuns' individual meditations, prayers, and even
accounts of mystical experiences. However, as Margaret does, the nuns
also include with their records of individual religious experience passages from other religious texts, interweaving accounts of others' personal experiences with their own. That multiple copies are recorded in
the catalog for many of these "collection books" suggests their role in the
nuns' devotional reading. As these volumes are produced and used by the
nuns, texts originating in writers' lived experiences become the lived

experiences of readers and then become texts again in an endless cycle, calling to mind the performative, incarnational imperative with which Julian closes the Long Text of the *Showings*. These texts that combine nuns' personal experience with the textual tokens of others' religious experiences become catalysts for nuns' contemplative unions with the divine and with each other. They are, in short, texts to be performed. The English Benedictine nuns' writings, like Julian's *Showings,* translate incarnational epistemology into incarnational textuality. These texts fundamentally seek to insinuate themselves into and to shape other lives, to become shared experiences in their own day and afterwards.[36]

The ways in which distinctions between self and other blur in the nuns' collection books resonate with the ambiguous nature of authorship in many texts associated with Augustine Baker and the English Benedictine nuns of Cambrai and Paris. Heather Wolfe notes that "Baker translated, modernized, and summarized the works of English and continental late medieval mystical writers . . . and often silently integrated their writings into his own commentary."[37] J. T. Rhodes too observes, "Whatever the status of Dom Augustine Baker's experience of contemplative prayer, when he wrote about it his teaching was dominated by texts rather than experientially based. Those texts, his own and the ones he cited, represent a bibliographical and editorial nightmare. . . . Baker incorporated substantial borrowings from other authors in his own writings, as well as quoting his own previous works, which he sometimes revised or adapted for different readers."[38] I would argue, though, that in their textual and devotional practices Baker and the Benedictine nuns of Cambrai and Paris do not differentiate as strongly as Rhodes does between textually based teachings and experientially based teachings. Indeed, such categories are perhaps not very meaningful ones in these monastic communities. Knowledge gained textually and knowledge gained experientially may well not be distinguishable from each other, because through reading texts one can not just learn of but actually reexperience others' experiences oneself. Correspondingly, the mixed qualities that lead Rhodes to call Baker's writings a "bibliographical and editorial nightmare" indicate something quite fundamental about the ways in which texts, reading, and writing—indeed, language itself—function in the spirituality of these monastic communities. One's embodied experiences, and the textual records of them, are not simply one's own. They are open to, and in vital respects exist for, have always existed for, one's "evynn cristene."[39]

The "collections" thus provide sustained evidence of the pervasiveness of interpenetrative modes of subjectivity and the place of textual encounters in processes of subject formation in these monastic communities. In the spirituality of the exiled English Benedictines, shared textual tokens and the shared sensations represented by those tokens continually work to constitute communal identity that transcends the space between self and other and the time between past and present. Margaret Gascoigne and her religious sisters perhaps also hoped that such shared communal identity would transcend the time between their present and that of future readers of their texts. This textual corpus bears witness to embodied human experience in history and simultaneously seeks reincarnation in the lives of readers through human history.[40]

Writing and reading correspondingly take on a quasi-sacramental aspects in the monastic communities of Cambrai and Paris, recalling the sacramental character of writing and reading in Aemilia Lanyer's *Salve Deus Rex Judaeorum* discussed in the first chapter. Textual inscription, the creation of an incarnational textual corpus, has a function rather analogous to that of transubstantiation. Inscription creates a textual corpus in which Christ and the writer alike are present in both spirit and body to be incorporated by the nuns into their individual and communal bodies.[41] In other words, something like a textual version of the doctrine of real presence operates. In the Catholic Mass, the Word made flesh is made over and over again through the priest's words, to be ingested and hence embodied by the members of the body of Christ that is the church. Likewise, these women's texts endlessly transform lived, fleshly experience into words (experience that may include becoming one with the incarnate Christ), words that are consumed and made into flesh and then into words endlessly through generations of readers and writers.

Significantly, in spite of the ambiguous nature of authorship in the texts in the nuns' library, the library catalog from Our Lady of Good Hope Priory in Paris insistently emphasizes the hand of the writer of a text, suggesting the presence of something of the writer's corporeal self on the page to be accessed by the reader. The hand's material traces on the page enable unions between the embodied selves of writers and readers, between past and present. For example, the copy of the *Imitation of Christ*, attributed to Jean Gerson as it commonly was at the time, is described as being translated "by R. F. Peter Saluin Monck of ye holy order of S. Benedict and is in his owne hand" (121r), and, as we have seen, the catalog entry for the Collection Books of Mother Clementia Cary precisely notes that "fower and part of the fift are of her owne hand writing" (31v). The cataloguer is particularly meticulous in recording which texts are written in Baker's own hand. Baker seems to be the priestly vicar of Christ who, through his textual labors, confects a holy body that offers access to Christ's body and Christian community. Simultaneously, lost to the nuns as their spiritual director, he is a Christ-like martyr present as a relic in the texts he has authored, transcribed, or inscribed.[42] The catalog's focus on the hand of the writer highlights that a textual corpus, when read, is understood to transfer something essential of its producers, present in its material body, into the body of the reader, transforming the reader, enlivening her, and forging a community of readers past and present.[43]

Baker's remarks on the nature of books in his treatise "Concerning the Librarie of this Howse" further establish the idea that in the monastic communities of Cambrai and Paris the textual corpus is a living body. In turn, consumed by readers, the text transforms the reader in body and spirit. He writes that books "are of farre more worth and more to be regarded then is transitory pellf of money or other temporal goodds, that neither have spirit, nor do cause spirit, but most commonlie are a cause (by the solicituds about them) to hinder and oppresse the spirit. I saie good bookes, being a more immediate and more effecacious meane for the good of our soules, are more to be tendred and cared for, then are other dumbe and spiritlesse transitorie goods."[44] That books, unlike other goods that are "dumbe and spiritlesse," possess spirit and are able to "cause spirit"—to inspire and so give life to (or, more literally, breathe spirit into) to readers—increases the close identification between embodied readers and the textual corpus that is so central to the Benedictine nuns' spirituality.

INSCRIBED BODIES, EMBODIED WORDS: THE PIETY OF
GRACE MILDMAY AND CROSSING THE "GREAT DIVIDE"

It does not disturb established understandings of confessional identities to find seventeenth-century English Catholic women reading Julian of Norwich's *Showings,* reinscribing her text, and even, as I have argued, reliving her experiences. That I would in a sense find Julian, and something of the spirituality of the Benedictine nuns who were so devoted to Julian's texts, in the writings of a Protestant gentry woman, is, though, more surprising, given that so much scholarship conditions us to expect far more differences than similarities in medieval—or even early modern—Catholic and early modern Protestant female spirituality. However, strong resonances between Protestant female spirituality and that of Julian of Norwich, as well as of her monastic readers and (re)writers, were precisely what I discovered when, at the suggestion of the eminent Reformation historian Norman Jones, I began reading the brief selections from Grace Mildmay's spiritual meditations and autobiography that have been published.[45] In the writings of this Protestant gentry woman, whom Linda Pollock, the editor of these selected excerpts, describes as "not a theologian, nor a female mystic, merely one of the many godly women of English Society," I came across the following account:

> When I lay in my bed of sorrow . . . then ugly shapes and a fearful view
> of hellish figures and monstrous apparitions presented themselves
> unto my mind. . . . And in the instant thereof there was the figure of
> the face of a man exulted and lifted up. Whereupon I settled the eye
> of my mind most fixedly, beholding well the countenance of that face
> which was so dolorous and sorrowful as no heart can imagine. . . .
> And in the very same instant of my beholding that face my heart was
> stirred up to apprehend with a deep impression, the sorrows of
> Christ's death, hanging upon the cross, sweating water and blood
> in the garden, his stripes, buffets and spittings in his face, with a
> meditation thereupon. And immediately in the same instant all the
> said fearful shapes vanished away to the great consolation of my
> mind. For I was most assuredly persuaded in my heart that Jesus

Christ together with God his heavenly father and the Holy Ghost . . . did vouchsafe to visit me in this my bed of sorrow.[46]

The experience Grace Mildmay describes here reminded me immediately of the sixteenth revelation (particularly chapters 66–69) in the Long Text of Julian of Norwich's *Showings,* in which she recounts being troubled by demonic visitations and being comforted by a vision of Christ sitting in the midst of the soul as well as by meditations on Christ's passion.[47] I was also struck by the ways in which Mildmay's descriptions, here and elsewhere, of different kinds of sight and methods of understanding (she speaks of figures presenting themselves to her mind, of beholding, of setting the eye of her mind on something) reminded me of Julian's sophisticated discussions of bodily and spiritual sight, of kinds of vision, descriptions echoed by the Benedictine nuns of Cambrai and Paris.[48] Suddenly, this Protestant gentry woman, like Julian of Norwich and Margaret Gascoigne, seemed to be, to return to Pollock's categories, both something of a mystic and something of a theologian.[49] These parallel scenes in Grace Mildmay's meditations and Julian's *Showings* led me to consider further areas of overlap, and I found several. Some, like their frequent reiterations of their orthodoxy and their insistence on their divine mandate to speak, are to be expected from women "talking about things of God," but others—especially the mutually imbricated natures of the female body, the communal body, the divine Word made flesh, and the word of the text—are less expected.

Some of the resonances between Grace Mildmay's meditations and Julian's *Showings* may well stem from the fact that one of the texts that Mildmay, like many of her Protestant co-religionists, read frequently and meditated upon was Thomas à Kempis's *Imitation of Christ.* She reports that "[t]he Bible, Musculus's *Common Places, The Imitation of Christ,* Mr. Foxe's *Books of Martyrs* were the only books" her mother encouraged her to read (28). Through reading the *Imitation of Christ,* and through reading Foxe as well, Mildmay was well steeped in the discourses of affective piety centering on visual and experiential engagements with Christ's passion—staples of the medieval devotional writings that informed Julian's spirituality and that of the Benedictine nuns of Cambrai and Paris.[50] Although sadly for me Grace Mildmay was not reading Julian's writings as the Benedictine nuns were (imagine what a coup such a discovery would have been!), she was reading texts that share important features with those recommended by Augustine Baker to his monastic charges whose community at Cambrai was founded the year Grace Mildmay died. And indeed, while Mildmay was not reading Julian of Norwich, the exiled English Benedictine nuns were reading Thomas à Kempis, just as she was. *The Imitation of Christ* appears in the library catalog from Our Lady of Good Hope Priory; furthermore, Augustine Baker is known to have "translated several of the works of Thomas à Kempis."[51]

Alexandra Walsham argues that "sharp polarities in church and society indicated by labels like 'Catholic' and 'Protestant' are, in many respects, invalid in the early modern environment."[52] Grace Mildmay provides an ideal case to explore the fuzziness of such categories during her lifetime.[53] She was of the gentry, so socially she fell somewhere between top and bottom, albeit rather closer to the top, despite the financial hardships she and her husband Anthony Mildmay endured. Her father-in-law Sir Walter Mildmay was socially and politically quite well connected, particularly through his service as chancellor of the exchequer under Elizabeth I. Her grandparents witnessed the dawning of the Tudor dynasty with the accession of Henry VII, and religion was, according to Grace Mildmay, of significant importance to members of that generation of her family.[54] Her parents, Henry Sharington and Anne Paget, experienced the religious tumult of the 1530s and 1540s during their youth and young adulthood and then benefited from the Dissolution of the Monasteries under Henry VIII.[55] As I mentioned, Grace Mildmay's mother in particular played a key role in shaping her daughter's piety, a process in which Anne's experiences, and those of her own mother, undoubtedly loomed large. Grace Mildmay's progenitors were thus implicated in the complexities of religious life in early modern England and transmitted those experiences to her; she in turn transmits this complex religious inheritance, further shaped by her own experiences, to subsequent generations through her writings.

One might, I would suggest, extend Walsham's argument about the invalidity of sharply polarized labels in church and society to ways of classifying devotional and textual practices as well. Significantly, an examination of the similarities in Julian of Norwich's and Grace Mildmay's writings calls into question the fairly widespread view of Catholic and Protestant piety summed up by Pollock: "Catholics employed more imagination, visualizing time and place, and strove to achieve a rapturous union with Christ," while Protestants "were more literary and scriptural in their meditative technique" (51). This seemingly clear distinction between Catholic and Protestant piety called into question by similarities between Julian of Norwich's and Grace Mildmay's writings becomes even more blurry when one brings into the picture the writings of the English Benedictines of Cambrai and Paris.

The literary and scriptural qualities that Pollock cites as hallmarks of Protestant meditations are indeed readily evident in Grace Mildmay's writings. Bible reading features prominently in her devotional life. She calls the Bible "the book of God, which above all earthly things is to be embraced, to be believed, obeyed, feared, loved, and praised; with continual delight, exercise and meditations therein whereby a good and virtuous life may be framed from youth to old age" (70). She goes on to declare, "In mine own study in the scriptures I have found most profit, comfort and delight to clear one scripture with another upon any point of doctrine whereby the mind might be replenished with plenty of divine matter fit for meditation" (71). Furthermore, her writings are filled with echoes and quotations of biblical language from the Old and New Testament alike.

Literary and scriptural dimensions are, however, far from absent in Julian's *Showings*, as other scholars have already done much to demonstrate, and Margaret Gascoigne frequently "speaks scripture" in her devotional writings, seamlessly incorporating biblical language much as Grace Mildmay does.[56] I thus want to examine the ways in which Grace Mildmay's meditations share with Julian's *Showings* and the writings of the English Benedictine nuns a commitment to purportedly "Catholic" practices, especially those involving imagination and visualization (both of which we have already seen in the extended passage from Mildmay's writings with which this section opens) as well as union with Christ. I will also examine the ways in which a comparative analysis of Mildmay's writings alongside those of Julian of Norwich and the English Benedictine nuns, all of which are profoundly personal but all of which attribute to the personal much larger theological and political significances, complicate ideas about selfhood, means of knowing God, and the nature of Christian community often marked out across the boundary of the Protestant Reformation as basic components of religious change.

In her fascinating recent book *Patterns of Piety: Women, Gender, and Religion in Late Medieval and Reformation England,* Christine Peters gives us one of the very few studies that engages in sustained examination of both medieval and early modern female spirituality.[57] At the heart of her argument is a claim that "evolving Christocentric devotion offered a bridge to the Reformation in terms of religious understanding."[58] One of the trends that Peters notes in exploring this evolution is what she terms "a growing realisation of the gulf between mankind and the incarnate Christ" that appeared in the fifteenth century in "Christocentric parish piety." She sees parish piety as quite different from the piety of the contemplatives and of the cloistered religious; additionally, she sees the evolution of Christocentric devotion among people of the parish as having had the effect of "reduc[ing] the significance of gendered patterns of devotion" as an emphasis on striving toward union with Christ gave way to less gendered forms of *imitatio Christi.*[59]

Reading Julian of Norwich and Grace Mildmay together and alongside the writings of the exiled Benedictine nuns confirms Peters's argument that Christocentric devotion forms a bridge between later medieval and post-Reformation religion. These women's writings also reveal, however, that the gulf Peters posits between humans and the incarnate Christ was not necessarily a large one either in the later Middle Ages or during the Reformation period. Reading the writings of the early modern Protestant woman and the medieval anchoress together and in conjunction with the texts of the early modern nun Margaret Gascoigne additionally provides evidence that the line between the piety of the cloister and that of the parish is not necessarily clear. Furthermore, comparative analysis of these medieval and early modern women's writings and devotional practices demonstrates that gender remains solidly in the picture as an animating force, shaping union with, and imitation of, Christ, modes of devotion that are themselves not always readily separable.

Grace Mildmay does at times uphold the importance of imitating Christ by using language that corresponds to a decorporealized mode of *imitatio Christi* focused on Christ's examples, a form of *imitatio Christi* that Peters associates with Protestantism. Mildmay says, for instance, that one must apply oneself "wholly and sincerely unto the same, his [Christ's] examples," which are "the ready way to a pure life and conversation" (82). That no large gulf separates Grace Mildmay from the incarnate Christ, any more than such a chasm separates Julian of Norwich or Margaret Gascoigne from Christ, is, however, evident when she describes the "sympathy and union" that exists "betwixt God and us in Christ Jesus" (80). Further suggesting that she shares with the anchoress and the Benedictine nuns a desire to go beyond Christ's examples to merging corporeally with Christ, she writes, "Oh, glorious Lord, which way so ever I turn me let me turn unto thee, from this world and all mortal vanities thereof. Let me open mine eyes, lift up my hands and my heart unto thee. Let me sit up and arise, walk, live and die unto thee. Let me continually taste, feel and find thee, retain, hold and keep thee, in all things and above all things" (74). The emphasis on senses and sensations in this passage highlights that for Mildmay, as for Julian of Norwich, as for the exiled Benedictine nuns, in order to know God and to know herself, more is necessary than following precepts drawn from Christ's life or striving to imitate Christ's virtues. Knowledge of Christ has to be embodied knowledge; Grace Mildmay accordingly seeks to experience Christ the Word made flesh in her own flesh.

In other words, Grace Mildmay shares the incarnational piety and incarnational epistemology that are so characteristic of Julian and of the English Benedictine nuns of Cambrai and Paris. In the emphasis placed by these women on the body as a site of and a means to knowledge, we see that imitating Christ, uniting with Christ, and knowing Christ overlap with each other and with the process of acquiring knowledge of oneself as a spiritual subject. Indeed, it seems that these women *must* imitate and be joined with Christ for knowledge of God and self to be possible. Grace Mildmay, Julian of Norwich, and the English Benedictine nuns all insist, furthermore, on the inseparability of the fallenness and the divinity of the body. Christ's divine body is a human body, and the women's human bodies, though subject to what Julian calls "synne and febylnes" or what Mildmay calls "mortal vanities," can access the divine by imitating and uniting with Christ.[60]

We also find that Grace Mildmay shares with Julian of Norwich and the English Benedictine nuns an understanding of subjectivity that inseparably connects inner and outer, soul and body. While the spiritual is clearly bodily for Mildmay, the bodily is also demonstrably spiritual. In this I find resonances with Julian's complex categories of substance and sensuality, aspects of our and of Christ's being that, as I discuss in chapter 1, do not correspond to a dichotomy of body and soul but rather involve body and soul together.[61] Mildmay often describes her relationship with Christ using language of bodies and medicine, language that, though conventional, has importantly literal qualities. She writes, for instance, that Christ is "our only doctor and teacher," and "our meat" and "medicine." She also declares that Christ's words are "unto me as a precious ointment poured out" (75). To give one further example, she describes "true faith" as "the oil of our larynxes" (70). Significantly, in addition to her voluminous spiritual meditations, Grace Mildmay produced substantial medical writings, and there is considerable linguistic overlap between her devotional and medical texts; the language of spirituality and devotion appears strikingly frequently in her medical writings.[62] In describing "[a]nother approved course by Mr Waters upon a sucking child," for example, Mildmay writes, "Take 5 spoonfuls of betony water and 5 of syrup of cowslips and 1 of syrup of poppy and 1 of the essence of the balm, fine powder of hart's horn 1 scruple and 20 drops of the oil of vitriol, all in the name of our Lord Jesus Christ" (115). Christ's name appears as an ingredient every bit as essential to the success of the remedy as the other botanical, animal, and chemical components.

The centrality of incarnational epistemology to the devotional practices of Julian of Norwich, the English Benedictine nuns, and Grace Mildmay provides a strong first indication that, to return to Peters's distinction, the piety of the medieval cloister (or the early modern cloister) and the piety of the early modern parish laity are not necessarily so different after all. The connections between these women's spiritualities go even further, though. Christopher Abbott argues that Julian's "integral sense of life lived in the body according to the dynamics of grace" manifests "certain themes which are recognizable key elements in the broad contemplative/monastic spiritual tradition."[63] Among these broad themes are some with particular significance for our purposes, including what Abbott describes as Julian's "experiential knowledge of God" (which is connected to her "meditation on the life and death of Christ" and her "desire for God; union of wills").[64] Abbott further calls attention to Julian's regard for "self-knowledge obtained through moral failure."[65] As has already begun to emerge, themes quite similar to these that Abbott outlines as part of the medieval contemplative/monastic tradition continue to feature importantly in the early modern monastic spirituality of the communities of Cambrai and Paris. But they also shape Grace's Protestant piety and her own "sense of life lived in the body according to the dynamics of grace."

To take up Abbott's first thematic strand, Grace Mildmay, like Julian, espouses "experiential knowledge of God," knowledge closely linked to "meditation on the life and death of Christ." While Grace Mildmay does not describe undergoing the sort of physical illness replicating Christ's pain that is so prominent in Julian's *Showings* and in Margaret Gascoigne's writings, she writes that she "think[s] often of the death of Christ and of his suffering" (71). She states that in her engagement with Christ's passion, she endeavors "patiently and thankfully to embrace his cross, for as much as I find it not a means to drive me from him but rather to draw me unto him" (82). This latter statement confounds any claim for a gulf between her and the incarnate Christ. Indeed, Mildmay here experiences the "desire for God" and "union of wills" to which Abbott calls attention in the *Showings*. Mildmay's meditation on Christ's life and death involves a merging of herself with Christ not unlike the merging Margaret Gascoigne describes when she speaks of leaving herself in Christ's wounds in the passage that opens her contemplative anthology. Interestingly, Mildmay dramatizes her struggle against sinful "works of the flesh" as an internalized reenactment of Christ's passion and resurrection. After providing an encompassing list of sins (ranging from adultery to witchcraft to sedition to gluttony), she writes, "[L]et them [works of the flesh] continually die in me & be plucked vp by the rootes. And fastened vnto thy crosse, & crucifyed, dead & buryed, through thy pretious death & passion. / And by the mightie power of thy gloryous resurrection let me continually aryse from them."[66]

Textual participation in Christ's passion forms Grace Mildmay, furthermore, as a particular kind of corporeal and spiritual subject. Echoing the monastic traditions of *ruminatio* and *lectio divina,* she writes, "It hath come unto my mind in my meditating in the word of God to think often of the death of Christ and of his suffering. . . . Whereby I found the same holy doctrine to make the deeper impression in my heart, as my feeding thereupon and chewing the cud" (72).[67] Elsewhere, she builds on her description of texts' feeding her and making an impression on her heart as she describes texts' bodily effects upon her in the process of gaining understanding. She writes, "Wherein I found that as the water pierceth the hard stone by often dropping thereupon, so the continual exercise in the word of God made a deep impression in my stony heart" (34–35).[68]

I submit that Grace Mildmay's repeated descriptions of her heart receiving an impression from her interactions with the Word of God are not merely metaphorical. Rather, they participate in what Abbott calls contemplative, "experiential knowledge of God." Her descriptions reflect perceived, corporeal experiences through which knowledge is acquired, experiences very like those described by Margaret Gascoigne in her involvement with Julian's textual record of imitation of and union with Christ. Grace Mildmay's description of her engagement with God's Word also does not sound unlike the paean to the transformational, affective aspects of encountering God's Word found in the commentary on parts of the Gospel in MS Mazarine 1062. In a passage concerning John the Baptist, Baker writes, "Wherefore I wish you only to remember and consider whose word it was. The word of God is not that enough. . . . It is Gods Word, his Instinct, his Call, His Inspiration, His Vnction, his Grace, his vocation. The most admirable affect which He worketh in the soule by which shee is illuminated with Light, inflamed with Love, ravished with delight" (24r–24v). Thinking, meditating, reading are all for Mildmay embodied experiences through which she knows God and herself. Just as in the monastic communities of Cambrai and Paris, for

Grace Mildmay textual and experiential knowledge cannot readily be differentiated because they are in the end ontologically the same; here too intellectual awareness is firmly yoked to, and categorically joined with, corporeal perception. The spiritual or intellectual and the bodily necessarily proceed together.[69]

That Grace Mildmay, like Julian of Norwich, aligns with a broad contemplative, monastic tradition of perceiving self-knowledge as accessible through moral failure is clear when she addresses the need to be aware of one's own sinful nature. Mildmay says, "The best man doth most condemn himself and turn his eyes from another unto himself. For what evil or wickedness can be in any one man, that he shall not find within his own heart by due examination?" (83).[70] Speaking more personally, she elsewhere laments, "{And now that} I have accused my flesh and admonished my earthly body and members, let me turn unto my heart and take an inward and sound view thereof. And consider if my heart be not the original of all the desires and evil carriage of my mortal body" (74).[71] In these passages that again highlight the connectedness of interior and exterior, Mildmay "reads" the text of the heart as a sort of script of sinfulness performed by the transgressive actions of her mortal body. Through reading the "original" inscribed in her heart, she fully knows her status as a member of sinful humanity, and, concomitantly, gains awareness of divine mercy and love.

Grace Mildmay's process of gaining self-knowledge through moral failure recalls aspects of Julian of Norwich's discussion of sin, as when, for instance, Julian says, "[I]f we felle not, we shulde not knowe how febil and how wreched we be of oureselfe nor also we shulde not so fulsomly know the mervelous love of oure maker" (315). Both women's understandings of this aspect of knowledge acquisition harmonize with the extended analysis of temptation and its role in the process of coming to know self and God in Margaret Gascoigne's *Devotions*. Throughout the first seventeen chapters of her "contemplative anthology," Gascoigne wrestles with what Baker calls "her greater sinns, and tempta[ti]ons about iterating of confessions" (*Devotions*, 44). However, she comes to understand herself and her sinfulness in the context of divine grace, an awareness that, appropriately enough, she sets out using Julian's language:

I doe vndoubtedly beleeue & confesse, that ther is noe sinn or defect soe little, but shall according to thy iustice be punished; doe I alsoe beleeue & confesse, that there is no sinn soe great but that thy sweet mercyes doe take delight to forgiue them . . . which I humbly beseech thee to doe with me for thy great mercyes sake. Thou only, my God, who are all-seeing and -knowing wisdome, dost see & know whether my soule be in this dangerous case which my fearefull conscience doth suggest me to be in, or noe; thou alsoe, who art almighty, canst deliuer me from such perillousnes soe farre as thou seest me to be in it; & thou who are all loue, shall I doubt but that thou wilt doe it? O noe; lett that neuer enter my heart, but in that & all other occasions & cases, let me euer conclude & satisfy my-selfe wth this, that <u>Thou are enough to mee</u>. (*Devotions*, 44, Baker's underlining)[72]

The self-knowledge Margaret Gascoigne gains through knowing Julian's language and experience, and, accordingly, knowing the sufficiency of God, supplants her need obsessively to attempt to exteriorize the interior and make the self knowable through too frequent confession.

Through these manifestations of the strands of the "broad contemplative/monastic tradition" that so fundamentally shape Julian of Norwich's spirituality and that of the Benedictine nuns of Cambrai and Paris, Grace Mildmay's meditations illuminate significant, far-reaching ways in which the cultures of the cloister and the parish blend. When one considers the place of gender in shaping overlapping imitations of and unions with Christ, one finds another key continuity linking Julian's medieval Catholic piety of the anchorhold, the early modern nuns' monastic spirituality, and Mildmay's early modern Protestant faith. Gender is at once a fundamental and a fluid component of these women's relationships with Christ. As we have seen, through their female bodies Catholic and Protestant women join with and imitate a male Christ who himself shares some of their female attributes, especially in his suffering flesh.[73] Furthermore, gender remains a fundamental and fluid interpretive category in understanding women's relationships with Christ because, while women's unions with Christ do continue to be framed in spousal terms in early modern Catholic and, as we shall see, also early modern Protestant female spirituality, such unions need not necessarily be framed in nuptial terms alone to be gendered experiences. Union with Christ may take the form of the dyad of mother and child, or of other familial relationships (brother and sister, father and daughter) in which gender remains a vitally important organizing principle.[74]

One of the words that Julian uses most frequently in describing her relationship with God is *homely,* as when she describes her astonishment that "he that is so reuerent and so dreadful will be so homely with a sinnfull creature liueing in this wretched flesh" (137). Similarly, calling attention to embodiment as an aspect of our intimate relationship with God, she says, "For as the body is clad in the cloth, and the flesh in the skinne, and the bones in the flesh, and the harte in the bowke, so ar we, soule and body, cladde and enclosedde in the goodnes of God. Yee, and more homely: For all these may waste and were away. The goodnesse of God is ever hole, and more nere to us without any likenes" (145). Julian's homely, bodily, and gendered understanding of intimacy with the divine carries over into her sophisticated familial Trinitarian theology (the terminology of which, as we have seen, is adopted by Margaret Gascoigne).

This Trinitarian theology famously includes Julian's highly developed understanding of Jesus our Brother who is simultaneously our Mother.[75] To cite one brief illustrative passage, Julian writes, "Thus oure lady is oure moder, in whome we be all beclosed and of her borne in Crist. For she that is moder of oure savioure is mother of all that ben saved in our savioure. And oure savioure is oure very moder, in whome we be endlesly borne" (305). Margaret Gascoigne echoes Julian's portrayal of divine maternity even as she again invokes Julian's phrase "Thou are enough to me." She writes,

> *Quis me separabit a charitate Christi? Who shall separate me from the charitie of Christ?* Whatsoeuer shall for that end present it-selfe to my soule, I hope that through thy holy assistance, it shall neuer make such seperation, that is most odious & tormenting to my soule so much as to thinke of. For if it come to trouble & disquiet me with griefe, how can it be? For to whom thou, my sweet Lord God, art pleasing, what can be displeasing? If it come to fright me, I will turne my-selfe to thee, as a child into the bosome of his mother,

crying out: *Responde pro me; Answer for me.* And if it come to flatter & please me, thow knowest I will none but thee; thou only suffisest me, my God; *Thou are enough to me.* (*Devotions*, 66)

It is such passages that I hear echo in Grace Mildmay's meditations when she addresses "glorious Lord Jesus, my dear father, my dear friend and my dear brother" (75), or when she praises Jesus, saying, "And I cannot remember any one day of my whole life wherein . . . thou has not showed me the way and stayed me therein, even as a mother stayeth up her infant from falling when it beginneth to go" (78).

It is worth noting that accounts of nuptial union with Christ in fact feature more prominently in Grace Mildmay's devotional writing than they do in Julian of Norwich's *Showings*.[76] Grace Mildmay describes her intimate relationship with Christ in language even more closely aligned with traditions of bridal mysticism than that used most frequently by Julian. In a section bearing the heading "Though we be afflicted, yet we are not forsaken," Mildmay writes as though quoting divine speech addressed to her, saying, "I will marry thee unto me for ever" (79). One might pass over this as pure metaphor but for the fact that she also includes in her meditations extensive passages of sensual language drawn from the Song of Songs. For instance, she writes, "Let me be so open to my welbeloved that my hands may drop down myrrh and my fingers pore myrrh upon the handles of the bars. Oh, let my welbeloved put his hand by the hole of the door and let my heart be affectioned unto him. Oh, let my welbeloved lay his left hand under my head and with his right hand embrace me" (74–75). Christ responds, "I am come into my garden, my sister, my spouse. I gathered my myrrh with my spice, I ate my honeycomb with my honey, I have drunk my wine with my milk" (75). Grace Mildmay then continues, "[L]et my sanctified soul continually and wholly love and be in love with him" (75).[77] Elsewhere, again adopting language of the Song of Songs, she positions herself as Christ's spouse: "My beloved is as a bundle of myrrh unto me, he shall lie between my breasts. My beloved is as a cluster of camphor unto me. His lips are like lilies, dropping down pure myrrh. His mouth is as sweet things and he is wholly delectable. . . . In my bed let me seek my welbeloved.

Yea, let me arise early to seek thee in all places, in all companies, in all opportunities and above all things, until I find thee and then let me take fast hold on thee and never leave thee" (79).[78] Such sensual, even sexualized, language features significantly in Margaret Gascoigne's devotional writings. For instance, Gascoigne exclaims, "Come, O come my lost sweet L[ord], into the garden of my soule, and gather the fruites of my labours" (*Devotions*, 58). She continues, "O most amiable beloued of my soule, let vs, I beseech thee, make and enter into a couenant betwixt vs two, which shall be this. Thou shalt haue my heart to be thy refuge, where into thou mayst retire thee for to rest & repose. . . . And on the other side I most humbly begg of thee, that thou wouldst be pleased to giue & bestow on me thy heart, to be my house & refuge & hauen of securitie" (*Devotions*, 59).[79] In their adoption of the language from the Song of Songs embraced by medieval contemplatives in recounting their nuptial unions with Christ, Grace Mildmay, Margaret Gascoigne, and her religious sisters re-embody the experience of these earlier spiritual subjects by employing the textual token that recorded such experience.

The commitment to reiterability and commonality evident in these passages from Grace Mildmay's meditations and shared by Julian of Norwich and the Benedictine nuns of Cambrai and Paris connects with these women's understanding that individual, corporeal knowledge of the divine is textually accessible to, and beneficial for, others. These related beliefs enables us to see another way in which gender is at once a fundamental and a fluid category in shaping female piety in the medieval and early modern periods. Embodied experiences of God may be *both* gendered *and*, via texts that can be brought to life again in readers' bodily practices, shared by people of different genders.[80] Julian says succinctly, "[F]or alle this sight was shewde in generalle" (151), and hence she is compelled to offer her text—her token of her experience—to her fellow Christians for them to enact in their lives.[81] Recalling the Benedictine nuns' attitudes toward individual nuns' collection books, Grace Mildmay expresses a similar sentiment regarding the value available to others through the textual record of her experiences of God. She offers through her writings access to herself and to the divine, saying, "[T]he book of my meditations written which book hath been to me as Jacob's ladder and as Jacob's pillar. . . . Thus have I given my mind unto my offspring as my chief and only gift unto them. And unto such of them . . . as shall receive and put the same in practice . . . I dare pronounce an everlasting blessing from God" (71). That women from both sides of historical and confessional divides understand their individual, embodied experiences as readily accessible and perpetually reiterable recalls Cavell's assertion that, however far one has gotten with the interior life (which is by no means separate from the bodily life), one will find that "what is common was there before you were."[82] Grace Mildmay's devotional life and her textualization of it suggest an important counterpoint to arguments that posit the increasingly private dimensions of lay people's religion in the later medieval period, a trend toward privatization that is typically understood as intensifying with the advent of Protestantism.[83]

That Grace Mildmay copied her own meditations with the intention of advancing the spiritual development of her daughter Mary Mildmay Fane and her grandson Mildmay Fane, and that her own meditations continued to be copied in commonplace books by generations of men and women alike in her family, attest to the presence of an early modern Protestant textual culture not unlike that of the Benedictine nunneries of Cambrai and Paris. Textual tokens of individual experience are read, performed, and reinscribed to be performed again. This aspect of the Mildmay family's textual culture also attests, not incidentally, to the spiritual as well as the textual authority that Protestant women could attain within their households. Grace Mildmay, her mother, Anne Sharington, and her daughter, Mary Fane, thus provide an important counterpoint to the arguments that in Protestant culture patriarchal authority within the family was bolstered by the Reformation and that lay men's religious authority was simultaneously enhanced at the dire expense of women's religious empowerment. Their examples present, furthermore, evidence to complicate the claim that "the importance of the written word disadvantaged women in Protestant households."[84]

In short, Grace Mildmay shares with Julian of Norwich and the English Benedictine nuns of Cambrai and Paris not only incarnational epistemology but a gendered commitment to incarnational textuality. In this regard, Mildmay's understanding of the nature of textuality runs counter to the "distrust" of writing "as a diluted, secondary and dangerous medium" characteristic of some of the godly.[85] As Tom Webster points out, Daniel Rogers, in his 1642 work *Naaman the Syrian,* claims, "You know no pencil can fully reach a living face: The Presse cannot comprehend the Pulpit, and writing of a Booke is but as the picture of a dead man."[86] Such a claim is antithetical to the understanding of the nature and function of texts present as much in the work of Grace Mildmay as in the writings of Julian of Norwich and the English Benedictine nuns.

The importance of the bodily in the spirituality of Julian of Norwich, the English Benedictine nuns, and Grace Mildmay alike, combined with their shared awareness of the open boundaries between embodied selves and others (human and divine alike), leads to strikingly similar, yet potentially doctrinally surprising, understandings of divine love and salvation. For Julian of Norwich, for Margaret Gascoigne, and for Grace Mildmay, as the divine love they have experienced is common to all, so too may salvation be. Julian's *Showings,* as many have noted, literally begins and ends with God's love. The opening words are "This is a revelation of love" (123), and her last words comprise the famous summation that Love is our Lord's meaning. This passage concludes, "In oure making we had beginning, but the love wherin he made us was in him fro without beginning, in which love we have oure beginning. And alle this shalle we see in God with-outen ende" (379–80). The primacy of divine love in Julian's spirituality drives her, as is also well known, to a view of salvation that pushes the boundaries of orthodoxy. In a section significantly headed with protective assertions of orthodoxy, Julian ponders Christ's promise that "[a]lle maner a thing shalle be wele" (221). She writes that "oure faith is grounded in Goddes worde, and it longeth to oure faith that we beleve that Goddes worde shalle be saved in alle thing. And one point of our faith is that many creatures shal be dampned" (223). Considering those who will be damned, she says, "[M]ethought it was unpossible that alle maner of thing shuld be wele" (223). She then declares, "And as to this I had no other answere in shewing of oure lorde but this: 'That that is unpossible to the is not unpossible to me. I shalle save my worde in alle thing, and I shalle make althing wele'" (223).[87]

Margaret Gascoigne overcomes her anxieties about her own sinfulness and salvation through her growing awareness of the encompassing extent of divine love. Extolling the power of divine love made manifest in the Incarnation, she says, "O loue, how strong art thou! Thou, O loue, I say, that wast able to draw my Sauiour & Redeemer into this vaile of mis-erie" (*Devotions*, 66). Like Julian, she considers divine love juxtaposed with the threat of damnation, and she optimistically says, "Although in my-selfe I see nothing but confusion & cause of feare, yes, that I can ex-pect nothing but hell & damnation, as iustly I may, & haue deserued it, yet returning to thee, O Lorde, I find soe great cause of hope, that it farre exceeds all whatsoeuer I could otherwise desire. Thou are more able to help & saue me, then mine enemyes & my sinfull soul be to damne me; & therefore I will for euer hope in thee" (*Devotions*, 34).

Grace Mildmay expresses a parallel view of the encompassing, sal-vific nature of divine love. Echoing scriptural language, she says, "God is love and he that dwelleth in love, dwelleth in God and God in him. . . . Herein is love, not that we loved God but that he loved us and sent his son" (79). Furthermore, she, like Julian, gives an overall assessment of her textual corpus as a witness of divine love, calling her book "a testi-mony to the love and presence of God" (24). Grace Mildmay's compre-hension of divine love leads her, like Julian of Norwich, to a view of salva-tion that departs from that of her co-religionists, namely, she does not embrace a stringent interpretation of the Calvinist doctrine of predes-tination and election. In spite of her emphasis on the primacy of God's Word, Mildmay's soteriology does not follow what might be considered the expected Calvinist path. In many godly Protestant writings, when the authors use the word *all* in referring to the recipients of divine grace and salvation, they simply mean all of the godly or elect. As Pollock notes, when Mildmay refers to the elect, she uses "such terms as the saints, the elect, God's chosen people and the faithfull" (60). But in understanding salvation, Mildmay has something different in mind. She writes:

> Our saviour Christ when he had called all the people and his disciples unto him, he said unto them, whosoever will come after me, let him deny himself and take up his cross and follow me, for whosoever will save his life shall lose it but whosoever shall lose his life for my sake and the gospels, the same shall save it. Here Christ speaketh universally to all, of what state or condition soever, high

and low, rich and poor whosoever. And as he speaketh generally so he speaketh lovingly whosoever will, as not scorning any but inducing all. Whoever will; here is no choice nor exceptions of persons. . . . [H]e that will shall be welcome to the inheritance prepared for him from the beginning. (59–60)

Pollock points out here that when Grace Mildmay says all, she means *all* (59).[88]

In spite of periodic expressions in her meditations of the sort of anti-Catholic sentiment that characterizes much religious writing by her Protestant contemporaries, for Grace Mildmay this "all" includes even Catholics—and potentially even the pope himself: "For, God is able to convert the papists and even the very Pope himself and to pardon their blindness" (90). She exhibits what I call a paradoxically optimistic Calvinism; it seems that somehow "all shall be well," as is so famously the case for Julian, a belief with implications both theological and political.[89] Grace Mildmay's belief system suggests a kind of irenicism (in her evident reluctance to embrace a strictly polemical Protestant identity) or at least a very broad view of what constitutes adiaphora, and her toleration is especially striking, given that she witnessed the dramatic, official hardening of the line against recusancy in the later sixteenth century.[90]

Grace Mildmay's spirituality, along with its theological and social corollaries, owes some of its optimism and toleration to her understanding of Christ's corporeal availability, something she shares with the "old religion's" Christology.[91] This availability comes not through consuming the transubstantiated host in the Eucharist but through consuming texts, imitating Christ, and uniting with Christ—through the practice of incarnational piety and through the processes of incarnational epistemology and incarnational textuality.[92] Grace Mildmay had, as Julian of Norwich and the English Benedictines of Cambrai and Paris had, the experience of being in, being one with, the body of Christ, an experience open to other Christians. Indeed, the writings of these women suggest that other Christians necessarily *must* be in and one with Christ because of the fundamentally open nature of Christ's incarnate body and the fundamentally permeable boundaries between human selves. Hence the body of Christ that is the church is for Grace Mildmay a rather more capacious, commodious body than it is for some of her co-religionists.[93]

To conclude, I would argue that Grace Mildmay's writings, considered in conjunction with Julian of Norwich's *Showings* and texts associated with the English Benedictine nuns of Cambrai and Paris, demonstrate that changes in female spirituality across the "great divide" are not always what one might expect, nor do they always proceed in the ways that one might expect. As we have seen, practices to which some scholars have pointed as evidence of new, Protestant modes of spirituality and subjectivity are clearly in play earlier on. At the same time, supposedly medieval and Catholic practices centering on the senses, the human body, and the body of Christ are, rather, catholic in the more general sense of the term. Such practices are embraced by an early modern Protestant gentry woman as well as by early modern nuns. Reading these women's texts together additionally reveals that the institutionally mediated relationship with God typically assigned to medieval Catholicism and the individual relationship with God typically assigned to reformed Protestantism were not the only kinds of relationships available. Julian of Norwich and the nuns, like Grace Mildmay, had individual and deeply personal relationships with the divine as gendered subjects, while Grace Mildmay, like Julian of Norwich and the nuns, simultaneously combined those individual experiences with an understanding of Christianity in which communality coexists with and is contiguous with, not simply subsidiary to, the individual.

Chapter Three

Embodying the "Old Religion" and Transforming the Body Politic

The Brigittine Nuns of Syon, Luisa de Carvajal y Mendoza, and Exiled Women Religious during the English Civil War

Augustine Baker, Gertrude More, and the Politics of Martyrdom

Within a decade of its foundation, the community of English Benedictine nuns of Cambrai found itself in conflict with figures of patriarchal authority over distinctive aspects of their spirituality and their textual production, a state of affairs that would have been quite familiar to St. Birgitta of Sweden and St. Catherine of Siena. English Benedictine officials objected to Augustine Baker's method of spiritual instruction and the nuns' use of texts associated with it. The first flare-up of trouble occurred in the early 1630s and culminated with Baker's removal from Cambrai as the nuns' spiritual director in 1633. In the same year, the Benedictine authorities also threatened to confiscate the nuns' manuscripts associated with Baker; however, "the manuscripts were examined and deemed to be free of any heretical tendency," and the nuns were permitted to retain them.[1]

This was not the end of the matter, though. In 1655 conflict erupted again, and "when . . . Father Claude White demanded the immediate surrender of all the Baker manuscripts, the nuns unanimously signed and forwarded a petition requesting that any examination be deferred until the forthcoming chapter. As a result, Father White arrived in person on Saturday, February 27, 1655, determined to enforce his demand."[2] The strength with which the nuns resisted White's efforts suggests they had taken to heart Baker's advice concerning the value of books in a document entitled "Concerning the Library of this Howse." Baker declares that "bookes in their own natures" are "more noble and more of worth then other goodds of fortun." He continues, "The time will come (said Thaulerus, as it were propheticallie) that soules will desire and seeke to have spirituall guids and directors, and will be able to find none, and it maie prove to be the case of this howse as well as of other howses, and how usefull will good bookes be then? And how will they then do without them?"[3] In spite of the great controversy that ensued in the wake of the nuns' resistance to Father White, the women religious ultimately retained possession of their manuscripts.[4]

In the nuns' texts produced in this environment of conflict, we see incarnational political visions emerge. The Benedictine authorities' threat to the nuns' distinctive monastic and textual cultures becomes for the nuns a joint suffering of the corporate body and the written corpus. Such suffering advances the nuns' processes of union with the divine, with each other, and, crucially, with their "evynn cristene" of the English past. The community's resistance to a Benedictine hierarchy that would alter their distinctive devotional traditions and the textual manifestations of that devotion merges with their opposition to the English Protestant nation. The nuns' individual bodies, those of their books, and the corporate body of their monastic community all stand in for, and have the potential to resurrect through their sufferings, a Catholic England.

Gertrude More's "exposition of the contemplative life as taught by Father Baker," published in Paris in 1658 under the title *The Spiritual Ex-*

ercises of the Most Vertuous and Religious D. Gertrude More, highlights the breaking down of boundaries separating individual bodies, communal bodies, Christ's body, and a textual corpus in ways as crucial to shaping the English Benedictine nuns' political vision as to forming their religious identity.[5] Much as Julian of Norwich relives Christ's suffering (his very pains) in her own body and in her text, and as Margaret Gascoigne re-embodies Christ's and Julian's pain in her life and text, this volume sets up a chain of explicitly English reincarnations of Christ's suffering in which those who successively re-embody Christ's passion also re-experience the sufferings of their English Catholic forebears.[6]

Placed before the dedicatory epistle to Brigit More (Gertrude More's biological sister and one of the scribes who copied Margaret Gascoigne's devotional writings) in *The Spiritual Exercises* is a likeness of Gertrude More by the French engraver René Lochon. On the page facing the engraving is a poem perhaps written, Geoffrey Scott asserts, by Dom Leander Normanton.[7] The poem begins with an apostrophe to Gertrude's ancestor St. Thomas More and transitions into praise for Gertrude:

> Renowned More whose bloody Fate
> England neer yet could expiate,
> Such was thy constant *Faith,* so much
> Thy *Hope,* thy *Charity* was such,
> As made thee twice a Martyr proue;
> Of *Faith* in Death, in Life of *Loue*
> View heer thy Grandchilds broken *Hart.*

By invoking More's martyrdom, the poem begins by aligning his suffering, like that of all the martyrs, with that of the crucified Christ. The poet then instructs More to view his grandchild's suffering (as we perhaps are to view it in the image on the facing page?); her "broken Hart" is positioned as a response to, even a reenactment of, More's "bloody Fate" at England's hands. Her suffering, and that of the community (in their exile from England and at the hands of those who would rob them of their manuscripts and Baker's spiritual direction), *are* More's suffering and, like Julian's, also Christ's. The past is written in and known through their bodies as well as in and through their books.

Such equations of past and present, of bodies and books, emerge even more strongly in the prefatory material to Gertrude More's *Spiritual Exercises*. In her letter "To the Reader" defending Augustine Baker and herself, she explicitly aligns Baker with Christ. She writes, "He who hath been my Maister, and Father in a spiritual life . . . is notwithstanding taxed now by the same words in a manner which were alleaged against our blessed Sauiour. *We have found this man subverting the people, and forbidding to give tribute to Cesar*" (8–9). And, as Christ's body suffered, so too can the textual body of books.[8] The dedicatory epistle to Gertrude More's *Spiritual Exercises* enhances the concept of incarnational textuality that animates the English Benedictine nuns' textual and political cultures. It sets up a textual experience of martyrdom, suggesting that the body of Gertrude More's text suffers in common with her, the monastic community, Baker, her martyred ancestor Thomas More, and, ultimately, Christ. The author, who signs the epistle "F. G." (that is, Francis Gascoigne, Margaret and Catherine Gascoigne's brother who was a secular priest and disciple of Baker), writes—making reference to another work of Gertrude More's published in 1657—"If it chance to fal into the hands of any such as may reiect, or cry it down: (as some did the Ideots Deuotions of the same Spirit lately set forth) it will (as that did) but receive the greater luster thereby, and be more highly prised" (4).

Francis Gascoigne's dedicatory epistle also emphasizes Brigit More's likeness to her sister Gertrude, positioning Brigit as the next heir to the text and as the next in the concatenated line of those who bring to life the form of spirituality the text embodies. He states, "[T]here is no other heire left to it but your deseruing self besids I know few or none do any way pretend to it, but you and your Religious flock who exactly trace by true practice (O Practice, divine practice, the only means) the same holy paths this booke treats of" (3). Significantly, under the engraving of Gertrude More that precedes the dedicatory epistle is the conceit "Magnes Amoris Amor" ("Love is the magnet of love"). This conceit's pun not only links the name of More with divine love but also, to an English speaker's ear, contains the phrase "A More is a More," a phrase that precisely encapsulates the idea of shared subjectivities and unitive reincarnation outlined in the poem and the epistle. Brigit and Gertrude More become one;

both are one with their martyred English ancestor, who features in the poem facing the image of Gertrude, and all are one with the incarnate Christ and with their fellow members of Christ's body.

The textual and corporeal lineages of simultaneous union with Christ and with the medieval past come together again in the "Approbation" added to the end of Gertrude More's letter "To the Reader." Here a priest refers to the text to follow in this fashion: "These Confessions or Soliloquies writen by the late deceased Dame Gertrude More . . . pious ofspring of that Noble and Glorious Martyr Sir Thomas More, Chancellor of England, contayning nothing but a true practise of that diuine Booke of the Imitation of Christ (restored of late to the true Author Iohn Gerson . . .)." The text's author, Gertrude, and the text itself, embody the imitation of Christ, either via a familial legacy of martyrdom for commitment to "the old religion" or via a textual ancestor, here attributed to a solidly medieval author, the fifteenth-century cleric Jean Gerson.

Individual, corporate, and textual re-embodiments of suffering make the past live in the present; suffering, however, is not the end of the story in the *Spiritual Exercises,* just as it is not for Julian of Norwich or for Margaret Gascoigne.[9] In the poem placed opposite Gertrude More's engraved portrait, her "broken Hart" is the fulcrum on which the poem makes an important turn. In the first part of the poem, the pain of her "broken Hart" is the pain of shared martyrdom. However, the poem continues:

> View heer thy Grandchilds broken *Hart*
> Wounded with a Seraphick Dart.
> Who while she liu'd mortals among
> Thus to her *Spouse Diuine* she sung.

The nature and meaning of her "broken Hart" shifts—the heart is broken because it is pierced, like that of St. Teresa in ecstasy, with a seraphic dart.[10] Martyrdom gives way to mysticism and prayer; indeed, the rest of the poem is Gertrude More's hymn to Christ. Suffering and union with the "Spouse Divine" are for More, as for Julian of Norwich, as for Margaret Gascoigne, inseparable.[11] Experiencing Christ's bodily suffering is the beginning, the beginning of a revelation of divine love, the beginning of knowledge of self and other, the beginning of a text, and, so the English Catholics in exile hope, the beginning of a reincarnation in England of "the old religion" that will transform the English body politic.

ENGLAND, SPAIN, AND EMBODYING THE "OLD RELIGION"

The English Benedictines of Cambrai show us, as do the English Carmelites of Antwerp, models of creating an English Catholic body politic across the English Channel. The English Brigittines of Syon also spent many years after the Dissolution of the Monasteries living as an English community on the Continent, eventually settling in Spanish-controlled Lisbon after traveling through the Low Countries and France. But during the reign of Elizabeth I, Syon, actually sent women religious back into England, including a nun named Marie Champney, whom I shall discuss shortly. Furthermore, in the early seventeenth century, when Catholic hopes were high in connection with the proposed "Spanish Marriage" between Charles, Prince of Wales, and the Infanta Maria of Spain, the nuns of Syon planned a wholesale return, a desire they expressed in a petition to the Infanta to enlist her help in achieving their aim.

The case of Syon in exile, supported financially by the Spanish crown and firmly enmeshed in Anglo-Spanish politics, calls attention to the fact that Spain as a nation has a place of profound importance alongside women as spiritual subjects in creating an oppositional English religio-political culture in the post-Reformation era. Here we find another set of permeable boundaries, another complex constellation of relationships of inner and outer, this time on a national rather than a personal scale. Though he is focusing on Shakespeare's *Hamlet*, David Hillman's remarks on subjectivity, the body, and politics are quite relevant to my argument here. He argues, "One could say, then, that from one perspective *the* project of early modern England was the renegotiation of inside/outside boundaries." He goes on to point out, however, that "instabilities . . . lie at the heart of all attempts to distinguish inner from outer." As he observes, "[T]he very act, the *process*, of distinguishing between the two undermines . . . its own declared goal, for while processes of incorporation and expulsion may ultimately be aimed at creating a perfect, closed interior, how can the body (of the individual, of the land, or of the nation) help but be seen as endlessly permeable if it at the same time allows—*needs,* in fact—so much taking in and letting out?"[12]

The Brigittine monastics who spent so much time in Spanish-controlled Lisbon capitalized on such instabilities, though not necessarily always in precisely the ways feared by the Protestant political establishment. Luisa de Carvajal y Mendoza, an embodiment of the Spanish Catholic Other that official Protestant England sought so passionately to exclude, also features prominently in this chapter. Luisa was a noblewoman with close ties to both the Spanish royal court and the Society of Jesus; these connections brought her into frequent interactions with such figures as Robert Parsons and other important members of Syon's circle of supporters. Luisa entered England in 1605 to advance the Jesuit "English Mission," and while in England she complicated boundaries and identities further by founding an unofficial, quasi-monastic organization for women called the Society of the Sovereign Virgin Mary, Our Lady.

The Brigittine nuns of Syon, Luisa de Carvajal y Mendoza, and the group of English women who joined Luisa's quasi-monastic Society all act upon the desires animating the poem preceding Gertrude More's *Spiritual Exercises.* That is, they strive through their practices of incarnational piety and incarnational textuality to transform the English body politic into a Catholic body politic. In their lived lives and in their writings, the Syon nuns, Luisa, and the English women of her Society perform revisions of the English body politic as a Catholic body at times represented by, and at times legitimated by, a variety of holy bodies from the past brought in diverse ways into the present. These bodies include those of saints (both officially canonized and popularly venerated), the Virgin Mary, the crucified Christ, individual women religious, and the corporate bodies of female religious communities. Luisa, the women of her Society, and the Syon nuns all embrace the hope that England will, through processes that simultaneously recall Christ's incarnation, passion, and resurrection, play a salvific, messianic role for the Catholic cause. As we shall see, these religio-political processes themselves depend, as do the incarnation, passion, and resurrection of Christ to which these women were devoted, upon female bodies and suffering bodies. In these processes, relationships between past and present, between interior and exterior, between domestic and foreign, are not simple ones. The women in question unite the past and the present, blend the interior and the exterior, and meld the domestic and the foreign. They do so by practicing in, projecting into, and disseminating from England forms of incarnational piety rooted in such later medieval religious practices as affective spirituality and Eucharistic devotion.[13]

SYON'S PASSION

After Henry VIII dissolved the monasteries, many of the nuns of Syon fled England together for the Continent, seeking to continue their distinctive form of monastic life while remaining an entirely English community despite their residence in foreign realms. Following their brief return home during the reign of Mary I, the nuns went again en masse into exile during the reign of Elizabeth I. While Syon was residing in Malines after fleeing England for the second time, they endured great poverty due both to Protestant hostilities and to the fact that their pension from the Spanish crown was paid only irregularly. Accordingly, the abbess and sisters decided to send a group of nuns covertly back into England to raise alms. This group included Elizabeth Sanders and Marie Champney. Elizabeth was imprisoned for nine years in England and ultimately escaped to rejoin her convent, which in the intervening period had moved on to Rouen. She wrote letters to Sir Francis Englefield describing her sojourn in England. Marie, who died in England, is primarily known through an anonymous account entitled *The Life and Good End of Sister Marie,* a generically hybrid text combining third-person biographical accounts of Marie's life with extensive first-person speeches.[14] The nuns also wrote a collective account of their troubles in France and their flight to Lisbon, which was translated into Spanish and published in Madrid in 1594 under the title *Relacion que embiaron las religiosas del monasterio de Sion de Inglaterra, que estaban en Roan de Francia, al padre Roberto Personio de la Compañia de Iesus, de su salida de aquella ciudad, y llegada à Lisboa de Portugal.*[15] Like the *Life and Good End of Sister Marie,* the Spanish version of the Syon nuns' account of their experiences addressed to Robert Parsons, with its long "Preambulo" by their confessor general Seth Foster setting out the history of their foundation from its fifteenth-century establishment, combines what might be called communal autobiography and institutional biography.[16]

As I have argued elsewhere, I believe more was at stake for Syon in sending nuns back to England than simply raising alms for the community. Elizabeth Sanders was the sister of Nicholas Sanders, and her time in England corresponded with the period of planning for his failed papal invasion through Ireland; furthermore, she was involved in distributing Edmund Campion's notorious *Brag.* Additionally, *The Life and Good End of Sister Marie* suggests Syon's support for Mary Stuart and possibly even hints at the community's involvement in Marian plots.[17] As the episode of Campion's *Brag* makes abundantly clear, writing is a highly political act, and textual representations have political consequences that may be every bit as great as plots or planned invasions. In what follows, I am therefore interested less in political intrigues in which the nuns of Syon may have been involved than in the textual representations of Syon's religio-political visions and the implications of those representations for the English Catholic cause in an international context. Specifically, I am interested in the ways in which the writings of Elizabeth Sanders, Marie Champney, and the community as a whole portray their understandings of the mutually informing dimensions of their convent's collective experiences of suffering in exile; individual nuns' bodily and spiritual experiences; and the suffering, as well as the potential redemption, of an English Catholic body politic.

The Life and Good End of Sister Marie highlights the interplay of incarnational piety and incarnational textuality in the English Brigittines' political vision.[18] Like the writings of Julian of Norwich, Margaret Gascoigne, and Grace Mildmay examined in chapter 2, *The Life and Good End of Sister Marie* is an account of a woman's complex engagement with past holy lives—in this case those of Christ, the Virgin Mary, and St. Birgitta— that simultaneously offers itself to others as a shareable religious (auto)- biography possessed of a strongly performative imperative.[19] In fact, I believe that a major component of the *Life's* raison d'etre was to encourage

precisely such re-embodying and reliving of holy lives by members of
the monastic community of Syon and by other English Catholics with
the aim of channeling textual performance into the creation of a transformed Catholic England.

The Life and Good End of Sister Marie first recounts Marie Champney's
departure from England as a young woman and the sequence of events
leading up to her monastic profession with the Brigittines in exile. In
these early experiences, Marie's processes of attaining self-knowledge
depend on corporeal experiences of the incarnate Christ. While Marie is
on the Continent, she experiences conflict and spiritual turmoil about
what course she should pursue. At one point she is filled with longing to
return home to England, and a "father of the Jesuites" advises her to pray
"with as much quietnes of minde as she coulde." He also directs her the
next morning to "heare Masse with as much devocyon as she coulde"
(2v). During Mass, at the elevation of the Host, she has a visionary experience of the sort that characterizes the Eucharistic piety of many later
medieval holy women. At the moment in the Mass when Christ's body
present in the transubstantiated Host is displayed to the gathered members of the congregation, that body is made manifest in its human form
to Marie: "When the preiste came to the blessed Elevation, this most
comfortable vision, God shewed her, that our Saviour Christ appeared
to her in visible shape over the Chalice (belike to confirme her in trewe
beleefe of those dreadfull misteries, besides the woing of her, as it were
to further perfeccion), lookinge most graciouslye towards her, and with
his twoo fingers (as the vse of the Byshopps is) blessinge her" (2v–3r).
These "livelie pictures" (3r), as Marie describes the visionary experience, provide divine confirmation of the Catholic doctrine of transubstantiation, simultaneously legitimating the Catholic office of bishop as
a vicar of Christ. They also, in "woing . . . her . . . to further perfeccion,"
reinforce Marie's religious vocation.

Ultimately, the "livelie pictures" have a physical effect on Marie,
somaticizing her vocation and uniting body, mind, and spirit. Upon perceiving the incarnate Christ over the chalice, "her hart seemed to be ravished halfe from her, and her fleshe also felte a kinde of tremlinge for
Reverence of so heavenlye a sighte" (3r). As if to mark the change in her

identity that her religious vocation demands, Marie's visionary experience leaves a lasting corporeal legacy, a form of somatic inscription not unlike those that Grace Mildmay describes receiving from her own experiences of Christ the Word made flesh. Marie's vision "vanished againe from her eyes," but the "perfecte shape & *printe* of his gracious countenaunce (as she woulde saye) coulde never while she liued out of her hartes remembraunce" (3r, emphasis added). In a scene reminiscent of many medieval saints' lives, her body becomes a text imprinted with the divine Word even as Christ's human countenance becomes flesh again in her.[20]

Marie's choice of the Brigittine order for her monastic profession involves another visionary experience, one that in a different way emphasizes the centrality of incarnational piety to Brigittine spirituality. Having spent time with a "cloyster of Nunnes aboute Antwerpe" where she learned "her Songe and her Grammer, for vnderstandinge of her lattin seruice," Marie is summoned by the abbess of Syon (then at Mishagen), who, "hauing hearde belike of this younge gentlewoman," was "somewhat desirous to haue a sight of her" (3r). When Marie sees the abbess's "blacke veyle on her heade lyned with pure white, and the white crowne withall spotted with five spotts of redd, which that order weareth, and no other sorte of nunnes but they" (3r), she is "astonyed" (3r) at the sight of this distinctive element of the Brigittine habit, which commemorates Christ's wounds. Her further reaction to the habit is an appropriately embodied one as she recalls an experience from her youth: "With teares ready to gushe out of her eyes, shee declared *what a suddayne impressyon there came into her harte* at the first sighte of the crowne, and the veyle . . . by remembraunce of a straunge dreame which she had in her youthe of the like weede and habitt to hers in all poyntes, to be putte by a Bishoppe vpon her" (3v, emphasis added). Once again Marie Champney describes her somatic response to a visual experience; like the sight of Christ's countenance, the sign of the abbess's crown and veil transforms her body, making an impression in her heart. Underlining the bodily dimensions of Champney's reaction to the sight of the abbess's habit, the author says that "her harte presently melted, as the spowses very worde is in the Canticles" (3r). The author's reference to the spouse of the

Song of Songs calls to mind the identity of Christ's bride that Champney will have as a Brigittine nun. Her somatic response to the sight of the abbess's habit serves as a profession *avant la lettre*. When she sees the abbess's outward signs of her identity as Christ's bride and her inward identification with Christ's passion (a dual self-conception simultaneously encompassing subject positions focused on the Virgin Mary and Christ that is so characteristically Brigittine), Marie Champney performs through her bodily reaction the identity of divine spouse that she will adopt formally when the bishop performs the consecration she saw in her earlier visionary experience.

Marie's identity as Christ's spouse is, as Ann Hutchison observes, an important point of intersection with the life of St. Birgitta.[21] Indeed, Hutchison details several aspects of the *Life* that suggest Marie Champney's "strong affinity with her Order's founder," including her gift of tears, the simplicity of her life, and her extended kneeling in prayer.[22] I would argue that Marie is doing more than simply "following the example of St. Birgitta,"[23] just as Margaret Gascoigne does more than simply follow the example of Julian of Norwich. Rather, as Margaret Gascoigne relives Julian of Norwich's life experiences, so Marie does with St. Birgitta's life, a life that encompasses a simultaneous, dual self-identification as "another himself" who relives Christ's suffering as Christ's spouse.

In its representation of Marie's last illness and death, the *Life and Good End of Sister Marie* thus quite fittingly emphasizes both Marie's status as Christ's bride and her status as one who re-embodies Christ's pains. The author reports various edifying conversations in which Marie takes part in the days just before her death, noting that on one "occasion of our talkinge" Marie foregrounds her identity as Christ's bride, declaring, "[W]hat a comforte it maye nowe be unto hir that she had forsaken all the allurements & delightes of creatures in this worlde from the pryme and flower of hir youthe, onelie for hir sweete spowses sake, to hope nowe more confidentlie for the ioyes of heaven" (14r). As Marie's death approaches, according to the author, the nun repeats the following words: "O my deere spowse o sweete Jesu Jesu now be to me a sweete Jesus" (15v). She is also comforted by the assurance that her sisters will celebrate her death as the consummation to her marriage to Christ. The author indicates that Marie is told that, following her funeral Mass, "[W]hen all this is fynished by the grace of god, we will have as it were a Bride cuppe, full of good spiced cakes, & sweete wyne, to reioyce agayne after mourninge" (15v).

Marie also brings together her role as Christ's spouse and the connection between her death and Christ's passion when she points out, as her last days approach, that she is thirty-three years old "even as my deere Lorde and spowse was at his crucyfyinge" (15v). Shortly before she dies, she recalls a vision concerning her death that she had earlier in her life. In this vision, she indicates, a taper, significantly shaped like a cross, appeared before her, lighted at the top, and she heard a voice announce that the hour of the flame's burning out would be the hour of her death. Significantly, the author of the *Life* strongly emphasizes both corporeality and intersubjectivity in aligning Marie's death with Christ's. He or she tells of a "learned preiste" who frequently attends Marie and who says "his ixth hower" immediately after dinner in accordance with "the custome of manye in Rome . . . in memorye of Christes yeelding up his blessed soule vpon the crosse at noone tyme" (16r). As the priest says his office, the author reports that Marie simultaneously feels intense pain: Marie "felte such gripes at hir harte that suddaynlye she repeated agayne these . . . wordes . . . 'O my deere spowse o sweete Jesu Jesu now be to me a sweete Jesus" (16r).[24]

Just prior to the author's prayers that conclude the manuscript, the narrative of Marie's "good end" wraps up with a detailed description of her body in death, pointing once again to the importance of embodiment in Brigittine spirituality. In a testament to the modes of epistemology that characterize Brigittine access to divinity in life, Marie's body makes her holiness, her union with her spouse Christ in death, knowable through physical signs. "Marie's coarse," the author observes, is "as white, as the white virgins waxe, her eyes as plumbe, as comelie, as any chyldes in a slumber, her cheekes no leaner then in tyme of healthe, & her cowntenaunce as sweete as the smyling Babes" (16v).

The detailed narration of Marie's corporeal suffering in the *Life and Good End of Sister Marie* is by no means the only place that accounts of the nuns' bodily pains have in their representations of their time in

England. Set into the description of Marie's experiences is what might be called a miniature *vita* of Ann Stapleton, featuring her own life and good end. Ann's sojourn in England also features in Elizabeth Sanders's letters. In these accounts of Ann Stapleton's life and death too, the body, and especially its pains, have important spiritual and political dimensions. Like Marie, Ann had a mystical experience (a "straunge dreame" [5r]) that prompted her to pursue profession "amonge the Englishe nunnes of S*aint* Brig*ittes* order" (5r). Ann too was sent back to England, and, as we learn from Elizabeth Sanders's letters, she suffered serious illness there. Indeed, this report of Ann Stapleton's illness and death opens one of Elizabeth's letters to Sir Francis Englefield and so sets the tone for the ensuing narrative of her English sojourn, shaping perceptions of the significance of the Brigittine nuns' experiences. Revealingly, the letter highlights the resonances between Ann's suffering and self-sacrifice for the Catholic cause and Christ's life and death. Elizabeth indicates that Ann arrived in England about a week after her, "very sick." Elizabeth continues, "w*ith* her I remayned all the tyme of her syknes, w*hich* was fro*m* St Symon and Jude day untill St Thomas day at w*hich* tyme I was sent away fro*m* her (for some respects) much agaynst myne owne mynd, for I would not haue left her by any meanes in that case fearyng greatly her death."[25]

Elizabeth's calling attention to the saints' feasts to mark the interval she spent with Ann during her illness may subtly suggest symbolic resonances between the community of Syon, and the community of persecuted English Catholics more broadly, and these saintly figures. St. Simon, St. Jude, and St. Thomas are all apostles, so Elizabeth may be drawing a connection between the small band of Syon nuns and these followers of Christ who traveled afar to preach the Gospel after Christ's death and resurrection.[26] In the western Christian tradition, both Simon and Jude are martyrs (both killed in Armenia or Persia), and St. Jude, famously, is the patron saint of desperate situations, a figure with potential special appeal to the English Catholics during periods of harsh persecution. Jude is also known for writing an epistle against heresy. St. Thomas, best known for his demand to touch the resurrected Christ's wounds to confirm his identity, is a figure who thus pointedly directs attention to Christ's tortured yet triumphantly raised body. Elizabeth indicates, furthermore, that Ann "dyed vppon Chrystmasse eue following," a detail that adds a further link to the chain of signification connecting Ann's suffering, that of the monastic community, and that of English Catholics as re-embodiments of the *vita Christi.*

The *Life and Good End of Sister Marie* provides further evidence that shared and shareable spiritual experiences can serve explicitly political ends. While Marie is in England, she hears of the horrors that befell the community of Syon in Mechlin in February 1578, when Protestant forces captured the city. She believes the convent may have been totally lost among the many religious houses that were destroyed in the violence. The author of the *Life* recounts that when Marie hears "of the losse of Machline, and of the captiuytye at leaste of her systers there remaynynge," her "harte" is "perced . . . with marveylous compassyon of their calamyte" (12v). The language of Marie's heart being pierced with compassion recalls the common medieval representation of her name saint the Virgin Mary's heart being pierced by the sword of sorrow at the Crucifixion— her own compassion—in accordance with Simeon's prophecy. The account's details thus highlight not only that Marie identifies with her community's troubles, sharing the experiences of her fellow women religious, but also that her suffering, like that of her religious sisters, is a simultaneous reiteration of Christ's and Mary's linked experiences of suffering at the Crucifixion.

Additional details emphasize that the physical valence of the language describing Marie's reaction to the news from Malines is more than figurative. The account of Syon's suffering, and that of the pain that Marie experiences with her sisters, call attention to the material, corporeal dimensions of the women's experiences, continuing to develop a sense of shared subjectivities and of overlapping temporalities combining a sacred past and a holy present. The author reports that one of Marie's friends reads to her "the prayer of Jeremy" from Lamentations "as fittest for her purpose" (12v) when she learns of the fall of Malines to the Protestants. The author continues, "[B]efore they could come to the end of it, namelie at these verye wordes Mulieres in Syon humiliaverint . . . Belike she both felte & perceaued the *nayle* of both theire sorrowes" (12v, emphasis added). Marie then reaches out to shut the book and does not speak until "after the *agonye* of it a little paste" (12v, emphasis added). Subsequently, "her frende was aduised to reade that prayer of Jeremie no more to her, for feare of *oppressinge her harte* with so much heavines" (13r, emphasis added). This language heightens the association of Marie's somaticized suffering, and that of her fellow women religious, with Christ's and the Virgin Mary's. It recalls the nails driven into Christ's body and his agony on the cross as well as Mary's maternal pain at the Crucifixion. This textual account inevitably aligns the Protestant forces who cause Syon's passion with the crucifiers of Christ. Marie and her sisters across the Channel thus become, like St. Catherine of Siena, "another himself," undergoing suffering that might potentially redeem and resurrect the English body politic, and even perhaps redeem those who cause its, and their, pain.

The *Life and Good End of Sister Marie* presents Marie's life as a reliving of past holy lives and offers her experiences as open to being relived by others. So too the *Relacion* construes the collective life and sufferings of Syon as sacred lives, and especially Christ's life, reenacted and reenactable, shareable by others. In creating this dynamic in the *Relacion*, the Syon nuns cause holy bodies both individual and communal to signify powerfully on the political stage. A large portion of the text is devoted to the nuns' discussion of their flight from Rouen to Lisbon, a flight necessitated by the rise to power in Rouen of hostile Protestant forces. The nuns recount their complicated negotiations to obtain passports and passage as well as their somewhat fraught departure from the city, events that correspond with Holy Week. As Elizabeth Sanders did in her report of Ann Stapleton's death on Christmas Eve, the nuns foreground this coincidence of timing to align their experiences with Christ's life and death. For instance, they recall that the following day, "que era el Domingo de Ramos" [which was Palm Sunday], their confessor general, after saying Mass, went "à casa del Gouernador de Roan" [to the governor of Rouen's house] to entreat him for passports for him and his religious family (" à el y à su familia") (32r). They report packing up their belongings on "Miercoles de la Semana Santa" (35r) [Wednesday of Holy Week], and, significantly, they finally depart from Rouen to begin their perilous sea voyage on Good Friday: "[D]os dias despues, que fue el Viernes Santo, nos embarcamos todos de nuestra familia y congregacion, que eramos veintitres Religiosas, y siete Padres Religiosos, y començamos à hazer nuestro camino" (35r) [Two days later, which was Good Friday, all our family and congregation embarked, twenty-three nuns and seven fathers, and we began to make our way].

The narrative then pauses for a description of the throng that gathers upon learning of the community's intended departure from Rouen. This interlude adds layers to the association of Syon's communal experiences with the events of Christ's passion. Recalling the witnesses to Christ's crucifixion, the account emphasizes that there are both mourners and mockers on the scene as the Brigittines prepare to leave. Upon hearing of Syon's plans, an amazingly large crowd gathers at the nuns' house ("fue cosa marauillosa el numero de gente de todas suertes que à nuestra casa concurrio"). Syon's friends and well-wishing strangers appear, lamenting their departure and weeping ("Venian los amigos, y conocidos tristes, desconsolados, y llenos de dolor, y otros à quien no conociamos, llorauan con grande sentimiento"). These are joined by heretics ("Los hereges") who laugh at the scene ("se reían") (36r). On Holy Saturday, after they have left Rouen, the nuns recall soldiers' taunting them, here again suggesting the abuse of Christ during the Crucifixion. The nuns say that on "Sabado Santo" a group of "soldados hereges" [heretic soldiers] begin "à cantar canciones torpes y deshonestas, llamando à las Religiosas con palabras indignas, y descomedidas" [to sing rude songs, calling the nuns improper, discomfiting names] (38r).

The nuns' description of an encounter between their vessel and hostile English ships on their way to Lisbon further enhances the *Relacion*'s connection of their experiences and Christ's sufferings on the cross. When they meet the English ships, the brethren dress as soldiers to attempt to fool their enemies into thinking the ship on which the religious of Syon are traveling is a warship. Meanwhile, "la señora Abadessa" [the lady abbess] and "las damas religiosas" [the women religious], becoming aware of their dangerous situation ("el peligro en que estauamos"), go below decks to seek divine aid through prayer ("al socorro diuino poniendose en oracion") (51v). Specifically, they undertake "el exercicio espiritual dela Cruz: que . . . ha sido vsado en nuestra orden desde su principio, con singular prouecho y consuelo de las religiosas della, y assi lo sentimos eneste nuestro viage muchas vezes" (51v) [the spiritual exercise of the Cross, which has been used in our order since its beginnings, with singular advantage and consolation to the religious of the order, just as we felt many times in this voyage]. According to Ann Hutchison, the current abbess of Syon indicates that "el exercicio espiritual dela Cruz" refers to the stations of the cross. The nuns thus enact in their time of peril a devotional practice that reiterates the events of Christ's passion, doubly bringing past sacred events to life in the present.[27]

Emphasizing the status of Syon as a holy body that undergoes suffering with salvific potential are the frequent references in the *Relacion* to the nuns themselves or to the corporate community as relics. In describing the community's first exile from England during the reign of Henry VIII, the "Preambulo" states that the nuns went to Flanders and "se conservasten como las reliquias de aquel su ilustre monesterio de Sion" (4v) [preserved themselves like relics of their illustrious monastery of Syon]. The nuns later indicate that the confessor general Seth Foster, in his efforts to persuade officials to permit their voyage to Lisbon, declares that his primary responsibility ("su mayor cuydado") is "guardar estas religiosas, como las reliquias de todos los monesterios de monjas, que salia auer en Inglaterra" [to protect these nuns, like relics of all the monasteries of nuns which used to exist in England] (49v). The Brigittine nuns take up similar language in their seventeenth-century petition to the Infanta to express the view that their experience in exile is a form of corporate martyrdom, which, they hope, will have redemptive value. They call themselves "esta Unica y sola Reliquia de todas las Religiosas de Inglatierra" [the unique and only relic of all the houses of religious Sisters of England], indicating that they are not only a reincarnation of Birgitta's holy body, as we have seen, but also part of the English, Catholic body politic that has suffered in Protestant hands.[28] Their hope is to return "al feliçe y mui deseado descanço en nuestra antigua Syon" (13) [to happy and greatly deserved rest in our former home, Syon] (25) and so to see the redemptive moment in which the suffering body of Christ, which they metonymically represent, is made whole once again in a Catholic England.

Martyrdom and Mission: Luisa de Carvajal y Mendoza

In addition to presenting the bodies of individual nuns and the communal monastic body as sacred relics possessed of salvific power, the *Relacion* illustrates the ability of holy bodies to transform political boundaries. In recounting their entry into Lisbon, the nuns of Syon emphasize the presence of holy English bodies in the city prior to their arrival:

> Fue en este punto nuestro gozo, y contento grandissimo, por vernos y a otra vez en Reyno tan Catolico y Christiano como es este de Portugal, con el qual hemos oydo muchas vezes, que el Reyno de Inglaterra antiguamente, quando obedecia à Dios, y à su Iglesia, auia tenido muy grande, y continua amistad: y concurrido tambien muy particularmente con la misma nacion Portuguesa en la conquista desta nobilissima ciudad de Lisboa contra los Moros, como nos dizen, que lo testifica vna principal iglesia, que oy dia ay aqui en esta ciudad de los santos martires Ingleses que en equella conquista murieron. (53r–53v)

> [In this point was our joy and greatest contentment, that is, to find ourselves once again in such a Catholic and Christian kingdom as Portugal, with him [the Spanish king] of whom we have heard many times that the king of England formerly, when he obeyed God and his church, had very great and continued friendship: and he [the English king] took part very particularly with the same Portuguese nation in the conquest of the most noble city of Lisbon against the Moors, as we are told that the principal church testifies, which still today contains in this city the holy English martyrs who died in this conquest.]

Holy bodies become the foundations for political alliances joining England, Spain, Portugal, and Rome. The Syon nuns use the relics of the English who died in Lisbon during the twelfth-century crusade to retake the city from Islamic forces to link their English community with Lisbon's Spanish Catholic rulers in the late sixteenth century. The bodies of the English martyrs also, in this account, pointedly represent a particular vision of the English body politic, as surviving fragments of an England that "obedecia à Dios" as a Catholic realm.

During James I's reign Luisa de Carvajal y Mendoza, a Spanish woman who shared with the exiled Brigittine nuns of Syon a dream of revivifying the Catholic past on English soil, undertook efforts in some ways even more audacious than those of the English women religious to manipulate holy bodies both English and Spanish, as well as political alliances involving England, Spain, and Rome, in order to recreate a "Reyno de Inglaterra" that, in the Catholic view, "obedecia à Dios." Born in 1556 in the province of Extremadura, Spain, Luisa was the daughter of a well-to-do and politically well-connected family. When she was still quite young, both of her parents died. Her father's will specified that she was to be sent to the household of her mother's sister Petronila Pacheco, Marquesa de Ladrada, until the age of ten, when she was to go into a convent. Once she reached the age of consent, she was then to choose either to take monastic vows or to live in the world. However, she was instead sent to live with her great-aunt Doña María Chacón at the royal court in Madrid. María served as governess to the Infant and Infanta, and from the ages of six to ten Luisa lived in royal quarters in the convent of Las Descalzas Reales. It was in this context that Luisa began her lifelong close relationship with the Jesuits.[29]

When Doña María Chacón died in 1576, Luisa's uncle Francisco Hurtado de Medoza, Marqués de Almazán, became her guardian. For the next sixteen years she remained in his household, where, largely thanks to her aunt's involvement, she "was given an outstanding education in domestic and intellectual matters" (*TE*, 2). Though relatively few scholars have written about Luisa, virtually all who have comment on the disturbing nature of the treatment she received at her uncle's hands. As Elizabeth Rhodes notes, "[U]nder the 'spiritual counsel' of the Marqués, Carvajal was obliged to participate in a series of violent and remarkable penitential activities" (*TE*, 3). In her spiritual autobiography, most likely composed at her confessor's behest, Luisa provides some details concerning her life with her uncle.[30] She writes:

> Y no se puede fácilemente creer el cuidado de mi buen tío en que yo
> fuese humillada y quebrantada con este género de penitencia. Y así,
> ordenaba algunas veces que me llevasen desnuda y descalza, con los

pies por la tierra friísima, con una cofilla en la cabeza que recogía
el cabello solamenta, y una toalla atada por la cintura, una soga a la
garganta . . . a atadas las manos con ella, de unos aposentos a otros,
como a malhechora. (*TE*, 102)

[And the care my uncle took to see that I was humiliated and broken
with this sort of penance cannot be easily believed. And thus he would
order at times that they lead me unclothed and barefoot, with my feet
on the extremely cold floor, with a cap on my head that only held my
hair, and a towel tied to my waist, a rope at my neck . . . and my hands
tied with it, from one room to another, like an evildoer.] (*TE*, 103)

Rhodes also correctly observes, "[W]ithout underestimating the dangerous nature of the penitential practices in which the Marqués engaged
his niece, it is important to recall the penitential mode of piety that dominated sixteenth-century Spain and Italy" (*TE*, 4). My concern with Luisa's
early life and her experiences with her uncle is not to attempt to diagnose
resultant psychological damage as a cause for her later devotion and political activities. As with the nuns of Syon, I am interested in how Luisa's
experiences of suffering—physical, emotional, and spiritual alike—bear
on her identification with Christ's suffering and with the suffering of
an English Catholic communal body. Her early life, and the connections
she was able to cultivate during the course of it, are also crucial in setting
the stage for her later political involvement in ecclesiastical and Anglo-
Spanish politics, both of which merge inseparably with her spirituality
and her modes of religious practice.

In 1591, when she was twenty-five, Luisa sought to escape her uncle's
control. He refused to grant permission for her to move into her own
household, but he did consent for her to live in "semiretirement from
the world with a few companions on the top story of his Madrid palace"
(*TE*, 6). The following year her uncle died, as did his brother, who had
hoped to become Luisa's guardian; her aunt died within a few months as
well. In the aftermath of these deaths, Luisa "began to plan for her life
of holy virtue, rejecting not only marriage and the convent, but Spain as
well" (*TE*, 6). Luisa's own words concerning this sequence of events are

revealing: "[A]lcé los ojos a Dios y dile inmensas gracias, porque ya me veía del todo sola y libre, para irme, sin ningún estorbo, tras los desprecios y desamparos de Cristo que tanto deseaba mi alma"[31] [I raised my eyes to God and gave Him immense thanks, because I saw myself then free to follow, without hindrance, in the scorn and abandonment of Christ which my soul so desired] (*TE*, 6).

In 1598, Luisa took a formal vow of martyrdom, extending her desire to follow Christ in experiencing scorn and abandonment to experiencing his death. She declares, "Yo, Luisa de Carvajal, lo más firmemente que puedo, con estrecho voto prometo a Dios Nuestro Señor que procuraré, cunato me sea posible, buscar todas aquellas ocasiones de martirio que no sean repugnantes a la ley de Dios" (*TE*, 118) [I, Luisa de Carvajal, as firmly as I am able, with a strict vow promise God Our Lord that I will procure, to the extent possible, to seek out all those opportunities of martyrdom which are not repugnant to the law of God] (*TE*, 119). This vow provides unmistakable evidence that Luisa, like Marie Champney, who also proclaimed her "thirste to suffer imprisonment yea or martirdome out righte for the Catholicke faythe" (10v), understands her life, Christ's, and those of generations of martyrs to be coterminous, inextricably melded.

The preamble that Luisa writes to this vow reveals her awareness of fluid relationships between self and others. As she explains, the vow is motivated by a desire that she perceives as a version of the very experience she seeks. Luisa's longing for martyrdom is itself a kind of bodily suffering: specifically, the desire makes itself felt as a wound in her heart. Recalling Marie Champney's and Grace Mildmay's descriptions of their hearts being pierced, melted, and inscribed by and in response to the divine, Luisa writes, "Viendo que los impetuosos y delicadísimos afectos de dar la vida por Cristo Nuestro Señor, siguiendo sus dulcísimas pisadas, uniéndome estrechamenta con El por este medio, tenían en gran manera apretado mi corazón y penetrado de una gravísima herida" (*TE*, 118) [Seeing that impetuous and most delicate inclinations to give my life for Christ Our Lord, following in His most sweet footsteps, joining myself closely to Him though this means, had my heart greatly pressed and penetrated it with a most critical wound] (*TE*, 119). Her yearning to imitate Christ's suffering and death makes her heart into a version of the wounded Sacred Heart of Jesus; the very impulse to imitate Christ trans-forms her body into his.[32]

In August 1604, after a protracted court battle through which Luisa gained control of her inheritance, she began to plan in earnest for the voyage to England that she desired to undertake in pursuit of martyr-dom. In her autobiography, she claims that travel to England and the path to martyrdom were associated in her thoughts since she first in her youth felt called to imitate Christ's sufferings and death. She says that when she was seventeen, she had a great desire "morir por el dulcísimo Señor que murió por mí" [to die for the most sweet Lord who died for me]. She further indicates that she believed that in England she would be able to approximate the state of the persecuted Christians of the primi-tive church ("casi haberme reducido al estado en la primitiva Iglesia, o persecuciones della antiguas").[33] In December of 1604, Luisa wrote her will in hopes that the trip on which she was soon to embark, reversing the track of Syon's peregrinations by traveling from the Iberian penin-sula through France and the Low Countries to England, would indeed lead to the fulfillment of her vow of martyrdom.

Luisa's will makes absolutely clear the extent to which her devo-tional desires and her political aims merge as a single holy calling to be fulfilled through the involvement of the Virgin Mary, the crucified Christ, and the bodies—including her own—that are sacrificed in the *imitatio Christi* of martyrdom. This document sets up a paradigm in which the Virgin Mary, Christ, and Luisa collaborate with the Jesuits in work-ing for the English Catholic cause.[34] The Virgin's interests, those of her Son, and Luisa's own perfectly align with each other in support of the Jesuits and the English Mission, which is itself represented as salvific work. In fact, the Jesuits feature prominently in her will as agents of inter-connected political and spiritual salvation. Luisa describes "los Padres ingleses de la Compañia de Jesús" [the English fathers of the Society of Jesus] as "fuertes columnas, apuntalando aquel reino, le detiennen y preservan que no dé de golpe en lo profundo, siendo eficasísimo medio de la salvación de millares de almas" [strong columns supporting that kingdom, holding it up and preventing it from receiving a fatal blow, being the most efficacious medium for salvation for thousands of souls].[35]

She has a similar role in the English Mission through the support she offers the Jesuits in the bequests in her will. She states that "Su Majestad" [His Majesty] has granted her "vivos sentimientos de que en mí lo sería, màs que otra ninguna cosa, acudir con toda mi posibilidad la conservación y aumento de los Padres ingleses de la Compañia de Jesús" [strong feelings that it would be up to me, more than any other thing, to carry out the conservation and augmentation of the English fathers of the Society of Jesus with all my capability].[36]

Luisa also plans a direct role for the Virgin Mary in the English Mission. She places all that she has "debajo el amparo de la soberanísima Virgin María, nuestra Señora" [under the protection of the most sovereign Virgin Mary Our Lady], the Virgin being, as she indicates, "mi universal heredera" [my universal heir]. To stand in the Virgin's stead on earth, she names "P. Roberto Personio de la Compañia de Jesús" [Father Robert Parsons of the Society of Jesus].[37] The Virgin's inheritance, as administered by Parsons, was immediately put to work to found the first novitiate of the English province of the Jesuits, located at Louvain (TE, 15). As Calvin Senning points out, this foundation "was an important institution. Not only was it set aside solely for the use of Englishmen, but it served as a preparatory school for colleges training priests to carry the Counter-Reformation across the Channel."[38] The foundation set up with Luisa's bequest thus not surprisingly "quickly became the object of particular concern to James's ministers in London and Brussels."[39]

In his preface to his life of Luisa, printed in Madrid in 1632, the Jesuit Michael Walpole, who served as Luisa's confessor for some time, capitalizes on Luisa's politically inflected devotion to the Virgin Mary in his own efforts to advance the cause of the English Catholics generally as well as that of the Company of Jesus specifically. Addressing himself to the Virgin Mary, he emphasizes the Jesuits' special connection with Jesus when he reiterates that Luisa "a vos escogió por heredere de todos sus beines, y si los dexó a los padres Ingleses de la Compania de vuestro hijo, hízólo en vuestro nombre, y como a hijos vuestros" [chose you as heir of all her goods, and so left them to the English fathers of the Society of your son, she gave it in your name and as if to your sons].[40] He gives divine legitimacy to the work of the English Mission in which Luisa put "manos a la obra" [hands to work] as efforts "cobrar vuestra dote las almas de Inglaterra, que los demonios y herejes vuestros enemigos os abian robado" [to recover your dowry, the souls of England, which demons and your enemies the heretics have stolen]. Calling Luisa "vuestra virgin, vuestra martyr, y vuestra Doctora, y sobre todo vuestra devota y fervorosa imitadora" [your virgin, your martyr, your doctor, and above all your devout and fervent imitator], he closes with a prayer that reiterates the bodily purity of the Virgin Mary. He implores Mary to intercede so that "vuestra limpyisima concepcion sin mancha de pecado original sea celebrada adonde començo esta solemnidad, como está oy dia con vuestro favor en España dulcisima y nobilisima patria desta vuestra sierva, paraque la paz y union fundada en vos sea firme e estable para el bien de ambos Reynos, y del de vuestro hijo, nuestra santa madre la yglesia Romana" [your most pure conception without stain of original sin might be celebrated where this solemnity began, as it is today with your favor in your servant's most sweet and most noble country of Spain, so that peace and union founded in you might be firm and stable for the good of both realms, and the kingdom of your Son our holy mother the Roman Church]. By calling attention to England as the place where celebration of the immaculate conception of Mary began, he aligns a Catholic England with virginal purity, with the locus where the divine Word could take on human flesh.[41] Like the Brigittine nuns who capitalize on the holy bodies of the English martyrs still in Lisbon to forge bonds between England, Spain, and Rome, Walpole, in speaking of "paz y union fundada en vos," imagines the pure, holy body of the Virgin Mary from which God's son issued as the vehicle, assisted by Luisa's efforts, for union between England and Spain that will entail England's return to Rome.

Some particular directives that Luisa makes in her will to the novitiate at Louvain further illustrate the importance of the bodily to her mutually informing political and spiritual aims. The will reminds the Jesuits of the sacrifice that they are called to enact in performing masses for English Catholics, and, ultimately, to emulate in seeking martyrdom in England. Luisa decrees that the novitiate there should have "in medio del retablo de su altar mayor una imagen de nuestra Señora, con su precioso Hijo en los brazos, y que, en cada una de sus nueve fiestas, le digan una misa cantada, solemne y devotamente" [in the middle of the retable of the high altar an image of Our Lady with her precious son in her arms, and, on each of their nine feasts, they perform a sung Mass, solemnly and devoutly].[42] She also says, "Y es mi voluntad que el santo Crucifijo vivo, que tengo . . . se ponga en el dicho Noviciado con particular veneración" [And it is my will that the holy, living crucifix that I have . . . be placed in the said novitiate with particular veneration].[43] Luisa envisions the Jesuits trained at Louvain as becoming incarnations in their own lives and deaths of the incarnate, crucified Christ whose body they reproduce in the Mass. They are to be, in effect, versions of the "holy living crucifix" that she bequeaths to them.

Jesuits and other priests in England did frequently enough follow the path of *imitatio Christi* to executions in England. When the priests John Roberts and Thomas Summer were executed, Luisa sent an account of their last days to the Marqués de Caracena—a letter accompanied by a piece of John Roberts's body intended as a relic. She recounts visiting Roberts in prison and dining with him and other imprisoned Catholics. She tells of sitting between Roberts and Summer, and reports, "La mesa estaba llena de alegría y devoción; y yo sumida en una profunda consideración de lo que tenía delante, que me representaba vivísimamenta la última cena de Cristo Nuestro Señor" [The table was full of happiness and devotion, and I was immersed in profound consideration of what was before me, which represented most vividly to me the Last Supper of Christ Our Lord].[44] In this scene, Eucharistic devotion blends with devotion to the Passion. The priests become the sacrificial victim whose body they confect in the Mass as Luisa describes Roberts and Summer preparing to reenact Christ's sacrificial suffering in their own Last Supper.[45] The priestly words of institution that echo the Last Supper and make Christ's body present in the Host—"this is my body"—hover over this mealtime scene, attaching themselves to the bodies of Roberts and Summer, who in their deaths are, in effect, themselves transubstantiated, becoming reiterations of Christ's crucified, sacrificial body as they are executed.[46]

Luisa subsequently provided transport for an English Benedictine to retrieve as many parts as possible from the dismembered corpses of Roberts and Summer after their executions, and the mangled bodies were then installed with honor in her house. She writes, "Yo me tuve por dichosa con tales huespedes, y de poderlos servir en tanta necesidad" (c. 125, p. 324) [I held myself fortunate to have such guests and to be able to serve them in such great necessity]. She describes her devotion before the corpses, saying, "Extraño espectáculo y motivo de oración, ver aquellas armas tan frágiles con que pelearon tan sin fragilidad, animosamente" (c. 125, p. 324) [Rare spectacle and motive for prayer, to see such fragile arms with which they fought bravely, without weakness]. Underlining the priests' transformation from earthly vicars of Christ to heavenly advocates with the Father who have attained saintly, even Christ-like status, she declares, "Volaron al cielo, aumentando allá los intercesores, e hicieron dichosa mi casa con tan ricos despojos" (c. 125, p. 324) [They flew to heaven, increasing the intercessors there, and they made my house fortunate with such rich booty].[47]

Executed priests' bodies were not only sources of spiritual value; they were also, like the miraculously preserved body of Mary Margaret of the Angels at the Antwerp Carmel, reservoirs of immense symbolic value, as is suggested by Luisa's referring to the bodies of Roberts and Summer as "tan ricos despojos." Similarly, she terms the bodies of two other executed priests, the Benedictine who used the alias William Escot and a secular priest (possibly Richard Newport), "nuestro tesoro" (c. 151, p. 369) [our treasure].[48] Her description of the aftermath of their execution suggests the value of these bodies to other English Catholics as well. She reports that those who aided in retrieving the priests' remains "no quisieron dinero ni otra alguna paga, que parte de los cuerpos" (c. 151, p. 369) [did not want money, or any other payment, except part of the bodies]. This might be a pious remark intended to suggest Catholic unworldliness and spirituality. However, another incident she recounts concerning the hours following the execution of Father Almond sheds a slightly different light. Rival bands of Catholics fired by "la furia de demasiada devoción" [the frenzy of too much devotion] competed to carry off his body in a scene of "gran peligro" [great danger], and, as it was difficult to tell friend from foe in the dark, they "pudieran matarse con los pistoletes unos a otros" [might have killed themselves with pistols] (c. 163, p. 389). Luisa's faction won the day, or rather the night, and managed to carry off the body parts revered as relics.[49]

Luisa's description of events following the executions of Escot and Newport intensifies the association between the bodies of the priests and the body of Christ. The priests' bodies were brought to Luisa's house at the Spanish embassy, and a ritualized "ceremony of admission" took place that sounds very much like a liturgical procession. This ritual involved "a processional candlelight welcome through the front door, followed by the bathing and vigil of the body parts by the women in Carvajal's Society" (*TE*, 22).[50] Luisa says, "[C]on devoción mezclado gozo y dolor, los pusimos sobre la alfombra, delante el altar . . . con muchas flores olorosas encima; hincadas de rodillas, tuvimos alguna oración allí" (c. 151, p. 369) [With devotion that mixed joy and sorrow, we placed them on the carpet, in front of the altar . . . surrounded by many fragrant flowers; kneeling, we said many prayers there]. Similarly, in a letter to Don Rodrigo Calderón, Luisa describes her intense devotion to the bodies of executed priests. She states that there are only two occasions upon which her life in England is sweet ("muy dulce"). One is when she receives "estos felices cuerpos" [these happy bodies] with which she spends entire nights ("las noches enteras"):

> aderezarlos con las especias aromáticas, de limpiarlos primero del lodo, coger la sangre que aún brota de algunas de las venas, besando muchas veces sus manos y sus pies, vendando los despedazados miembros con holanda nueva, velando delante dellos y puniéndolos en su sepulcro de plomo, para que puedan conservarse, si así lo quiere conceder nuestro soberano señor, esperando acepta este pequeño servicio, a vueltas de su gran sacrificio y holocausto dellos, que fuego se hace do queman sus entrañas y corazón. (c. 163, p. 389)[51]

> [adorning them with aromatic spices, first cleaning them of the mud, catching the blood that still spurted from some of the veins, many times kissing their hands and feet, bandaging the shattered members with new linen, keeping vigil in front of them and putting them in their lead sepulchre, so that they might be preserved, if our most sovereign lord wishes to grant it, hoping that he might accept this small service in exchange for his great sacrifice and their holocaust, which fire caused their entrails and hearts to burn.]

The "pequeño servicio" that Luisa says she renders to her Lord in the veneration of the priests' bodies resembles something close to monastic or ecclesiastical divine service. Like the Host transubstantiated in the Mass, the priests' bodies that are torn apart by officials of the Protestant regime become the means through which a community is incorporated. The act of making and then breaking Christ's body in the Mass (through the words of institution and the fraction of the Host) and the process of distributing the consecrated Host to the recipients paradoxically create union through fragmentation as the communicant who consumes the body of Christ is incorporated into the body of Christ that is the church.[52] So too in engaging in acts of devotion centering on the fragmented bodies of the executed priests, Luisa and the women of her Society are joined as a quasi-monastic community and as members of the larger community of the English Catholic body politic. In fact, in the same letter to Rodrigo Calderón discussed above, Luisa emphasizes the connection between the Mass and the veneration of the priests' corporeal fragments. She recounts having made "un altar grande, hueco y con puertas que se quitan y ponen" [a large altar, hollow, and with doors that open and shut]. On Christmas and other feast days, the doors were removed, and "sirvieron de frontal las reliquias" [the reliquaries served as the frontal]; in other words, the lead caskets ("cajas de plomo") containing body parts of executed priests ("los santos cuerpos") served as the altar frontal (c. 165, p. 391).

Indeed, the politically inflected interplay among the priests' bodies, Christ's body, and communal bodies in the devotional rituals performed by Luisa and the women of her Society has a close parallel in the ways that bodies interact in Luisa's intense Eucharistic piety. Like many medieval female saints and mystics, Luisa passionately desired the privilege of daily communion, and in 1597 she received permission for this from her confessor (*TE,* 8). Caroline Walker Bynum has, as is well known, written extensively about the spiritual and cultural implications of the Eucharistic devotion so widespread among later medieval holy women.[53] Luisa's version of this practice has an additional layer of significance that brings together incarnational piety and her own performative iteration of incarnational politics. For Luisa, the consecrated Host is a means to reembody the "old religion" in Protestant England.[54] Much as Luisa glories in having the bodies of martyred priests in her house, so too she rejoices at the presence of the consecrated Host at the Spanish embassy where she resides. At the end of a long letter to Magdalena de San Jeronimo written in May 1606, in which she recounts in detail the trial of Father Garnet for his involvement in the Gunpowder Plot, Luisa writes,

> Dícenme que no hay en otro ningún cabo el Santísimo sacramento, sino en esta casa, y que, ha mucha cantidad de años que no le ha habido así de asiento en toda Inglaterra. Yo he tenido gran dicha en esto; que, después que estoy en esta casa, se ha puesto Su Majestad en ella. (c. 46, p. 169)

> [I am told that the blessed Host is not kept anywhere else except in this house and that, for many years, it was not kept anywhere at all in all of England. I have been very fortunate in this, for since I have been in this house, His Majesty has been put in it.] (*TE*, 243)

The reference to Christ present in the Host as "Su Majestad" sheds light on the political ramifications of Luisa's Eucharistic devotion, since there is easy slippage between "His Majesty" Christ, who is present in the Host, and His Majesty the Spanish king, who might intervene by force or through arranging a royal marriage to reintroduce Catholicism into England. The location in question—the Spanish ambassador's house, an outpost of the Spanish royal court in England—is a place where the king might be said symbolically to be present, and indeed, Rhodes notes that late in Luisa's life she "no longer distinguished" the divine majesty of God "from His Majesty the Spanish King" (*TE*, 24).[55]

Try though English Protestants might, the Spanish embassy, where Luisa practiced the "old religion" and where the body of Christ was present in the consecrated Host she venerated, was an unwelcome reminder that England had not escaped its past, had not created a body politic free of Catholic bodies. On the contrary, the past was all too present, materially and temporally. The presence of Christ's body in the consecrated Host in the Spanish ambassador's house gave this outpost of Spain in England a status rather like that of the corporate body of Syon in exile in Lisbon, or of the English communities of Benedictine nuns in Cambrai and Paris. It stood as a solitary, enfleshed fragment of the past living in the present, at once English yet at the same time paradoxically foreign. The presence of Christ's body in the Host at the Spanish embassy thus reminds us—as it did Luisa and her contemporaries—that the national boundaries separating England and Spain, the separations between the domestic and the foreign so often demarcated in confessional terms, are only tenuous, despite the Protestant regime's best efforts to fortify them practically and symbolically. The porous subjectivity characteristic of the incarnational paradigms of piety, epistemology, and textuality is here writ politically large, with potentially terrifying implications to the English Protestant regime, anxieties that I will explore in a variety of manifestations in chapters 4 and 5.

Luisa's suffering body, and the reincarnations of Christ that are the priests whose dismembered bodies she reveres, exhibit the same capacity to remap bodies politic—to redraw, erase, and transcend borders—as do the bodies of the English martyrs in Lisbon described by the Syon nuns in the *Relacion,* or as does the consecrated Host at the Spanish embassy in London. As Doreen Massey has argued, "[T]he spatial is integral to the production of history, and thus to the possibility of politics."[56] When Luisa sends corporeal fragments abroad in lead caskets, their circulation creates communities within and beyond the borders of England, so traducing the boundaries of Christ's body that is the Catholic Church and creating a map with new borders that defy those drawn by secular powers. For Luisa, as for the Brigittines of Syon, the sanctifying and remapping of space through the distribution of Catholic bodies has profound implications.

In her emphasis on communities and territories created through and sanctified by bodies that reenact Christ's life and death, Luisa resembles not only the Brigittine nuns of Syon but also her fellow "female Jesuit" Mary Ward. David Wallace argues that Mary "spatialize[s]" her Catholicism "onto the landscape" and engages in a "Catholic remapping of English space," and so too does Luisa.[57] Indeed, both women's concepts of a sacred geography predicated upon bodies, and the political possibilities inherent in the creation of such a geography, resonate with the important relationship accorded to place, history, and the body in Jesuit spirituality, particularly in the Spiritual Exercises.[58]

In the first meditation in the Spiritual Exercises, the exercitant is directed as the "First Preliminary" to undertake the "composition of place" (compositio loci). Loyola states: "It should be noted here that for contemplation or meditation about visible things, for example a contemplation on Christ our Lord (who is visible), the 'composition' will consist in seeing through the gaze of the imagination the material place where the object I want to contemplate is situated. By 'material place' I mean for example a temple or mountain where Jesus Christ or our Lady is to be found—according to what I want to contemplate."[59] As Nicholas Standaert point out, the compositio loci in the Spiritual Exercises is "a special occasion for facilitating" a "personal encounter with Jesus," an encounter that is "not simply the product of . . . imagining or the projection of a personal emotion" but rather "a coming up against . . . a definite historical person."[60] The composition of place, furthermore, prepares the reader to imitate and unite with Christ. Christ's life is not simply something one encounters as history but rather something that one lives in one's own body in one's own historical reality. As the early Jesuit Jerónimo Nadal's text Annotations and Meditations on the Gospels (1595) makes clear, the composition of place "give[s] a universal dimension to the Incarnation."[61] Appropriately, then, the First Preliminary leads to the Second, which emphasizes experiential identification of the exercitant with Christ, with particular reference to Christ's sufferings. In the Second Preliminary, "I ask our Lord God for what I want. This prayer must be appropriate to the subject matter. If I am contemplating . . . the Passion, I will ask for suffering, grief, and agony, in the company of Christ in agony."[62]

In the Spiritual Exercises, meditation upon a place where Christ's body was present in his historical time is thus connected to the meditating individual's own spiritual, and even bodily, union with Christ in his or her own historical time. Not only do holy bodies create a sacred geography, but that geography also has the power to transform the internal landscape of the exercitant, who can then perform Christ's life in her or his own historical moment and so in turn transform that historical moment. The incarnational thus influences the very nature of spatial and historical relations.

In Luisa's writings, Christ's life clearly has both universal significance and a placement in a historical context—the latter being the historical framework of Jacobean England. And the descriptions of events in England in Luisa's letters, with their accounts of the executions of priests and the presence of the Host in the Spanish embassy, have the ability to serve in turn for their recipients as something like aids for *compositio loci*. The letters are full of Catholic bodies reenacting Christ's life on English ground that accordingly becomes holy ground, and, in reading the accounts, the readers are drawn into the scene. Luisa's letters enable those with whom she corresponds to participate in sacred history as lived experience. The letters catalyze a series of identifications with and reiterations of holy lives quite similar to those encapsulated in the Brigittine divine service and in texts associated with the English Benedictines of Cambrai and Paris. Luisa and the persecuted English Catholics relive Christ's life; they share his biography. Their experiences are then recorded in the letters that are, like Julian's *Showings* and Margaret Gascoigne's devotional writings, textual tokens whose function is to enable the recipients to access these experiences, and subsequently to embody them for themselves in their own lives. Luisa's letters enable the "oneing," to borrow Julian's language once more, of Christ, the writer, and the readers in seamless community. The letters are fragments of herself that open out to other lives, seeking to be embodied and so to play a generative role in constituting community. This is a role not unlike that performed by the bodily members of executed priests that Luisa sometimes sent with her correspondence, or the role performed by the fragments of Christ's body disseminated in the Eucharist. Her letters too are, in short, incarnational texts.

In this capacity, Luisa's letters also share with Aemilia Lanyer's *Salve Deus* something of the status of scriptural reiteration. Her letters not only present repetitions of the *vita Christi* but also resonate with an ancient Christian understanding of the religious place and function of the letter. As Alain Boureau observes, the epistles of Paul have their own incarnational dimension: "The epistolary form itself neatly represents the essential originality of Christianity: the Incarnation brought God to the earth at an ordinary moment and among ordinary people."[63] Boureau further states that Paul "taught (or obliged) the West to believe in the life-giving power of the letter" (32). The Jesuits who played such a key role in disseminating accounts of the tribulations of the Syon nuns and who were so influential in shaping Luisa's spirituality had a particular faith in the ability of a letter to "give life" by making absent people present and distant events available for being experienced. The *Regulae Societatis Iesu*, first published in 1561, is illustrative. It contains an extensive section devoted to setting out "when, why, and to whom letters should be written within the society."[64] These regulations include requirements that superiors of residences and college rectors write weekly letters to their provincials so that each provincial will, through the letters, be able to "see 'everything as if he were present.'"[65]

Luisa's letters, like Paul's, link one group of true believers to another, giving life to an embodied community. Aligning Luisa's letters and the Pauline epistles is particularly apt, given Luisa's representation of the sufferings of the English Catholics as a reenactment of the sufferings of the early Christians. For instance, in a letter to Don Rodrigo Calderón, she writes, "Las casas de los cristianos eran sus iglesias en la primitiva Iglesia . . . ; y en Inglaterra, las de los católicos" (c. 137, p. 344) [The Christians' houses were their churches in the primitive church . . . ; and in England, it is thus with the Catholics]. It seems particularly appropriate, therefore, that Luisa's journey to England was reportedly inspired by another woman's experience initially transmitted in letters: those of Elizabeth Sanders to Sir Francis Englefield.[66] These letters, with their descriptions of persecution and prison, have a strongly Pauline dimension of their own. In traveling to England to embrace persecution and court imprisonment, Luisa thus revives Elizabeth's story, making the autobiographical aspects of Elizabeth's letters part of her own story that she in turn transmits in letters to those back on the Continent, making (re)lived experience open to performance and re-embodiment.

Another important step in Luisa's efforts to bring about the rebirth of an English Catholic body politic was to seek conversions and reconciliations to Catholicism among the "heretics." Luisa's letters are filled with her accounts of endeavors of these sorts that foreground corporeal details concerning the converts and reconciled Catholics themselves as well as the processes of their conversions and reconciliations. These descriptions emphasize the primacy of embodiment to religious faith as well as the importance of Catholic bodies' physical presence in England. In a letter from November 1609, written to Inés de la Asunción, Luisa recounts the reconciliation to Catholicism "de una vieja de ochenta o noventa años" [of an old lady of eighty or ninety years]. She explains that the old lady periodically passed by her window, and on one occasion Luisa took it upon herself to call out to her, informing her that she was "bien cerca del infierno" [very near to hell]. Three weeks later, the lady came to Luisa's door asking to see the "monja" [nun] and reporting that Christ had appeared to her twice in her dreams. He had instructed her that if she would save herself, she must return "a la santa Iglesia" [to the holy church], and accordingly he directed her to "la española que viviá . . . junto a don Pedro" [the Spanish woman who was living . . . near don Pedro] (c. 111, p. 294).

Luisa continues her account of the events leading up to and following the old lady's reconciliation by foregrounding her physical condition in contrast to her spiritual capacities. She writes, "[E]stá acabadísima y toda inclinada y temblando, y los sentidos medio muertos, y desflaquecidísima el habla y aliento, pero capaz de absolución" (c. 111, p. 294) [She was totally used up and entirely stooped and trembling, and her senses half dead, and extremely weak in speech and breath, but capable of absolution]. This description could virtually substitute for a portrait of the condition of the English Catholic body politic—weakened and pitiful, but still capable of being rescued and achieving salvation in political as well as religious terms. Indeed, Luisa's estimate of the woman's age ("ochenta o noventa años") significantly places her birth in either 1529 or 1519—in either case prior to Henry VIII's break with Rome—indicating that the lady herself is a fragile remnant of the Catholic past extant in the present and awaiting a return to full spiritual life through reconciliation.

Luisa goes on to report locating a priest and approvingly notes the old lady's full confession and absolution. The rest of the account highlights details of the old lady's pious bodily practices following her reconciliation, giving special attention to matters of eating and fasting. Luisa indicates that the lady received "el santísimo sacramento" [the most holy sacrament] and then immediately notes that she "no está para pecar en nada y ayuna los viernes, sin ser posible hacerla comer ni un bocado de pan a la noche, que la pone en el extremo de su vida" [is not at all inclined to sin and fasts on Fridays, without it being possible to force her to eat even a mouthful of bread in the evening, which puts her in mortal peril] (c. 111, p. 294). In closing this section of the letter, Luisa observes that the old lady sustained herself "de limosna, que poca basta, porque come como un pajarito, no más" (c. 111, p. 295) [with alms, which were quite small, because she eats nothing more than a little bird]. Luisa's description of the newly reconciled Catholic thus resonates with the *vitae* of so many medieval female saints who dramatically restricted their food intake, sustaining themselves on the consecrated Host alone. Once the lady has become part of Christ's body through her return to Catholicism, and has been incorporated into it through the consumption of the Host, "oneing" (to return to Julian of Norwich's terminology) is complete and seamless, and further bodily sustenance seems superfluous.

Luisa's letters also call attention to her own embodiment as she narrates her spiritual life. Though she was not to achieve her hope of a spectacular death to match those of the executed priests whose bodies she venerated, she writes into existence a martyr's identity for herself in her letters, which exude a characteristically Jesuit "ethos of martyrdom and aesthetic of suffering."[67] In a letter to Rodrigo Calderón written in May 1613, Luisa says, "Ya vuestra señoría sabe lo que me duelen aflicciones de la Santa Iglesia, cuyas cosas están tan eslabonadas y entretejidas con esas del Rey nuestro señor, que son indivisibles; y esto ha tenido en pie la monarquía de España" (c. 170, p. 400) [Your lordship already knows how the afflictions of Holy Church hurt me; affairs so interconnected and interlaced with those of our lord the king that they are indivisible, and this has kept the monarchy of Spain standing].[68] As we have seen occur in the writings of the English Benedictine and Brigittine nuns, in this letter Luisa interprets the collective suffering of Christ's ecclesiastical body as being reproduced in her own individual, corporeal suffering that is a form of *imitatio Christi*.[69] Furthermore, in this letter, "El rey nuestro Señor" seems once again, as is so often true in Luisa's writing, simultaneously to be Christ and the king of Spain, both of whom are united, foundationally and indivisibly, with Luisa.[70] As in the poem printed in the prefatory material for Gertrude More's *Spiritual Exercises,* in Luisa's letter the suffering female body merges with a national body politic—in Gertrude More's case, Catholic England, here the monarchy of Spain—that itself replicates Christ's suffering. Indeed, in Luisa's letter the suffering female body even seems to play a crucial role in bringing the body politic into existence, suggesting a potentially maternal valence for her incarnational political vision.

"Soldados Doncellas": The Society of the Sovereign Virgin Mary, Our Lady and Militant Monasticism

Luisa shares more with Mary Ward than a commitment to what Wallace calls "a Catholic remapping of English space." Luisa's Society of the Sovereign Virgin Mary Our Lady, like Mary Ward's Institute of the Blessed Virgin Mary (sometimes called the "English Ladies"), was during the founder's lifetime an unofficial female "branch" of the Society of Jesus. Both groups lacked the approval of the Jesuits; as Rhodes observes, "Ignatius of Loyola's prohibition of a women's branch of the Jesuits before his death tormented both of these determined Catholic apostles" (*TE,* 25 n. 21). Luisa's Society was organized as a quasi-monastic institution, though Luisa strongly rejected the norms of post-Tridentine female monasticism, particularly enclosure.[71] Writing to Rodrigo Calderón, she declares, "[N]o es mi vocación de anacoreta, sino la contrario" (c. 170, p. 398) [My vocation is not that of an anchoress; indeed, just the opposite]. In another letter to Calderón she contrasts the women of her Society to nuns who seek "por solo acomodarse en lo temporal y vivir quietamente" [only to make themselves comfortable temporally and to live quietly]; she then dryly observes that it is customary "henchir un monasterio de gente de flaquísima virtud y espíritu y de poca edificación y importancia" [to cram a monastery with people of extremely flaccid virtue and spirit and of little edification and importance] (c. 146, p. 357).[72]

To the Protestants in England, Luisa and her group of women *were* nuns, whatever Luisa and her supporters might claim. Luisa reports

that reasons given in the Council of State to support the call for her banishment from England included the assertions that "soy monja y he fundado algunos monasterios dentro de Inglaterra" (*TE,* 288) [I'm a nun
and I have founded several monasteries within England] (*TE,* 289), and
in writing to Lorenzo da Ponte, she states, "[S]epa vuestra merced que
los herejes me llaman monja" (c. 96, p. 257) [Your grace should know
that the heretics call me a nun].[73] Edward Waldegrave, the agent of the
elector palatine in England, writing in 1613, describes Luisa as "the abbess,"[74] and one of her primary antagonists, the archbishop of Canterbury George Abbot, is quite firm in his view that Luisa and her companions are monastics. In a letter of October 1613 he states that Luisa "hath
set up a nunnery in London near the Spittle, gathering young women
unto her, and using them as in a monastery. She is herself a Jesuitess,
and so are all her disciples, apparelled in every respect as the Jesuits'
women."[75] James I makes the same assessment; in the response he gives
to the Spanish Ambassador Gondomar's pleas on Luisa's behalf, he states
that Luisa and the women of her Society "call each other sister in her
house, without other name or appellation."[76]

Though she sought to distance herself from female monasticism,
Luisa did include recognizably monastic elements in the Society's mode
of life. In fact, on more than one occasion, she refers to her community as
a monastery. Writing to Joseph Creswell, she declares, "[N]uestra casa es
un chiquito monasterio" (c. 123, p. 139) [Our house is a little monastery].
Similarly, in a letter to the duchess of Rioseco, she states, "[N]uestra casa
es como un monasterio" (c. 131, p. 333) [Our house is like a monastery],
and she tells Calderón that "nuestra casa es verdaderamenta un conven-
tico" (c. 137, p. 344) [our house is truly a convent]. Margaret Rees notes
that the members of the Society "found themselves dressed in nun-like
habits" and further observes, "So clear was the signal given out by their
dress that Luisa thought it prudent, when it was time for Mass, to send
them out two at a time, in case the sight of a whole posse of nuns should
provoke a riot."[77] As Luisa tells Lorenzo da Ponte, "[C]omo traemos ves-
tido más modesto que se usa, es necesario enviar dos de mis compañeras
a la capilla de don Pedro primero que yo vaya, porque no vean tantas jun-
tas; y la que queda va conmigo" (c. 96, p. 257) [As we clothe ourselves

more modestly than is the custom, it is necessary to send two of my companions to Don Pedro's chapel before I go, so that they do not see so many of us together, and the one who remains goes with me].

Even more significant to the Society's corporate identity than their quasi-monastic apparel is the fact that the Society is a religious community organized around modes of spirituality in which devotion to the Virgin Mary and the incarnate Christ exist tightly bonded to a version of incarnational politics, just as is the case for the Syon nuns and for the English Benedictine nuns of Cambrai and Paris. Strikingly, Luisa uses explicitly corporeal language to describe the ideal communal identity that she envisions for the group. The women are to be united as one body with only "un corazón entre todas" (*TE*, 198) [one heart among you all] (*TE*, 199).[78]

Furthermore, in spite of Luisa's rejection of traditional female monasticism for herself (though her male associates frequently tried to persuade her to enter a nunnery), there are notable Brigittine parallels in her vision of her Society. As is the case in the Brigittine order, the head of the religious corporate body of the Society is to be the Virgin Mary. The Brigittine abbess holds the place of the Virgin Mary in the monastery; as the *Rewyll* declares, the abbess "for the reue*r*ence of the most blessid virgyn marie to whom this ordre ys halwyd. owith to be hedde & ladye. ffor that virgyn whose stede the abbes beryth in eerth. Cryst ascendynge in to heuyn. was hedde and qwene of the apostelis & disciples of cryst."[79] Luisa similarly declares in the document of "Instrucción espiritual" she crafted for the Society that the members of her Society are to choose one of their number to serve "en nombre y lugar de la soberanísima Virgen María Nuestra Señora, que será vuestra más dulcisima y especial superiora y Madre de misericordia" (*TE*, 200) [in the name and place of the most sovereign Virgin Mary Our Lady, who will be your most sweet and special superior and Mother of Mercy] (*TE*, 201). The superior is, furthermore, instructed to "dejará su primer puesto vacío" (*TE*, 200) [leave Her first seat vacant] (*TE*, 201)] in the oratory "en señal de la suma reverencia y respecto debido a esta celestial Señora" (*TE*, 200) [as a sign of the maximum reverence and respect due to this heavenly Lady] (*TE*, 201). The Virgin Mary and her representative the superior play central roles in guiding the community's collective labor, which is to "trat[ar] de veras de toda la perfección posible aquí en Inglaterra, para que el olor suavísimo de vuestros ferverosos deseos y santas obras suban al cielo y pidan misericordia contra tanta abominación de herejías y otras maldades que se cometen cada día e incitan a su divina majestad para tomar venganza" (*TE*, 208) [attempt truly, and in all possible perfection here in England, to make the sweet fragrance of our fervent desires and holy works rise to heaven and seek mercy for as many heretical abominations and other evils as are committed daily and incite His Divine Majesty to vengeance] (*TE*, 209).

In its emphasis on the efficacy of feminine labor in a redemptive enterprise that will result in birth (or, perhaps better, rebirth) and salvation, in this case of England, Luisa's vision of the Society again exhibits a strong affinity to the Brigittine order. As we have seen, Brigittine monastic culture places the Virgin Mary at its heart and emphasizes in divine service her redemptive work in making Christ's incarnation possible. As we have also seen, the Brigittines' monastic identity encompasses identification not only with the Virgin Mary but also with Christ crucified. Similarly, the members of Luisa's Society are aligned both with the Virgin Mary in salvific labor and with the incarnate Christ, whose example they are to hold before their eyes. Luisa instructs the women, "Poned delante de vuestros ojos el ejemplar de Cristo en un pesebre, y muerto en una cruz" (*TE*, 206) [Put before your eyes the example of Christ in the manger, and dead on a cross] (*TE*, 207).

Not only did the Society incorporate itself using models strongly redolent of medieval female monasticism, especially Brigittine monasticism, but the Society also resembled the English Brigittine community of Syon in its combativeness. As I have argued elsewhere, the Brigittine nuns, especially those who returned illegally to England, engaged in symbolic battles against the Protestant regime, and, given their close ties with Nicholas Sanders and their support for Mary, Queen of Scots, they may well have been involved in more direct forms of armed struggle.[80] Like the Brigittine nun Elizabeth Sanders, who was, at the very least, involved in the affair of distributing Edmond Campion's *Brag*, Luisa and members of her Society evidently desired to move beyond symbolic battle to more direct, active methods of combat to enact a transformed English body politic. The women of the Society were committed to "violent and fortunate death for the confession of the holy Catholic faith" (*TE,* 199), a commitment that at times prompted them to violent acts of their own. In a letter to Rodrigo Calderón Luisa assigns the women of her Society a characteristically Jesuit militant, even military, identity as soldiers for Christ. She says, "[L]os soldados . . . son unas pobres doncellas. ¿No es este caso, señor, de grande gloria de Dios . . . ?" (c. 137, p. 344) [The soldiers . . . are some poor maidens. My Lord, is not this case to the great glory of God?]. More succinctly, she refers to the women of her Society as "soldados doncellas" (c. 152, p. 371) [soldier maidens]. Luisa claims that two of her women would, if she permitted them, beat up the pursuivants: "Dos tengo que, si quisiere darles licencia y viniesen los bellacos de las pursivantes, les darán ellas muy buenas bofetadas primero que sepan de dónde les viene, y muy buenos palos también" (c. 150, p. 367) [I have two who, if I were to give them permission and if the pursuivants' agents were to come, would give them many good clouts before they knew what hit them, and many strong kicks too]. Ann Garnet seems to have been especially feisty. Luisa describes her as "un leoncillo en la religión" [a little lion in religion], and she recounts an episode in which "Ana" takes on a Protestant passerby who has attempted to snatch Luisa's rosary: "Un día, salía yo de misa de casa de don Pedro . . . con mi rosario en la mano, y uno de los que pasaban por la calle, hereje vino a quitármelo, y ella, al punto, arremetió a él y dióle grandes puñadas, diciendo: '¡Mal hombre! ¿Que queréis el rosario?' " [One day, I left Mass at don Pedro's house . . . with my rosary in my hand, and one of those who was passing by in the street, a heretic, came to take it from me, and she immediately assailed him and gave him great blows with her fists, saying, "Bad man! What do you want with the rosary?"] (c. 98, p. 267).

In the opening section of the document laying out her spiritual instructions, Luisa directs the English women who make up the Society to implore God to receive "su santísimo amor y gracia" (*TE,* 198) [His most holy love and grace] (*TE,* 199), which will render them "pura y aceptable ofrenda a su mayor gloria y salvación de las almas de vuestra patria, necesitada de espirituales ayudas en el grado que sabeís" (*TE,* 198) [a pure and acceptable offering to His greater glory and the salvation of the souls of your country, needy of spiritual assistance to the degree that you are aware] (*TE,* 199). Luisa's charge shapes the members of the Society not simply as fighters for the English Mission but as sacred, sacrificial bodies whose passion will redeem England and English souls. Her language echoes the Eucharistic rite, as when, just prior to the moment of transubstantiation, the priest describes Christ's death on the cross as a "full, perfect, and sufficient sacrifice, oblation, and satisfaction for the sins of the whole world." The very next sentence confirms this "transubstantiated" spiritual identity for the women, joining them simultaneously with Christ and with the executed priests whose bodies they venerate. Luisa declares, "¡Ojalá rematásemos nuestro camino con violenta y dichosa muerte por la confesión de la santa fe católica!" (*TE,* 198) [Would that our road might end with a violent and fortunate death for the confession of the holy Catholic faith!] (*TE,* 199).[81] Like the English Brigittines and Benedictines in exile, the members of Luisa's Society perform with their bodies an England in which the body of Christ that is the Catholic Church and the body of the state are one, a body that will, through suffering and death, be reborn.[82]

Luisa herself died in the Spanish embassy, a guest of the Ambassador Gondomar, following her release from the prison in which she and her companions were incarcerated as the result of a raid on her house in Spitalfields by pursuivants under the explicit direction of the extremely hostile archbishop of Canterbury George Abbot. Luisa's incarnational piety colors her dying, as does incarnational politics. On her deathbed she repeated the words "My Lord, My Lady," and in her last hours "Michael Walpole and the ambassador's confessor, Diego de la Fuente, remained at her bedside and together they read aloud the Passion of Christ."[83] Just as the narrative of Christ's passion informs her accounts of the deaths of English priests, so too is her passing shaped by it. Upon learning of her death, the English Jesuit John Blakfan wrote, "Verily I take her to be a martyr," a status he attributed to the fact that "her end was hastened by this affliction."[84] Much as she had faith in the intercessory ability of the executed priests, Luisa's servant Diego Lemeteliel had such faith in her, imploring her, "My lady, remember Diego Lemeteliel when you are in heaven," and in a scene straight out of a saint's life, the English carpenter who had long been attached to her household, a staunch Protestant, began to contemplate conversion to Catholicism witnessing the moving spectacle of her final hours. His making the coffin "and seeing her at peace was what made him finally decide to ask Michael Walpole to accept him into the Catholic faith."[85] In death her body thus continued creating Catholic bodies in England.

The funeral rites involving Luisa's corpse too were an occasion for a scene of resurrection of a kind. The funeral took place at the Spanish ambassador's chapel. "Her emaciated body was placed on top of a sepulcher next to the high altar,"[86] taking a place similar to that she had accorded to the remains of executed priests. An international crowd attended to mourn her death. As Glyn Redworth indicates, "[I]n addition to mourners from all the great Catholic mercantile nations, 'there was also a great number of English Catholics who attended the honours with great devotion, full of admiration at seeing the ceremonies and listening to a sermon and a sung mass at such a large gathering of people, something which had not been seen in England for many years.'"[87] For at least this brief moment, in this scene Luisa's body in death brought to life in England the Catholic community of her hopes and prayers.

INCARNATIONAL PIETY, INCARNATIONAL POLITICS, AND
THE ENGLISH CIVIL WAR ON AN INTERNATIONAL STAGE

Though the English Catholic community gathered at Luisa's funeral was only fleetingly constituted, English women religious exhibited a remarkably durable commitment to bringing about the rebirth of a Catholic England. Their faith in the efficacy of incarnational piety to bring about political change, even in the face of daunting setbacks, was tenacious. As we have seen, the English Carmelites of Antwerp mobilized the symbolic resources available from the incorrupt body of Mary Margaret of the Angels, and from the textualization of the lives of members of the community, in the aftermath of the failed Jacobite rebellion of 1715. The nuns of Syon too sought to advance their long-lived hopes in sending a petition to the Infanta Maria in the early 1620s when it seemed she would marry Charles, Prince of Wales. This marriage did not, of course, take place, and Charles's marriage to the Catholic Henrietta Maria equally did not result in the fulfillment of Catholic desires for reconversion of the realm, or even for reliable toleration. Still, when Charles I was executed, English monastics in exile lamented his demise. Anne Neville of the English Benedictine community at Ghent characteristically "referred to the execution of Charles I as 'that horrible sacrilegious murther.'"[88]

During the Civil War era and the years of the Protectorate, English monastic communities on the Continent suffered a decline in postulants and funds coming from England, but they did not despair. Rather, many communities of nuns engaged in practical, textual, and spiritual work on behalf of the English Royalist party, which they saw as potentially sympathetic to their aims of returning the monastic foundations to England. In these efforts, we see the continuing importance of Spain in oppositional English Catholic affairs. The Infanta Isabella and her husband the archduke of Austria were, as governors of the Spanish Netherlands, important financial and political supporters of many of the English monastic communities in their realm.[89] When the future Charles II was in exile and seeking military aid from the Spanish, English monastic communities' close connections to the Infanta and archduke were doubtless a political asset to him. As Caroline Bowden observes, in the summer of 1656, Charles was in the Spanish Netherlands. Philip IV of Spain, "angry at the refusal of Cromwell to give up Jamaica," promised Charles "sanctuary on Spanish soil" as well as troops and a pension.[90] Letters from this period between the abbess of the Ghent Benedictines, Mary Knatchbull, and Charles's advisors reveal she "had a sound appreciation of the complexities of the political situation in the royalist court in the Spanish Netherlands" and that she was "involved in high level political affairs."[91] Indeed, a letter between Edward Hyde, first Earl of Clarendon, and George Digby, Earl of Bristol, from October 1656 outlines Charles's sense of obligation to the abbess for her political aid. Hyde writes, "[H]is Majesty is very desirous to gratify my Lady Abbesse, in the businesse of which she says she gave you a memoriall, and in which she takes her selfe to be very much concerned."[92]

Indeed, Mary Knatchbull was, as Caroline Bowden and Claire Walker have shown, a tireless worker for the Royalist faction, even as she made the most of her political connections to advance her house's well-being.[93] The abbess and her community served as a valuable conduit of information, receiving and passing along details of Royalist activities. In these political engagements, Mary Knatchbull and the Ghent Benedictines benefited from their gendered monastic identity. As Bowden observes, "[U]sing the convent as an address for mail meant that letters were less likely to attract suspicion. The female pseudonyms adopted for the chief protagonists in the planned restoration by both male and female correspondents as an alternative to using ciphers, suggests that male politicians were using current concepts of the female gender role to their advantage, hiding serious political planning behind preconceived notions of female activities."[94] And, as Claire Walker notes, "[G]ender assumptions which denied women any capacity for political cunning, coupled with Protestant stereotypes of the 'silly nun,' might well have enhanced the convents' ability to engage in English affairs of state."[95] Perhaps as early as 1654, Mary "was receiving regular visits from Charles, discussing Crown business, giving him advice, acting as security for loans and dispatching letters on his behalf."[96] Anne Neville records in her "Annals," "The King of england often entred ye monastery and exprest much esteeme and respect to ys worthy lady [ie, Mary Knatchbull] conferring with her and intrusting her; with many affayres of great concern & consequence in ye transport of his letters and ye dispatch of much business yt most imported his maiesty."[97]

In the involvement of English nuns like Mary Knatchbull in Royalist politics, we see not only a continuation of the long history of English women religious involving themselves in high-level political affairs but also the ongoing legacies of incarnational piety and incarnational politics. The Ghent Benedictines operated with a strong awareness of the political dimensions of a spirituality in which the body is central, as emerges clearly in Anne Neville's "Annals." Just prior to recounting the "King of england's" frequent visits, Anne provides an account of Abbess Knatchbull's spiritual reforms in the community. These reforms prominently involve bodily regulations, including matters of diet, observance of the Rule, and practices of devotion. Anne writes:

> I was then thow vnworthy pryoress and I can affirm it was soe
> inuyolably obserued as I can say with truoth [sic] there was not an
> aple or a nut eaten out of order but was acknowleged with as much
> humility and sincerity as if it had binn some great fault; and . . .
> good practis of regularity & mortification setled so good a custom
> in ye Community as gaue great edification to all and tru aduaunsment
> in vertu; . . . and euery yeare when she and ye Community took ye
> spirituall exercys. she layd hold of some one espetiall Rule to take
> to hart; to improue ye Communitys vertu by.[98]

She then turns to Mary Knatchbull's political engagements with Charles,
saying, "[I]t pleased God to bless her with such good success as neuer
any of thos affayres she had ye conduct of in sending letters or ye lik,
euer came to miscarry." The "Annals" thus suggest that God's pleasure
and the corresponding blessings of success he bestowed on Mary Knatchbull's political activities have to do not only with divine support of those
activities themselves but also with the holiness and bodily purity of the
nuns working on Charles's behalf.[99]

The benefits available from the nuns' holiness were evidently quite
attractive to Charles. Though Protestant, during his exile he seems to
have taken advantage when he could of rumors of his purported Catholic leanings, forging ties with his fellow exiles the English recusants.
Charles's connection with the Ghent Benedictines may have been particularly beneficial in making him and his cause all the more attractive to
exiled English Catholics, since the English monastic houses on the Continent were an extremely potent symbol to members of this group. Exiled recusants saw the convents as "markers of recusant definace and
confidence."[100] Walker argues, "[I]n the face of continued Protestant as-
cendancy, the cloisters evidenced recusant determination to preserve
Catholic institutions, which in the event of a Catholic restoration could
easily be transferred to English soil."[101] Charles's close relationships
with the Ghent Benedictine nunnery itself preserved something of the
past. His cultivation of the symbolically valuable relationship echoed the
strategy of his medieval royal English predecessors, especially members
of the Lancastrian dynasty, who regularly drew upon the symbolic value

available from their connections with St. Birgitta and the Brigittine foundation of Syon, as I discuss in chapter 5.

Mary Knatchbull's desire to found a daughter house foregrounds the same sort of interpenetration of the spiritual and the political so central to the activities of the Syon nuns and of Luisa de Carvajal y Mendoza and her Society.[102] Charles's support for a new English Benedictine foundation at Dunkirk was, as Walker recounts, "Mary Knatchbull's chosen reward for her years of royalist assistance." That the abbess chose Dunkirk is highly significant; "Dunkirk was an English territory, so the foundation of a religious house there was a politically charged act on Knatchbull's part." Furthermore, she persisted in pursuing the foundation even though Charles did not keep his promises of support following his restoration to the throne. Her determination to establish the community "strongly implies that she saw it as the preface to the return of monasticism to England's shores, where it would be tolerated along with Catholicism generally."[103]

In spite of its initial difficulties, the Dunkirk foundation was a success. The ongoing roles of incarnational piety and incarnational politics in English Catholic affairs are abundantly clear in this act of foundation and in the devotional life of the nuns there. The Dunkirk house saw its identity as fundamentally—quite literally foundationally—connected to the re-Catholicization of England.[104] As the community (which ultimately returned to England to reside at St. Scholastica's Abbey, Teignmouth, Devon) reports in their unabashedly pious and partisan history written in the nineteenth century, "Tradition tells us that our foundation at Dunkirk, an English possession, at least close to English shores, was owing in great measure to the earnest desire felt that our holy Order might once again settle in England, and the hope that the return of our country to the ancient Faith was not far off, a hope that has ever been cherished in a special manner by our Community from that day to this."[105] Accordingly, since their foundation the nuns engaged in special forms of divine service that, like the Brigittine divine service and the devotions practiced by Luisa and members of her Society, emphasized devotion to the incarnate Christ and the Virgin Mary. In the case of the Dunkirk Benedictines, the linkage of incarnational piety and incarnational politics was quite explicit. Using language that calls to mind Michael Walpole's description of England in the life of Luisa de Carvajal y Mendoza, the community indicates:

> To obtain this great grace [i.e., the re-Catholicization of England] it has been the custom ever since the beginning of our House, for two religious to offer weekly special prayers and Communions. The ceremony of offering "Oblations," each Saturday, has been for the community to sing the antiphon, *Sancta Maria,* in the Chapter House, after which the two, whose turn it is, kneeling before Our Lady's statue, first touch the hand of Our Blessed Mother, and then that of her Divine Son, with the "Oblations," those offering them through Mary to Jesus, to obtain the recovery of "Our Lady's Dowry."[106]

In light of these customs, it is equally telling that the first corporate acts of worship at Dunkirk were, by Mary Knatchbull's design, timed to highlight the community's politicized devotion to the Eucharist, the incarnate Christ, and the Virgin Mary: "August 12, the feast of that special lover of the Blessed Sacrament, St Clare, was, in accordance with the wish expressed by Lady Abbess Knatchbull, fixed for the celebration of the first Mass; again in accordance with the Abbess's wish, the recitation of the Divine Office in Choir was begun on the Feast of the Assumption of Our Blessed Lady, on that day when her voice was added to the heavenly chorus."[107] Though after his restoration Charles II neglected to provide the exiled Benedictine nuns the sort of aid and support that Mary Knatchbull had expected, the conversion of Charles's brother James to Catholicism fueled further hopes.[108] Walker notes, "James II had befriended the recusant exiles during the Interregnum. His conversion to Catholicism exalted the nuns' regard for him, and in the 1680s they eagerly anticipated his accession to the throne."[109] Of course, history did not see these hopes come to fruition either; James II was deposed in the "Glorious Revolution" of 1688, and the Protestant William and Mary took the throne. English nuns in exile, however, still refused to give up. The extraordinarily somatic, politicized form of devotion practiced by Luisa de Carvajal y

Mendoza and the women of her Society in their veneration of the body parts of executed priests also lived on. "Abbess Anne Tyldesley of the Paris Augustinians obtained a relic of the deposed king's arm, which the nuns venerated in their chapel" even as they continued to support the claim to the throne of his son,[110] the very son whose military efforts to transform the English body politic coincided, as we have seen, with the discovery of the incorrupt body of Mary Margaret of the Angels at the English Carmelite house in Antwerp and the foundation of a systematic program of life writing there.

Chapter Four

Women's Life Writing, Women's Bodies, and the Gendered Politics of Faith

Margery Kempe, Anna Trapnel, and Elizabeth Cary

THE DEVOTIONAL PRACTICES AND TEXTUAL PRODUCTIONS OF THE English Benedictine nuns of Ghent and Dunkirk illustrate ways in which modes of spirituality rooted in the medieval past shape political relations in the nuns' present, the era of the Civil War and Protectorate, with an aim of bringing a version of that past back to life in the future. In this chapter, one of the chief figures is a very different woman from the period of the Civil War and Protectorate, the Fifth Monarchist prophet and preacher Anna Trapnel. She shares with the nuns of Ghent and Dunkirk, though, legacies from the medieval period that influence her spirituality, her visions of a sociopolitical future, and the ways in which she participates in her contemporary cultural milieu. In this chapter I examine the larger implications of what Anna Trapnel shares with the English nuns of Ghent and Dunkirk in their negotiations between past and present and in their performances of gendered religious identity in the political sphere by reading Trapnel's texts in conversation with the life writings of another set of medieval and early modern women: *The Book of Margery Kempe* and the biography of Elizabeth Tanfield Cary written by one of her daughters who was a nun at the English Benedictine house at Cambrai.

Multivalenced body language plays a central role in the spiritual, social, and textual lives of Margery Kempe, Anna Trapnel, and Elizabeth Cary. By the term *body language* I mean first the bodily signifying gestures and practices of the women themselves that make such powerful meaning in their times and in their texts. I also mean the language spoken by the women and inscribed in the pages of their texts, language that is so strongly connected to the locus of its production in the female body. I want to stress that my central point in choosing to focus on embodied piety and body language in texts associated with Margery Kempe, Anna Trapnel, and Elizabeth Cary is not to revisit well-established arguments about the pervasive associations of women with the body in medieval and early modern cultures. Rather, my aim is to explore the ways in which bodies and texts interact in these medieval and early modern women's life writings, forming a complex nexus that has profound theological, social, and political ramifications.

In their embodied lives and the textualizations of these lives, Margery Kempe, Anna Trapnel, and Elizabeth Cary create conditions for powerful sociopolitical critiques and revisions. As they do in the texts considered in chapter 3, bodies and bodies politic intersect in these women's lives and life writings; these women's relationships with the Word made flesh generate imperatives for sociopolitical reform and spark attendant sociopolitical anxieties. Though in some ways these critiques and revisions are different in content from each other, they share much in form and function. These women's bodies intervene symbolically in political relations, represent oppositional visions of the English body politic, and serve as a catalyst for political action. Correspondingly, uneasiness about women's involvement in the politico-spiritual arena manifests itself in strikingly similar ways in these women's lives and texts. Furthermore, even though the politico-spiritual contexts in which Margery Kempe, Anna Trapnel, and Elizabeth Cary practiced their faiths are, like their devotional practices themselves, in some respects quite different, in the face of hostility these three women also share strategies for establishing female authority.

The Book of Margery Kempe scarcely needs introduction, at least to scholars of Middle English. The *Book* describes Margery's devotional life, mystical experiences, travels, and repeated run-ins with clerics and political officials, including numerous accusations of Lollardy. Most of what we know of Margery comes from this text, which was most likely written in the later 1430s. It exists in only one manuscript, which belonged to the Carthusian Charterhouse of Mount Grace, though a radically abridged version was printed in 1501 by Wynkyn de Worde.[1] Margery identifies herself in the *Book* as the daughter of John Brunham, a man whose name "appears frequently and with increasing prominence" in the records of the East Anglian town of Lynn, where he served in a variety of offices: "jurat, chamberlain, member of parliament, mayor, coroner, justice of the peace, and alderman of the Trinity Guild."[2] The name Margery Kempe too appears in the records of the Trinity Guild, and she indicates that she married a man named John Kempe, for whom there are numerous extant references in fifteenth-century documents.[3]

Anna Trapnel is a somewhat more obscure figure than Margery Kempe, though she is relatively well known to scholars interested in seventeenth-century radical Protestantism. Anna was the daughter of William Trapnel, a shipwright from Stepney, Middlesex; her mother, Anne, a strongly "godly" woman, played an influential role in the development of her spiritual life. She remained unmarried, and her career as a visionary and prophet flourished between 1642 and 1660. During the tumultuous years of Oliver Cromwell's Protectorate, she became involved with the movement known as the Fifth Monarchists. This was a group composed largely of religious Independents, and Trapnel herself was a member of a Baptist congregation. The group's name is a biblical reference to Daniel 2:44, a prophecy in a dream of King Nebuchadnezzar in which he envisions five kingdoms, the last of which will usher in a new kingdom on earth. Anna Trapnel and her fellow Fifth Monarchists, disillusioned with the Protectorate, regarded Cromwell as impeding the coming of the fifth monarchy, that of King Jesus. In 1647, she experienced an illness that was followed by a series of prophetic visions concerning the New Model Army's entry into London and the dissolution of the Barebones Parliament. In December 1653, she traveled to Whitehall when the Independent Welsh minister Vavasour Powell was examined for treason. In a neighboring inn, she fell into a trance of several days' duration in which she pronounced prophecies regarding Cromwell's corruption and the corruption of ecclesiastical institutions. These prophecies were published as *The Cry of a Stone* in 1654. In the wake of her experiences at Whitehall, Trapnel claimed that she was commanded by God to travel to Cornwall to preach and prophesy on behalf of the Fifth Monarchist cause. *Anna Trapnel's Report and Plea*, also published in 1654, gives her account of this journey, including her arrest as a voice of sedition and her imprisonment at Bridewell. The same year also saw the publication of her spiritual autobiography entitled *A Legacy for Saints*, produced during her imprisonment at Bridewell.

Elizabeth Tanfield Cary was born at Burford Priory, Oxfordshire, in 1585 to Lawrence Tanfield and Elizabeth Symonds, and in 1602 she married Sir Henry Cary. She is perhaps best known today for her conversion to Catholicism and for her authorship of the closet drama *The Tragedy of Mariam*, a text often read as reflecting upon her conversion and her subsequently difficult relationship with her husband, though in fact her writing the drama preceded her conversion.[4] She also wrote or translated several other texts, including *The Reply of the Most Illustrious Cardinall of Perron, to the Answeare of the King of Great Britain*, published in Douai in 1630, and, perhaps, *The History of the Life, Reign, and Death of Edward II*. Like Margery Kempe, Elizabeth Cary was the mother of numerous children—eleven in Elizabeth's case, six of whom eventually converted, like her, to Catholicism (though her son Patrick would eventually return to the Protestant faith).

The lives of these three women span roughly two hundred years filled with religious and political tumult, including the height of anxieties over the heretical Lollard movement, a crucial phase of the Hundred Years' War with France, the civil strife known as the "Wars of the Roses," the seventeenth-century English Civil Wars, and the period of the Protectorate. The women's respective faiths, furthermore, legitimately appear quite divergent: we are dealing with medieval affective devotion and mysticism, radical Protestant millenarianism combined with ecstatic prophecy, and recusant Catholicism. But these women have important links with figures examined thus far in this study. One of the best-known episodes in *The Book of Margery Kempe* recounts Margery Kempe's visit to Julian of Norwich to seek spiritual counsel. Though Julian does not provide her own account of the visit, her response to her visitor as set out in the *Book* resonates, as such scholars as Nicholas Watson have observed, with passages of the *Showings*.[5] St. Birgitta of Sweden and the community of Syon are also important for Margery Kempe. Numerous critics have pointed out that Birgitta—like Margery Kempe a married woman many times a mother, yet also an accepted mystic and canonized saint—served as a role model for Kempe, and, as I have argued elsewhere, Brigittine spirituality pervades *The Book of Margery Kempe*.[6] Kempe visits St. Birgitta's haunts in Rome (*Book*, 94–95), and late in the *Book* she tells of traveling to Syon to obtain its famous pardon. In the course of that visit she reinforces a young man's vocation to seek profession as a Brigittine brother (246). Anna Trapnel also has an oblique Brigittine connection. One of her opponents disparagingly compares her to Elizabeth Barton, the "Holy Maid of Kent," who may have been inspired in her political prophecies against Henry VIII's divorce by the example of St. Birgitta and who enjoyed significant support from the Syon community.

Elizabeth Cary's biography *The Life of Lady Falkland* originates, as I mention previously, in the English Benedictine nunnery of Cambrai where women religious preserved and so complexly engaged with Julian's *Showings*. Elizabeth's daughters Anne, Lucy, Mary, and Elizabeth all became English Benedictine nuns in the Cambrai community; Anne (in religion Dame Clementia) would go on to help found the daughter house of Our Lady of Good Hope in Paris in 1651. One son, Henry, also became a Benedictine at Paris. Though there is some debate about which daughter served as the biographer, the *Life* has strong ties with the traditions of life writing as devotional writing that animate the culture of this monastic community.[7] The *Life*, which was "most likely written between February and August 1645," is nearly contemporary with Anna Trapnel's writings,[8] and spiritually, Elizabeth is something of a mediating figure between Margery and Anna, since she began life as a Protestant (though one of a very different sort than Anna Trapnel) and then became Catholic, embracing devotional practices that have important connections with the medieval realm of affective devotion so significant to Margery Kempe and, as we have seen, to the Benedictine nuns of Cambrai, where the *Life of Lady Falkland* was written.

Furthermore, important historical and textual connections exist among medieval mysticism, radical Protestantism, and Counter-Reformation Catholicism. As we have already seen, there are strong ties between Counter-Reformation female spirituality and medieval female spirituality, particularly the medieval female mystical tradition. In chapter 2, we additionally saw that both the English Benedictine nuns of Cambrai and Paris and the Protestant gentry woman Grace Mildmay were reading works of Thomas à Kempis, especially the *Imitation of Christ*. In *Perfection Proclaimed,* Nigel Smith also establishes links between radical Puritanism and medieval mysticism. As Smith indicates: "Radical religious writers, especially learned ones, were using medieval and sixteenth-century Catholic, reformed and radical, mystical and spiritual writings in order to extend the boundaries of their own spiritual experiences, both psychologically and politically. That Catholic works were used should come as less of a surprise when it is realized that the emphasis upon direct divine inspiration put them in the same position as Catholic spiritual writers."[9] While Anna Trapnel would not typically be called "learned" (though she does emphasize her literacy), it is also the case that, as Smith points out, "[g]ifted sectarian women displayed particular types of expression and languages which are not dissimilar to those of medieval female mystics and anchoresses."[10]

Smith's fascinating analysis of radical Protestant translations of and uses of medieval and Counter-Reformation mystical texts focuses primarily on works that embrace the "negative" mystical tradition (see chapter 3 of *Perfection Proclaimed*). These works did undoubtedly inform the spirituality of medieval and early modern women, Catholic and Protestant alike. Indeed, Smith takes as one of his key examples radical Protestant versions of Tauler, and, as we saw in the second chapter, Augustine

Baker invokes Tauler in directing the English Benedictine nuns of Cambrai and Paris. My focus in this chapter is on a different sort of medieval legacy, however. I am interested in "positive" mysticism and affective devotion, in forms of spirituality committed to the presence of, rather than the negation or transcendence of, the corporeal in seeking union with God. *The Book of Margery Kempe*, Anna Trapnel's texts, and *The Life of Lady Falkland*, like the corpus of life writings prompted by the discovery of the incorrupt body of the English Carmelite nun at Antwerp and like Luisa de Carvajal y Mendoza's letters sent with fragments of executed priests' bodies, manifest complex, tight connections between texts and bodies, "Lives" and lives.[11]

The texts associated with Margery Kempe, Anna Trapnel, and Elizabeth Cary are generically hybrid, blending the autobiographical with the biographical.[12] The status of the access they provide to the women's lives is complex, since they involve not only the contributions of the women themselves but also mediating figures: the scribe in the case of Margery Kempe, the unnamed male "relator" in the case of Anna Trapnel, and the daughter biographer who spent considerable time away from her mother in the case of Elizabeth Cary.[13] Adding to the complexity is the fact that Margery and Anna refer to themselves in the third as well as in the first person; indeed, Margery Kempe uses third-person formulations, especially her signature phrase "this creature," almost exclusively.[14] The texts that represent Margery Kempe's, Anna Trapnel's, and Elizabeth Cary's lives are thus not simple, uncomplicated records of the lived experiences of their central figures (though indeed whether any record of lived experience could be simple or uncomplicated is an open question). They may nevertheless be construed as some species of life writings, even as we keep in mind the difficult question "[W]hat is the relation of a 'self' to a 'life'?"[15]

The nature of the relationship between fact and fiction in the accounts of these women's lives is also critically fraught and further complicates their generic status.[16] One might say of the texts associated with all three women what Lynn Staley says of *The Book of Margery Kempe*: these texts do "not report a world" but rather "mak[e] a world."[17] The fact that Kempe's, Trapnel's, and Cary's lived lives, as well as the texts about those lives, are "made" in ways that rely upon others' lived lives and other texts does not, however, mean that relationships do not exist among the "made" texts and the women's actual lived experience.[18] Indeed, it is precisely the interaction of texts recounting the lives of others with the women's lived experiences—the ways in which, as in the case of Mary Frances of St. Theresa discussed in the Introduction, women's lives and texts about lives intersect and inform each other—that are my concerns.

BRIDES OF CHRIST OUTSIDE THE CLOISTER: MARGERY KEMPE AND ANNA TRAPNEL

The presence of a legacy derived from medieval female spirituality no doubt has much to do with why, just as I was insistently reminded of Julian of Norwich's *Showings* when I first encountered the writings of Grace Mildmay, so too my impression of Anna Trapnel upon reading her texts was of a latter-day Margery Kempe. Not only are the medieval traditions that Nigel Smith discusses operative in Anna Trapnel's texts, but striking parallels also exist in the experiences Margery Kempe and Anna Trapnel recount. Both women have divine revelations, insistently participate in public religious discourse, and are as a consequence frequently detained and persecuted. The ways in which they live and textually represent their relationships with Christ also exhibit compelling similarities.

In *The Book of Margery Kempe* and the writings of Anna Trapnel, the women's female bodies are the first and primary means by which they achieve unions with the incarnate Christ.[19] In both women's writings, accounts of the sort of nuptial union that is so important in medieval and early modern female monastic spirituality feature prominently. Margery Kempe makes a dramatically public statement of her marriage to Christ by wearing a ring with the inscription "Ihesus est amor meus" (78), which she describes as "my bone maryd ryng to Ihesu Crist" (78). In one of the *Book*'s most famous—or perhaps notorious—passages, Kempe recounts Jesus's declaration of her status as his bride and their corresponding bodily union. Jesus tells her:

For it is conuenyent þe wyf to be homly wyth hir husbond. Be he
neuyr so gret a lorde & sche so powr a woman whan he weddyth hir,
ȝet þei must ly to-gedir & rest to-gedi in joy & pes. Ryght so mot it
be twyx þe and me, for I take non hed what þu has be but what þu
woldist be. . . . Þerfore most I nedys be homly wyth þe & lyn in þi
bed wyth þe. . . . [Þ]u mayst boldly, whan þu art in þi bed, take me
to þe as for þi weddyd husbond. . . . & þerfor þu mayst boldly take
me in þe armys of þi sowle & kyssen my mowth, myn hed, & my fete
as swetly as thow wylt. (90)[20]

In such descriptions of her encounters with Christ, we see that for Margery, as for "many female and some male mystics, the corporeal aspect
of mystical meditation was neither metaphorical nor symbolic."[21]

As it does in Julian of Norwich's *Showings,* in *The Book of Margery
Kempe* the term *homely* that occurs in the passage quoted above appears
frequently to characterize the intimate bond between Margery Kempe
and Christ. Descriptions of the sensual, corporeal dimensions of Kempe's
relationship with Christ as spouse and lover also echo the intricate relationships between bodily and ghostly modes of perception in Julian's
Showings.[22] Telling of one mystical experience with Christ's body, Kempe
says, "[A]-non in þe syght of hir sowle sche sey owr Lord standyng ryght
up ouyr hir so ner þat hir thowt sche toke hys toos in hir hand & felt hem,
& to hir felyng it weryn as it had ben very flesch & bon" (208). Though
the encounter takes place spiritually, it is irreducibly an encounter with
bodily manifestations, as the juxtaposition of her perception of Christ in
the "syght of her soule" and her touching of his toes "as it had ben very
flesch & bon" in "her felyng" demonstrates. Margery Kempe, like Julian
of Norwich, thus exhibits quite a complex system of incarnational epistemology, even though Julian's spirituality is often held up as a more orthodox, sophisticated, and intellectual foil to Kempe's purportedly simple,
or simple-minded, "positive" mysticism.

The highly developed workings of Margery Kempe's incarnational
epistemology are equally evident when she undergoes a mystical marriage with the first person of the Trinity, adding a dimension to her
identity as the bride of Christ. When she is in "þe Postelys Chirch at
Rome on seynt Laterynes Day" (86), God "þe Fadyr of Hevun" proposes

marriage to her, saying, "I wil han þe weddyd to my Godhede, for I schal schewyn þe my preuyteys & my cownselys, for þu schalt wonyn wyth me wyth-owtyn ende" (86). She is reluctant and remains silent because "al hir lofe & al hir affeccyon was set in þe manhode of Crist" (86). Christ, however, intercedes for her, excusing her silence, and the marriage ensues with a heavenly version of the fifteenth-century wedding service. With the entire Trinity, the Virgin Mary, and a vast company of saints and angels present, God says, "I take þe, Margery, for my weddyd wyfe, for fayrar, for fowelar, for richar, for powerar, so þat þu be buxom & bonyr to do what I byd þe to do. For, dowtyr, þer was neuyr childe so buxon to þe modyr as I xal be to þe boþe in wel & in wo,—to help þe and comfort þe. And þerto I make þe suyrte" (87).

Later in the *Book*, Margery Kempe returns to this scene of mystical marriage to interpret it, much as Julian returns again and again to her revelations in the *Showings* to enlarge upon their meaning. Kempe says that the affection she felt for the Godhead after their nuptial union was "more feruent in lofe & desyr & mor sotyl in vndirstondyng þan was þe Manhood" (209). This shift does not, though, represent a movement away from the body, or indeed from the incarnate Christ, in favor of the intellect, or the spirit, or a disembodied divinity. Her "more subtle" relationship with the Godhead through which she learns God's privities and counsels is still one with corporeal dimensions. As she declares, describing her relationship with the Godhead, "And neuyr-þe-lesse þe fyr of loue encresyd . . . & . . . it was . . . plentyuows in teerys as euyr it was beforn" (209). She continues to perceive union with the divine sensually and to gain knowledge of God through her body.

James Holstun starkly contrasts Anna Trapnel's spirituality with that of early modern nuns who became brides of Christ. He claims, "Like their sisters entering arranged marriages, novice nuns tended to enter monastic life under the pressure of families. . . . But Trapnel freely chose her status as an ascetic virgin, asserting her own bodily self-propriety in a public and sacramental refusal of the sacrament of marriage."[23] This assessment of early modern nuns not only is overly generalized and troublingly dismissive of the possibility of sincere piety in the early modern convent but also draws too sharp a distinction between Anna Trapnel and early modern women religious (not to mention the overly strong difference that Holstun implicitly posits between Trapnel and the medieval women religious whose forms of devotion were so important to monastic piety in the early modern period).[24] The ways in which Anna Trapnel constructs a spiritual identity in fact draw on many of the same gendered patterns of devotional practice that signify so powerfully for medieval and early modern women entering monastic life, as well as for Margery Kempe who, like Anna Trapnel, lived as a bride of Christ not within convent walls but aggressively in the world.

Anna Trapnel's texts devote considerable attention to her nuptial union and bodily intimacy with Christ, experiences through which she simultaneously gains knowledge of herself and of God.[25] Much as Christ and God the Father proclaim their marriages to Margery Kempe, in *A Legacy for Saints* God calls Anna Trapnel to be his prophet and servant using language that resembles a marriage proposal.[26] She says that during a period of doubt and spiritual torment a "small voice made such a report in my soul, which made me to listen; it was such a speaking that I had not heard before, therefore it was very strange to me; the word I had was this, *Christ is thine, and thou are his.*"[27] This unitive formulation of mutual possession recurs throughout the opening section of *A Legacy for Saints* and also appears repeatedly in *The Book of Margery Kempe,* as when Jesus tells Margery Kempe, "þu art myn & I am thyn, & so xalt þu be wyth-owtyn ende" (182). Like Margery Kempe making an open declaration of her status as the bride of Christ with her white clothes and her "bone maryd ring," Anna Trapnel publicly proclaims her nuptial union with Christ in a ceremonial statement of her identity.[28] She reports that when her aunt informs her that her mother has died, her aunt instructs her, "[N]ow labour to be married to Christ, you have nothing to take up your time, but to labour for Christ." Trapnel replies, "I hope I am married to Christ" (*Legacy,* 10).[29]

To characterize her relationship with Christ, Anna Trapnel, like Margery Kempe, employs overtly corporeal, sensual descriptions that draw on the language of the Song of Songs. In the *Report and Plea,* Trapnel states, "And the second day my heart was heat also with the flame of love, which many waters cannot quench, as the spouse saith in the Canticles."[30]

Language drawing on the Canticles again features prominently in the untitled volume of Trapnel's spiritual songs and prophecies preserved in the Bodleian Library (Bodleian S1.42 Th.). For instance, she identifies with the spouse of the Canticles when she adopts the well-known language of the *hortus conclusus*:

> A garden enclosed in my Spouse
> Is my sister, saith he;
> A fountain sealed, and there is
> Delightful harmonie.
> A garden enclosed is my Spouse:
> O it is not a common place:
> It hath a peculiar beauty,
> O it hath special grace.
>
> (353)[31]

Furthermore, she highlights the bedchamber as the locus of intimate union with Christ. In *Report and Plea*, just prior to her journey to Cornwall, she says that "the Lord greatly ravished my soul with his smiling looks on me. . . . I lay all that night in a rapture of great joy" (9). Similarly, she casts the chamber in Lieutenant Lark's house in which she is imprisoned in Plymouth as a bridal bedchamber where she joins with Christ, saying, "[C]oming into my chamber, I found the Lord Christ opening his love to me from that Scripture, in *Hosea* the 2.19. I have betrothed thee to my self in mercy and loving kindnesse for ever. And I had some inlargement upon that, and likewise from Scripture expressions in the *Canticles*, and in *Habbakuk*" (*Report and Plea*, 30).[32]

VITAE CHRISTI: MARGERY KEMPE AND ANNA TRAPNEL (RE)LIVE THE GOSPEL

Nuptial union is not the only mode of bodily intimacy with the incarnate Christ present in Margery Kempe's and Anna Trapnel's texts. Nor are their identities as brides of Christ the only relationships Kempe and

Trapnel have with the divine in which both gender and corporeality are constitutive. Once again, as we saw in the second chapter, union with and imitation of Christ are overlapping phenomena, and gender plays significant roles in both. In particular, Margery Kempe and Anna Trapnel unite with and imitate Christ through bodily suffering, and they undertake salvific maternal labor associated with both Christ and the Virgin Mary.

Many scholars have examined the role of illness in the experiences of seventeenth-century female prophets, concentrating particularly on the strong authorizing function of physical suffering. As Diane Purkiss argues, for example, "Illness and physical incapacity stage the body as the passive prey of external forces, hence an authentic site of divine intervention."[33] Hilary Hinds similarly claims that "writing and serious illness mark out the sectarian woman as different from her fellows. . . . As markers of difference . . . these parallels only become significant when we return to the texts themselves and find the underlying common factor of both phenomena: namely, God."[34] Illness and the subsequent textualization of the experience may perhaps make Anna Trapnel "different from her fellows," but they make her very like many medieval holy women, including, as we have seen, St. Catherine of Siena and Julian of Norwich, who become one with Christ through bodily suffering.[35] Like Julian's and St. Catherine's experiences of suffering, Margery Kempe's and Anna Trapnel's bodily pain thus has spiritual as well as social meaning beyond confirming their divine inspiration, important though such an authenticating function is.

The Book of Margery Kempe begins with the well-known description of Margery's suffering—physical, spiritual, and mental—following the difficult birth of her first child. This opening episode sets the stage for the numerous accounts of Margery's bodily pain throughout the *Book*. In chapter 56, for example, Margery tells of her "many gret & divers sekenes," which she attributes to divine punishment (137). In the grip of illness, she fears for her life, and Christ "spak to hir in hir sowle & seyd þat sche xulde not dey ȝet" (137). She recovers, only to fall ill again. She understands her subsequent suffering, which includes a long-lasting pain in her "ryth syde" (137) that recalls the wound in Christ's side, not as divine retribution but instead as a means to enhance the closeness of her relationship with Christ. Kempe indicates that in her sickness Christ's pain displaces hers: "Sumtyme, not-wythstondyng þe sayd creatur had gret bodily sekenes, ȝet þe Passyon of owr merciful Lord Crist Ihesu wrowt so in hir sowle þat *for þe tyme sche felt not hir owyn sekenes but wept & sobbyd in þe mend of owr Lordus Passyon* as thow sche sey hym wyth hir bodily eye sufferyng peyne & passyon be-forn hir" (138, emphasis added). As when Julian of Norwich has Christ's very pains in the aftermath of an episode of illness, illness thus provides for Margery Kempe a catalyst for the merging of her experience with Christ's.

Margery Kempe's suffering also merges with Christ's in an extended account (chapters 78–82) of her mystical experiences of the events of Christ's passion corresponding to the liturgy of Holy Week: "Many ȝerys on Palme Sonday, as þis creatur was at þe processyon wyth oþer good pepyl in þe chirch-ȝerd & beheld how þe prestys dedyn her obseruawnce, how þei knelyd to þe Sacrament & þe pepil also, it semyd to hir gostly syght as þei sche had ben þat tyme in Ierusalem & seen owr Lord in hys manhod receyuyd of þe pepil as he was whil he went her in erth" (184). Her engagement with Christ's body present in the consecrated Host shifts into engagement with Christ's body in his earthly incarnation. While during her illness Christ's suffering replaces hers, this mystical sequence takes the (re)incarnational dynamics aligning Margery Kempe's and Christ's pain a step further.[36] She here offers herself to replace Christ, to suffer in Christ's place: "þe forseyd creatur thowt þat sche cryid owt of þe Iewys and seyd, 'ȝe cursyd Iewys, why sle ȝe my Lord Ihesu Crist? Sle me raþar & late hym gon'" (192). Like St. Catherine of Siena, Kempe identifies as "another himself." Revealingly, the account continues, "And þan sche wept & cryid passyngly sor þat myche of þe pepil in þe chirche wondryd *on hir body*" (192, emphasis added). The reference to her body as a spectacle that arouses wonder in the other churchgoers reveals that her experience of the Passion, like her experience of nuptial union, is not disembodied, even though it involves "gostly syght." The body and the soul, the interior and the exterior, are inseparable; Margery Kempe's intersubjective experience of Christ's passion is made manifest in, and is known both to herself and others through, her body.

Anna Trapnel's physical suffering advances her ability to know God and to unite with Christ, even as it authorizes her prophetic utterances for others. In the autobiographical preface to *The Cry of a Stone*, Trapnel associates her becoming God's prophet with bodily pain and divine intervention in an account that aligns her experience with Christ's crucifixion and resurrection. She tells of having a "feaver" from which she was "given over by all for dead" and then of experiencing recovery in accordance with God's promise on the symbolically significant third day: "[T]he Lord then gave me faith to believe from that Scripture. After two days I will revive thee, the third day I will raise thee up, and thou shalt live in my sight" (*Cry of a Stone*, 3). Furthermore, like *The Book of Margery Kempe*, *A Legacy for Saints* begins with an account of inseparably overlapping spiritual, mental, and physical torment followed by Christ's intervention. Anna Trapnel writes: "I was strongly tempted to destroy myself, which had not divine power prevented, I had been as murderer of my own life, and of their lives that I loved most intirely; I have been waked in the night by the devill for this very purpose, and directed where to have the knife, and what knife I should take; & these assaults followed me not seldom but very often, which made my poor soul and body exceedingly to tremble" (*Legacy*, 2–3). She goes on to present her condition using the language of physical disability, saying, "I was now as a cripple when his crutches are taken from him he falls" (*Legacy*, 3). It is while she is in this state that she hears the divine voice speak to her, announcing, "Christ is thine, and thou art his" (*Legacy*, 7). She describes her subsequent recovery resulting from this divine revelation by invoking both the process of Christ's incarnation and, as in *Cry of a Stone*, his bodily resurrection. Trapnel declares, "[I]n the fulness of time, Almighty power brought Christ into the world, and into the grave, it raised Christ also out of the grave; this same power was a hand by Divine appointment, leading me through varieties of inward bitter desolations, untill it brought me not onely to the gate, but into a heaven of sweet consolation" (*Legacy*, 8).

In the *Report and Plea*, Anna Trapnel provides extensive descriptions of her suffering in prison in which she makes clear that suffering for her is not simply God's punishment or a means beneficially to mortify the flesh.[37] Rather, it functions to merge her life with the *vita Christi*, to

join her experiences with his. She revealingly recounts her imprisonment in Bridewell as a Passion narrative. She initially fears she will be
mocked as "a Bridewell bird," but her fears disappear when, she says,
"my Father kept me, and gave me a discovery of my Saviour as he was
hung, between two thieves, and also brought those scriptures to my
thoughts which makes a report of Christ, as he was ranked among trans-
gressours" (*Report and Plea*, 40). Much as he does for Margery Kempe,
Christ provides personal reassurance to Trapnel in her distress, talking
with her about his own suffering: "[T]he Lord talked with me about my
Saviours suffering much for me, and therefore do not hearken to Satan
said the Lord, but look to him that suffered the contradiction of sinners
for they sake" (*Report and Plea*, 40). She becomes ill almost immediately
once she is confined to Bridewell; she says, "I grew very sick, for the
hard damp bed struck much into my stomach, and the cold sheets; so all
this set me into an Ague, and I shook much, and my limbs smarted with
cold. . . . [M]y heart panted, and lay beating, and my stomack working,
and my head aching exceeding much" (*Report and Plea*, 40). Anna Trapnel, like Christ on the cross, cries out to God the Father in her suffering,
saying, "[D]ear Father, hast thou brought me to Bridewell to dye" (*Report and Plea*, 40). As in the accounts of suffering that begin *A Legacy for
Saints* and the autobiographical preface to *Cry of a Stone*, in this narrative too her recovery results from divine intervention and is figured as a
repetition of Christ's resurrection. God tells Trapnel, "I have taken away
thy sicknesse, thou shalt be sick no more, While thou art here" (*Report
and Plea*, 42). The Lord also tells her, significantly, that on the third day
of illness he "would take me into the mount that day, for the perfect
cure of my sicknesse, and so the Lord did, and I spake by way of prayer
and singing from morning till night, and felt no sicknesse nor pain, nor
faintnesse, not all that day nor at night when I came to my self, to be capable of a body" (*Report and Plea*, 42).

Margery Kempe and Anna Trapnel emphatically perform their intersubjective, embodied relationships with Christ in the world, and as a
result both women fall victim to frequent slander and rejection by those
who witness, or even merely hear reports of, their devotional practices.
Margery Kempe, for instance, says she "had so many enmys & so mech
slawndyr þat hem semyd sche mythe not beryn it wyth-owtyn gret grace

& a myghty feyth" (43). While she is on pilgrimage she is abandoned by her fellow English travelers, who are so frustrated by her paroxysms of tears and cries that they "wold not go wyth hir for an hundryd pownd" (76).[38] Similarly, Anna Trapnel reports that when she arrives at Captain Langdon's house she receives a "sowre greeting" from many gathered there because her reputation has preceded her (*Report and Plea*, 11), and she says she is "mocked and derided" when she is sent to trial in Cornwall (*Report and Plea*, 23).

As happened in the cases of many medieval female mystics, both Margery Kempe and Anna Trapnel also face a variety of accusations— including fakery, demonic possession, and sorcery—from those who doubt the authenticity of their experiences. Kempe has a confessor who, as she says, "wyl not levyn my felyngs; & he settyth nowt by hem; he heldyth hem but tryfelys & japys" (44). She also reports being tested by clerics to see if her weeping and cries are put on just for show (200).[39] When the steward of Leicester interrogates her, he demands to know "wheþyr þu hast þis speche of God or of þe Devyl" (113), and when she is questioned by the archbishop of York, clerics in attendance declare, "[W]ot we wel þat sche hath a deuyl wyth-inne hir, for sche spekyth of þe Gospel" (126).[40] In the prefatory letter "To the Reader" in *Anna Trapnel's Report and Plea*, Trapnel indicates that "England's Rulers and Clergie do judge the Lord's handmaid to be mad" (A3r). She too tells of being tested to determine whether her ecstatic trance is a sham: "[T]hey caused my eye-lids to be pull'd up, for they said, *I held them fast, because I would deceive the people:* they spake to this purpose. One of the Justices pincht me by the nose, and caused my pillow to be pull'd from under my head, and kept pulling me, and calling me; but I heard none of all this stir and bustle; neither did I hear Mr. *Welsted* which I was told called to the Rulers, saying, *A whip will fetch her up*" (*Report and Plea*, 21, italics in original). She says that the clergy in Cornwall labeled her an imposter, and she states that the people "spit forth venome against me; but it did me no hurt, because my Father made it work for good" (*Report and Plea*, 18). Justice Tregegle, who interrogates Anna Trapnel in Cornwall, similarly expresses doubt, saying to her, "Oh you are a dreamer," an accusation to which she quickly retorts, "[S]o they called Joseph" (*Report and Plea*, 27).

Anna Trapnel's response to Justice Tregegle's assertion that she is a "dreamer" shows how adept she is at turning accusations back upon those who hurl them. When Justice Lobb demands information from her about the prophecies she spoke at Whitehall, Trapnel, invoking biblical language, queries in turn his right to interrogate her on that subject. She says:

> I am not careful to answer you in that matter, touching the whole book, as I told you before, so I say again: for what was spoken, was at White-Hall, at a place of concourse of people, and neer a Councel, I suppose wise enough to call me into question if I offended, and unto them I appeal: but though it was said, I appealed unto Caesar, and unto Caesar I should go; yet I have not been brought before him which is called Caesar: so much by the by. Again . . . I supposed they had not power to question me for that which was spoke in another county. (Report and Plea, 25; italics in original)

In the same interrogation, Justice Launse says to her, "*But had you not some of extraordinary impulses Spirit [sic], that brought you down? pray tell us what those were.*" She replies, "*When you are capable extraordinary of impulse of Spirit [sic], I will tell you; but I suppose you are not in a capacity now*" (Report and Plea 26, italics in original).

This is a skill Anna Trapnel shares with Margery Kempe. In dealing with the opponents who react skeptically or hostilely to their embodied piety, both women adopt strikingly similar rhetorical strategies, and they prove similarly successful in their quick-witted responses, successes both women connect with divine grace.[41] When Kempe is interrogated before the archbishop of York, a clerk objects to an exemplum she narrates in which a sinful priest is likened to a bear who eats blossoms and then voids "hem out ageyn at þe hymyr party" (127), calling it one of "þe werst talys of prestys þat euyr I herde" (126).[42] She responds to this cleric by making his objections the sign of his own sinfulness, saying, "A, worschipful doctowr, ser, in place wher my dwellyng is most, is a worthy clerk, a good prechar, whech boldly spekyth ageyn þe misgouer-nawns of þe pepil & wil flatyr no man. He seyth many tymes in þe pulpit, 'ȝyf any man be euyl plesyd wyth my prechyng, note hym wel, for he is gylty.' And rith so, ser . . . far ȝe be me, God forȝeue it ȝow" (127–28). Margery similarly impugns the mayor of Leicester when he interrogates her. She tells him, "Sir, ȝe arn not worthy to ben a meyr" (116), and in response to his demands that she explain her white clothing, she answers, "ȝe xal not wetyn of my mowth why I go in white clothys; ȝe arn not worthy to wetyn it" (116).

In considering the significance of continuities in female spiritualities across confessional and temporal gulfs, the parallel ways in which Margery Kempe and Anna Trapnel transformatively interpret experiences of slander and contempt are perhaps even more interesting than their similar rhetorical strategies in the face of hostility. For both women, the rejection they undergo becomes a further means to re-embody Christ's incarnation. When a "preste þat is her enmye" (85) engages in an argument with Margery Kempe, Christ describes Kempe's experience of scorn as something that joins her with him in a reenactment of the Crucifixion. He says, "[H]erby mayst thow knowyn þat I suffyr many schrewyd wordys for I haue often-tymes seyd to þe þat I schuld be *newe crucifyed in þe be schrewyd wordys*, for þu schalt no oþer-wyse ben slayn þan be schrewyd wordys sufferyng" (85, emphasis added). Note that Christ does not say that her experience is merely *like* his; rather, referencing their intersubjective, empathetic bond, he says he experiences the Crucifixion *again in her* as she is subjected to "schrewd wordys." Furthermore, her suffering "schrewyd wordys" is *her* passion as well, for she "schalt no oþer-wyse ben slayn." Margery Kempe makes the same equation between her experience and Christ's when her fellow churchgoers in Bristol are offended by her "plentyuoys terys & boystows sobbyngs . . . lowde cryingys and schille *[sic]* schrykyngs." In response to her outbursts, they "skornyd hir & despised hir, bannyd hir & cursyd hir, seyde meche euyl of hir, slawndryd hir" (107). Kempe in turn adopts Christ's identity at the moment of the Crucifixion: she weeps and prays "forȝeuenes for hem seying to owr Lord, 'Lord, as þe seydyst hangyng on þe Cros for þi crucyfyerys, "Fadyr, forȝeue hem; þei wite not what þei don," so I beseche þe, forȝeue þe pepyl al scorne & slawndrys & al þat ei han trespasyd, ȝyf it be thy wille'" (107).[43]

In the *Report and Plea* Anna Trapnel casts not just her physical suffering in prison but her entire voyage to Cornwall, a trip fraught with conflict and rejection, as a reiteration of Christ's suffering.[44] After she meets with a "sowre greeting" at Captain Langdon's house, she says that she "had a minde to walk in the Garden by myself" (*Report and Plea*, 11), where, like Christ in the Garden of Gethsemane, she prays and, as she says, experiences "communion in the Garden" (*Report and Plea*, 13). Trapnel also relives Christ's interlude in the Garden of Gethsemane prior to her interrogation, which she in turn presents as a reiteration of Christ's appearance before Pontius Pilate. Like Christ before his arrest and trial, Anna Trapnel, before she is taken to be questioned, "rose up, and prepared to go before them at the Sessions-house." She tells of "walking out in the garden before I went . . . thinking what I should say before the Justices, but I was taken off from my own thoughts quickly. . . . So I was resolved to cast myself upon the Lord, and his teaching" (*Report and Plea*, 23). She subsequently presents herself as a sacrificial Lamb of God. Trapnel reports, "[A]s I went to the Sessions house I was never in such a blessed self-denying lambe like frame of Spirit in my life as then; I had such lovely apprehensions of Christ's suffering" (*Report and Plea*, 23). During her trial, she makes the link between her persecutions and Christ's quite explicit, declaring to the justice, "You may suborne false witnesses against me, for they did so against Christ" (27). The hostile responses to Margery Kempe's and Anna Trapnel's embodied piety thus accrue layers of spiritual significance and are transmuted into something to be sought and embraced.[45] Social rejection interpreted as suffering aligned with Christ's passion becomes for each woman a paradoxical kind of empowerment, an authorization of their multivalenced body language that does so much to cause hostility toward them.

The multilayered connections of Margery Kempe's and Anna Trapnel's experiences with Christ's exhibit still another shared quality. Recalling the maternal Jesus so powerfully present in Julian's *Showings* and the feminized Christ of Lanyer's *Salve Deus Rex Judaeorum*, both women's texts strongly associate their pain that reiterates Christ's suffering with maternity. They bring together their gendered, embodied experiences with an understanding of Christ's body as a feminine, life-giving, suffering body. In this respect, Margery Kempe's and Anna Trapnel's texts illustrate further the persistence of gender as an important, though fluid, interpretive category in understanding women's incarnational piety both before and after the Reformation as well as both inside and outside the cloister.

Furthermore, in their maternal suffering, Margery Kempe and Anna Trapnel simultaneously unite not only with Christ but also with the Virgin Mary, who, at the Crucifixion, experiences her own maternal pain that merges with Christ's suffering. Mary's maternal compassion at Christ's crucifixion empowers her as a powerful co-redeemer. So too through their maternally inflected pain Margery Kempe and Anna Trapnel become salvific figures who make divine grace accessible to others.

The place of maternity in *The Book of Margery Kempe* is complex, and I have devoted a great deal of attention to Margery Kempe's physical and spiritual maternity elsewhere, as have numerous other scholars.[46] I want to focus here chiefly on two episodes to consider the ways in which Margery Kempe's experiences align with Christ's and the Virgin Mary's maternal suffering to shape Kempe as a salvific figure. While she is on pilgrimage in the Holy Land, she visits "fro [on] place to an-oþer wher owyr Lord had sufferyd hys [peynys] and hys passyons" (68). When she arrives at Calvary, "sche fel down þat sche mygth not stondyn ne knelyn but walwyd & wrestyd wyth hir body, spredyng hir armys a-brode & cryed wyth a lowde voys as þow hir hert xulde a brostyn a-sundyr, for in þe cite of hir sowle sche saw veryly & freschly how owyr Lord was crucifyed" (68). As Karma Lochrie has argued, Margery's bodily posture and violent physical gestures at once call to mind Christ on the cross and a woman in labor. This process of multilayered experiential reiteration echoes the process examined in the first chapter through which Brigittine nuns participate jointly in Christ's and Mary's pain at the Crucifixion. It is also similar to the process by which, as we saw in chapter 2, the dying Margaret Gascoigne at once reenacts the shared pain of Julian of Norwich and Christ. Later in the *Book*, the Virgin Mary underlines the link between Margery Kempe's pain, Christ's, and her own, announcing the redemptive dimensions of Kempe's suffering. Mary says, "Dowtyr, all þes sorwys þat þu hast had for me & for my blissyd Sone xal turne þe to gret joye & blys in Heuyn wyth-owtyn ende. . . . & þe same pardon þat was grawntyd þe befor-tyme, it was confermyd on Seynt Nicholas Day, þat is to seyn plenowr remissyon, and it is not only grawntyd to þe but also to alle þo þat beleuyn & to alle þo þat xul beleuyn in-to þe worldys ende þat God louyth þe and xal þankyn God for þe" (175).

Anna Trapnel undergoes bodily and spiritual travails every bit the equal of Margery Kempe's dramatic experiences on Calvary. These manifestations of Trapnel's embodied piety align, like Kempe's on Calvary, with the labor of childbirth, creating an identity for Trapnel as one whose redemptive power comes from maternal suffering with Christ-like dimensions. In discussing Anna Trapnel's trance at Whitehall, Holstun argues, "By lying in bed for twelve days and giving spiritual life to others while risking her own mortal life, Trapnel conjured up the authority of protracted childbirth."[47] Trapnel reinforces the maternal, life-giving aspects of her Christ-like maternal suffering when she casts herself in "the role of the laboring woman clothed with the sun / Son of Revelation 12,"[48] as she does in her prophetic songs recorded in the untitled Bodleian volume. For example, she says:

> And such a wonder *John* in Heaven saw,
> A poor woman cloathed with the Sun,
> And having the Moon under her feet,
> And with bright stars she come.
>
> She had a Crown, and she did shine,
> Fit to sit on a Throne,
> And on a chair of State: for she
> is an exalted one.
>
> (873)[49]

As Christ and the Virgin Mary do with Margery Kempe, so too the Lord informs Anna Trapnel that her experiences of suffering make her a means of access to God for others. Trapnel says that after her recovery/ resurrection on the third day of her life-threatening fever, "the Lord made use of me for the refreshing of afflicted and tempted ones, inwardly and outwardly" (*Cry of a Stone*, 3). The Lord assures her, "I will make thee an Instrument of much more; for particular souls shall not only have benefit by thee, but the universality of Saints shall have discoveries of God through thee" (*Cry of a Stone*, 3).

WRITING CHRIST, UNITING WITH CHRIST

The maternity that is a central component of Margery Kempe's and Anna Trapnel's spiritual identities also plays a key role in the ways in which both women represent the processes of textual production. Like Lanyer's *Salve Deus Rex Judaeorum*, considered in chapter 1, these women's life writings valorize the place of the female (and especially the maternal) body in the textual economy while foregrounding the crucial places of maternal work and the female body in salvation history. Margery Kempe's and Anna Trapnel's life writings begin, significantly, with accounts that link bodily suffering and maternal reproduction with textual production.

The Book of Margery Kempe tells us nothing of Margery Kempe's early life but rather begins with her marriage at approximately age twenty and her nearly immediate pregnancy (which follows her marriage within the first sentence of the first chapter): "Whan þis creatur was xx ȝer of age or sumdele mor, sche was maryed to a worschepful burgeys and was wyth chylde wyth-in a schort tyme, as kynde wolde" (6). The first chapter then recounts, as is well known, the details of her physical, mental, and spiritual suffering that follow the difficult delivery of her first child. A vision of Christ who "aperyd to hys creatur . . . in lyknesse of a man, most semly, most bewtyuows, & most amyable . . . clad in a mantyl of purpyl sylke, syttyng up-on hir beddys syde" (8) subsequently heals her. Margery Kempe's mystical career and the *Book* itself thus quite literally begin with the suffering maternal body; the *Book* is born through her travail.

Anna Trapnel's texts similarly include accounts of their origins that connect maternity with the processes of textual production. The first of Anna Trapnel's texts to appear in 1654, *The Cry of a Stone*, begins with a much discussed description of her physical state provided by the unnamed male "relator." He annotates in detail the condition of her fasting, entranced body as the locus from which her prophetic voice speaking God's words issues forth. Waiting to learn Vavasour Powell's fate, Anna was carried forth in a spirit of Prayer and Singing, from noon till night, and went down into Mr. *Roberts* lodging, who keeps the Ordinary in *Whitehall*; And finding her natural strength going from her, she took to her bed at eleven a clock in the night, where she lay from that day, being the seventh day of the month, to the nineteenth day of the same month, in all twelve days together; The first five days neither eating nor drinking any thing more or less, and the rest of the time once in 24 hours, sometimes eat a very little toast in small Bear, sometimes only chewed it, and took down the moysture only, sometimes drank of the small Bear, and sometimes only washt her mouth therewith, and cast it out, lying in bed with her eyes shut, her hands fixed, seldom seen to move, she delivered in that time many and various things. (*Cry of a Stone*, 1–2)

This scene obviously underlines the need to establish the divine authenticity of Trapnel's prophetic voice by situating its origin in a particular sort of female body, as Diane Purkiss has persuasively argued. Purkiss observes, "Just as prophecy could authenticate fasting, so fasting could authenticate prophecy."[50] The fact that the relator describes Anna Trapnel's laboring body in the bed as "delivering" many things, however, specifically associates the process of Anna's production of prophetic language with the labor of childbirth.[51]

The correlation between maternal suffering and the creation of Anna Trapnel's texts becomes even clearer in her first-person preface that precedes the relator's account of her prophetic utterances at Whitehall. This section, like the first chapter of *The Book of Margery Kempe*, stages a scene of textual origin centering on the suffering maternal body. The *Cry of a Stone* begins: "I am *Anna Trapnel*, the daughter of *William Trapnel*, Shipwright, who lived in *Poplar*, in *Stepney* Parish; my father and mother living and dying in the profession of the Lord Jesus; my mother died nine years ago, the last words she uttered upon her death-bed, were these to the Lord for her daughter. Lord! Double thy spirit upon my child; These words she uttered with much eagerness three times, and spoke no more" (3). As Purkiss observes, "This story, in explaining Trapnel's gifts as the product of her mother's prayer, associated Trapnel's mother with the power of words" (143). The language issuing forth from Trapnel's mother's dying body is the catalyst for the divinely inspired language that will in turn issue forth from Trapnel's own entranced body to be recorded in her textual corpus. Indeed, after establishing her good standing in her congregation, Anna Trapnel turns in the second paragraph to the origins of her prophetic language in her own experience of illness and miraculous recovery, an episode that, as we have already seen, connects her divinely instigated recovery on the third day with Christ's resurrection. In these opening scenes, Trapnel thus associates the origins of the texts that record her speaking God's words both with her mother's body, the labors of which grant her spiritual as well as earthly life, and with her own bodily suffering, which takes on maternal dimensions in that it leads to spiritual rebirth and new life as God's servant and prophet after her "resurrection" from her illness.

In the spiritual songs recorded in the Bodleian volume, Anna again associates textual origins with maternity, in this case the maternal role of the Virgin Mary. She says, in a passage that foregrounds embodiment as the Word becomes flesh:

> This Body the Father sent out
> It was prepared of old,
> And came forth in sweet Virgin-state,
> Though laid in manger mold.
> This prepared Body, dear God,
> It was compleat and choice.
> And thou didst send it forth in time
> With a choice Virgin-voice.
>
> (346)

As Matthew Prineas observes, "Trapnel identified her song and her voice . . . with the Virgin Birth. Perhaps we are to infer a parallel between her pouring forth of the Word with Mary's giving birth to it."[52] The dynamics of textual production at once replicate the bodily experience of the Word made flesh himself and the maternal labor through which Christ's incarnation transpired.

The connections between textual production and maternity in Margery Kempe's and Anna Trapnel's life writings foreground the close ties between the textual corpus and spiritual experiences lived in the body.[53] Even more significantly, though, as texts that accordingly offer access to the divine Word (re)made flesh in Margery Kempe's and Anna Trapnel's lives, these life writings present themselves as textual reiterations of Christ's incarnation. We have in both the medieval Catholic mystic's and the early modern Protestant prophet's writings once again something like a textual version of the doctrine of the real presence at work. *The Book of Margery Kempe* and Anna Trapnel's texts take on a status like that of Aemilia Lanyer's poetry, or the incarnate, spirit-filled texts of the English Benedictines of Cambrai and Paris, or Luisa de Carvajal y Mendoza's letters. Margery Kempe and Anna Trapnel live lives they experience as reiterations of Christ's life. Similarly, their textual lives are, in effect, sacramental documents. Like the transubstantiated Host, these texts contain Christ's body, *are* Christ, and so enable readers simultaneously to join with the women whose lives are their subject and to become one with Christ, part of the body of Christ, by consuming them.[54]

Margery Kempe's and Anna Trapnel's lived and textual lives equally exhibit complex engagements with the divine Word of scripture. Like Lanyer's *Salve Deus,* Margery Kempe's and Anna Trapnel's texts retell scriptural events and present themselves as new iterations of the divine Word, "gospels according to Margery and Anna," to recast Achsah Guibbory's description of *Salve Deus Rex Judaeorum*. We have already seen the ways in which for Kempe the Nativity and Passion sequences, and for Trapnel the Passion sequence, become parts of their lives. In a process that Hilary Hinds, in her work on Anna Trapnel, calls "self-inscripturation," both women's identities also blend with those of women and men from the Bible as they write themselves into God's Word and write God's Word anew in their texts.[55] For Margery Kempe, the life of Mary Magdalene is especially significant. She recounts retracing the steps of Mary Magdalene during her pilgrimage to the Holy Land, when she visits "Betanye þer Mary & Martha dwellyd" and stands "in þe same place þer Mary Mawdelyn stode whan Crist sayd to hir 'Mary why wepyst þu?'" (75). She also participates in this latter scene in her extended mystical experiences of the events of Holy Week (see chapter 81). Christ invokes Mary Magdalene's status as a penitent sinner to comfort Kempe when she laments her much-mourned virginity; indeed, the first appearance of Mary Magdalene in *The Book of Margery Kempe* occurs when Christ tells her that he loves "wyfes also," going on to instruct her not to despise herself for her lack of sexual purity because "þow xalt neuyr be despysed of God. Have mend, dowtyr, what Mary Mawdelyn was" (49). The Virgin Mary also connects Margery with Mary Magdalene in offering reassurance concerning Margery's weeping and crying aloud. She tells Margery, "Be not aschamyd, my derworthy dowtyr, to receyue þe ʒyftys whech my Sone xal ʒeue þe. . . . Mary Mawdelyn was not aschamyd to cryen & to wepyn for my Sonys lofe. And þerfor, dowtyr, ʒyf þu wylt be partabyl in owyr joye, þe must be partabil in owyr sorwe" (73). Later Christ aligns Margery with Mary Magdalene more directly still. Margery says, "A, blysful Lord . . . I wolde I we as worthy to ben sekyr of they lofe as Mary Mawdelyn was" (176). Christ responds, "Trwely, dowtyr, I loue þe as wel, and *þe same pes þat I ʒaf to hir þe same pes I ʒeue to þe*" (176, emphasis added). This passage makes clear that the connection between Margery Kempe and Mary Magdalene is not simply one of similarity, or even of *imitatio*, either through temporal pilgrimage or mystical experience. Rather, the *Book* presents Kempe as a reincarnated Mary Magdalene.[56] As we have seen, Julian of Norwich and Margaret Kempe have the same pain as Christ (not analogous or similar pain, but his actual pain), and here Kempe receives from Christ the same peace as Mary Magdalene received. The saint's experience becomes Margery's experience as Margery lives Mary Magdalene's life again. The *Book* is a record not just of Margery Kempe's life but also of the reiteration of the *vita* of a saint whose experiences have unassailable scriptural authority.

Anna Trapnel also reanimates the biographies of biblical figures, in the process highlighting the divinely authorized status of her life as both lived experience and text. Her namesake Hannah is especially important; in fact, Trapnel sometimes spells her name Hannah, emphasizing her identification with the female prophet. In her epistle "To the Reader" in her *Report and Plea,* she says, "[M]y desire is to imitate that approved *Hannah* in 1 *Sam.* 1" (A2v). Here too, though, *imitatio* is not the whole story. Anna Trapnel *becomes* Hannah, perhaps even out-Hannahs Hannah, when she experiences "malice and envie uttered and acted by the Clergie and Rulers" (A3r). She says, "I am sure they have sinned far more then old *Eli,* who said of *Hannah,* She was Drunk. This grieved her and made her reply and say, *Don't count thy hand maid for a daughter of Belial, for out of the abundance of my complaint and grief have I spoken"* (A3r, italics in original).[57]

Much as Christ and the Virgin Mary reassure Margery Kempe by connecting her with Mary Magdalene, so to the Lord reassures Anna Trapnel by interpreting her experiences as reiterations of episodes in the lives of biblical figures. In a dialogue resembling that in which Christ tells Kempe she will have the "same pes" that he granted Mary Magdalene, the Lord tells Trapnel, *"Thou shalt have the same word as I gave to my servant Abraham; I told him when he went he knew not whither, that I would be his shield and exceeding great reward"* (*Report and Plea,* 12, italics in original, underlining added). The Lord also aligns what Trapnel calls her "vision of my Cornwal-journey" (*Report and Plea,* 2) with Paul's experience.[58] She recounts, "[T]his I saw, and heard this saying, *That as sure as Paul in Act.16.9. had a vision appeared in the night: There stood a man of Macedonia and prayed Paul, saying, Come over into Macedonia and help us;* and the Lord said, *as truly do I thy Lord call the to Cornwal by this vision"* (*Report and Plea,* 3, italics in original). Anna responds, *"Paul was to preach there, what is that word to me?"* She subsequently reports, "[T]hen reply was, *But as sure as his was a vision from the Lord to go to Macedonia, so as sure had I a call and true vision to go to Cornwal"* (*Report and Plea,* 3; italics in original).[59] That the Lord connects Anna Trapnel with Paul to legitimate her public religious speech is highly significant, and the careful formulation of the equation is quite important. Her initial reaction ("What is that word to me?") acknowledges her awareness of the long-standing barriers to women's preaching, a prohibition rooted, of course, in Pauline writings, particularly to the passage that states, "But I suffer not a woman to teach, nor to use authority over the man: but to be in silence. For Adam was first formed; then Eve. And Adam was not seduced, but woman being seduced, was in the transgression"' (1 Tim. 2:12–14).[60] The divine answer to Trapnel's query at once evades the issue of preaching by its strategic omission of the key term and authorizes her as a new Paul, called by a divine vision just as surely as he was.

This alignment of the divinely inspired woman with Paul, and the careful framing of that alignment, resemble episodes from *The Book of Margery Kempe*. When Margery Kempe is being questioned before the archbishop of York, "a gret clerke browt forth a boke & leyd Seynt Powyl for his party a-geyns hir þat no woman xulde prechyn" (126). In response she declares, "I preche not, ser, I come in no pulpytt" (126). Like the Lord's response to Trapnel, Kempe's reply evades the charge by distancing herself from the term *preaching* even as Kempe, like Trapnel, engages in an activity that for all intents and purposes looks precisely like preaching.[61] And just as the Lord connects Anna Trapnel's preaching mission to Cornwall with Paul's divinely ordained mission to Macedonia, Christ links Margery Kempe's actions with those of Paul in a discussion of her public religious speech. In an exchange that might easily refer to Kempe's experiences before the archbishop of York, Christ, who also avoids using the term *preaching,* tells her, "Dowtyr, I sent onys Seynt Powyl vn-to þe for to strenghtyn þe & comfortyn þe þat þu schuldist boldly spekyn in my name fro þat day forward. And Seynt Powle seyd vn-to þe þat þe haddyst suffyrd mech tribulacyon for cawse of hys wrytyng, & he behyte þe þat þe xuldist han as meche grace þer-a-ʒens for hys lofe as euyr þu haddist schame er reprefe for hys lofe" (160). As Lochrie argues, "Paul's endorsement of Kempe's bold speech undermines those very writings which have caused her suffering. In effect, he interdicts his own writings in order to authorize Kempe's speech. Ironically, the same Pauline texts so often cited as authorities against woman's speech become for Kempe the source of her grace."[62]

In addition to reframing scripture to legitimate women's suspect preacherly speech, Margery Kempe's and Anna Trapnel's life writings specifically foreground the ways in which both women "speak scripture" in their public religious discourse. Such "speaking scripture" recalls the ready adoption of biblical language by Julian of Norwich, Aemilia Lanyer, Grace Mildmay, and the English Benedictines of Cambrai and Paris. At Canterbury, Margery Kempe meets a monk who asks her, "What kanst þow seyn of God" (27). She replies, "I wyl boþe speke of hym &

heryn of hym," and she continues by "rehearsyng þe monk a story of Scriptur" (27). Anna Trapnel says that she speaks to a gathered crowd "in Scripture language" (*Report and Plea,* 28), and she frequently adopts biblical formulations, as when she states, "[Y]et I can say with *Paul,* Through grace I am what I am; and I live, yet not I, but Christ lives in me" ("To the Reader," in *Report and Plea*; italics in original). Trapnel additionally calls the spiritual songs recorded in the Bodleian volume "prophetic epistles" and "psalms."[63]

Such use of scripture serves to make Margery Kempe's and Anna Trapnel's speeches all the more controversial, and both women accordingly provoke strong responses when they adopt biblical language. The people to whom Trapnel speaks react by giving, she says, "a great shout," and she continues, "The people said, they used to do so at some strange sight" (*Report and Plea,* 28). In the environment of anxiety concerning the Lollard movement in which Kempe operates, reactions to a woman speaking scripture are especially hostile (though pamphlets about female "tub preachers" in Anna's time show plenty of their own hostility). As Kempe departs from Canterbury, for instance, a group follows her "crying up-on hir, 'þow xalt be brent, fals lollare. Her is a cartful of thornys redy for þe and a tonne to bren þe wyth'" (28). The monk to whom Kempe rehearses a Bible story reacts by saying, "I wold þow wer closyd in an hows of ston þat þer schuld no man speke wyth þe" (27). In her interrogation before the archbishop of York, one of the clerks adds a charge of demonic possession to the allegations of heresy as a result of her speaking scripture, saying, "[H]er wot we wel þat sche hath a deuyl wyth-inne hir, for sche spekyth of þe Gospel" (126).

An episode from Anna Trapnel's *Cry of a Stone* provides a useful final example of the recursive, cyclical interactions of bodies and texts, selves and others, characteristic of both her and Margery Kempe's engagements with scripture. In one of her spiritual songs, Anna speaks as Christ, serving as his stand-in and saying:

And look into the written Word,
and there you shall behold
How I have beautified, and have
made you bright as gold.

O look into the written Word,
and there drink you of me,
for I am flagons of Wine, and
you shall partake of me.

(40)

The status of the first-person pronoun in this passage is complex. The
"I" is Christ and Trapnel at once; he and she are inseparably present together.[64] Given the lack of clear differentiation between human self and
divine Other, in the passage from Trapnel's spiritual song the written
Word of God is simultaneously the scriptures and the text of the song itself. The written Word is, furthermore, at once the means of access to
knowledge of the self (as indicated by the first stanza, which tells the
reader to behold her beautified self in "the written Word") and to the
body of Christ (as signaled by the second stanza, which tells the reader to
partake of Christ in "the written Word"). In "the written Word" reader
and Christ are simultaneously present, even as Anna and Christ are simultaneously present in the "I" that voices the song. The language of this
song, recalling the Eucharistic poetics of Lanyer's dedicatory poems,
presents the reader's encounter with the written Word jointly as a corporeal, epistemological, and sacramental experience. By looking into
the written Word, the reader incorporates Christ (who is "flagons of
Wine ") into her or his own body and is thus united with Christ, acquiring knowledge of self and God in the process.[65]

False Strumpets and Ranting Sluts

The controversy associated with Margery Kempe's and Anna Trapnel's
public religious discourse, as well as the hostile reactions their embodied pieties so often generate, call us to examine the precise nature of the
religio-political threats both women were deemed to pose. Appropriately, given the salvific aspects of their incarnational spirituality, and
given their production of texts that make God's incarnate and scriptural
Word accessible, both women express an awareness of the commonality
of their experiences. Like Julian of Norwich's revelations, these women's

intimate interactions with Christ, while unquestionably individual, are also at the same time for their "evencristen." Their being "oned" with Christ corresponds to being "oned" with the larger, corporate body of Christ and so underwrites visions of reformed communal, social bodies.[66] This commonality contains the seeds of far-reaching, and potentially disturbing, social revisions.

Lynn Staley argues that though Kempe uses "autobiographical apparatus to shape an account of Margery as a representative type, she uses those details as a screen for an analysis of communal values and practices."[67] In contrast to Staley, however, I see a more continuous relationship between the accounts of Margery Kempe's experiences or Anna Trapnel's experiences and these women's redefinitions of community. The "autobiographical apparatus" is not just a screen for the analysis of communal issues but rather the very site where, and the very material through which, issues of community or commonality are (re)negotiated.[68] In the relationships of the individual or personal to the communal lies an important structural dimension to both women's envisioned reforms. The commonality, the reiterability, of the personal, the open relationships between one's own embodied experience and that of others both human and divine, are what make possible the reformist social gospel that both Kempe and Trapnel advance.[69]

In a scathing dismissal of *The Book of Margery Kempe* as a "proper" work of religious contemplation, Stephen Medcalf says, "Many have treated it as a treatise on contemplation. . . . To be that, it should have focused not on her idiosyncrasy but on God. But she does not know the difference."[70] Though my reading of the *Book* differs radically from Medcalf's, the lack of differentiation between knowledge of God and knowledge of individual experience to which he points is in a way key to my argument. Part of the central point of Margery Kempe's and Anna Trapnel's reformist visions of society is that in writing about their idiosyncratic experiences they *are* writing about God as well as about human others.[71]

Staley notes that *The Book of Margery Kempe* provides a model of community different from the one found in "official pronouncements about the nature of English society." Margery Kempe, she says, defines "community in terms of what it can include and thus in terms of those individuals who can now be accommodated in this new society whose foundation is love." The representation of her life in the *Book* "translates into her mother tongue . . . a *vita Christi* in the form of a social gospel that breaks down, rather than erects, boundaries."[72] Margery Kempe's embodied experience of the incarnate Christ recorded in her reiterable, incarnational (auto)biography contains the script to perform a capacious Christian community not unlike that represented in Grace Mildmay's meditations or in Julian's *Showings*. In other words, Margery posits a reformed social body grounded in the accessibility to all of Christ's body, one avenue of access to which is through her own body and her text. One might describe her reformed social vision by adopting the language of the scribal prologue, which describes Margery Kempe's life being turned "vp-so down" (a phrase that in many ways could serve as an organizing principle for *The Book of Margery Kempe*) in that established power dynamics and social relations are radically transformed.

As a Fifth Monarchist, Anna Trapnel of course explicitly advocates for social reform in a radical sense. She embraces a "social and political vision involving the complete reformation of society" and "offers a forceful prophetic critique of contemporary realities."[73] What I want to call to particular attention are not the specifics of her attitudes toward the monarchy, Cromwell, or the events of the English Revolution. Furthermore, her political allegiances and sympathies are different from Margery Kempe's in very important ways. Consider, for instance, the good relationship that Margery Kempe had, even in spite of the suspicions of Lollardy that persistently clung to her, with Archbishop Arundel of Canterbury, a connection that for Anna Trapnel would have been abhorrent and impossible in equal parts. Instead, I want to emphasize what might be called the *form* of Trapnel's reform, a reform grounded upon the *bodily* return of King Jesus and advanced through her bodily experiences and their textual representations. I would suggest that Anna Trapnel's redefinition of community predicated on an encompassing social gospel shares much in this respect with the social vision embraced by Margery Kempe.

The *vita Christi* reincarnated in Anna Trapnel's life and openly available through her writings undergirds a radically egalitarian social vision in which the political and the spiritual exist in harmony. In *The Cry of a Stone*, for instance, the Lord tells Trapnel that "particular souls shall not only have benefit by thee, but the *universality* of saints shall have discoveries of God through thee" (9; emphasis added). And in the prefatory epistle to *Cry of a Stone*, Trapnel dedicates the text "To all the wise Virgins in Sion," adding, "It was the desire of this Maid to present this her Testimony to you, *though it is not for you only, but for all*" (emphasis added).[74]

For both Margery Kempe and Anna Trapnel, this new, encompassing social gospel is ripe for (re)creation in the world via the performance of that which their texts contain. These women, with their embodied piety and their body language, with their relivings of Christ's life and their insistence that such experiences are inherently shareable, problematically refigure and break down boundaries. At the heart of their reformed visions of society are new paradigms that expose the constructed, artificial dimensions of the supposedly immutable, natural nexus of masculinity, divinity, and political authority.[75] Tellingly, Margery Kempe and Anna Trapnel are not simply accused of doctrinal error or unauthorized preaching (though they certainly are accused of both of these things). Rather, as they perform their embodied spirituality and publicize the imperatives for social and ecclesiastical reforms demanded by their relationships with the divine Word made flesh, they are also explicitly accused of engaging in treasonous activities.[76]

In fact, both Margery Kempe and Anna Trapnel attract the attention of the most politically powerful men in England in their respective periods.[77] John, Duke of Bedford, acting as lieutenant for Henry V while the king is in France, seeks Kempe's arrest, while the Protector Cromwell concerns himself with Trapnel. When the Duke of Bedford's yeomen apprehend Kempe, they declare, "þu art holdyn þe grettest loller in al þis countre er a-bowte London eythyr" (129). They highlight the treasonous dimension of her suspected Lollardy when they subsequently call her "Combomis dowtyr" and say she "was sent to beryn lettrys abowtyn þe cuntre" (132). Their accusations link her with Sir John Oldcastle, Lord Cobham, the notorious Lollard rebel leader who was, at the time of her arrest, on the loose following his escape from the Tower of London.[78]

Treason and sedition figure equally prominently in the accusations that swirl around Anna Trapnel. Marchamont Needham, whom Hinds describes as "a journalist, pamphleteer, and government supporter," clearly articulates the threats Trapnel and her texts are deemed to pose to the Protectorate.[79] In a letter to Cromwell, he says:

> There is a twofold design about the prophetess Hannah [Trapnel], who played her part lately at Whitehall at the ordinary; one to print her discourses and hymns, which are desperate against your person, family, children, friends and the government; the other to send her all over England, to proclaim them *viva voce*. She is much visited, and does a world of mischief in London, and would do in the country. The vulgar dote on vain prophecies. I saw hers in the hands of a man who was in the room when she uttered them day by day in her trance, as they call it. He promised to lend me them; if he does, I will show you them. They would make 14 or 15 sheets in print.[80]

When Anna Trapnel learns that two warrants are out for her arrest, she explains, "[T]he report was, I went from place to place, aspersing the Government" (*Report and Plea*, 19), and when she is brought to Bridewell, the matron directly accuses her of seditious activity, saying, "I warrant you are one of the plotters" (*Report and Plea*, 38). Ensign Owen, who serves as Trapnel's jailer at one point, indicates that he too is aware of the widespread opinion that she is a traitor. She reports, "Ensign Owen was my keeper, and he was very carefull to fulfill his office, and he was loath to let in my friends to see me, but charged them at the gate with trespasse, if they let in any of my friends, saying, they had best to be traytors too; so that he was as severe, as if I had been a traytor; yet he spake me very fair to my face, but I saw he indeavoured to catch my words, and to ensnare me" (*Report and Plea*, 32–33). She also asserts that the "*Cornwall* Jurors, who say they are for the Lord protector of the Commonwealth," level the charge of treason against her, since "upon their Oaths" they "present *Anna Trapnell* to be a dangerous, seditious Person" (*Report and Plea*, 52). The jurors, she states, further say that she is not only "imagining, but devising and maliciously intending the peace, tranquility and felicity of the good people of this Commonwealth of *England* to disturb" (*Report and Plea*, 52; italics in original).

Both clerical and secular authority figures fear that Margery Kempe will lead others to follow her into heresy and rebellion. In her interrogation before the archbishop of York, the clerks admit that she "can þe Articles of þe Feith" (125), but they still say, "[W]e wil not suffyr hir to dwellyn a-mong vs, for þe pepil hath gret feyth in hir dalyawnce, and perauentur sche myth peruertyn summe of hem" (125). Even more pointedly, the mayor of Leicester says to Kempe, "I wyl wetyn why þow gost in white clothys, for I trowe þow art comyn hedyr to han a-wey owr wyuys fro us & leden hem wyth þe" (116). As Ruth Nissé Shklar observes, the mayor here "transform[s] her supposed Lollardy from a heretical reinterpretation of property and power to a domestic revolt or sexual treason—essentially an all-women's version of Oldcastle's Rebellion."[81]

Anna Trapnel is similarly suspected not only of being a traitor herself but also of instigating others to rebellion. The Cornwall jurors believe she intends "to move, stir up, and raise discord, rebellion and insurrection among the good People of *England*" (*Report and Plea*, 52; italics in original). Indeed, a fear that she will, like Margery Kempe, "pervert" people through her embodied piety and her body language, making them into versions of herself, accompanies her everywhere. When she is on her way to Cornwall, for instance, Trapnel meets a man who, as she says, declares, "[I]f he had known me, and had known I was going into his county, he would have procured the Councils Order to have stopt my journey, for the love he bore to his county: which sure he thought I would corrupt, and make like my self" (*Report and Plea*, 7). Similarly, she indicates that clerics fear she has Pied Piper–like qualities similar to those the mayor of Leicester attributes to Kempe. Trapnel says that "the Clergie, with all their might, rung their jangling bells against me, and called to the Ruler to take me up. . . . [O]thers said, *The people would be drawn away, if the Rulers did not take some course with me*" (*Report and Plea*, 18; italics in original).

Erica Longfellow argues that "the men in charge seem to have viewed Trapnel first as a political danger and only secondarily, if at all, as an unruly woman."[82] While the clerical and governmental authorities certainly viewed Anna Trapnel as a political danger, I would argue that her femaleness plays a crucial role in *making* her a political danger, and much the same holds true for Margery Kempe. Margery Kempe's and Anna Trapnel's opponents revealingly link charges of sedition with charges of improper speech and sexual impropriety. The mayor of Leicester, for instance, calls Kempe a "fals strumpet, a fals loller. & a fals deceyuer of þe pepyl" (112), and the matron of Bridewell calls Trapnel a "ranting slut" (*Report and Plea*, 38).[83] The juxtaposition of such accusations sheds light on the nature of the crimes Margery Kempe and Anna Trapnel are perceived to have committed. The anxiety that is so frequently expressed about these women's capacity to convert or pervert others is a fear of a gendered form of reproduction—a disturbing, symbolic maternity. Margery Kempe's and Anna Trapnel's bodies and their words have an incarnational quality with dangerous implications for those in power: their bodies and words have the power to create more (oppositional) bodies and words that will continue to perform their visions of reformed bodies politic.

By representing Margery Kempe's and Anna Trapnel's female bodies as sexually impure, their opponents strive to devalue the very medium through which the women unite with Christ and relive the *vita Christi*. As a result, the women's language becomes corrupt rather than inspired, profane rather than prophetic.[84] These yoked accusations of corporeal corruption and suspect speech simultaneously undermine Margery and Anna's reincarnations of the Word made flesh that are the foundations of their social critiques and their reformist visions of the body politic. In other words, the accusations assert the commonality of Margery and Anna's bodies in a sexual sense, so negating the reformed communities born from and figured by those bodies and disseminated through the incarnational texts produced by those bodies.

THE LIFE OF LADY FALKLAND: CONVERSION, CONVERGENCE, AND CONTINUITY

To end this chapter I return to the milieu of convent life writing with which I began this book and, indeed, to the very monastic community of Cambrai under consideration in chapters 2 and 3. Admittedly, the

Life of Lady Falkland is different from the life writings of Margery Kempe and Anna Trapnel, as it is a straightforward biography rather than a more generically ambiguous work. The figure at its center too might seem a very different sort of woman from the visionary Margery Kempe or the prophetic Anna Trapnel. Yet Elizabeth Cary's lived experiences and her textual *Life* have much in common with the lives and life writings of Margery Kempe and Anna Trapnel. Specifically, the *Life of Lady Falkland* presents extensive evidence for the centrality of the body in Elizabeth Cary's devotional life and for the female body's irreducible place in the text. The paradigm of turning life into text and text into life once again serves as a fundamental organizing principle. We continue to see, furthermore, strong socially reformist dimensions to female spirituality lived in the body and recorded on the page. Additionally, in the *Life of Lady Falkland* we find evidence of ongoing political anxiety about the larger implications of such embodied female piety and the textual productions that make it accessible to others.

In focusing detailed attention on the bodily dimensions of Elizabeth Cary's spirituality, *The Life of Lady Falkland* gives special prominence to her fasting. Indeed, the treatment of fasting grants important insights not only into Elizabeth's devotional life but also into the perceptions of her monastic daughter biographer. This emphasis on fasting's spiritual importance, whether the fast is undertaken as penance or necessitated by poverty, recalls the religious significances given to food, as Caroline Walker Bynum has shown, in the piety of many medieval holy women. It is worth noting too that fasting features significantly in the religious practices of both Margery Kempe and Anna Trapnel.[85]

The author of the *Life* dwells at length on the extreme want that Elizabeth Cary experienced following her conversion when both her husband and her mother cut her off from material support. The biographer reports that at one point Cary is sustained only by the table scraps smuggled home by her faithful servant Bessie Poulter (who also converts to Catholicism and in 1643 is professed as a choir nun at the very nunnery at Antwerp that produced the miraculously preserved body and the corpus of life writings with which this book begins).[86] When Elizabeth Cary is "in such extreamity, as she had not meat of any sort to put in her mouth," she sends Bessie "to my Lord of Ormonds to meales, but with a charge to conceale her case." Bessie, "to giue her Lady what helpe she could and yet obey her, did from the table privatly take and put into a handkerchef some peeces of pyecrust or bread or other such thinge, which bringing home to her were all she had to liue on some days (so much did she seeme to be forgoten by all the world, and all the frinds she euer had had)."[87] The *Life* portrays Cary's hunger resulting from her postconversion poverty as suffering endured for her faith, suggesting the endurance of the saints and martyrs.[88]

Elizabeth Cary's biographer also returns repeatedly to the topic of Cary's Lenten fasting. She says that her Cary observes "most exactly the fasts of the Church, never eating butter nor milke in Lent, as long as she was a catholike . . . and some Lents she did confirme her observance of the obliged fast by resolving and observing some farther abstinence, as particularly one Lent, when her table was filled with flesh for her protestant children, she forbid herself any thing with sugar in it, save on Sundays, which in the maner of her diet (especially Lenten) had a great part" (144). She also indicates that one Lent her mother "lived for the most part (if not only) on the watter in wich fish had bene boyled, with bred sopped in it, and her woman eate the fish" (139). The detailed accounts of these Lenten fasts obviously illustrate Cary's punctilious obedience in Catholic penitential practices. Because the Lenten fast of forty days is associated both with the forty days Christ spent in the wilderness and with the forty hours he lay in the tomb, the attention given to Cary's fasting during this penitential season links her food practices with Christ's suffering.

In a section in which the daughter biographer discusses Elizabeth Cary's childbearing, fasting and maternal suffering come together in ways that recall both the unnamed relator's description of Anna Trapnel's laboring, fasting body at Whitehall and Margery Kempe's torment associated with her first pregnancy. The biographer reports that while Cary is pregnant with Lucius (her second child), and again while she is pregnant with Anne (her fourth child), she "lost the perfect vse of her reason." She then recounts that Cary "one of these times for fowerteene days together . . . eate nor drunke nothinge in the world, but only a little beare with a tost, yet without touching the tost, so as being greate with child and quicke, the child left to stirre and she became as flate as if she had not bene with child at all yet after coming out of her malancholy the child and she did well" (118). This episode represents one of the most heavily edited sections of the *Life*. Whole sentences are deleted and, as the editor Heather Wolfe points out, the phrase "she lost the perfect vse of her reason" is "deleted twice, the second time in a broad criss-crossing stroke" (118 n. 47). Wolfe observes that this deletion, like other deletions of references to "erratic, confused behavior" consistently made through-out the *Life*, reflects an editorial concern to remove any unedifying material, to suppress anything that might lead critics to impugn Cary's Catholic faith or accuse her of madness.[89] In this context, it seems quite important that the description of Cary's restricted eating has *not* been deleted in any way. In spite of the fact that the pregnant Elizabeth Cary's refusal of food is connected with a period in which she lost her reason, the daughter biographer, as well as the text's later editor, evidently interprets it through the lens of an approved tradition of female embodied piety. Though it is not motivated by a devotional impulse, Elizabeth's fasting during pregnancy closely resembles her very strict Lenten fast during which she consumed only bread and the water in which fish was boiled. It also resonates with recognized evidence for female holiness (witness the authorizing function of Anna Trapnel's long fast accompanying her trance at Whitehall, where she too survived only on small beer and limited amounts of bread, and Luisa de Carvajal y Mendoza's emphasis on the minute quantities of food consumed by an elderly English woman after her reconciliation to Catholicism). That the child "does well" in spite of Cary's inedia has the air of the miraculous. In her monastic daughter's quasi-hagiographical account, Cary's fasting thus aids, rather than harms, the causes of edifying readers and promoting Catholicism.

Not surprisingly, given that one of Elizabeth Cary's daughters authors the *Life*, Elizabeth's maternal role occupies a central, complex position in the text. Though in the *Life of Lady Falkland* we do not find precisely the same alignment of textual production with maternal reproduction that appears so prominently in the writings of Margery Kempe and Anna Trapnel, the terms of the equation are in effect reversed. Elizabeth Cary as the subject of the *Life* in multiple senses comes into being through textual operations. As Frances Dolan notes, the figure of Elizabeth Cary in the *Life* "may have as much to do with what her daughters read as with Cary's actual life"; furthermore, "The *Life* presents Elizabeth as being born through or in conjunction with reading."[90] After spending some time on Elizabeth Cary's father's career as a judge, the biographer writes, "Her mothers name was Elisabeth symondes. she was thier only child. she was christened Elizabeth. she learnt to read very soone and loved it much" (*Life*, 105). The account continues with details of Elizabeth's extraordinary ability in learning languages and her skill at translating texts. Dolan additionally observes that in recounting the end of Elizabeth Cary's life the biographer also emphasizes reading: "[T]he biographer addresses the extent of her reading first so that Cary's life seems to begin and end with reading."[91]

The *Life of Lady Falkland* casts Elizabeth Cary's maternal labor as providential and salvific, a perspective not unusual from a daughter who understood her own religious conversion and monastic profession to have been enabled by God and her mother alike.[92] Much as Margery Kempe and Anna Trapnel provide a means of access to God through their redemptive maternal suffering, so too Elizabeth Cary appears in *The Life of Lady Falkland* as an agent through whom others, particularly her children, gain their salvation through conversion to Catholicism (as perhaps her husband does as well, since the text suggests he converted to Catholicism on his deathbed, prompted in part by Cary's translation of Perron).[93] Part of the maternal labor in which Elizabeth Cary engages, as does Margery Kempe, is intercessory prayer. The biographer indicates that Cary sets aside time each day to pray "for the conversions of her Lord and children" (144).

Furthermore, as Dolan observes, the central conflict in the *Life* is not that between Elizabeth Cary and her husband over her Catholicism. Rather, it is her conflict with the clergyman Chillingworth and her eldest son, Lucius, over the faith to be practiced by her younger children. Her struggles to keep her children in her custody, and so have the opportunity to influence them toward Catholicism, include the dramatic episode in 1636 when she arranged to have her sons Patrick and Henry removed from Lucius's house to be smuggled illegally out of England (see 197 ff). For these actions, Elizabeth Cary is called before the Star Chamber and the King's Bench, and in her interrogations there she shows rhetorical skill very reminiscent of the quick-witted responses of Margery Kempe and Anna Trapnel in their respective interrogations. For instance, the officials charge Cary with sending her sons abroad without permission, "shewing some orders made to officers of Ports to lett none passe without licence" (201). In response, "she alleaged that this concerned not her, nor was she bound to know or take notice of it being no such officer to whom this was directed; that this was no command to her not to send, but to those officers not to lett passe, which if they had done, their lordships might please to question them, not her" (201). Such maternal linguistic labors of prayer and argument coalesce with the bodily labor entailed in her repeated childbirths when the biographer states, "What she did undergoe, to keepe them [i.e., her younger children] with her . . . may well give them cause to acknowledge she was their mother in faith as well as in nature" (158).[94]

Further sacralizing maternity and at the same time introducing the subject position of Christ's spouse for Elizabeth Cary, *The Life of Lady Falkland* emphasizes Cary's identification with the Virgin Mary. By integrating the Virgin Mary's holy life into her own, Cary follows a pattern seen not only in Margery Kempe's and Anna Trapnel's lives but also in the monastic culture of the Brigittine nuns of Syon. The author indicates that Cary was devoted to the Virgin Mary even before she became a Catholic, a devotion that manifested itself through an experience of pregnancy and birth. She says that Cary "bore a great and high reverence to our Blessed Lady, to whom, being with child of her last daughter (and still a protestant) she offred vp that child, promising if it were a girle it should (in devotion to her) beare her name, and that as much as was in her power, she would indeavour to haue it be a Nunne" (119). Not only did Elizabeth Cary name her last daughter Mary, but she also adopted the Virgin Mary's name herself at her confirmation, marking her new identity that came with her conversion (a move reminiscent of Mary Birbeck's taking St. Teresa's name as part of her religious name after her profession with the Antwerp Carmelites). Wolfe's introduction to the *Life* notes that "beginning in 1632, Lady Falkland, in quiet defiance, signed her letters 'EM Falkland' instead of 'E Falkland' to emphasize the name 'Maria.'"[95]

Because the *Life of Lady Falkland* presents, not Elizabeth Cary's own description of her relationship with God, but rather her daughter's account of that relationship, it is not unusual that we do not find the intimate accounts of nuptial union with Christ that are so central to Margery Kempe's and Anna Trapnel's life writings.[96] As Elizabeth Cary's identification with Mary, Christ's mother as well as his heavenly spouse, shows, however, the paradigm of nuptial union with Christ is not entirely absent from the *Life*. Like the relationship of maternity and textual production, this paradigm too appears in the *Life of Lady Falkland* in a somewhat different guise than in Margery Kempe's *Book* and Anna Trapnel's works. The *Life* repeatedly stresses not Elizabeth Cary's marriage to Christ but her marriage to her earthly husband, foregrounding her submission and obedience to him in all things save the one matter of her Catholic faith crucial to the health of her soul. For instance, the biographer says that Cary "seemed to preferre nothing but religion and her duty to God, before his [i.e., her husband's] will" (117). When the biographer comes to the account of Elizabeth Cary's conversion to Catholicism, however, she frames the episode as a romantic tryst, or even as an illicit elopement. Her narrative strategies perhaps reveal the effects of her understanding of her monastic identity as that of a bride of Christ; they also may hint at her intimate knowledge of medieval female hagiographical conventions. The author indicates that Elizabeth Cary believes her friend Lady Denbigh is going to join her in changing religions, but Lady Denbigh keeps delaying. While she is visiting Lady Denbigh at court, Cary makes a final attempt to push her friend to take the plunge, declaring that if Lady Denbigh persists in procrastinating she will take the step alone. Lady Denbigh remains reluctant and indeed tries to prevent her friend from proceeding. The biographer writes: "[T]he Lady sayd, well, I haue you now in the court, and heere I will keepe you, you shall lye in my chamber and shall not goe forth; giuing order to have a bed sett vp there for her; she was amazed to see herself thus surprised, little expecting it; but thought it best then to seeme content to stay there" (129). Elizabeth Cary, confined in a bedchamber like a romance heroine locked away by a jealous husband (or, like St. Christine, a martyr-to-be shut up by her angry father), looks for an opportunity to escape. One presents itself when Lady Denbigh "left her alone . . . to fecth [sic] one that should confirme her stay" (129). The biographer reports that Cary seizes the moment: she "lett not this opportunity slip, but gott her ways in the Ladys absence, going withall speed to my Lord of Ormonds" (129–30). There, in a clandestine assignation in the stable, she is received into the Catholic Church: "[F]inding black Father Dunstan there, she was, the soonest she could, reconciled by him in my Lord of Ormonds stable (who continved her ghostly father till he was taken)" (130).

After her conversion to Catholicism Elizabeth Cary finds herself, like Margery Kempe prior to the dramatic scene that transpires on Midsummer's Eve on the road to Bridlington, in another position familiar to the heroines of many later medieval saints' lives. That is, with regard to the disposal of access to her body, she is caught between obedience to God and to a figure of earthly masculine authority. In a scene of masterful, divinely aided negotiation, Margery Kempe manages to get her husband to agree to a formal vow of chastity so that, as her husband declares, "As fre mot ʒowr body ben to God as it hath ben to me" (25). Elizabeth Cary's husband proves far less accommodating to her religious convictions. In fact, Henry Cary tellingly interprets her conversion as a kind of marital infidelity deserving of censure, heightening the sense that her conversion entails her entry into a competing nuptial relationship with Christ. In the letter Lord Falkland writes to Lord Conway on July 5, 1627, in which he requests "a fayre and a legall separacion," he declares that he has "become notorious ouer all the Christian world for this *defection* of his Wiues, and hir preualent contestacion with him, *ageynst duty and the lawe Matrinomiall.*"[97]

With Henry Cary's description of Elizabeth's conversion as marital infidelity, we are on familiar territory. His accusations resonate with the linked charges of sexual impropriety and sedition made against Margery Kempe and Anna Trapnel. Indeed, female piety once again proves to be a political threat on the national as well as the domestic front, since Elizabeth Cary's faith also explicitly raises the question of treason. Wolfe observes, "Surviving documents show that Lady Falkland's wayward actions instigated more than just a family drama, and in fact were a source of concern, frustration, and fascination for a considerable number of Stuart nobility and clergy. The conversion of an outspoken viscountess was no small matter—theoretically, it was treasonable, and could potentially open the floodgates for further conversions if it were condoned."[98]

Elizabeth Cary, like Margery Kempe and Anna Trapnel, provoked nervousness about the reproductive, reformist forces nascent in female spirituality, and her influence on her children was a particular flashpoint for such anxiety. The convergence of fears about her faith and her maternal influence highlights the incarnational power of women's spiritual and corporeal labors. Speaking of Elizabeth's relationship with her son Lucius, Edward Hyde, Earl of Clarendon, echoes the accusations made against Margery Kempe and Anna Trapnel as he describes Elizabeth's efforts to "*pervert* him in his Piety to the Church of England, and to reconcile him to that of Rome."[99]

Elizabeth Cary provides yet another case, in yet another religiopolitical configuration of authority, in which female embodied piety and body language are feared to have the power to destabilize the English body politic. As the faiths of Margery Kempe, Anna Trapnel, and Elizabeth Cary might superficially seem utterly different, so too might the regimes in question: the fifteenth-century Lancastrian monarchy of Henry V, Cromwell's radical Protestant Protectorate, and the Anglican Protestant rule of Charles I. Indeed, Cromwell's radical Protestant government, which was responsible for Charles I's execution and the abolition of the monarchy, aimed to rid England of the very concept of divinely ordained kingship so highly valued by Henry V. Much as there are important continuities in the women's embodied pieties, and much as their life writings exhibit overlapping textual strategies, there is also an important continuity to be found in the fact that these political regimes, for all their differences, have precisely the same point of instability. That embodied female spirituality and textual representations of it are such an effective force for putting pressure on this shared fault

line reveals something constitutive of English national identity as it un-
folds in the later medieval and early modern periods. While the specific
content of the women's religious beliefs is certainly at times a source of
anxiety for various authority figures (Margery Kempe's suspected Lollardy, Anna Trapnel's association with the Fifth Monarchists, Elizabeth
Cary's Catholicism), the overarching political threat their embodied
piety implies is one of form.

Because they foreground subjectivities predicated upon open boundaries between selves and others both human and divine, all of these
women's spiritual lives entail, even demand, revisions of social relations.
Not only do these women undermine political and ecclesiastical power
structures by putting women in direct, even privileged, relationships with
God, but their incarnational spirituality and the incarnational texts also
threaten to break down gendered hierarchies altogether. Christ's body is
in some ways female, and female bodies are in some ways Christ's. The
Word of God made flesh and the Word of scripture are fully accessible
to all and perhaps even especially accessible to women. The fundamental threat stems from the radical sociopolitical potential of empathetic
hermeneutics and intersubjectivity. Put another way, Margery Kempe's,
Anna Trapnel's, and Elizabeth Cary's lives, along with their life writings,
represent the profound political threat contained in the idea that in Christ
"[t]here is neither Jew nor Greek, there is neither slave nor free, there
is neither male nor female" (Galatians 3:28) when the English body politic constitutes itself precisely by striving to maintain distinctions between Jew and Greek (or, rather, Catholic and Protestant or orthodox
and heterodox) and between male and female.

Chapter Five

The Embodied Presence of the Past

Medieval History, Female Spirituality,
and Traumatic Textuality, 1570—1700

The Traumatic Middle Ages

In the responses to the lives and life writings of Margery Kempe, Anna Trapnel, and Elizabeth Cary, we see political instabilities magnified when these women suggest options for alternative systems of social relations as they relive past holy lives, make their own lives textually accessible to others, and destabilize binary relationships of past and present, male and female, self and other. In the early modern period, the domestic and international political threats posed by the 1570 papal bull *Regnans in excelsis,* the Elizabethan succession crisis, the controversy surrounding the "Spanish Marriage" in the 1620s, and the English Civil Wars of the mid-seventeenth century mark the return in successive generations of a tightly intertwined complex of anxieties concerning religion, lineage, monarchical legitimacy, and gender, anxieties resembling those that swirl around Margery Kempe, Anna Trapnel, and Elizabeth Cary.

Male writers attempting to cope with such political uncertainties found history, and especially the history of the recent, medieval past, to be an especially valuable tool for asserting legitimacy. Rival factions strove mightily to own medieval history, to produce definitive versions of it, and to turn the past lives—including holy women's lives—that constituted it to partisan purposes.

As a resource for enhancing claims of legitimacy, however, history was hardly trouble-free. The anxieties involved in the aforementioned early modern crises are fundamentally the same ones that shaped and animated the very medieval history to which politicians and propagandists so readily turned. In particular, coming to terms with female bodies and the roles those bodies play in legitimating or delegitimating dynastic lineages is of primary concern in both the works of early modern writers and the medieval histories upon which these writers rely. Early modern writers who mobilize medieval history have to negotiate the same fraught demarcations of past and present, male and female, self and other, that are at stake in the lives and texts of the women discussed in the previous chapter. As the cases considered in chapter 4 have begun to suggest, such negotiations are constitutive of distinctively English modes of forging competing versions of national identity at the interface between past and present.

The texts under consideration here include works of pro-Elizabethan Lancastrian propaganda, Robert Parsons's *Conference Concerning the Next Succession* and his history of Syon Abbey, John Foxe's *Acts and Monuments*, Thomas Robinson's *Anatomie of the English Nunnery at Lisbon in Portugal*, Thomas Goad's *Friers Chronicle*, and Thomas Pomfret's *The Life of the Right Honourable and Religious Lady Christian, Late Countess Dowager of Devonshire*. These texts, which are linked by complex networks of readership and citation, illustrate that laying claim to the Middle Ages in the early modern period is no easy task. The good news and the bad news for these writers who turn to medieval history to achieve political aims are in effect one and the same: the past and the present resemble each other. Medieval history is available to answer questions in the early modern present because it provides precedents, but the medieval past also raises questions in the early modern present because it is so replete with the unresolved.[1] The texts that I analyze in this chapter invoke the past and strive to establish definitive versions of history; at times they also recycle representational strategies from the past. In the process, their textual accounts, invocations, and representations are disturbed by the traumatic aspects of the very past that they wish to manipulate to their own ends. In these texts, medieval history often transforms claims to define it and overtakes efforts to make it straightforwardly serve political purposes. For early modern writers, the Middle Ages are indeed valuable to claim and to define, in both positive and negative guises, but the Middle Ages can also, in fact, prove to do the claiming.

The Lancastrian Line and the Lancastrian Repressed: Elizabeth I, Robert Parsons, and the Claims of the Past

The Lancastrian era began in an act of deposition with the triumph of Henry Bolingbroke over Richard II, and when Edward IV triumphed over Henry VI for the second time in 1471 it also ended, at least temporarily, in one. Lancastrian revival, however, came thanks to another act of deposition when Henry Tudor defeated Richard III at Bosworth Field in 1485. Originating with an episode so closely recalling the earlier Henry's dethroning of the earlier Richard, the new Tudor dynasty found itself contending with an all-too-familiar crisis of legitimacy. Remedies were, somewhat paradoxically, sought through what John N. King has called the "incessant Tudor claim to Lancastrian descent."[2]

In his account of the last days of Richard III's reign, Polydore Vergil—no stranger to Tudor Lancastrianism—presents a series of encounters that highlights both the desirability and the ambivalent status of the Lancastrian inheritance at the moment the Tudor dynasty was being born. Leading up to his discussion of Henry Tudor's arrival in England from France, Vergil discusses the conflict between Richard III and Henry, Duke of Buckingham, who in Vergil's version of events appears as a key agent in engineering Henry Tudor's return. Vergil first traces Buckingham's own connections to the Lancastrian line. Henry, Duke of Buckingham, was the son of Humphrey, Duke of Buckingham. Humphrey's father was Edmund of Stafford, and his mother, Anne, was the daughter of Thomas of Woodstock and Alienor of Hereford. Anne had been heir to her mother's inheritance after Richard III executed Woodstock and confiscated his possessions. Alienor's sister Mary had married Henry of Darby (who became Henry IV). As Vergil reports, "And so by the maryage of Anne and Mary was therle of Herefords inherytance devydyd, thone moytie to thowse of Lancaster, thother to the bloode of Staffords, from whome the dukes of Buckingham deryve ther pedygre."[3] Since the line of Henry IV ended with the death of Henry VI and his son Edward, Prince of Wales, "Henry of Buckingham thowght that he might by good right demand that part of therle of Herefords patrimony which in the right of Mary had coommyd to the howse of Lancaster, which whan King Richard held the right of the crown, with thother possessions of the howse of Lancaster" (193). Buckingham thus demanded what he perceived as his rightful inheritance from Richard III, who, according to Vergil, did not respond favorably: "To this king Richard . . . ys reportyd to have answered furthwith in great rage: 'What now, duke Henry, will yow chalenge unto you that right of Henry the Fourth wherby he wyckedly usurpid the crowne, and so make open for yourself the way therunto?'" (193). The Lancastrian inheritance, for Buckingham something of great value worth claiming, was for Richard III a legacy of usurpation and illegitimacy.

The royal response to Buckingham's demand almost prophetically envisions a recurrence of Lancastrian trauma in positioning Richard III as a potential new Richard II. The monarch's retort indeed suggested precisely such an association between the two Ricardian monarchs to Buckingham, who reportedly was motivated by Richard III's scornful answer to seek the king's deposition and the triumph of the house of Lancaster by means of Henry Tudor. Vergil says: "Which king Richerds answer settlyd depe into the dukes breste, who from that time furth, movyd muche with ire and indignation, began to devyse by what meane he might thrust owt that ungratefull man from the royall seat. . . . Than the duke unfoldyd all thynges to the bisshop of Ely, and dyscoveryd himself wholy, shewing how he had devysyd the meane wherby both the bloode of king Edward and of Henry the Sixth that yeat was remaining, being conjoignyd by affynytie, might be restoryd to the domynion dew unto both their progenyes" (193–94). The plan, of course, was that "Henry erle of Richemond . . . might be sent for in all hast possyble . . . so that he wold promyse before by solemne othe, that after he had once obtaynyd the kingdom he wold take to wyfe Elyzabeth, king Edwards eldest dawghter" (194).

Vergil's partisan account throws into sharp relief—albeit perhaps unwittingly—the paradox inherent in the fact that the first monarch of the Tudor dynasty would invoke Lancastrian heritage, a heritage replete with anxieties about legitimacy concerning its origins in an act of deposition, to legitimate a reign also founded on deposition. Furthermore, the paradox of Tudor Lancastrianism as inaugurated by Henry VII was heightened by the fact that Henry's connection to the Lancastrian line was so fragile and relied on female descent. The questionable legitimacy of female descent, like the problem of usurpation, persistently troubled earlier generations of Lancastrians. The medieval Lancastrian kings depended for their claim to the French throne on descent through the female line. However, the necessity that the English royal line be an exclusively masculine one uncontaminated by a feminine presence was something upon which the Lancastrians insisted quite forcefully, an insistence that only intensified once the Yorkist faction began to advance its claim.[4]

Buckingham's involvement of the bishop of Ely in his plans to enable the return of Henry Tudor, offspring of the Lancastrian line, echoes a strategy characteristic of earlier Lancastrians, especially Henry V—that is, turning to the realm of religion to enhance the credibility of monarchs and causes. Though this strategy would prove to be a favorite of early modern kings and queens, as throughout much of the sixteenth and seventeenth centuries Catholic and Protestant rivals struggled mightily to assert that they enjoyed the right to the throne by divine mandate as well as by Lancastrian blood, spiritual assets had, like the Lancastrian inheritance, their own paradoxical dimensions. For example, as Henry V consolidated the Lancastrian hold on the throne of England and pressed the English claim to France in the early fifteenth century, he worked to maintain a delicate balance between forms of holy kingship at odds with each other as he negotiated the aforementioned contradictory stances on women in the line of succession. On the one hand, Henry claimed to be descended from a holy line of English priest kings—a sacerdotal model of kingship that excluded women from the royal succession. On the other hand, he embraced "incarnational kingship"—a model that granted women a legitimate place in the royal line by pointing to the example of the Virgin Mary and Jesus as a case in which a virtuous woman transmitted a divine inheritance to a male heir. The inherent trickiness of managing spiritual assets was intensified when those assets were combined with the Lancastrian inheritance: for instance, as I shall discuss shortly, Protestant propagandists wrestled with the awkward fact of their Lancastrian ancestors' Catholicism while early modern Catholic partisans strove to cope with the presence of Henry VIII among the descendants of the house of Lancaster.

The benefits of the Lancastrian inheritance were thus forever complicated by mutually reinforcing anxieties concerning gender, religion, legitimacy, and lineage. The glories of the Lancastrian past brought with them traumas only ever partially repressed and incompletely resolved. Since repression is, as Freud instructs us, "the precondition for the construction of symptoms," it is not surprising that the return of the Lancastrian dynasty in the person and propaganda of Henry VII was accompanied by another sort of return—the return of the Lancastrian repressed.[5]

Henry VII's grand-daughter Elizabeth faced challenges to her reign on multiple grounds—the legitimacy of her birth, her Protestant religion, and her gender. The Lancastrian inheritance offered virtually irresistible material to use in holding these challenges at bay, providing a means of foregrounding both Elizabeth's dynastic and her divinely ordained rights to the throne. Accordingly, the pageants staged to mark Elizabeth's entry into London preceding her coronation in 1558 prominently exploited her Lancastrian ties. An anonymous account of the processions and pageants, entitled *The royall passage of her Maiesty from the Tower of London, to her palace of White-hall with all the speaches and deuices,* reports that early in the ceremonies, in "Gracious street . . . at the upper end, before the signe of the Eagle," a stage was erected consisting of "three Parts; and over the middlemost was aduaunced three severall stages in degrees."[6] The pageant bore a wreath inscribed with its title:

"The vniting of the two houses of Lancaster and Yorke" (A4r), and it displayed a classic version of Elizabethan Lancastrianism, the oft-used imagery of the Tudor rose tree. Invoking the iconography of the Tree of Jesse, as well as the elaborate Lancastrian genealogical propaganda that circulated during the reign of Henry VI, the Tudor rose tree had been used by Elizabeth's father Henry VIII to proclaim his own legitimacy.[7]

In the version of the image incorporated into the pageants, on the lowest of the three stages, Henry VII and his wife Elizabeth appear. Henry is enclosed in the red rose of Lancaster, Elizabeth in the white rose of York, and the figures' hands are joined. The author reports, "Out of the which two Roses, sprang two branches gathered into one, which were directed upward to the second stage or degree: wherein was placed one, representing the valiant & noble Prince King Henry the eight" (A3v). He is accompanied by a figure representing Anne Boleyn, and from the two of them a single branch extends to a representation of Elizabeth I on the uppermost stage. The interpretation given for this pageant seeks to minimize the problematic dimensions of the Lancastrian past by underlining, and uniting, past and present concord. Noting that the queen shares the name Elizabeth with the one whose marriage to Henry VII ended "the long warre between the two houses of Yorke and Lancaster," the author invokes a paradigm not at all unlike St. Catherine of Siena becoming "another himself" of Christ, or Gertrude More becoming a reincarnation of St. Thomas More. He declares: "So since that the Queenes Maiesties name was Elizabeth, and forsomuch as she is the onely heire of Henry the eight, which came of both houses, as the knitting up of concord, it was deuised, that like as Elizabeth was the first occasion of concord, so shee another Elizabeth might maintaine the same among her Subiects; so that vnitie was the end where at the whole deuise shot, as the Queenes Maiesties names moued the first ground" (A4r). Elizabeth is heir not only to the Lancastrian heritage, a heritage that is embraced even as its traumas are elided in its representation by the red rose surrounding Henry VII, but also to a Tudor legacy of peace and unity.

A particularly interesting example of Elizabethan Lancastrianism appears in Richard Grafton's discussions of the aforementioned pre-coronation pageant series. In his *Abridgement of the Chronicles of England*, Grafton discourses at some length on the same pageant described above.[8]

Grafton's description, like that in the anonymous pamphlet, emphasizes Queen Elizabeth's connection to the Lancastrian line; Grafton also engages, like the pamphlet author, in a sort of typological reading. In this case, it is not Elizabeth I's reign of concord that is prefigured by an earlier Elizabeth who unified warring factions. Instead, confounding those who deny Elizabeth's right to rule on grounds of faith, Grafton imaginatively posits that the Lancastrian line enjoys a sort of retroactive Protestantism. Grafton had been appointed King's Printer under Edward VI and had been imprisoned under Mary I, so this stance is not unexpected. Grafton glosses the nuptial union of Henry VII and Elizabeth of York as a symbol of "the coniunction and coupling together of our soveraigne Lady with the Gospell and veritie of Goddes holy woord, for the peaceable gouvernement of all her good subiectes."[9] Henry VII's place in relation to Elizabeth of York is thus taken by the Gospel and Word of God, which are coupled with Elizabeth I. Elizabeth I's representation as the bride of the Gospel and the Word of God—a significant modification of the nuptial identity of bride of Christ the Word made flesh—confirms her divine mandate to reign. Furthermore, the description of Elizabeth I united with the Word of God suggests that Elizabeth, succeeding the Catholic Mary I, caused true religion to displace a false ecclesiastical regime in the same way that Henry VII displaced the false reign of Richard III with his true one.

Elizabethan propaganda does not only highlight the queen's resemblance to figures in the reign of Henry VII. Elizabeth and her supporters alike also work very hard to emphasize her ties with and resemblance to her father, Henry VIII, thus claiming Elizabeth's place as the heir to the Lancastrian line while at the same time providing ammunition to resist those opposed to female rule. A striking example of efforts to forge a strong connection between Elizabeth I and Henry VIII occurs in *The royall passage of her Maiesty:* "In Cheapside her Grace smiled: and being thereof demanded the cause, answered, for that she had heard one say, Remember olde King Henry the eight. A naturall child, which at the very remembrance of her fathers name took so great a ioy, that all men may well thinke, that as she reioyced at his name, whome this Realme doth hold of so worthy memory: so in her doings she will resemble the same"

(D3r). Such representations illustrate that Elizabeth had received not only a genealogical inheritance from Henry VIII but also a gendered one; she possessed from him the mantle of specifically English masculinity so highly prized and hard won by Lancastrian kings. Accounts like this one have added value since they enhance her self-representation as the virago "Virgin Queen," an identification that comprises her distinctive method of claiming a valuable legacy of medieval female spirituality.[10]

Elizabeth's Catholic opponents saw her complex construction of an identity dependent in some respects on transforming the incarnational piety on the cult of the Virgin Mary quite differently than her supporters did. So too they remembered much differently "olde king Henry the eight," whose "doings" the author of *The royall passage of her Maiesty* hopes Elizabeth will reiterate. For English Catholic writers opposed to Elizabeth's reign and concerned with restoring a Catholic monarch to the throne, the specifics that constituted cultural crisis coalesced around a different moment of rupture—not that of Henry Bolingbroke's deposition of Richard II but that of Henry VIII's break with Rome. Similarities, however, underlay the divergent understandings of what constituted a critical break. For Catholics, as for Protestants, the results of rupture were deep concerns with the interplay of religion, lineage, legitimacy, and gender, all of which shaped their perspectives on Elizabeth's rule and the question of who should succeed her.

The Jesuit Robert Parsons, writing as R. Doleman, addresses this knotty complex of issues directly in *A Conference about the Next Succession to the Crowne of England*, published in 1594.[11] This work might equally be entitled "A Revisionist History of the House of Lancaster," and it makes abundantly clear how valuable the Lancastrian inheritance was. Parsons faces a daunting task in staking his claim, however. He is in a position similar to that of the exiled communities of English nuns discussed in previous chapters in that he finds it necessary to argue that authentic Englishness resides outside Protestant England. He also, like the fifteenth-century Lancastrian monarchs laying claim to the throne of France, needs to make a persuasive case for women's rightful place in dynastic lineages while at the same time forestalling the anxiety-provoking scenario of a female monarch ruling independently.

The *Conference* "is in the form of discourses by a civilian and a tempo-ral lawyer respectively," and it is divided into two sections. The first sec-tion, in the voice of the civilian lawyer, treats political philosophy. The second section (the one with which I am concerned) is "the discourse of the temporal lawyer" and "deals with the claims of various pretenders to the succession."[12] From Parsons's perspective, Henry VIII represents the real problem point in Lancastrian history, while the originary trauma of Richard II's deposition becomes an asset rather than a liability. Parsons argues that "both by reason authority and examples of all nations Chris-tian" it is lawful that "vppon iust causes" a monarch "may be deposed" (61). He goes on to present the arguments of the Lancastrian and Yorkist factions concerning whether Richard II was deposed by just cause. In the case of Richard II, Parsons concludes, usurpation was a justified, and in fact a divinely approved, political action.

One might be led to believe that such a line of argument would in fact aid the cause of pro-Elizabethan Lancastrianism, since an obvious point to be drawn is that the Lancastrians need suffer no loss of legiti-macy as a result of the deposition that established their dynasty. But in Parsons's account of the deposition of Richard II, Elizabethan ver-sions of medieval history, and Elizabeth's representational strategies that rely on such versions of history, come to be troubled by the legacies of Lancastrian trauma. Parsons argues first that Richard never should have reigned; rather, John of Gaunt should have succeeded Edward III (77–78). Accordingly, Gaunt's descendents should bear no taint of usurpation, because Henry IV simply reclaimed what should always have been his rightful inheritance.

Parsons also argues that *real* Lancastrian ancestry can be claimed only by those who descend from John of Gaunt's first marriage to Blanche of Lancaster. He observes that "Iohn of Gaunt third sonne of king Edward being duke of Lancaster by his wife . . . had three wiues in al, and by euery one of them had issue"; however, he goes on to note that since "only the first wife was daughter and heyre of the house of Lancaster and iohn of Gaunt duke thereof by her, it followeth that the children only that were borne of her can pretend properly to the inheritance of that house" (41). The line descended from John of Gaunt and his first wife, and the right to legitimate inheritance of the English throne that went with it, ended in England in the aftermath of Henry VI's deposition.[13] In Parsons's version of Lancastrian history, one must look elsewhere than England to find *true* Lancastrians descended from John of Gaunt and Blanche of Lancaster in the sixteenth century. Hence, Parsons deals with the problem of Henry VIII's presence in the Lancastrian line by removing him and his descendents, including Elizabeth I, from that line.

In Parsons's view, the only royal legacy Henry VIII and Elizabeth I can claim is that of the house of York, which was joined to the "pseudo-Lancastrian" line when Henry VII married Elizabeth, daughter of Edward IV. Far from being a moment of union that prefigured the harmony to be solidified by Elizabeth's reign, this marriage was the impetus for the perpetuation of a false Lancastrian line and a nefarious Yorkist one. The Yorkist line, in which Henry VIII is firmly placed, emerges as a conduit of trouble and misrule as Parsons sets up a comparison between the monarchs that he deems to be authentically Lancastrian and those "that have bin of the house of York, to wit Edward the fourth, Richard the third, *Henry the eight*, and Edward the sixt" (97, my emphasis). He calls attention to "al their acts both at home & abroade, what quitnes or troobles haue passed, and what the common wealth of Ingland hath gotten or lost under each of them" (97), concluding that "we shal finde, that God hath seemed to prosper and allow much more of those of Lancaster than of those of Yorke, for that under those of Lancaster the realme hath enioyed much more peace, and gayned far greater honor, and enlarged more the dominions of the crowne then under those of Yorke" (97–98).

Although Parsons never states it directly, the intended conclusion the reader is to draw is obvious—Elizabeth I is heir to a legacy of misrule, misrule is grounds for justified deposition, and Elizabeth should be deposed. This perspective is strengthened by the list of rightly deposed monarchs Parsons musters to support his argument that Richard II was rightfully dethroned. The last two in the list are not kings but queens—Jezebel and Athalia. If it is true that, as John Bossy argues, Parsons was directly involved in a plot to kill Elizabeth, the Jesuit's account of Athalia's fate is especially sinister:

> And in the same booke of kings within two chapters after, there is
> other example how God moued Ioïada high priest of Ierusalem to
> persuade the Captaines and Coronels of that cittye to conspire against
> Athalia the Queene that had reigned six years, and to arme them
> selues with the armor of the temple, for that purpose, and to besiege
> the pallace wher she lay, and to kill al them that should offer or goe
> about to defend her, & so they did, and hauing taken her aliue, she
> was put to death also by sentence of the said high priest, and the fact
> was allowed by God, and highly commended in the Scripture. (71)[14]

Immediately upon concluding this account, Parsons declares summarily,
"And this seemeth sufficient proofe to these men, that king Richard of
Ingland might be remoued by force of armes, his life and gouerment
being so euel and pernitious as before hath bin shewed" (72).

In Parsons's exposition of Lancastrian history, Elizabeth I is not a
Henry IV or a Henry V—she is a Jezebel, an Athalia, or, indeed, a Richard II. That possible parallels might be drawn between Elizabeth and
Richard II did not escape Elizabeth herself; in an often-quoted conversation with the historian William Lambarde she purportedly remarked,
"I am Richard II, know ye not that?"[15] Interestingly, the title page of the
Conference declares that the work is "Directed to the Right Honorable
the earl of Essex of her Maiesties priuy councell, & of the noble order of
the Garter." As Ronald Corthell notes, with this direction "Parsons boldly
politicizes his own excursion into English history."[16] At the time of publication, this mention caused Robert Devereux, Earl of Essex, certain
trouble and embarrassment.[17] In time, though, he perhaps took some of
Parsons's arguments to heart, much as Vergil reports the Duke of Buckingham having taken up the inadvertent hint dropped by Richard III.
Famously, on the eve of his rebellion, Essex announced his dissent from
both Elizabeth's rule and pro-Elizabethan historiography, asserting her
connections with Richard II as a monarch ripe for deposition by spon-
soring a performance of Shakespeare's *Richard II* at the Globe Theatre.

It is not only in the Lancastrian histories produced by Elizabeth's
opponents that the traumatic aspects of the past resurface as that past is
harnessed for present ends. Even in presentations of medieval, Lan-

castrian history designed to advance Elizabeth's legitimacy as queen, such elements ultimately prove inescapable. The woodcut border of the title page of John Stowe's *The Annales of England* (figure 1), published in 1592 and reissued during Elizabeth's reign in 1600 and 1601 with the same title page, bears witness to the truth of Paul Strohm's remark that "those texts which try hardest to ignore or exclude an event—to 'forget' history—tend to be the very places where the absent event stages its most interesting and complicated return."[18] The border once again uses the image of the Tudor rose tree, revising one included in the *Union*. In the woodcut in the *Annales*, twining branches springing from the recumbent form of Edward III depict the Lancastrian line on the left and the Yorkist line on the right; these join in a crowned circle bearing the name of Henry VIII. At the top, connected to that circle, are pictures of his three children who wore the crown—Edward VI on the left, Mary I on the right, and Elizabeth I in the center, directly above Henry VIII. Elizabeth's picture is flanked by the words VIVAT REGINA.

Clearly, the message of this image is that Elizabeth is the rightful heir of the combined Lancastrian and Yorkist lines, as was her father before her. By placing her image directly above Henry VIII's name, the artist indicates her closeness or likeness to her father, echoing the representational strategies discussed earlier; she is "another himself." However, the strong vertical axis of the tree, in which the text's title is centered in a rectangular frame, runs from Elizabeth to Henry VIII directly to Richard II. The full title—*The Annales of England, faithfully collected out of the most autenticall Authors, Records, and other Monuments of Antiquitie, from the first inhabitation untill this present yeere 1592*—which both names the history at hand and makes reference to historical sources, is placed between Henry VIII and Richard II, standing in the place of rupture (that is, the deposition of Richard II). In the very act of naming itself as history, history recalls trauma into being. The image links Elizabeth directly with the traumatic past and foregrounds the possibility that she will reenact that past. An image designed to assert Elizabeth's Lancastrian inheritance ends up asserting as well that she is, at least potentially, another Richard II, another victim of Lancastrian trauma, another manipulator of the past claimed by history.

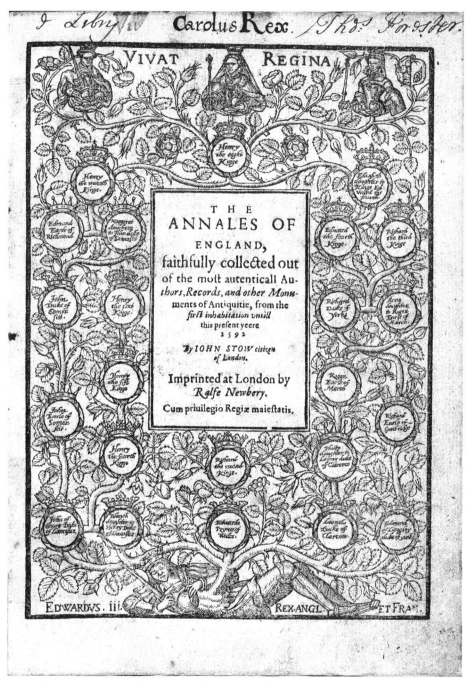

Figure 1. Title page of John Stowe's *The Annales of England* (1592). Reproduced by permission of The Huntington Library, San Marino, California.

Parsons equally cannot escape the claims of history, and in the *Conference* he cannot ultimately assign all of the inconvenient baggage of the past to the Protestants. Just as the woodcut on the title page of the *Annales* casts into sharp relief that which it would likely rather conceal, the *Conference*, though often seeming at pains to deny it, is troubled by some of the very issues that bedeviled Lancastrian monarchs in their struggles for legitimacy. As I indicated earlier, Parsons holds that to find *true* Lancastrians in the sixteenth century one must look outside England, specifically in Spain and Portugal. He describes the authentic Lancastrian line—that of the offspring of John of Gaunt's first marriage to Blanche of Lancaster—as immediately moving into Portugal with their daughter Philippa's marriage to John I of Portugal; the line then continues through Edward I of Portugal, Alfonsus V of Portugal, and on to his present time.[19] Weighing evidence, Parsons presents the cases of other claimants to the Lancastrian inheritance as well, but he ultimately concludes that the Iberian claim is the best.

Parsons similarly outlines the pros and cons of the possible successors for Elizabeth. He never makes an absolutely definitive statement in favor of any one candidate.[20] There is no doubt, though, that he sees the best claim to be that of the potential successor who is most authentically Lancastrian; accordingly, one can readily discern his preference for the Infanta Isabel (eldest daughter of Philip II) as that successor. Parsons's preference for a Spanish successor is made all the more clear by the fact that "[e]ven before the news of the execution of Mary, Queen of Scots, reached Rome in March 1587, Parsons had begun researching the descent of the House of Lancaster with the intent of supporting Philip II's claim to the English throne."[21] Parsons insists that the Infanta "is of the ancient blood royal of Ingland, even from the conquest" (150); he also claims that her father King Philip of Spain, who is "at this day king also of Portugal," is "the cheife titler of that house vnto Ingland" (161).[22] He underlines the fact that the heir to the throne of Portugal is also heir to the throne of England, saying, "I haue byn the longer in setting downe this contention about the succession to the crowne of Portugal, for that it includeth also the very same pretence and contention for the crowne of Ingland" (186). In the years after the Armada in 1588, arguments for

Philip himself as the right monarch of England would have been un-
palatable even to many who might otherwise have been sympathetic
to Parsons's arguments; choosing Philip's daughter as the successor
undoubtedly seemed a politic compromise. The Infanta presented the
further advantage of a "French connection," bearing the royal blood of
France on her mother's side, since she descended "as wel from Queene
Blanch as from Lewys" (24).[23]

It is in making his case for the Infanta that Parsons is in his own turn
troubled by unresolved issues from the Lancastrian past—the anxieties
raised by the presence of women in the line of succession. Legitimating women's transmissive abilities requires for Parsons, as it did for the
earlier Lancastrian monarchs, dealing with the troubling possibility of
independent female rule. Parsons thus finds himself in precisely the
same dilemma the fifteenth-century Lancastrians had to face in balanc-
ing contradictory approaches to women in the line of succession in relation to their English and French claims. Like the fifteenth-century
Lancastrians, Parsons wishes in effect to have it both ways—he wants a
woman to be a legitimate heir, but he does not want her fully to possess
that inheritance.

Uneasiness about female rule and about including women in the
line of succession surfaces even as Parsons puts forward a female candidate for succession whose claim depends on descent through the female
line. For instance, in making his case for the greater legitimacy of those
of true Lancastrian descent, he denigrates the Yorkist title because it is
"by a woman" (75), seemingly forgetting that what he purports to be the
real Lancastrian line also enjoys that title "by a woman."[24] Furthermore,
in presenting the downsides of Arabella Stuart as a successor to Elizabeth, he includes a fairly lengthy diatribe against female rule, even though
he ultimately holds up another woman as the best candidate to occupy
the English throne. Parsons says: "It should be hurtful to the realme to
admit this lady Arbella for Queene, as first of al for that she is a woman,
who ought not to be preferred, before so many men as at this tyme do or
may stand for the crowne: and that it were much to haue three women
to reigne in Ingland one after the other, wher-as in the space of a-boue a
thousaid [sic] yeares before them, there hath not reigned so many of that

sexe, nether together nor a sunder" (128). He goes on to point out that between the time of "king Cerdrick first king of the west Saxons" and the reign of "Egbright the first monarch of the Inglish name and nation," a period of more than three hundred years, no woman reigned. Then, from the time of Egbright until the coming of William the Conqueror, another period of approximately three hundred years, no woman occupied the throne. Furthermore, in the five hundred years after the Conquest, "one only woman was admitted for inheritrix, which was Maude the Empresse," and she was a special case, since "she neuer receaued by the realme, vntil her sonne Henry the second was of age to gouerne himselfe, and then he was receaued with expresse condition, that he should be crowned, and gouerne by himself, and not his mother" (128).

In facing the quintessentially Lancastrian dilemma of negotiating women's place in royal lineages, Parsons borrows a page from the Lancastrians' book. As did the genealogical propaganda of Henry VI's reign, Parsons stresses women's subordination to men.[25] To mitigate the consequences of arguing a case that might well enable ongoing female rule in England, he emphasizes that in Spain, where the Lancastrian line has devolved, women who are the heirs in a royal line are, like the English Empress Maude, merely placeholders for a male who will *actually* rule. He follows his discussion of Maude quoted above by remarking that this "very condition was put also by the spaniards not long after, at their admitting of the lady Berenguela yonger sister of lady Blaunch neese to king Henry the second, wherof before often mention hath bin made, to wit the condition was, that her sonne Fernando should gouerne, and not she, though his title came by her" (128–29). He suggests that the Infanta will follow this same pattern, stressing her desirability as a wife and suggesting that, should she succeed Elizabeth, a husband will be brought into the picture with all due haste. Indeed, he turns the Infanta's marriageability into an asset that strengthens the case for her as a successor to Elizabeth. Parsons writes, "My reasons for the former part, about the Lady Infanta, are, that she is a woman, and may easely ioyne (if her father will) the titles of Britany and Portugal together, she is also vnmarried, and by her marriage may make some other composition, either at home or abroade, that may facilitate the matter, she is a great Princesse and fit for some great state, and other Princes perhapps of Christendome would more willingly yeald and concurr to such a composition" (263).

Working to emphasize that women's role, while necessary, is necessarily subordinate to male authority is not the only Lancastrian-style move that Parsons makes in legitimating a line of succession that depends on women. Like Henry V, he turns to female spirituality, especially to Brigittine spirituality, to lend support to his cause. Henry V found St. Birgitta and the Brigittine order to be especially useful in constructing his self-representational strategy centering on "incarnational kingship" because not only did Birgitta's revelations suggest that God was on the English side in the dispute over who should rule France, but the Brigittine order's particular form of monastic life also emphasized the role of the Virgin Mary in salvation history, placing particular stress on her role in the Incarnation.[26] Parsons repeats his argument that the true heirs to the house of Lancaster, and so to the English throne, are to be found on the Iberian peninsula, in what might, if one were not aware of the significance of the Brigittine order to the Lancastrian dynasty, initially seem a rather unlikely place—an account of the foundation, history, and exile of the English Brigittine community of Syon.[27]

As we have seen, Syon, after repeatedly fleeing Protestant forces in the Low Countries and France, settled in Lisbon in 1594. The Spanish monarchs who held sovereignty over Lisbon at that time were important financial supporters of the English monastic community in exile. One obvious motive for Parsons to incorporate into his history of Syon his argument that the heirs of Lancaster were to be found in Spain and had the right to claim the English throne might thus be to curry favor with the king who had for so long trained his gaze on England. But Parsons's rehearsal of the argument of the *Conference* in miniature in a Brigittine text that is precisely contemporaneous with the *Conference* suggests that his discussion in this particular context of the Lancastrian line's continuance in Spain has greater significance than flattering the Spanish monarch. As he does in the *Conference,* here Parsons insists on the Catholic orthodoxy of the Lancastrian line, stressing that Syon's founder Henry V was renowned "for matters of religion and piety."[28] More pointedly, he writes: "And now, considering the circumstances of these Religious, it certainly seems not to be without a mystery that by the particular Providence of God they have been brought through so many travels and banishment to the kingdom of Portugal, there to repose themselves securely within the protection of the descendants of the House of Lancaster and the blood royal of their founder King Henry the Fifth: for the kings of Portugal descend in a right line from the royal house of Lancaster."[29] In this passage, Parsons's reference to Henry V as founder of Syon helps us to see that Parsons is himself using a representational tactic that the fifteenth-century ruler mobilized to great effect. As Henry V did by founding Syon, Parsons draws on the symbolic resources of Brigittine spirituality to enhance the legitimacy of a genealogy that depends on descent through the female line. In his day Edward IV had made generous grants to Syon, becoming the house's "second founder" and tapping into the symbolic benefits of Syon's distinctive brand of female spirituality, something every bit as useful to the Yorkists in bolstering their claim to the English crown as it was to the Lancastrians in representing their French claim.[30] In his history of Syon, Parsons positions the king of Spain not only as the heir of Syon's first founder Henry V "descend[ed] in a right line" but also in effect the house's third founder, thanks to his role as protector of the community.[31] Philip is thus the rightful inheritor both of the throne of England and of the symbolic benefits of Brigittine spirituality that aided his Lancastrian ancestors nearly two centuries earlier.

Virgin Martyrs: Foxe's *Acts and Monuments*, Elizabethan Legitimacy, and the Specter of Spain

On a far more massive scale than Parsons's history of Syon, John Foxe's *Acts and Monuments* lays partisan claim to the past, retelling holy lives for political ends. The earliest version of what would become the sprawling vernacular collection of accounts of Protestant and proto-Protestant martyrs is the *Comentarii rerum* of 1554, a Latin work "conceived during the reign of Edward VI as part of a historical justification of the Reformation."[32] In subsequent years, the project expanded and shifted, responding to the unfolding of Protestant reforms and Catholic opposition to those reforms. During the Elizabethan era, the *Acts and Monuments* appeared in four versions, in 1563, 1570, 1576, and 1583, each different and differently pointed.[33] My focus in what follows is on the most overarching revision of the project, the edition of 1570. This edition appeared in the context of a particularly fraught political moment, in the wake of the 1569 rebellion of the Northern Earls and at the precise moment that Pius V promulgated the bull *Regnans in excelsis,* which excommunicates Elizabeth I and encourages her deposition.[34]

In the 1570 edition of the *Acts and Monuments* Foxe is especially interested in combating the charge of Protestant novelty and in countering "Roman Catholic allegations that Protestants were innovators who departed from tenets of early Christianity."[35] The work is an important contribution to the intense, long-lived struggle between Catholics and Protestants to embrace the past of the early church as their own, and accordingly Foxe added to the 1570 edition "hundreds of pages of documentation concerning the first millennium of the Christian era. . . . [T]he first volume of the 1570 version begins at a chronological point much earlier than the era when the 1563 version had effectively begun."[36]

Foxe's additions of material, his organizational strategies, and his illustrative choices in the 1570 edition also highlight his increased interest in more recent history, especially the reign of Henry VIII, as he seeks to defend the legitimacy of an English church and English monarchy independent from Rome. The 1570 edition of the *Acts and Monuments* accordingly takes a much stronger antipapal stance than the 1563 edition. One of the additions is a sequence of twelve woodcuts added at the end of what becomes in the 1570 edition the first of two volumes created out of the single volume of the 1563 version. This sequence of woodcuts, entitled "The Proud Primacie of Popes," is unpaginated, a fact that, as John King notes, is "consonant with its addition after the completion of the printing of the text *per se.*" "The late addition of this portrait gallery of excommunications and depositions of secular rulers implicitly glorifies Henry VIII and Elizabeth I as monarchs who countered papal usurpation of temporal power."[37]

The new second volume begins with the accession of Henry VIII, a choice that "create[s] a textual hinge that places great emphasis upon his reign at the time when England declared its independence from the Church of Rome."[38] The frontispiece for volume 2 of the 1570 edition is another newly added image, one of Henry VIII in council. Though the "woodcut *per se* is non-polemical," its origins are significant: none other than Richard Grafton originally commissioned the image "as an illustration for a book with a notably Protestant bent"—that is, Hall's *Union of the Two Noble and Illustrate Families of Lancaster and York*,[39] which is also an important source of the sort of Elizabethan Lancastrianism discussed above.

In the 1570 edition, Foxe's interest in more recent history extends back somewhat further than the reign of Henry VIII. As other strategically designed changes to the 1570 edition illustrate, Lancastrian history, medieval female saints, the genre of hagiography, and Spain all play important roles in Foxe's project, much as they do in Parsons's *Conference* and his history of Syon. In book 5, Foxe includes a discussion of the law of praemunire, recounting that Edward III "[n]ot onely reuiued the sayd statute made by Edward the first his graundfather, but also inlarged the same."[40] Foxe immediately follows the discussion of Edward III's expansion of this statute with something rather unexpected, given his general hostility toward saints other than those whose lives have scriptural warrant. Whereas Parsons mobilizes the life, revelations, and monastic order of St. Birgitta to support his Catholic revision of Lancastrian history and his argument for a Spanish claimant to the English throne, Foxe joins Edward III, the monarch to whom the competing Lancastrian dynastic arguments all look for the source of their ultimate legitimacy, with two saints—St. Birgitta of Sweden and St. Catherine of Siena. He then makes these two saints, who were, as we have seen in chapter 1, passionately committed to the cause of the Roman papacy, serve the Protestant aim of undermining papal authority and bolstering English monarchical independence.

Foxe says, "About thys tyme, being þe yeare of our Lord. 1370. lyued holy Brigit, whom the churche of Rome hath canonised not onely for a saynt, but also for a prophetis: who notwithstanding in her booke of reuelations, which hath bene oft times imprinted, was a great rebuker of the Pope, and of the filth of his clergy, calling hym a murtherer of soules, a spyller, and pyller of the flocke of Christ" (517). He proceeds to incorporate various elements of her critiques of clerical and papal corruption (which are admittedly plentiful in her revelations, though they are never targeted at denying the authority of the papacy or the priesthood as offices). Then, stating, "It were long and tedious to declare" all that she writes against the clergy, he concludes, "Among the rest which I omit, let this suffice for all, where as the sayd Brigit affirmeth in her reuelations, that when the holye virgine should say to her sonne, how Rome was a fruitfull and fertile field: yea, sayd he, but of weedes only & cockle.&c" (517). Foxe pits Brigittine incarnational piety, the characteristic dual focus on the Virgin Mary and the incarnate Christ, against the church that claims to be Christ's true body and against its head, who claims to be Christ's earthly representative.

Foxe then turns to St. Catherine of Siena. His strategy with St. Catherine is to transform her revelations that, as we saw in the first chapter, call for reforms of the Catholic Church framed by her experience of Christ's body into propaganda for and prophecies of the Protestant Reformation. Foxe writes:

> To this Bridget I wyll ioyne also Catherina Senensis, an holy virgin, which lyued much about the same tyme, an. 1379. Of whom writeth Antininus part. historie 3. Thys Katherine hauing the spirite of prophesye, was woont muche to complayne of the corrupt state of the church, namely of the prelates, of the court of Rome, and of the pope: prophesieng before of the great schisme, which then folowed in the churche of Rome, and dured to the councell of Constance, the space of .xxxix. yeares. Also of the great warres and tribulation, which sneud vpon the same. Ane moreouer declared before and foretold, of this so excellent reformation of religion in the church now present. (517)

Foxe's revised versions of the lives and revelations of these two medieval saints gesture toward a larger revisionary project of the *Acts and Monuments*, a project that is part and parcel of the Catholic and Protestant competition for the ownership of the past. Even though a central aim of the project is to deny the validity of most saints venerated by Catholics, the *Acts and Monuments* is profoundly indebted to medieval Catholic hagiographical traditions and conventions, to the extent that I would argue it is perhaps the most Catholic of Protestant polemical works. In the 1563 edition, Foxe included a calendar that became the source of immense controversy. This calendar omits "almost all nonbiblical saints, whose lives filled collections such as the *Golden Legend*," and it "follows the Protestant calendar in the Book of Common Prayer by retaining selected Christian festivals, evangelists, and apostolic saints."[41] Additionally, "The days of each month are filled with the names of medieval and contemporary individuals whom Foxe honors as proto-protestant or Protestant martyrs."[42] Foxe seeks to forestall the charges of innovation and novelty his calendar invites in his Latin preface *Ad doctum Lectorem*, strenuously rejecting the argument of "some papists, who . . . shout against me that while I expunge ancient and old divines, martyrs, confessors, and virgins, I cram new martyrs and confessors in their place."[43]

Despite Foxe's preemptive efforts, the calendar led to such massive Catholic criticism, including criticism from Robert Parsons, that in the 1570 and 1576 editions Foxe omitted it. Foxe did not, however, omit the apparatus of medieval hagiography from the 1570 edition. Indeed, though the *Acts and Monuments* exists in a "counter-generic relationship" with the *Golden Legend*, Foxe actually makes aspects of medieval hagiographic convention part of his defense against Catholic criticism.[44] In addition to omitting the calendar from the 1570 version, he revises the prefatory material. He incorporates a dedication to Elizabeth I in which he explicitly addresses the controversy stirred by the 1563 edition with the calendar. Comparing the uproar generated by the 1563 edition to Herod's response to the birth of Christ, Foxe writes: "But certaine euill disposed persons, of intemperant tounges, aduersaries to good procedynges would not suffer me so to rest, fumyng and freatyng, and raising up suche miserable exclamations at the first appearyng of the booke, as was wonderfull to heare. A man would haue thought Christ to haue bene new borne agayne, and that Herode with all the Citie of Ierusalem had bene in an uproare" (7). Foxe thus connects the appearance of the *Acts and Monuments* to the appearance of the divine Word made flesh "newe borne agayne," a formulation that combines an ironic and wry tone with, perhaps, a more serious suggestion that the *Acts and Monuments* shares something of the incarnational, quasi-scriptural dimensions of Margery Kempe's and Anna Trapnel's writings. He also equates the criticism of that text with the passion of Christ and the martyrs whose lives the text recounts. Somewhat paradoxically, though by this point I hope not too surprisingly, Foxe echoes the language with which, as we saw in chapter 3, Francis Gascoigne describes the critical response to Gertrude More's writings. Foxe states: "Such blustryng and styrring was then against that poore booke through all quarters of Engalnd, euen to the gates of Louaine: so that no English Papist almost in all the realme thought him selfe a perfect Catholicke, unless he had cast out some word or other, *to geue that booke a blow*" (7, emphasis added).

In addition to the expansions discussed previously, Foxe enlarges the 1570 edition with "a considerable amount of heterogeneous material concerning the final years of the reign of Henry VIII."[45] Much of this material helps to enhance the enlarged focus in the 1570 edition on "images of the persecuting church."[46] Newly incorporated condemnation of the Spanish Inquisition, along with added descriptions of executions of Protestants in Spain, is useful in this regard. Foxe includes brief accounts of the sentences pronounced against a series of men and women and ends with a detailed description of the execution of the condemned. In a section bearing the marginal annotation "xiiij Martyrs in Spain, burned," he writes:

> After these sentences beyng thus pronounced, they whiche
> were condemned to be burned . . . were committed to the secular
> magistrate, & to their executioners, which were commaunded to
> do their endeuour. Then were they all incontinent taken, and euery
> one set vpon an asse, their faces turned backeward, with a great
> garison of armed souldiours, vnto the place of punishement, which
> was without the gate of the towne called Del Campo. When they were
> come to the place, there were xiiij stakes set vp of equall distance
> one from an other, wherunto euery one seuerally beyng fastened,

accordyng to the fashion of Spayne, they were all first strangled,
and then burned, and turned to ashes. (1062)

These additions reflect increasing anxieties following the promulgation of *Regnans in excelsis* about possible alignments between the papacy
and Spain as forces striving to end English Protestant rule.

Foxe's inclusion of these accounts of the Spanish martyrs enables
us to see not only the ways in which the text responds to its own historical moment but also the ways in which the text intervenes in the unfolding of history. When Francis Drake set off on his circumnavigation of
the globe, one of the books he took with him was Foxe's *Acts and Monuments.* Thanks to records of the trial of Nuño da Silva (a Portuguese pilot
whom Drake had taken captive and whom he subsequently left in the
port of Guatulco) before the Inquisition in Mexico, we learn of Drake's
use of the *Acts and Monuments,* and particularly his use of the material
concerning the Spanish martyrs, in his interactions with the Spanish
in the New World. In February 1580, Francisco Gomes Rengifo was deposed for da Silva's trial in the Cathedral of Antequera (now Oaxaca,
Mexico). In his deposition, he describes Drake's men's activities in
plundering the port of Guatulco in 1579. Rengifo reports that the Englishmen took all the silver furnishings from the church, stamped upon
the unconsecrated wafers, and "smashed to pieces an image of Our
Lady, with Our Father and the Holy Ghost, and hacked and scratched
and made holes in it. Together with the cross to which it was attached,
they smashed a crucifix to pieces."[47] Rengifo and other Spaniards were
taken prisoner on Drake's ship, where they witnessed an English prayer
service in which Drake had a book on the table, a book about which Rengifo was quite curious. Rengifo reports that Drake "sent for a book of
the size of the *Lives of the Saints* and when all this was in place he struck
the table twice with the palm of his hand. Then, immediately nine Englishmen, with nine small books the size of a breviary, joined him and
seated themselves around him and the table. Then the said Francis
Drake crossed his hands, and, kneeling on the cushion and small box,
lifted his eyes to heaven and remained in that attitude for about a quar-
ter of an hour."[48] After the service was over, Drake questioned Rengifo

about his evident interest in the book and directed Rengifo to examine it. Rengifo reports:

> [A]fter a little while, he said to the witness "that book is a very good book," and, saying this, he opened it again, after having already shut it, and said to this witness: "Look at this book. You can see here those who were martyred in Castile," and he pointed out to this witness a figure representing a fire and a man therein, and he said "that this represented those who had been martyred and burnt in Castile." Turning over the pages of the book he showed witness, further on, another picture which he said "figured the astounding [arrogance] of the Supreme Pontiff."[49]

The book that Rengifo tellingly compares to the *Lives of the Saints* (the very work from which Foxe seeks to differentiate his project) is of course the *Acts and Monuments*. The Spanish executions of Protestants and the pope's humiliation of secular rules described there serve for Drake as justifications of plundering the church at Guatulco and, more broadly, for English taking of Spanish lands and possessions in the New World.

Drake then introduces Elizabeth I into the picture as further justification for his actions. Rengifo says:

> And when he finished reciting the psalm, Francis Drake said to the witness, "You will be saying now This man is a devil, who robs by day and prays at night in public. This is what I do, but it is just as when King Philip gives a very large written paper to your Viceroy, Don Martin Enriquez, telling him what he is to do and how he is to govern, so the Queen my Sovereign Lady, has ordered me to come to these parts. It is thus that I am acting, and if it is wrong it is she who knows best and I am not to be blamed for anything whatsoever."[50]

This rather curious passage may suggest Drake's ambivalence not simply about the propriety of his actions in Guatulco, as the deposition suggests, but also about his subordination to a female monarch, an attitude not unlike that expressed by Elizabeth's other great sailor and New World explorer Sir Walter Raleigh.[51] Drake reportedly says, in effect,

"Don't blame me; I'm just doing what the queen tells me to do, even if what she tells me is wrong." Drake's apparent ambivalence resonates with the uneasiness that Parsons, as we have seen, displays toward female rule. Equally, it harmonizes with Foxe's own ambiguous attitude toward the monarch whom his *Acts and Monuments* aims to serve and support. By the time of the 1570 edition Foxe saw Elizabeth I as having "failed to fulfill expectations that she would not only restore the Edwardian settlement of religion, but also go beyond it by implementing a full set of ecclesiastical reforms."[52] Drake seeks to deflect blame from himself by highlighting the limits of his authority, emphasizing that errors in his actions, if there be any errors, have their source in the authority of the female monarch, who, if she "knows best," may also "know worst," so to speak. Foxe in contrast subtly reminds Elizabeth of the limits of her own authority, particularly in the religious sphere. For instance, Foxe addresses Elizabeth not as the "supreme governour" of the church, as he does in the 1563 version, but rather as "the 'principall governour . . . under Christe the *supreme head* of the same, &c' (1570, *1r)."[53]

Drake's and Foxe's uneasy attitudes toward their female monarch direct us once again to the problematic convergence of gender, religion, and monarchical legitimacy in English politics. The juxtaposition of Drake's exhibition of Foxe's Spanish martyrs, his speech to Rengifo concerning Elizabeth's ultimate authority for English actions in the New World, and Rengifo's tellingly apt comparison of Drake's copy of the *Acts and Monuments* to the *Lives of the Saints* illuminate a fundamental ambiguity in the *Acts and Monuments.* Though Foxe turns St. Birgitta of Sweden and St. Catherine of Siena against the papacy they supported, and though he appropriates hagiographical mechanisms, in the process placing Catholic critics of his text in the position of Herod and the persecutors of saints, the *Acts and Monuments* is in the end troubled by the very hagiographical material it simultaneously seeks to co-opt, transform, and deny. Once again, the past that Foxe strives to have for his own purposes in the end overtakes the *Acts and Monuments* with its irrepressible embodied presence. Though the *Acts and Monuments* explicitly excludes virgin martyrs, there is a potential virgin martyr in the text—the Virgin Queen herself, to whom Foxe dedicates the work and whose early life he recounts. When we, like Rengifo, are put in mind of the *Lives of the*

Saints even as we are confronted with the Spanish martyrs juxtaposed with the English Protestant queen, a possibility inevitably suggests itself—the possibility that the narrative trajectory followed by so many saints' lives may overtake not only the writing of history but history itself. Especially in the years between the papal bull of 1570 and the triumph of the English over the Spanish Armada in 1588, the idea that the Spanish king might do to the Protestant church the equivalent (or, better, the reverse) of what the English did to the church in Guatulco, and might do to the Protestant queen what the forces of the Inquisition did to the martyr in Castile whose image Drake shows Rengifo, was not an idle flight of imagination.

Even if the threat of Elizabeth's death at the hands of the Spanish is not immediate, another threat from the medieval past inhabits Foxe's account of the Spanish martyrs. In addition to those executed, there were, he indicates, many others imprisoned and sentenced to other punishments by the Inquisition. Among these was an Englishman named Antonie Basnor. Foxe writes: "Last of all was produced Antonie Basnor, who for that he was an Englishe man, he was iudged to beare his mantell of yellow, to the towne house, in penaunce for his crime, and incontinent was thrust into a cloyster for one yeare, to the entent hee myght there be instructed in the catholicke ordenaunces of the Church of Rome, as they be called" (1065). So even if the Virgin Queen were not to be made a virgin martyr, she might still be made subject to claustration like those Catholic virgins enclosed in convent walls. Foxe might consciously abhor this option, given his disdain for the monastic life; unconsciously, however, he and others who, though pro-Protestant and pro-English, resented subordination to a powerful queen might find it paradoxically attractive.

PROTESTANT PROPAGANDA, THE SPANISH MARRIAGE, AND THE MEDIEVAL PAST

Parsons's efforts to mobilize the symbolic value available from the English Brigittines in exile to advance the case for a Spanish succession to the English throne came back to cause difficulties for the English Catholic cause a generation later, in the era of the controversial Spanish Marriage. The Protestant James VI of Scotland had of course succeeded Elizabeth as James I of England, but the hopes of English Catholics were raised when the proposal for his son Charles to marry the Infanta Maria of Spain (daughter of Philip III) emerged. While for Protestants the specter of Spain and all the dangers it represented again loomed large, the Brigittine community of Syon strongly supported this plan. As discussed in chapter 3, the nuns and abbess directed a petition to the Infanta, hoping she would make it possible for the community to return to England. In this petition, they address her as the Princess of Wales ("La Altissima Señora Prinçesa de Walia") in advance of the marriage and set out a view of the Lancastrian descent that harmonizes precisely with Parsons's.[54] Indicating their belief that the Catholic, Spanish monarchs are the true Lancastrian heirs and, accordingly, the heirs to the throne of England, they thank the Spanish kings for their financial support. Expressing their gratitude to Philip III, they say:

> [F]altando la su dicha Real fundaçion hecha y dotada por los Reyes de Inglatierra predeçeres de V*uestra* Mag*ista*d como consta por los Anales del dicho Reyno todauia Nuestro Señor no falto a estas sus siervas de inspirar y tocar El Real pecho de V*uestra* Mag*ista*d y de su Zelossissimo padre El Rey Phelippe segundo como verdaderos descendientes de los dichos Reyes jnglezes sus fundadores dellas Romarlas a sus quenta y sustenallas. ("Petition," 21–22; italics indicate expansions)

> [Driven out from their royal foundation, *founded and endowed by Your Majesty's predecessors the Kings of England,* these servants of Our Lord did not lack protection, for he touched and inspired the royal hearts of Your Majesty and of Your Most Zealous father, King Philip II, *true descendants of their founders the English Kings,* to take them to your charge and sustain them.] ("Petition," 33, emphasis added)

The nuns likewise declare their hopes that the Infanta Maria, like Mary Tudor before her, will prove to be a savior for the community in exile and "lo redusiera esta segunda vez de los Reynos estraños para adonde [e]stava otra vez desterrado" ("Petition," 12) [resettle it a second time from the foreign kingdoms to which it had again been exiled] ("Petition," 24).

As we have seen, an emphasis on repetition of past holy lives characterizes the devotional life and communal identity of the English Brigittines in exile. In their petition to the Infanta Maria, the abbess and nuns of Syon turn this emphasis to their political cause. Capitalizing on the symbolic value of St. Birgitta and the Brigittine line, they explicitly identify their communal life, and particularly their suffering in exile, with the life of St. Birgitta. In publicizing their support for the proposed marriage between the Infanta and the Prince of Wales as well as their corresponding hopes for their return to England, the abbess and nuns of Syon represent themselves as reliving St. Birgitta's life, saying:

> [A]unque se pueden hallar cosas majores ni mas altas que se
> descubran en este primero Testimonio: Todauia el segundo de
> la dicha Santa muger como no es menos del primero assi el sirue
> muy proposito a este nuestro prezente intento porque el claramente
> trata de Su Santa y Exemplara peregrinaçion, y consequentemente
> de nos otras sus Verdaderas hijas que sequimos y Caminamos
> por sus dichosos passos y destierros y peregrinaçiones El qual
> Testimonio esta Contenido en la dicha bulla de Su Canonizaçion
> En estas palabras (Iella siendo auisada del Spiritu Sancto de dexar,
> y salir fuera de su tierra y parentesco se fue a Roma y Hierusalen).
> ("Petition," 15; italics indicate expansions)

> [Although better and higher things cannot be found than those
> displayed in this first Testimony, nevertheless the second Testimony
> of the aforementioned Holy Woman, no less valid than the first,
> serves our present intent more aptly, because it clearly treats of her
> holy and exemplary pilgrimage, and consequently, of us, her true
> daughters, who follow and journey in her auspicious footsteps, and
> in her exiles and wanderings. This testimony is contained in the
> aforesaid Bull of her Canonization, in these words, "She, being told

by the Holy Ghost to leave and to depart from her native land and
family, went to Rome and Jerusalem."] ("Petition," 27)

They drive home their union with their order's founder, a saint who,
though not English, was embraced in the fifteenth century as a patron
saint of England, saying:

> [P]or cujos y enterçession creemos y tenemos por cierto averse
> hecho que este solo convento sobre todos los otros monasterios
> de su orden mas ymite aesta heroica obra de su peregrinaçion y
> que mucho mas insiste en los Trabajosos passos y sudores de
> aquella su dichosa salida de su tierra y parentesco por tantas y
> tan varias tierras y provinçias agenas. ("Petition," 16)

> [Through her intercession we believe and know that we have
> made this convent alone, above all other convents of her Order,
> approximate more exactly to the heroic labour of her pilgrimage
> and more closely exemplify the painful steps and toil of her
> auspicious departure from her native land and family for so many
> different foreign countries and provinces.] ("Petition," 28)

St. Birgitta's life is not the only holy *vita* that the nuns of Syon represent as being linked to their current situation as they make a case for
the "Spanish Match," the re-Catholicization of England, and their return from exile. Syon puts its hope in persuading the Infanta Maria to be
a savior for the community, acting, as Mary Tudor did, to "resettle it . . .
from the foreign kingdoms to which it had again been exiled." In expressing their desires, the Brigittines capitalize on the shared name
"Mary." They present a paradigm in which the Infanta revives the Catholic reign of Mary I of England and simultaneously enacts the Virgin
Mary's identity, a figure with whom, as we have seen, the nuns themselves closely identify, to bring religio-political salvation.[55] The abbess
and nuns stress that the order "fue comensada y dedicada al honor de
nuestra Señora Maria Madre de Dios, y Reyna de los cielos" ("Petition,"
12) [was commended and dedicated to the honour of Our Lady, Mary

Mother of God and Queen of Heaven] ("Petition," 24) and claim that divine providence has ordained that the order "sea favoreçida y conser-
vada por estas otras Reynas Marias muy devotas a la dicha divinissima
Maria, y Reina de los Angeles" ("Petition," 12) [might later be favoured
and protected by these other Queen Marys themselves most devoted to
the Most Divine Mary, Queen of the Angels] ("Petition," 24). A strong
sense of connection between past and present holy lives thus informs
both Syon's self-representation in their petition to the Infanta and their
suggestion of a politico-spiritual identity for the Infanta Maria. The petition thus further illustrates that a porous, permeable model of selfhood has for the Brigittines, as for the Benedictines, political as well as
spiritual dimensions.

For English Protestants opposed to the Spanish Marriage, this tie
between the Infanta and English women in Iberia who embodied the
"old religion" was at once anxiety provoking and useful. Cristina Mal-
comson argues that during the period in which the Spanish Marriage
looked likely, there was a strong association "of women with Spanish
infiltration."[56] Gender and religion once again combined with anxieties about lineage and legitimacy to emerge as a locus of crisis. Among
English Protestants "a powerful fear" existed "about . . . the Spanish
princess, who as queen would be mother to the future English king. . . .
[T]he Spanish Infanta was seen as the avenue through which the Catholic Church and the Spanish Empire would enter the English state and
rob it of its national strength."[57]

Thomas Robinson's *The Anatomie of the English Nunnery at Lisbon in
Portugal* represents the Protestants' strategy for turning the troubling
nexus of fears raised by the Spanish Marriage to their advantage.[58] Robinson claimed to have been forcibly detained by the confessor general
Seth Foster and put to work as a copyist (1), another Englishman purportedly thrust, like Antonie Basor, into a cloister in Spanish territory.
Robinson, though, makes the most of this situation, treating it as an opportunity to tell all the scurrilous secrets of convent life. The *Anatomie*,
first published in 1622, appeared at precisely the same time as the nuns'
petition described above.[59] Thus, if Robinson did work as a copiest in the
community, he may well have known the nuns' petition, a possibility that

makes it all the more difficult not to read the *Anatomie* as a response both to the Spanish Marriage and to English Catholic versions of medieval history like those set out by Parsons and the nuns.

In the *Anatomie,* medieval female spirituality and medieval history taint, rather than support, the cause of the Infanta and her English Catholic supporters. Playing off the widespread Protestant representation of the Catholic Church as the "whore of Rome" or the "whore of Babylon," and mobilizing strategies resembling those used by the accusers of Margery Kempe, Anna Trapnel, and Elizabeth Cary, Robinson portrays the Brigittine community of Syon in exile as a nest of sexual vice. The explanation of the title Robinson gives in his address "To the indifferent Reader" makes immediately evident his interest in female bodies—the actual bodies of the nuns and the symbolic, feminized body of the Catholic Church—as well as in these bodies' corrupt excesses. He first warns that the reader should not expect the sort of medical work possibly signaled by his title, saying, "Reader, if the Title of this booke, being The Anatomie of the English Nunnery at Lisbon, doo make the expect some Chyryrgicall mysteries, or profound Lecture upon a dissected body, let me satisfie thee, and saue thee a labour in reading it." He goes on to indicate that bodies are, however, in fact a central topic of discussion in the text, claiming that the treatise "hath truly anatomized this handmaid of the Whore of Babylon; laying open her principall veins and sinews."

The image included on the title page of the 1623 edition, which is accompanied by an explanatory poem, further indicates Robinson's concern with in female bodies (figure 2). The title page bears a series of pictures (conveniently labeled with letters keyed to corresponding passages in the explanatory verses) in which a nun enters a cleric's chamber through the grate where he hears her confession. Subsequent images unflinchingly reveal their debauched activities within the chamber. As the poem gleefully explains:

> So on a bed they wanton, clippe, and kisse,
> There's nothing in a Nunnery amisse.
> Then doth a banquet on a Table stand,

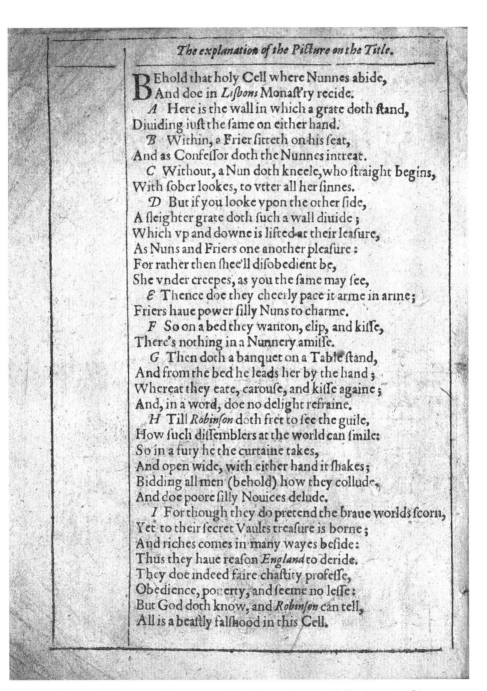

Behold that holy Cell where Nunnes abide,
And doe in *Lisbons* Monaſtry recide.

   A Here is the wall in which a grate doth ſtand,
Diuiding iuſt the ſame on either hand.

   B Within, a Frier ſitteth on his ſeat,
And as Confeſſor doth the Nunnes intreat.

   C Without, a Nun doth kneele, who ſtraight begins,
With ſober lookes, to vtter all her ſinnes.

   D But if you looke vpon the other ſide,
A ſleighter grate doth ſuch a wall diuide ;
Which vp and downe is lifted at their leaſure,
As Nuns and Friers one another pleaſure :
For rather then ſhee'll diſobedient be,
She vnder creepes, as you the ſame may ſee,

   E Thence doe they cheerly pace it arme in arme;
Friers haue power ſilly Nuns to charme.

   F So on a bed they wanton, clip, and kiſſe,
There's nothing in a Nunnery amiſſe.

   G Then doth a banquet on a Table ſtand,
And from the bed he leads her by the hand ;
Whereat they eate, carouſe, and kiſſe againe ;
And, in a word, doe no delight refraine.

   H Till *Robinſon* doth fret to ſee the guile,
How ſuch diſſemblers at the world can ſmile:
So in a fury he the curtaine takes,
And open wide, with either hand it ſhakes;
Bidding all men (behold) how they collude,
And doe poore ſilly Nouices delude.

   I For though they do pretend the braue worlds ſcorn,
Yet to their ſecret Vaults treaſure is borne ;
And riches comes in many wayes beſide :
Thus they haue reaſon *England* to deride.
They doe indeed faire chaſtity profeſſe,
Obedience, pouerty, and ſeeme no leſſe :
But God doth know, and *Robinſon* can tell,
All is a beaſtly falſhood in this Cell.

Figure 2. Title page with facing poem from Thomas Robinson's *The Anatomie of the English Nunnery at Lisbon in Portugal* (1623). Reproduced with permission of The Rare Book and Manuscript Library of the University of Illinois at Urbana-Champaign.

THE
ANATOMIE
OF THE ENGLISH
NVNNERY AT Lisbon
in PORTVGALL:

Diffected and laid open by one that was
fometime a yonger Brother of the *Couent* :

Who (if the grace of God had not preuented him) might haue
grovvne as old in a wicked life as the oldeft amongft them.

Publifhed by Authoritie.

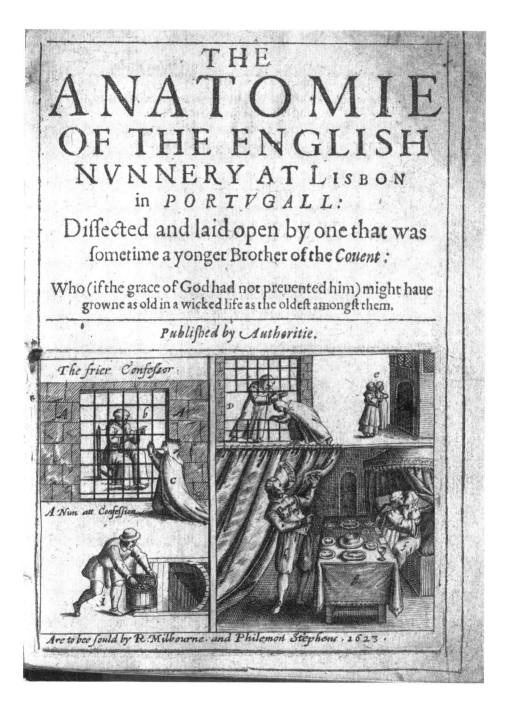

The frier Confeffeor

A Nun att Confeffion

Are to bee fould by R. *Milbourne and* Philemon *Stephens* . 1623 .

And from the bed he leads her by the hand;
Whereat they eate, carouse, and kisse againe;
And, in a word, doe no delight refraine.

Robinson's interest in female bodies extends to an interest in lineage. He notes that, although Syon was founded by women of royal blood and was previously populated by women from well-born families, the women in the house now are personally corrupt and derived from undistinguished backgrounds. He says, "[A]t this present it is not of any extraordinary repute; neither are the people of it for birth and parentage equall to their predecessors, who were wont to be of good descent: whereas now (saue only a few) they are Recusants daughters of the meaner sort" (7). Furthermore, he claims that many of the postulants flee to the Continent because they have "ministered to their spirituall fathers in all things: and by such means having gotten a clap, diuers of them become Nunnes" (7). In a marginal note on this passage, Robinson bitingly observes, "It is no great miracle for a whore to become a Nunne; nor for a Nunne to become a whore" (7 n. b). The only lineage to be found at Syon is fundamentally illegitimate in every sense of the term; in fact, Robinson makes unmistakably clear that Syon is characterized by female carnality, sexual corruption, and a tainted inheritance when he reports his discovery of the bones of nuns' illegitimate children within the nunnery walls.[60] By emphasizing feminine corruption and the nuns' undistinguished parentage, Robinson is himself embracing a strategy with a long medieval history, a strategy that had particular appeal to Lancastrian monarchs. Robinson does to the Brigittine nuns, whose spirituality has the potential to aid the cause of his Catholic enemies, the very thing that the Lancastrians did to Joan of Arc during her trial and Tudor propagandists did to her after her death in the pages of chronicles. The mayor of Leicester played this hand with Margery Kempe when, as we saw in the previous chapter, he called her a "fals strumpet, a fals loller. & a fals deceyuer of þe pepyl," and Henry VIII's "reformers" too adopted this strategy in the course of the Dissolution of the Monasteries.[61]

Robinson strikingly suggests that Syon's present sexual corruption is rooted in the Brigittine order's medieval past. Indeed, the nuns' vice appears to be the direct result of their continuing to employ the practices of that age. Again directing attention to lineage and origins, Robinson notes that "in the Catholique *Romane* Church, amongst all the disordered Orders of swarming Locusts . . . there is none but take their beginning from one supposed Saint or another" (4). Robinson then turns to a central figure in Parsons's, and indeed in Henry V's, symbolic programs—St. Birgitta herself. The Brigittines, Robinson notes, "take their beginning from their holy Mothers Saint *Bridget,* and her daughter Saint *Katherine*" (6). He admits that these women were of royal blood and that Birgitta was "a woman (questionlesse) of a good vnderstanding and singular memory" (6). However, far from being a visionary who founded a monastic order on God's command and who received that order's rule from Christ, she was "miserably seduced and led away by the subtil allurements of her ghostly Father, by whose perswasions and counsell she went to *Rome* as a Pilgrime, and coming before the Pope, she pretended to haue diuers reuelations from God; amongst which, one was for the founding of this Order of Nunnes" (6).

The sexual connotations of the language in this passage (in particular, the references of seduction and subtle allurements) make St. Birgitta appear to be much the same as the postulants who come to Lisbon after being seduced by seminary priests, or, indeed, like the nuns who dally with their confessors (as in the text's opening image) only to bear illegitimate children. The idea that the legacy to be had at Syon is not one of a distinctive, Marian form of medieval female spirituality but rather one of stereotypical feminine sexual corruption reaching back to the house's fifteenth-century foundation, emerges even more strongly when Robinson stresses that Syon, unlike other English monastic communities in exile, has an unbroken connection to the medieval past. He points out that English nunneries exist in Bruxelles, Gravelines, and Lisbon, "but none that haue continued euer since the suppression of Abbeys in England, saue only that at Lisbon" (8 n. b).

In Robinson's *Anatomie* St. Birgitta and the nuns of Syon do not lend symbolic support to a case for women's legitimate place in a line of succession. Rather, they model a corrupt female lineage and demonstrate that medieval female spirituality is simply a guise for feminine carnality.

Instead of emphasizing likeness between the Infanta Maria and the Virgin Mary, as the Syon nuns' petition does, the *Anatomie* seems to make, at least indirectly, a claim like that of William Prynne, who writes that the Spanish hoped to cause England's downfall through the "project of marrying us to the whore of Rome by matching the heire of the crownse of England to a *Romanist.*"[62] For Robinson, the saintly founder of the Brigittine order, the English nuns of Syon living in Lisbon, the Infanta Maria with whom they are closely tied, and the Roman Church to which all these women belong are all, in effect, whores.

Robinson thus categorically denies to the supporters of the Spanish Marriage all symbolic value deriving from female purity and holiness. He similarly denies the Catholic cause the benefits to be obtained through Syon's strong links to Lancastrian royalty. Indeed, while he cannot dismiss the house's foundation by the Lancastrian Henry V "at his returne from his famous Conquest in France" (2), he portrays the break with Rome and the Dissolution of the Monasteries as being a more glorious Lancastrian triumph. He writes: "[I]t pleased the lord of his infinit mercy to disperse and scatter those thick clouds of ignorance and superstition, which had long time bedimmed the eyes, and darkend the vnderstanding of our forefathers, and that the glorious light of the Gospell began to be more and more resplendent in the latter end of the reigne of King Henry the 8" (3). Whereas Parsons seeks to give the Spanish monarch legitimating symbolic capital by positioning him, like Henry V, as a patron of Syon, Robinson inverts this strategy, making dissolution, rather than foundation, a source of symbolic value. As we have seen, Grafton imaginatively crafts on Elizabeth I's behalf a Protestant Lancastrian line, and Parsons emphasizes on the Infanta's behalf the *true* Lancastrian line's Catholic orthodoxy. Robinson, on behalf of those opposed to the Spanish Marriage, in turn creates a Lancastrian line cleansed of Catholic taint by Henry VIII's heroic action in doing God's work of banishing "ignorance and superstition."

Thomas Robinson was not, of course, alone in his method of responding to the dynastic fears central to the Spanish Marriage controversy by resorting to anti-Catholic propaganda targeted at the intersections of gender, religion, and history. Thomas Goad too took the height of the Spanish Marriage tumult as an occasion to write the history of England's Catholic past and that past's present continuance, with special emphasis on Catholic Spain. In 1623, his work *The Friers Chronicle or The Trve Legend of Priests and Monkes Lives* appeared. Much as Robinson's title signals his interest in female bodies, Goad's title signals his interests in a textual corpus and historiographical traditions. Calling the text *The Friers Chronicle* evokes the ancient, authoritative genre of the monastic chronicle. Goad's aim is to take that which Catholic works wrongly (from a Protestant perspective) present as truth and, by revealing these works' falsity, to make his chronicle the rightful heir to the authority inherent in a genre of writing history that has been tainted by Catholic practitioners. Goad observes, "[T]here is not a step I make, but I have warrant for my footing; no story I relate, but is extracted out of the bookes of their owne *Magazines,* and Authoritie of their former Writers."[63]

Goad's alternative title for his work, *The Trve Legend of Priests and Monkes Lives,* highlights the simultaneous meanings of *legend* as something to be read, a saint's life, and something fabulous or false. The title emphasizes that Goad will tell the truth about the lives of priests and monks in contrast to hagiographical accounts that are filled with falsehood. Adopting a strategy much like Foxe's, he explicitly situates his *Trve Legende* in contrast to "their Golden Legend," which is authored by "the father of Lyes" (B2r).[64] By invoking the *Legenda aurea* Goad does to hagiography what he does to the monastic chronicle, appropriating the genre to turn it against itself. Goad writes antihagiography; his text predictably derides miracles purportedly effected by saints and their relics, and, like Robinson's *Anatomie,* presents scurrilous tales of the sexual misdeeds of the religious—priests, friars, monks, and nuns alike.

Also like Robinson, Goad sees the continuity of Catholic tradition, especially in Spain, as a present threat to England in the 1620s, a view that surfaces in a somewhat unexpected interjection into his titillating disquisition on fornication among the religious. After presenting accounts of nunneries turned into brothels and cardinals consorting with married women, he states: "Againe, whereas it may be obiected, these were the times of old, there is now great reformation since these enormities were looked into: I answere plainely and directly; the same superstition remaines at this houre, and the Priests doe so preuaile with coozening deceit, and farre-fetcht deuices, that in *Spaine* this present yeere 1622 the doctrine of the conception of our *Lady* without sinne, and assumption into Heauen, is newly divulged and ratified, and the contrary opinion reputed Heresie, and the repugners hunted, and hissed at in euery Towne and Citie" (C2v). Immediately after this digression concerning the Immaculate Conception and the Assumption, he returns to the more salacious topic at hand. He continues, "Concerning their Whoredome; or if you will haue the cleanlier terme, Fornication; Who knowes not, that there is a common allowance of Stewes (more then a conueniencie) vnder all the Catholike gouernment" (C2v).

What are we to make of Goad's expression of dismay about these particular points of Catholic doctrine at this particular textual juncture? I would argue that the convergence of sexuality, the female body (that of Mary's mother, St. Anne, and that of Mary assumed bodily into heaven), the Catholic faith, Spain as a place where past abuses continue in the present year 1622, and an interest in fornication among the religious point to one thing: Goad, like Robinson, strives to undermine any potential positive association among the Catholic Infanta, English nuns in Spanish territory, and the benefits of Marian identity. Goad's strategy is in a sense the inverse of Michael Walpole's in his life of Luisa de Carvajal y Mendoza discussed in chapter 3; in that work, Walpole makes a case for the restoration of Catholicism in England by associating Catholic England with a historical alliance with virginal purity. He calls attention to the fact that the Feast of the Immaculate Conception, still in his time celebrated in Spain, actually originated in England even as he invokes the traditional appellation of England as the "Virgin's dowry." Goad in contrast subtly suggests that the Virgin Mary herself is perhaps not so pure as the Catholics would have her, and in any case that those who claim to imitate her, or revere her, are in fact whores and fornicators. The model of the Incarnation, the claim to Marian identity, and the value of female spirituality rooted in the medieval past are all devalued as symbolic resources available to the Catholic cause. In Goad's *Friers Chronicle*, the legacy of the Middle Ages is one of contamination, of corruption transmitted through a corrupt line; to permit a Catholic woman to enter the English royal lineage will be to corrupt it with all the evils of the past made incarnate in the Catholic present.

St. Birgitta, Christian Cavendish, and the English Civil War

It is no accident that Goad shares so much with Robinson. Goad clearly knew and approved of the *Anatomie*, since in the *Friers Chronicle* he praises "that true and wel written Discourse of the *Anatomie of the English Nunnery at* Lisbone *in* Portugall" (A4r). Another evidently approving reader of the *Anatomie* was "The Right Honorable The Countesse of Devonshire" (A2r) to whom Goad dedicates *The Friers Chronicle*. He addresses her at the beginning of *The Friers Chronicle,* saying that the *Anatomie* "hath not onely had a gracious acceptation with you, but wrought vpon your iudgements and vnderstanding, as farre as the abhorring their impieties [sic] and lamenting the seduction of silly Ignorants" (A4r).

Christian Cavendish, daughter of Edward Bruce of Kinloss and wife of William Cavendish, second Earl of Devonshire, has a significant connection not only with the *Anatomie* and *The Friers Chronicle* but also with the material covered in Parsons's *Conference,* although in this latter case the tie is familial rather than textual. Her father was the Scottish ambassador who did so much to ensure that James VI of Scotland reigned after Elizabeth as James I of England; indeed, James I contributed part of her marriage portion of £10,000 in gratitude for her father's services.[65] Furthermore, William Cavendish was cousin to Arabella Stuart, whose status as a potential successor to Elizabeth I Robert Parsons discusses at some length, and who was, as we have seen, one of Aemilia Lanyer's desired patrons.

These family connections, along with her evident taste for anti-Catholic literature, situate Christian Cavendish firmly in the camp of those who would seem most likely to see the medieval past as a negative foil for the Protestant present and to see any continuance of that past in present practices as dangerous. Indeed, in an anonymous elegy commemorating her death at "a Hundred and odd Years of Age," a rather unexpected—but perhaps in a sense inevitable—reference to St. Birgitta appears in connection to Christian Cavendish.[66] The same things that made St. Birgitta valuable for fifteenth-century Lancastrians, for Parsons, and for the nuns of Syon also made her valuable as a placeholder for a medieval religious legacy, an embodiment of the benighted past, to Christian's elegist as well as his Protestant contemporaries and precursors. The elegist declares:

> Her life so *Straight,* it shames the *Popish* square
> Prescrib'd in Rules of saint *Bridget* or *Clare*;
> Whilst *Pilgrimageing* here, she stood possest
> Of Heav'n in *part,* For her Rich furnisht Brest
> Was a fair *Temple,* and her heart a shrine,
> So *Purg'd,* that she appeared *All Divine*;
> Strictly *Religious,* of firm loyalty,
> In discourse *Pleasant,* without *vanity.*
>
> (emphasis in original)

Unexpected though a reference to St. Birgitta might seem in this context, in using St. Birgitta as an iconic representation of all that is wrong with medieval Catholic spirituality Christian's elegist is far from idiosyncratic. Indeed, doing so goes back to the days of Protestant attacks on Robert Parsons. In *A Caueat for Parsons Howlet . . . ,* a response to a piece by Parsons published under the pseudonym John Howlet, John Fielde describes the Jesuits as inheriting, and indeed surpassing, the falsity of their medieval forebears St. Francis, St. Clare, and St. Bridget.[67] The sort of Brigittine affinities that infuse Luisa de Carvajal y Mendoza's would-be Jesuit Society of the Sovereign Virgin Mary, Our Lady, become, in Fielde's hands, a liability for the Jesuits. Among works by closer contemporaries of Christian's elegist, William Guild's *Anti-Christ pointed and painted out . . .* (1655) describes the cross speaking to St. Birgitta in Rome as an example of a false popish miracle, and Walter Pope's satirical "The Catholick Ballad: or an Invitation to Popery . . ." (1674) includes a mocking reference to St. Birgitta.[68] So too does John Oldham's "Satyr IV. S. Ignatius his Image brought in . . ." (1684). Like Christian's elegist, Oldham dismissively pairs St. Birgitta with St. Clare, mocking Catholic devotion to relics: "These Locks S. *Bridget's* were, and those S. *Clare's* / Some for S. *Catherine* go, and some for *her's* / That wip'd her *Saviour's* feet, wash'd with her tears" (emphasis in original).[69] An especially interesting later seventeenth-century negative reference to St. Birgitta appears in Edward Fowler's *A Friendly Conference between a Minister and a Parishioner of his, Inclining to Quakerism* (1676). In this text, Fowler ridicules the Quakers as heirs to the sort of Catholic falsity and superstition embodied by St. Birgitta and her "miraculous inspirations." He writes, "That the spirit helpeth us to understand old truths already revealed in Scripture, we confess and pray for his assistance therein, but to pretend to such miraculous inspirations as the Apostles once had, or to new revelations beyond what was discover'd to them, is a horrible cheat set up at first by St. Francis and St. Bridget, and some other Fanatical Friers and Nuns of the Romish Church, whose steps the Quakers now do follow."[70]

During her life Christian Cavendish not only was renowned for her piety, as the elegy claims, but also was a passionate supporter of the Royalist cause, the same cause that so occupied the English Benedictine nuns of Ghent and Dunkirk considered in chapter 3. Her son Charles died leading Royalist forces at Gainsborough in 1648, and she after the battle of Worcester took charge of the king's effects. During the Protectorate she was known for harboring Royalist partisans at her house at Roehampton, and, like the English nuns of Ghent and Dunkirk, she was in active communication with English Royalists on the Continent. Her support for the Royalist cause and her piety are celebrated in a biography of her entitled *The Life of the Right Honourable and Religious Lady Christian Late Countess Dowager of Devonshire*, by Thomas Pomfret, written for presentation to Christian's son William after her death.

In the context of the Civil War and the Protectorate, Christian's Royalist politics and her evident anti-Catholicism form a complicated nexus, since Pomfret portrays her to be as strongly opposed to Presbyterians as she is to Catholics. Pomfret incorporates a vigorous denunciation of the Presbyterian faction in his *Life*, including a comparison of Presbyterianism with "Mahumetism."[71] Pomfret also praises Christian for her support of Anglican clerics during the Civil War. He writes: "The War had made Loyalty poor; and Sequestrations upon the Priests of God had reduced the Clergy to such lamentable wants, that they had nothing left to cloath them, but their own Righteousness; or any thing to feed on, but a good Conscience, and their passive Vertues. Here our noble Lady saw, and pitied; and as ever she had been the Defender, so now she became the succourer of the Righteous Cause; Fed, and Cloathed, and Comforted all, that lived within the Vicinage of her Charity" (68–69). Pomfret must walk a fine line in making Christian's virtuous and pious life distinct *both* from models taken from the Catholic past *and* from modes of life espoused by antipopish Presbyterians. Pomfret's representations of Christian's piety align with Charles I's religious views; the monarch that Christian so strongly supported "identified Popery with tyranny and Puritanism with anarchy." Tellingly, in an anti-Puritan speech to Parliament, Charles "called for the Church's return to the 'purest times of Queen Elizabeth's days.'"[72] Charles's gesture to a time in the past when the nature of English religion was, in fact, far from pure (although it laid claim to the purity of the early church) and was indeed actually quite mixed, being as it was engaged in constant negotiations among Catholicism and versions of Protestantism, heightens the push-pull dynamic with the Catholic past to which Christian's biography bears witness.

In the end, the line separating Christian from the Catholic past blurs. In spite of the stance taken by her elegist, in Pomfret's *Life* Christian ends up looking a great deal like the very medieval, Catholic saints from whom her elegist seeks to distinguish her. Although by all available evidence both Christian and those who wrote about her rejected "popery," language and generic elements of medieval female hagiography pervade Pomfret's life of her. Such echoes may, on the one had, be evidence of a strategy like that employed by Goad with the genres of chronicle and legend, a strategy of adopting a genre of the Catholic past and adapting it by rescuing it from that past's presumed corrupting force. On the other hand, the presence of such textual elements also reveals, I would suggest, ways in which "the medieval" continues to assert a kind of ownership on the present of the later seventeenth century. Just as the traumatic legacies of the past overtake those who seek to embrace the past, they also emerge, in a time of political crisis, to attach to those who would distance themselves from those same legacies.

Pomfret's *Life* evokes the language of hagiography early on when he says that he has "chosen a Noble Personage, out of the number of the

Dead, of incomparable Piety and Prudence, (intended by Providence to make Vertue lovely and imitable) to speak truth of whom, can Regret none; and whom too, as her Merits were above, so it hath pleased God to remove from the Opportunities of being flatterd" (2–3). The object of his praise—a dead exemplar of virtue providing a model for imitation—sounds precisely like a Catholic saint. Even more tellingly, he claims that he will relate her life "for the Admiration of this, and the Imitation of Posterity" (4), reminding us of the formula of admiration and imitation given to readers of hagiography. Pomfret further calls Christian "an Ornament to her Sex, and . . . a just Model of all Vertues" (7). The lurking presence of all about the past that is excluded so resolutely by Christian's elegist when he contrasts her with St. Birgitta is suggested by some fairly surprising appearances in the catalog of virtuous women Pomfret includes as fit company for his subject. We find in this catalog the expected biblical women (much like Aemilia Lanyer, he cites Deborah, Judith, Esther, Mariam) and women from the early church. Rather unexpected, though, is "Leucy," who "plucked out her eyes, that she might extinguish the inraged flames of unlawful Love inkindled at them" (9). Additionally, among those distinguished "for private Uertues" we find "S. Agnes" and "S. Cicely" (11). These are all saints who enjoyed widespread popular devotion in the Middle Ages and whose lives are, of course, included in the *Legenda aurea* so summarily dismissed by Goad, following Foxe, in the *Friers Chronicle* (B3r), where events like those in these same saints' lives are derided as prime examples of "the lying Miracles of Popish Prelates."

In Pomfret's life of Christian Cavendish, even if the presence of medieval female hagiography is part of an attempt to transform a Catholic tradition for Protestant ends, the generic elements seem to take on a life of their own. Christian's life as Pomfret tells it sounds very much like none other than that of St. Birgitta, with whom Christian's elegist contrasts her and who stands as an embodiment of all that is wrong with the religion of the medieval past in so many early modern texts. Christian and Birgitta share royal family connections, unusual and auspicious circumstances of birth, and a holy youth. When St. Birgitta's mother was pregnant with her, she was shipwrecked. As Birgitta's *vita* reports, "And when many of either sex had already drowned, a duke of the kingdom,

Lord Eric, the king of Sweden's brother, who was there at the time, saw her in peril, and, by every means in his power, brought her alive to shore. Then that very night, a person in shining garments stood by that same mother of Lady Birgitta and said: 'You have been saved for the sake of the good that you have in your womb.'"[73] Her *vita* also tells of Birgitta's extraordinary piety in childhood, outlining her visionary experiences beginning at age seven and her intense nocturnal devotions.[74] Pomfret says of Christian's birth and childhood: "Several Sons he had; and but this only Daughter; she born to him on *Christmas* day, and for that reason had the name of *Christian*: answering up to the highest measures, the glorious *Omen,* both of the Day and of her Name; appearing so soon to be *Christian,* as if indeed, she had been born one; expressing in her younger years, such vigorous Demonstrations of Goodness, that the World might easily see, she had a Soul, and Body, made at first to all possible Perfections" (*Life,* 18–19). Both women marry well, have children and experience their children's deaths (coincidentally, both experience the loss of adult sons named Charles), and have long widowhoods filled with religious devotion. Most strikingly, however, Birgitta and Christian themselves interweave their spirituality with their political participation, and after their deaths their spirituality is put to political ends by others. Much as Birgitta involved herself with the events of the papal schism and the Hundred Years' War, Christian, moved by "the deplorable condition of the King and Church," worked "with her utmost skill, and diligence" for "the Recovery of her Prince, and the Nation from those usurpations that were upon his Crown" (59). While St. Birgitta's holiness was used by Lancastrians and by Parsons for support their political causes, Pomfret allies Christian's pious virtue to the Royalist and Anglican causes.

To illuminate the problematic dimensions of the close connections between Christian and the very saint against which her elegist defines her, and to illustrate the ways in which Pomfret's *Life* is haunted by the past it at once adopts and rejects, it is worth considering the circumstances of the text's publication. In the latter part of Christian's life, in the 1670s, anxieties about gender, religion, lineage, and succession once again came to trouble English political culture. In 1649, those issues had dramatically emerged front and center in yet another act of deposition when Charles I was executed and his French, Catholic wife Henrietta Maria fled to the Continent with their children. This act of rupture was at least superficially healed with the restoration of Charles II in 1660. But the politico-cultural environment of the 1670s was troubled by the looming succession of a Catholic monarch in Charles II's brother James (who had become Catholic in 1671 under the influence of Henrietta Maria) and by the rumored "Popish Plot" of 1678 (which was, as I discuss in the Introduction, such a momentous event for the English nuns of the Antwerp Carmel). In many respects, the 1670s were thus characterized by tumult similar to that of the 1620s during the Spanish Marriage controversy, or to that of the still earlier Elizabethan succession crisis.[75] While Pomfret's life of a virtuous, pious Protestant woman who reportedly approved of such virulently anti-Catholic writings as the *Anatomie of the English Nunnery at Lisbon in Portugal* could well be taken as a symbolic asset for the Anglican, Royalist political cause, her unlikely likeness to the very saint who founded the Brigittine order would have been a liability. Such a likeness would have become even more unwelcome at the very moment Pomfret's text appeared in print; the title page of the *Life* proclaims that it was "Printed by *William Rawlins* for the Author, 1685." This is the year in which Charles II died, James II came to the throne, and Protestants rebelled (the Monmouth rising) against the new Catholic monarch.

Lest it seem that only the Royalist faction found itself unsettled by the persistence of the medieval, I want to end by calling attention to another striking set of publication circumstances. In an act demonstrating that the medieval past was still very much worth appropriating, those in favor of ending monarchical rule in England turned to a most surprising resource—Robert Parsons's *Conference*. The first part of Parsons's text was "plagiarized and . . . reappear[ed] unexpectedly in 1648 in a pirated version under the pen of Oliver Cromwell's own publicist, Henry Walker."[76] The *Conference* obviously appealed to Republicans for its prodeposition arguments. Indeed, they clearly wanted to suggest that Charles was yet another Richard II. For instance, witness the argument that

> King Richard the second . . . forgetting the miserable end of his
> great Grandfather for evil government, as also the felicity, and
> vertue of his Father and Grandfather for the contrary, suffered
> himselfe to be abused and misled by evill councellours, to the great
> hurt and disquietnesse of the Realme. For which cause after he
> had reigned 22 yeares, he was deposed by act of Parliament holden
> in *London,* and condemned to perpetuall prison in the Castle of
> *Pomfret.* . . . [A]nd in this man's place by free election was chosen
> for King the noble Knight *Henry* Duke of *Lancaster,* who proved
> afterwards a notable King.[77]

It is difficult to imagine, however, anything more incongruous than a
Jesuit work committed to making a case for the divine legitimacy of a
Catholic monarch being turned to Republican ends. This republication
of the *Conference,* like the appearance of Pomfret's *Life* in the political
ferment on 1685, casts into sharp relief not only that it is impossible to
escape the legacies of the medieval past by rejecting them, but also that
the unresolved traumas of the past never cease to reemerge to unsettle
present invocations of it.

Notes

The following are abbreviations used in the notes:

EEBO   Early English Books Online
EETS   Early English Text Society
STC (2nd ed.)   A. W. Pollard and G. R. Redgrave, *A Short-Title Catalogue*
                of Books Printed in England, Scotland, and Ireland, and of
                English Books Printed Abroad, 1475–1640, 2nd. ed., 1986–91,
                accessed via EEBO
TEE   The English Experience: Its Record in Early Printed Books
                Published in Facsimile
Wing (2nd ed.) Donald G. Wing, *Short-Title Catalogue of Books Printed*
                in England, Scotland, Ireland, Wales, and British America
                and of English Books Printed in Other Countries, 1641–1700,
                2nd ed., 1982–84, accessed via EEBO

INTRODUCTION

   1. Thomas Hunter, *An English Carmelite: The Life of Catharine Burton,*
Mother Mary Xaveria of the Angels, of the English Teresian Convent at Antwerp (London: Burns and Oates, 1876), 272–73.
   2. Quoted in Nicky Hallett, *Lives of Spirit: English Carmelite Self-Writing*
of the Early Modern Period (Aldershot: Ashgate, 2007), 166, her ellipses and

brackets. In accordance with editorial policy for the series in which this volume appears, I have expanded contractions in quotations from this edition; such expansions are indicated by italics.

3. Hunter, *English Carmelite*, 273.

4. Hallett asserts, "[T]he Antwerp papers were most probably compiled directly as a result" of the discovery of the incorrupt body of Mary Margaret of the Angels (*Lives of Spirit*, 9). The texts, which include first-person accounts by the nuns as well as accounts written by others, were compiled by Mary Howard (in religion Mary Joseph of St. Theresa), who remained "anonymous until the point in the narrative at which her own Life appears, some 26 years after she began" (10).

5. Ibid., 98; Hallett's ellipses and brackets. It is to the "Life of Mary Xaveria" (Catherine Burton, who lived from 1668 to 1714) that Thomas Hunter appends his account of the discovery of the incorrupt body of Mary Margaret of the Angels.

6. Ibid., 9.

7. Ibid., 147.

8. Ibid., 2.

9. Ibid., 98–99.

10. Ibid., 11. Hallett points out the wider presence of such a concept of the self in the Christian tradition, saying, "Ideas of a reiterative, relational self are at the heart, of course, of a biblical interpretive typology of fulfillment and salvation in which successive selves co-exist with others in a figurative, teleological framework founded on Christ as the second Adam. They are therefore naturally central to the mimetic tradition this in turn draws upon—of Christians mirroring their Saviour in exemplary lives, and of later devout individuals following a saintly precursor" (28–29). My focus, though, as should already begin to be clear, is not on simple mirroring or imitation.

11. Hunter, *English Carmelite*, 275.

12. Ibid., 276.

13. Ibid.

14. As Hallett observes, in the "Carmelite papers . . . Catholics represent themselves as true patriots, praying for the 'poor distressed country of England,' and it is the apparently marginalized who occupy positions of perceived centrality, claiming continuity within a pre-lapsarian spatial poetic, their 'paradise upon earth'" (*Lives of Spirit*, 2).

15. Ibid., 5.

16. Ibid., 5 n. 2. I include an extended discussion of exiled English nuns' involvement with the English Royalist cause in chapter 3. The Antwerp nuns' own interest in publicizing the divine blessing bestowed on their community through

the body's preservation, as well as in cultivating the community's long-term and ongoing reputation for holiness (an interest attested by the fact that some of the life writings seem to have been destined for wider circulation than simply among the nuns) is connected not only to their involvement with English politics but also to their involvement in power struggles within the Carmelite order. As Hallett notes, the Discalced women religious faced "successive challenges from the friars of the Order" and correspondingly sought "consistently" to "restate their rights in a line of succession from the Saint [i.e., St. Teresa]" (29).

17. For information on the nuns' family connections, see ibid., 5, 193–94.

18. Such binarism, though still pervasive, is not, of course, universal, and I am certainly not the first to challenge it. An excellent departure from this either/or perspective is Anthony Milton's *Catholic and Reformed: The Roman and Protestant Churches in English Protestant Thought, 1600–1640* (Cambridge: Cambridge University Press, 1995). Alexandra Walsham's scholarship also provides exemplary models of a more nuanced stance: see, for example, *Church Papists: Catholics, Conformity, and Confessional Polemic in Early Modern England* (Woodbridge: Boydell, 1999). For more recent efforts to paint a more subtle picture of the religious landscape in early modern England, see the essays collected in the volume *Catholics and the "Protestant Nation": Religion, Politics, and Identity in Early Modern England*, ed. Ethan Shagan (Manchester: Manchester University Press, 2005).

19. Jonathan Dollimore, in *Radical Tragedy: Religion, Ideology, and Power in the Drama of Shakespeare and His Contemporaries* (Brighton: Harvester, 1984), presents what I see as an especially problematic interpretation of medieval and early modern subjectivities when he describes the Middle Ages as a period in which "Christian essentialism . . . simply disallowed the idea of the autonomous, unified self-generating subject" (155). The widespread view that the Renaissance discovered the past's alterity is related; just as the individual was purportedly merely an element of an undifferentiated whole in the Middle Ages, so too, as Catherine Sanok summarizes the view, "the Middle Ages knew only one 'homogenous' or undifferentiated 'temporality' structured by typological correspondences between events or by eschatology, in which the temporal order of the secular world is dissolved" (*Her Life Historical: Exemplarity and Female Saints' Lives in Late Medieval England* [Philadelphia: University of Pennsylvania Press, 2007], 176).

20. Dollimore, *Radical Tragedy*, 155–56. The quote from Walter Ullmann comes from *The Individual and Society in the Middle Ages* (London: Metheun, 1967), 48.

21. Dollimore, *Radical Tragedy*, 179.

22. Rachel Fulton and Bruce Holsinger, introduction to *History in the Comic Mode: Medieval Communities and the Matter of Person*, ed. Rachel Fulton and Bruce Holsinger (New York: Columbia University Press, 2007), 4.

23. Though the figures and forms of community under consideration are rather different from the ones I analyze in this project, Michael Questier's magisterial book *Catholicism and Community in Early Modern England: Politics, Aristocratic Patronage, and Religion, c. 1550–1640* provides a useful account of a politically involved and textually engaged segment of the English Catholic population.

24. In other words, not only do I wish to reiterate David Aers's "whisper in the ear of the early modernists" that "their" form of the subject exists in the medieval period, but I also want to stress that the early modern subject was not always, and not simply, one that, to adopt Catherine Belsey's influential description of Hamlet (that icon of a supposedly new form of Renaissance subjectivity), is possessed of "an authentic inner reality defined by its difference from an inauthentic exterior" (quoted in David Aers, "A Whisper in the Ear of Early Modernists; or, Reflections of Literary Critics Writing the 'History of the Subject,'" in *Culture and History, 1350–1600: Essays on English Communities*, ed. David Aers [Detroit: Wayne State University Press, 1992], 189).

25. Like Fulton and Holsinger, as well as the contributors to their collection of essays, I seek to "tak[e] up the category of the person, and in particular . . . the 'matter of person' in relation to community: the forms of mediation, materiality, incarnation, representation, and transcendence that go into the making of the . . . human being in all its individual and collective complexity" (Fulton and Holsinger, introduction, 5). My approach differs from that of the editors of and contributors to *History in the Comic Mode* in that my focus is on the medieval and the early modern together.

26. Susanne Woods, introduction to *The Poems of Aemilia Lanyer: Salve Deus Rex Judaeorum*, ed. Susanne Woods (New York: Oxford University Press, 1993) xv.

27. I take the term *(auto)biographical* from Douglas Catterall, who says, "The term (auto)biography is used to indicate that from the perspective of the present we are looking at biographical information; it was also autobiographical with respect to its contemporary generation" (Douglas Catterall, "Drawing Lives and Memories from the Everyday Words of the Early Modern Era," *Sixteenth Century Journal* 36.3 [2005]: 652 n. 8).

28. See Carolyn Dinshaw's observations on this point in her essay "Margery Kempe," in *The Cambridge Companion to Medieval Women's Writing*, ed. Carolyn Dinshaw and David Wallace (Cambridge: Cambridge University Press, 2003), 222–39.

CHAPTER 1. THE INCARNATIONAL AND THE INTERNATIONAL

1. Some scholars have made arguments concerning potential influences among Birgitta, Catherine, and Julian. Mary Ann Folmarr discusses the potential role Catherine might have played in shaping Julian's spirituality, noting ties between East Anglia and Siena ("St. Catherine of Siena and Julian of Norwich: A Message of Hope for the Church," *Congresso Internazionale di Studi Cateriniani [1980 Siena]*, 110–20). Julia Bolton Holloway suggests that book 5 of St. Birgitta's *Revelations* may have influenced Catherine's *Dialogue* ("Saint Birgitta of Sweden, Saint Catherine of Siena: Saints, Secretaries, Scribes, Supporters," *Birgittiana* 1 [1996]: 35–36). She also compares the writings of Julian, Catherine, and Birgitta, saying that the *Dialogue* "is closer in strategy to Julian's *Showings*, though Julian, like Birgitta, uses intensely memorable images and parables. But Julian's images are homely ones, rather than regal, private, rather than public" (36). As my subsequent discussion of these figures will reveal, I do not necessarily see the same sorts of dichotomies (especially between private and public) that shape Holloway's interpretation. F. Thomas Luongo also notes the close connection between St. Birgitta and St. Catherine, even as he contrasts their writings, saying, "Catherine was recruited as a second Birgitta by churchmen who must have seen her as the inheritor of a tradition of visionary women in Italy and Europe. But Catherine's letters in their form, content, and style were a very different sort of literature than Birgitta's *Revelations*. Catherine's letters show almost no interest at all in eschatological claims or predictions, and show little if any influence of Joachimite and other traditions of prophetic literature current in Italian culture" (*The Saintly Politics of Catherine of Siena* [Ithaca: Cornell University Press, 2006], 73). Other considerations of potential influence include that suggested by Jane Chance, who argues that the vineyard imagery that shapes the Middle English translation of Catherine's *Dialogue* for the Brigittine nuns of Syon may have come from Birgitta's revelations ("St. Catherine of Siena in Late Medieval Britain: Feminizing Literary Reception through Gender and Class," *Annali d'Italianistica* 13 [1995]: 168–69). However, such imagery also appears frequently in Catherine's writings, so it also seems possible to me that the translator chose it precisely because it is shared by Catherine and Birgitta.

2. Holloway, "Saint Birgitta," 33, 37.

3. Luongo, *Saintly Politics*, 73.

4. Holloway says of this image, "In a remarkable fresco, painted in 1368, over twenty years later than Birgitta's initial papal diplomacy, we see living supporters of the Church and the Empire, at the centre of which are Pope Urban V and the Emperor Charles IV of Bohemia, who were both in Rome on October 21,

1368. . . . Flanking the Pope and Emperor are such figures as King Peter of Cyprus, to be murdered in 1369, and whose widow, Queen Eleanor, Birgitta of Sweden would meet in 1372 and to whom Catherine of Siena would write . . . while on the left we see a humble Dominican *mantellata*, who is thought to be St. Catherine, and on the right an aging widow, who is most likely St. Birgitta" ("Saint Birgitta," 31).

5. Suzanne Noffke, ed., *The Letters of Catherine of Siena*, 3 vols., Medieval and Renaissance Texts and Studies, vols. 202, 203, 329 (Tempe: Arizona Center for Medieval and Renaissance Studies, 2001–7), T140, 1:80. Hereafter I will cite St. Catherine's letters from these volumes parenthetically in the text, indicating the letter number (beginning with "T"), followed by the volume number and the page number.

6. There is some evidence St. Catherine of Siena may have corresponded with Richard II in support of Pope Urban VI and the Roman papacy, and, as Jeremy Finnegan points out, "Catherinian material" may have been sent to Henry IV for the same purpose (Jeremy Finnegan, "St. Catherine in England: *The Orcherd of Syon*," *Spirituality Today* 32 [1980]: 14).

7. On the use of St. Birgitta's revelations in Anglo-French political affairs, see Nancy Bradley Warren, *Spiritual Economies: Female Monasticism in Later Medieval England* (Philadelphia: University of Pennsylvania Press, 2001), ch. 5, especially 113–14.

8. Jane Chance notes, "There abound manuscripts of breviaries in Scotland dating from the fifteenth and sixteenth century whose provenance is marked by the telltale coupling in their calendars of St. Catherine of Siena . . . and St. Birgitta" ("St. Catherine of Siena," 171). Holloway, in "Saint Birgitta," points to a further connection between the Brigittine and Caterinian circles, indicating that the Latin text of the *Dialogue* used for the base text of the Middle English *Orcherd* was that made by Ser Christofano di Gano Guidini, who was responsible for translating Brigittine texts into Sienese Italian. Jane Chance, in "St. Catherine of Siena," suggests that Guidini's Latin text likely came to England through the Dominicans or perhaps through the Carthusians of Mountgrace of Sheen (175), the latter community having, as is well known, close ties with Syon. Elizabeth Armstrong suggests that this translation has important political ramifications. She argues, "The addition of Katherine's text to Bridget's Syon . . . suggests an unusual, perhaps daring, programmatic intention if we consider, as Phyllis Hodgson does, how unwelcoming the times were for such texts or such foundations: 'The new interest in women mystics was to remain a matter of controversy. The very year of the foundation of Syon (1415)

and only seven months after the canonization of St. Bridget was confirmed at the Council of Constance, Gerson was to assert that 'All words and works of women must be held suspect.'. . . The mighty translation of St. Catherine's Book no less than the royal foundation of Syon can be regarded as an English affirmation of credence" (Elizabeth Psakis Armstrong, "Informing the Mind and Stirring up the Heart: Katherine of Siena at Syon," in *Studies in St. Birgitta and the Brigittine Order*, vol. 2, Analecta Cartusiana 35:19, ed. James Hogg [Salzburg: Institut für Anglistik und Amerikanistik, Universität Salzburg, 1993], 171).

9. Finnegan, "St. Catherine in England," 14.

10. Ibid.

11. Holloway, "St. Birgitta," 43–44.

12. Aubrey Gwynn, *The Austin Friars in the Time of Wyclif* (London: Oxford University Press, 1940), 144–45.

13. Benedict Hackett, "Catherine of Siena and William of England: A Curious Partnership," *Proceedings of the Patristic, Mediaeval, and Renaissance Conference* 5 (1980): 32–33. For extensive further discussion of the relationship between St. Catherine and William Flete, see Benedict Hackett, *William Flete, O.S.A., and Catherine of Siena: Masters of Fourteenth Century Spirituality* (Villanova, PA: Augustinian Press, 1992).

14. Hackett, "Catherine of Siena," 39.

15. I also discuss the role of the circulation of letters as incarnational texts in creating communities founded on incarnational spirituality in the section of chapter 3 dealing with Luisa de Carvajal y Mendoza.

16. Aemilia Lanyer, "To the doubtfull Reader," in *The Poems of Aemilia Lanyer: Salve Deus Rex Judaeorum*, ed. Susanne Woods (New York: Oxford University Press, 1993), 139. All further quotations from Aemilia Lanyer's *Salve Deus Rex Judaeorum* are taken from this volume and are cited parenthetically in the text, by line numbers for poetry and by page numbers for prose. As Woods's introduction points out, in this passage, "[a] generation before Milton, Aemilia Lanyer professes herself to be God's poet" (xii).

17. "The Description of Cooke-ham," one of the first (and quite possibly the first) English country house poems, focuses on the time Lanyer spent at this estate with a group of women including Margaret, Duchess of Cumberland, and Margaret's daughter Anne Clifford.

18. John Henry Blunt, ed., *The Myroure of Oure Ladye*, EETS, e.s., 19 (London: Kegan Paul, 1873), 18; hereafter cited parenthetically in the text.

19. On the Virgin Mary as "translator" of the divine Logos in Brigittine devotional culture, see Warren, *Spiritual Economies*, 53–54.

20. Incarnational piety pervaded St. Birgitta's own devotional life. As her *vita* reveals, the Virgin Mary aided St. Birgitta in one of her childbirths, and Birgitta's *imitatio Christi* included re-embodying Christ's passion through such ascetic practices as creating wounds in her palms with hot candle wax and placing the bitter herb gentian in her mouth (see "A Life of St. Bridget," in *The Liber celestis of St. Bridget of Sweden*, ed. Roger Ellis, EETS, o.s., 291 [Oxford: Oxford University Press, 1987], 1—5). She participates mystically in Christ's birth and crucifixion, and in the latter sequence of events she experiences the Virgin Mary's suffering as well as Christ's (on St. Birgitta's well-known mystical experience of the Nativity, see *Liber celestis*, 485—87; for examples of her many mystical engagement with the Passion, see, for instance, *Liber celestis*, 20—22, 313—15). Incarnational paradigms also pervade the origins, texts, and daily devotional practices of the monastic order that St. Birgitta founded. Christ mystically revealed the order's rule to St. Birgitta, though during the papal confirmation process for the rule ecclesiastical officials required references to the rule's divine origins to be removed. On the origins of the rule and the complex process of papal approval, see Roger Ellis, *Viderunt eam filie Syon: The Spirituality of the English House of a Medieval Contemplative Order from Its Beginnings to the Present Day*, Analecta Cartusiana 68 (Institut für Anglistik und Amerikanistik, Universität Salzburg, 1984).

21. James Hogg, ed., *The Rewyll of Seynt Sauioure*, vol. 2 of *The Rewyll of Seynt Sauioure and Other Middle English Brigittine Legislative Texts*, Salzburger Studien zur Anglistik und Amerikanistik 6 (Salzburg: Institut für Englische Sprache und Literatur, Universität Salzburg), 42r, hereafter cited parenthetically in the text; expansions are indicated by italics. In her analysis of the Anglo-Saxon lyric sequence *Christ I*, Lara Farina makes observations about the treatment of the Virgin Mary and the body in that text that are startlingly applicable to the *Myroure*. She says that the text "focuses on the embodiment of the Word and on the uses of material bodies as a way to knowing God." The body is "a tool in the production of knowledge. . . . Mary's body is positioned as an epistemological medium for sacred understanding" (*Erotic Discourse and Early English Religious Writing* [New York: Palgrave Macmillan, 2006], 30—31).

22. St. Birgitta had her own experience of reliving an aspect of Mary's experience in the process of Christ's incarnation: "It fell on þe Cristemas night þat þe spouse, with one passing gladsomnes of hir hert, felid as it had bene a whike childe sterringe in hir hert. And at þe hye mes, þe modir of merci apperid to hir and saide, 'Doghtir, right as þou wote noȝt how þat gladnes and stirynge com so sodanli to þe bi þe sonde of God, so þe comminge of mi son to me

was wondirfull and sodaine. And also sone as I assentid to þe aungels message, I felid in me a wondirfull whike steringe child'" (*Liber celestis*, 460).

23. Nicholas Watson and Jacqueline Jenkins, eds., *The Writings of Julian of Norwich: A Vision Showed to a Devout Woman and a Revelation of Love* (University Park: Pennsylvania State University Press, 2006), 147; hereafter all quotations from Julian of Norwich's writings are from this edition and are cited parenthetically in the text. Similarly, Julian recounts a vision of the dying Christ with almost clinical attention to corporeal detail: "After this, Crist shewde a parte of his passion nere his dying. I saw the swete face as it were drye and blodeles with pale dying; and sithen more deade pale, languring; and than turned more deade into blew; and sithen more browne blew, as the flesh turned more depe dede. For his passion shewde to me most properly in his blessed face, and namely in his lippes, there I saw these four colours—tho that were before fresh and rody, lively and liking to my sight. This was a swemfulle change, to se this depe dying" (179). Julian's mystical participation in the Passion also includes involvement with Marian compassion. She says: "Here I saw in parte the compassion of our lady, Saint Mary. For Crist and she was so oned in love that the gretnes of her love was cause of the mekillehede of her paine. For in this I saw a substance of kinde love, continued by grace, that his creatures have to him, which kinde love was most fulsomly shewde in his swete mother, and overpassing. For so mekille as she loved him more then alle other, her paine passed alle other. Forever the higher, the mightier, the swetter that the love is, the more sorow is to the lover to se that body in paine that he loved. And so alle his disciples, and all his tru lovers suffered paines more than ther awne bodely dying" (185). As I hope my subsequent discussion of Julian's text will make clear, I agree with David Aers that Julian's experience of the Crucifixion is not simply an iteration of "the dominant commonplace of late medieval devotion" (David Aers, "The Humanity of Christ: Reflections on Julian of Norwich's *Revelation of Love*," in *The Powers of the Holy: Religion, Politics, and Gender in Late Medieval English Culture*, ed. David Aers and Lynn Staley [University Park: Pennsylvania State University Press, 1996], 82). I do, though, see rather more of a role for affect, and a stronger connection between affect and "theological reflections on the trinity" (Aers, "Humanity of Christ," 82), than does Aers.

24. As Chance notes, "English readers in the fifteenth and sixteenth centuries perceived the Christlike bridge as an important unifying metaphor for the whole book and therefore also as a symbol for St. Catherine as author and mediator" ("St. Catherine of Siena," 176).

25. Phyllis Hodgson and G. M. Liegey, eds., *The Orcherd of Syon,* EETS, o.s., 258 (London: Oxford University Press, 1966), 62.

26. Ibid., 70–71.

27. Frederick Bauerschmidt, *Julian of Norwich and the Mystical Body Politic of Christ* (Notre Dame: University of Notre Dame Press, 1999), 50.

28. Stanley Cavell, *The Claim of Reason: Wittgenstein, Skepticism, Morality, and Tragedy* (New York: Oxford University Press, 1999), 356. I am very grateful to my colleague Ralph Berry for introducing me to Cavell's work and for many illuminating conversations about both Wittgenstein and *The Claim of Reason.* Claudia Papka's observation about St. Catherine seems equally applicable to Julian's *Showings* and to at least some Brigittine texts (though Birgitta does at times portray herself as a conduit or channel for divine messages). Papka states, "But while Caterina did experience mystical ecstasies, and did speak and act publicly, she does not make the rhetorical connection between the two through self-annihilation, as Raimondo would have it, but rather through somaticized assimilation to Christ" ("The Written Woman Writes: Caterina da Siena between History and Hagiography, Body and Text," *Annali d'Italianistica* 13 [1995]: 145).

29. Mary O'Driscoll, "Women and the Dominican Charism, with Particular Reference to Catherine of Siena," *Angelicum* 81 (2004): 450. Thomas McDermott observes that Catherine makes a related assertion of the connections linking knowledge of God, oneself, and others in the *Dialogue,* in which Catherine speaks "of the 'knowledge of yourself and of me in yourself' or 'the goodness of God in oneself' and of the necessity of keeping both kinds of knowledge together" ("Catherine of Siena's Teaching on Self-Knowledge," *New Blackfriars* 88 [2007]: 643).

30. Caroline Walker Bynum, *Holy Feast and Holy Fast: The Religious Significance of Food to Medieval Women* (Berkeley: University of California Press, 1987), 175. As Papka points out, Catherine "persistently emphasize[s] body . . . as integral to the mystical experience, empowering and sanctifying, signifying the presence of Christ in human flesh" ("Written Woman Writes," 132).

31. Suzanne Noffke argues, "Catherine's understanding of the incarnation of the Word, and of redemption as the whole object of that incarnation, is nested inextricably in her understanding of our creation in God's Trinitarian image and likeness. . . . Incarnation/redemption is a divine, a Trinitarian affair. . . . But it is also a human, physical affair" (Suzanne Noffke, "The Physical in the Mystical Writings of Catherine of Siena," *Annali d'Italianistica* 13 [1995)]: 113).

32. Mary Zimmer, "'Two Bodies with One Soul': Catherine of Siena's Incarnational Model of Christian Mysticism," *Studia Mystica* 19 (1998): 25 n.15.

33. Ibid.

34. C. Annette Grisé has discussed the importance of the written word in defining communal identity at Syon. In her account of the Brigittine nuns' ritual for profession, for example, she observes that the "formal submission to practically every legal and regulatory document that the Abbey possessed marked the importance accorded to textual expressions of the house's governance and rule. The nun's public and oral declaration of her acceptance of this practice seals her obedience to the written word; she further promises to uphold the written word in her behaviour" ("The Textual Community of Syon Abbey," *Florilegium* 19 (2002): 152–53). The interplay of texts and bodies in Brigittine monastic life creates, however, a community that is something more than a textual community in the sense that Grisé, following Brian Stock, uses the term, important though such a conception of communal life no doubt was for Syon.

35. Armstrong, "Informing the Mind," 176.

36. Cavell, *Claim of Reason*, 369. David Hillman has argued that the "problem of certainty and doubt is intimately tied to the so-called problem of other minds, which . . . is in turn inseparable from the problem of other bodies" ("The Inside Story," in *Historicism, Psychoanalysis, and Early Modern Culture*, ed. Carla Mazzio and Douglas Trevor [New York: Routledge, 2000], 305). Hillman also turns to Cavell's work in grappling with these issues of knowledge, minds, and bodies. In positing the relationship between the problem of other minds and the problem of other bodies, he states, "I am relying here upon the work of Stanley Cavell, who, following the later work of Wittgenstein, has characterized the problem as one of finding 'the correct relation between inner and outer, between the self and society'" (305–6).

37. As E. Catherine Dunn indicates, the "method of reading advocated" in the *Myroure* "is much in the spirit of the *lectio divina* prescribed in the *Rule* of St. Benedict, although the writer does not cite such an original. He makes practical suggestions for the choice of reading material, e.g., that a person should not select a severe ascetical treatise at a time when he or she is suffering from melancholy or tribulation. He distinguishes clearly between books that are directed to the understanding, with a cognitive approach, and those that are meant to stir the emotions with an affective appeal (69–70). He indicates that the Bridgettine office and its lectionary move freely back and forth from cognitive to affective address, and it is clear that he envisions not only the community recitation of this office but also an individual program of frequent private reading" ("*The Myroure of Oure Ladye*: Syon Abbey's Role in the Continuity of English Prose," in *Diakonia: Studies in Honor of Robert T. Meyer*, ed. Thomas Holten

and Joseph P. Williman [Washington, DC: Catholic University of America Press, 1986], 115). Roger Ellis views the joining of heart and mind in Brigittine spirituality as "twin movements of the soul" ("A Note on the Spirituality of St. Birgitta of Sweden," in *Spiritualität Heute und Gestern*, 3 vols., Analecta Cartusiana 35 [Salzburg: Universität Salzburg, 1982–83], 1:157–66).

38. In their notes on this passage, Watson and Jenkins observe, "In contemplative theology, self-knowledge is a stage on the way to God. . . . Here, however, the model is daringly reversed, as the quest for self-knowledge becomes a quest for the integration of sensuality and substance in which God is for a few lines seen, not as the end of contemplation, but as the means by which the self comes to know the self" (*Writings of Julian*, 300). Christopher Abbott argues that an important theme in Julian's writings is the "theme of the indivisibility of self-knowledge and knowledge of God," an idea that is "particularly strong in medieval monastic tradition" and "is nevertheless especially associated with St. Augustine and brought into sharp focus in his autobiographical *Confessions*" (*Julian of Norwich: Autobiography and Theology* [Cambridge: D. S. Brewer, 1999], 10). In an essay on Julian of Norwich in a collection entitled *A History of Women Philosophers*, Elizabeth N. Evasdaughter says the Long Text of the *Showings* contains "a treatise on knowledge, covering the possibility of knowing God, the sources of such knowledge, its limits, and its value" ("Julian of Norwich," in *A History of Women Philosophers*, vol. 2, ed. Mary Ellen Waithe [Dordrecht: Kluwer Academic Publishers, 1990], 191). On Julian and the processes of knowing God, self, and other, see also Nancy Coiner, "The 'Homely' and the Heimlich: The Hidden, Doubled Self in Julian of Norwich's *Showings*," *Exemplaria* 5 (1993): 302–23, and Andrew Sprung, " 'We neuyr shall come out of hym': Enclosure and Immanence in Julian of Norwich's *Book of Showings*," *Mystics Quarterly* 19 (1993): 47–62.

39. Evasdaughter, "Julian of Norwich," 194. Hugh Kempster's analysis of Julian's theology concerning "bodily sights" supports this assessment. He observes that in the Long Text "the phrases 'shewyth hym to vs,' 'see owght of hym,' and 'desyer to see hym' are all packed with immediate corporeal visionary significance (C and W, 325–6)" ("Julian of Norwich: The Westminster Text of *A Revelation of Love*," *Mystics Quarterly* 23.4 [1997]: 191). Kempster goes on to align Julian's position on bodily sights with that of Thomas Aquinas in the *Summa theologica*. He states, "Aquinas is faced with a dilemma: traditional Augustinian orthodoxy holds that the highest form of vision is intellectual, yet the most Christologically significant biblical vision, the Annunciation, is profoundly corporeal. He resolves the tension by asserting that 'The angel of the Annunciation

appeared in a bodily vision to the Blessed Virgin' and backs this up by a broader reading of Augustine's theology. In these instances both Aquinas and Julian move beyond a simplistic understanding of Augustinian mystical theology in order to reconcile their fresh insight with traditional orthodoxy. In place of an inflexible hermeneutical model, both theologians construct an original and lively re-interpretation" (192). He also notes that rather than simply warning against the unorthodoxy of bodily sights and the desire for them, as Ruysbroek does in his *Spiritual Espousals,* "Julian embraces the tension between mystical experience and traditional orthodoxy, and a deeper theological understanding is born as a result." On Julian's adoption of, and also her challenges to, Augustinian epistemology, especially her revisions of the Augustinian hierarchy of reason and sensuality, see Jennifer Bryan, *Looking Inward: Devotional Reading and the Private Self in Late Medieval England* (Philadelphia: University of Pennsylvania Press, 2008), 146–48. Marion Glasscoe also discusses Julian's epistemology with reference to the incarnation of Christ. She observes that Julian "uses the language and assumptions of medieval theology but illuminates them through her psychological understanding of the realities they seek to discover. Her text is grounded in an understanding—she would say 'connyng'—of the Incarnation, not apprehended primarily in intellectual terms but experienced as a catalyst which transfigures everyday experience" ("Means of Showing: An Approach to Reading Julian of Norwich," *Analecta Cartusiana* 106 [1983]: 156). Later, she continues, "Julian's epistemology, whether consciously or unconsciously, is Augustinian in its confidence that despite the ineffability of God, the Incarnation has not only revealed his word in Christ, but made it possible to use the medium of language, limited as it is to the created world of sense impression and natural reason to provide signs whereby we may know God, not directly or completely, but as in a mirror by faith. . . . [T]he perception of reality of which the words are signs is God-given through incarnation" (176). Karma Lochrie's discussion of *imitatio Christi,* the body, and cognition in the first chapter of her *Margery Kempe and Translations of the Flesh* (Philadelphia: University of Pennsylvania Press, 1991) is also relevant to my understanding of Julian's epistemology.

40. Nicholas Watson, "'Yf Wommen Be Double Naturelly': Remaking 'Woman' in Julian of Norwich's *Revelation of Love,*" *Exemplaria* 8.1 (1996): 5. Abbott makes a related argument regarding Julian's processes of acquiring knowledge. He focuses on chapter 24 of the Long Text, in which Julian enters Christ's side, stating, "[A]lthough the literary illusion here is substantially the discovery of a space within the Christ-figure, it is, more significantly, the means

by which Julian conveys her discovery of a space within herself. . . . According to the logic of the image, understanding grows to the extent that it is led further into Christ" (*Julian of Norwich*, 72).

41. As Ludwig Wittgenstein observes, "[A]n 'inner process' stands in need of outward criteria" (*Philosophical Investigations*, 153e sec. 580). My thinking about the implications of incarnationality for epistemological processes, as well as my thinking about the relationships of medieval and early modern, has been deeply influenced by the work of Sarah Beckwith and David Aers. Particularly important here are Aers's essay "New Historicism and the Eucharist," *Journal of Medieval and Early Modern Studies* 33.2 (2003): 241–59, and Beckwith's essay "Stephen Greenblatt's *Hamlet* and the Forms of Oblivion," *Journal of Medieval and Early Modern Studies* 33.2 (2003): 261–80.

42. P. M. S. Hacker, *Wittgenstein on Human Nature* (London: Weidenfeld and Nicolson, 1997), 43. One might also argue, to adopt Elizabeth Grosz's evocative conceptualization, that the inner and the outer exist in a relationship comparable to a Möbius strip: "Bodies and minds are not two distinct substances or two kinds of attributes of a single substance but somewhere in between these two alternatives. The Möbius strip has the advantage of showing the inflection of mind into body and body into mind. This model also provides a way of problematizing and rethinking the relations between the inside and the outside of the subject, its psychical interior and corporeal exterior, by showing not their fundamental identity or reducibility but the torsion of the one into the other, the passage, vector, or uncontrollable drift of the inside into the outside and the outside into the inside" (*Volatile Bodies: Toward a Corporeal Feminism* [Bloomington: Indiana University Press, 1994], xii).

43. Watson and Jenkins write of this passage, "God's dwelling place in the soul is at the point of union between the substance, which dwells in him, and the sensuality, which is separate, fallen, and redeemed. The place is analogous to the union between divine and human in Christ" (*Writings of Julian*, 298, note to lines 21–22). In their introduction, they also call attention to the significance of this passage, saying, "As the work expounds a new model of the human soul (divided into substance and sensuality), its solution to the controversial problem of how creature and creator can be imagined as one without violating their distinctness finally turns on the most academically subtle shift in word order: 'For I saw full sekerly [very surely] that oure substance is in God. And also I saw that in our sensualite God is'" (8).

44. Nicholas Watson, "Desire for the Past," in *Maistresse of My Wit: Medieval Women, Modern Scholars*, ed. Louise D'Arcens and Juanita Feros Ruys (Turnhout: Brepols, 2004), 162.

45. Karl Frederick Morrison, *"I Am You": The Hermeneutics of Empathy in Western Literature, Theology, and Art* (Princeton: Princeton University Press, 1988), xxvi.

46. Joab Rosenberg, review of *The Claim to Community: Essays on Stanley Cavell and Political Philosophy,* ed. Andrew Norris, *European Journal of Philosophy* 16.1 (2008): 154. Bauerschmidt makes an observation about Julian that clarifies the nature of intersubjectivity. He says that Julian advances a "participatory model of knowing, in which there is a mutual interpenetration of subject and object" (*Julian of Norwich,* 34).

47. This episode from the *Showings* prompts me to add a corrective "whisper" of my own to scholars who argue for the emergence in the early modern period of a dramatically new understanding of the relationship of selfhood and embodiment. For instance, in an analysis of Caravaggio's *Incredulity of St. Thomas* and Dürer's self-portraits, Jonathon Sawday writes of the emergence in the seventeenth century not of "'selfhood' but the modern idea of 'corporeality'" (*The Body Emblazoned: Dissection and the Human Body in Renaissance Culture* [New York: Routledge, 1996], 48). He states that "'Embodiment'. . . is the object of enquiry in Caravaggio's depiction of St. Thomas searching the wounds of his saviour. . . . '[E]mbodiment' now meant far more than the representation of the surface of the body" (36). Sawday calls Dürer's depiction of himself pointing at the source of his pain in his side "a generalized meditation on Christ's passion, interiorized to the point where it has become part of the subjective experience of the individual believer. . . . Pointing to his own wound, Dürer has re-enacted Christ's passion; he has discovered the Christ within" (42). Julian's reincarnation of Christ's pains in her own body, and the sophisticated incarnational epistemology that proceeds from this experience, clearly anticipate the ideas and modes of knowledge that Sawday interprets as something new in the works of Caravaggio and Dürer. Hence, understandings of corporeal subjectivity and an emphasis on embodiment are not necessarily, as Sawday indicated, connected to autopsy and the rise of anatomy as a subject of study. Embodiment is therefore not, as he claims, "a project of a Europe-wide artistic, philosophical and scientific programme which spanned nearly 150 years" in the sixteenth and seventeenth centuries (48). Rather, it has a much longer history, and early modern interest in embodiment ought to be explored in dialogue with medieval considerations of embodiment.

48. David Aers's discussion of the role of Christ in catalyzing knowledge in *Piers Plowman* is revelant to my argument. In *Salvation and Sin,* Aers writes, "Only *after* Wille has seen the Samaritan, with Faith and Hope, does he become aware of the true consequences of the violent activity of thieves in what is now

perceived as a 'wilde wildernesse.' He discerns a man beaten, stripped naked, and bound so that he cannot move. . . . This is . . . Semyuief (XIX. 53–58). The point . . . is that only in the light of Christ's way, the way to his 'ioust' on the Cross against the powers of evil, can humans adequately discern the effects of sin. Through Christ's presence we are enabled to see what has not been seen in the poem's multivarious, inventive representations of vice: *semivivus*, in English, *semyuief*. That is, humanity has unmade God's good creation into a dangerous wilderness in which the very potentialities of this life are utterly crushed: 'he ny myhte stepe ne stande ne stere foet ne handes / Ne helpe hymsulue' (XIX. 56–57). Only the divine vision, the life of Christ, discloses this reality and the need for God's own journey into the far country where the source of love and life was crucified" (David Aers, *Salvation and Sin: Augustine, Langland, and Fourteenth-Century Theology* [Notre Dame: University of Notre Dame Press, 2009], 100). It is highly significant, I would add, that this epistemological breakthrough so centrally involves an encounter with the suffering, wounded body of Semyuief, and with the divine Word made flesh on the way to his own experience of bodily suffering. Knowledge, as with St. Catherine of Siena, depends on Christ's, and our own, embodiment.

49. Catherine of Siena, *The Dialogue*, ed. and trans. Suzanne Noffke (New York: Paulist Press, 1980), 25.

50. My view of interiority thus contrasts with that of Elaine Scarry. In *The Body in Pain*, Scarry argues that pain, and indeed all that is inner, whether bodily or otherwise, is "something that cannot be denied and something that cannot be confirmed" (*The Body in Pain: The Making and Unmaking of the World* [New York: Oxford University Press, 1985], 13). As David Hillman comments, for Scarry this assessment provides "a good working definition of 'the inner'" ("Inside Story," 305).

51. Jennifer Bryan observes that Julian states "quite plainly that her intimate vision of the Passion was not, in fact, meant to remain private—that as personal and subjective as her visions were, they can mean for humanity in general as much as they mean to her" (*Looking Inward*, 157).

52. Eric Jager, *The Book of the Heart* (Chicago: University of Chicago Press, 2000), 33.

53. My thanks to Anne for this perceptive insight made as a response to a version of this material I presented as a talk at the Faculty Research Lecture Series of the Florida State University Department of English. I would like to thank as well Leigh Edwards for her work in organizing this very helpful and always interesting venue for the exchange of ideas. My analysis of the ways in which

bodies and texts operate as they mutually inform each other builds on the groundbreaking work of Eric Jager in *Book of the Heart* and is indebted to Karma Lochrie's influential *Margery Kempe and Translations of the Flesh*. However, my views depart from Jager's and Lochrie's in some important respects. *The Book of the Heart* largely preserves segregations between medieval and early modern, Catholic and Protestant, manuscript and print cultures, that I strive to break down. For example, in chapter 7, Jager focuses on Flemish paintings representing devotional reading and Eucharistic devotion; he moves in chapter 8, tellingly entitled "After Gutenberg," to address Protestant print culture (though to be fair, Jager does note that the Flemish "portrait of the scribe was actually created several decades *after* the birth of printing" [137], so he does signal that the boundaries between the cultures in question are not entirely firm). Following Terence Cave and Stephen Greenblatt, Jager argues: "For Protestants in particular, new hermeneutical models articulated by scholars such as Erasmus encouraged 'a dynamic imitation or reproduction of Scripture' whereby the text was to be 'wholly absorbed by the reader and located in the *pectus,* that intuitive focus on the self which is presumed to guarantee profound understanding and living expression.' Noting the reciprocity of heart and book in early Protestantism, Stephen Greenblatt described how spiritual writings were 'precisely designed to be absorbed,' so that it is not always clear 'where the book stops and identity begins'" (139). Jager further indicates that print "actually reinforced the Protestant immediacy of self and text" (139). As I will argue—indeed, as I hope I have already begun to make clear—"dynamic imitation and reproduction of Scripture" resulting from a union of reader and text, as well as a difficulty in distinguishing the beginning of the book from the beginning of identity, are not new in the age of Protestantism and print. Nor are they confined in the early modern period either to Protestant culture or to print culture.

While Lochrie concentrates specifically on mystical experience and its textual records, I am interested as well in other forms of female religious experience (for instance, prayer, contemplation, meditation, monastic divine service) and their textual records as loci for, and catalysts of, women's interactions with God. Additionally, Lochrie interprets the mystical text as always necessarily incomplete; in her view, mystical experience of the divine by nature cannot fully be translated into texts, into human language. Mystical experience conveyed textually remains only partially accessible to a reader. For example, she argues: "If mystical desire to utter always exceeds the power to utter God, the divine remains unread as well as unuttered. It is the fissure between flesh and word, utterance and desire which initiates the reader's rapture. Reading the body of Christ leads to a crisis, a hiatus between the living presence of the Word and its Resurrection, for, as Kristeva argues, the Crucifixion occupies that 'caesura' or rupture at the center of the Passion narrative. The mystical text only reproduces this hiatus in and through language. Utterance is 'choked marvelous communication which silences it'" (75). As my exploration of chains of textual relations, of the interactions involving bodies of writers and readers, should already suggest, my focus is on the ways in which texts *can* make embodied experience of the divine accessible for others to reenact. The texts, and the textual relations, upon which I focus do, I contend, achieve that of which the Monk of Farne despairs: "Would that my longing might imprint its own characters on the hearts of them that hear, just as the hand that writes presents them, to the eyes of readers" (quoted in Lochrie, *Margery Kempe,* 56).

54. Papka, "Written Woman Writes," 141–42.

55. F. Thomas Luongo, "Saintly Authorship in the Italian Renaissance: The Quattrocento Reception of Catherine of Siena's Letters," *Journal of the Early Book Society* 8 (2005): 6.

56. Quoted in Martha W. Driver, "Nuns as Patrons, Artists, Readers: Bridgettine Woodcuts in Printed Books Produced for the English Market," in *Art into Life: Collected Papers from the Kresge Art Museum Medieval Symposia,* ed. Carol Garrett Fisher and Kathleen L. Scott (East Lansing: Michigan State University Press, 1995), 237; Driver quotes Patrick O. Moore's translation "in the *Doom of Kings,* from the *Revelations of St. Birgitta of Sweden,* a limited edition of unbound single-leaf prints designed, illustrated, and printed by Jeanette Olender-Papurt (Toledo: The Clarino Press, 1982)" (261 n. 1).

57. Julian writes, "And fro the time that it was shewde, I desyrde oftentimes to witte what was oure lords mening. And fifteen yere after and more, I was answered in gostly understonding, seying thus: 'What, woldest thou wit thy lordes mening in this thing? Wit it wele, love was his mening. Who shewed it the? Love. What shewid he the? Love. Wherfore shewed he it the? For love'" (379). Evasdaughter points out that knowledge and love are bound together for Julian: "Julian held that knowledge of God results in love, that knowledge is necessary to love God, that knowledge is characteristic of divine love and that knowledge is among the gifts God's love gives us" ("Julian of Norwich," 217).

58. My emphases on affect and the performance of texts in my discussion of incarnational textuality resonate in some respects with Stanley Fish's analytical method of "affective stylistics." I do not adhere to his step-by-step approach to tracing the reader's evolving process of making meaning of a text. Broadly, however, my understanding of incarnational textuality shares with Fish's methodology a concern with the text as "an *event,* something that *happens*

to, and with the participation of, the reader" (Stanley Fish, "Literature in the Reader: Affective Stylistics," *New Literary History* 2.1 [1970]: 125, his emphasis). My view of incarnational textuality's performative imperative also shares something with Fish's understanding of "kinetic art," which, as Fish argues, "does not lend itself to a static interpretation because it refuses to stay still and doesn't let you stay still either" (140). However, the incarnational textual paradigm in which I am interested demands adding another set of questions to the one central to Fish's methodology. Fish insists on asking readers to answer the question "What does that . . . do?" (rather than "What does that . . . mean?") (161). Incarnational textuality requires further questions: What does the reader, having read the text, then *do herself or himself*? What does she or he *become* as a result of the textual encounter with another's lived experiences of the divine?

59. Bauerschmidt argues that Julian actually "seeks to *create* readers who will endeavor to perform the drama of divine love scripted in her *Revelation*" (*Julian of Norwich*, 193). Abbott makes a related point, stating that Julian "discovers a unity in Christ between herself and her presumed audience of fellow Christians, a unity upon which the rhetorical character of the text as a whole is predicated and through which it claims an intrinsic theological authorization" (*Julian of Norwich*, 71).

60. Once again, the philosophy of Stanley Cavell is useful, suggesting the ways in which the political enters the picture. Considering Cavell's understanding of the individual, the communal, and the place of language, Joab Rosenberg, in his review of *The Claim to Community*, notes that the "Cavellian blend of individualism and communitarianism is achieved by an emphasis on the role of conversation in the political making of a society. The combination of inherited language with the individual's ability to project new meanings onto words allows for an understanding of both the communal aspects of language and the individual's contribution to its growth" (153–54).

61. Abbott, *Julian of Norwich*, 3.

62. Karen Scott, "Mystical Death, Bodily Death: Catherine of Siena and Raymond of Capua on the Mystic's Encounter with God," in *Gendered Voices: Medieval Saints and Their Interpreters*, ed. Catherine M. Mooney (Philadelphia: University of Pennsylvania Press, 1999), 138; Anna Maria Reynolds, "Some Literary Influences in the *Revelations* of Julian of Norwich," *Leeds Studies in English and Kindred Languages* 78 (1952): 26 n. 40, www.umilta.net/courtesy.html.

63. Contrasting Julian of Norwich's vision of Christ's crucifixion with William Langland's, Aers argues in *Salvation and Sin* that Julian's "choices systematically desocialize and depoliticize the Crucifixion" (147); he indicates that her "treatment of the Crucifixion eliminates the human agency and collective

social practices making this event" (167). Aers makes a compelling case for the theological implications of this vision for the meanings and workings of sin and atonement in Julian's writings. While I agree that Julian's vision of Christ's passion contrasts sharply with Langland's "strange and densely populated joust" (149), I do not fully share Aers's view that Julian's representation of the Crucifixion is depoliticized, dehistoricized, and desocialized. Granted, the social is much smaller in scope for Julian than for Langland at the scene of the Crucifixion; society for Julian at that moment involves her and Christ. However, the possibility of social relationships involving a range of individuals and the crucified Christ enlarges as she meditates upon and theologizes her experience, opening to include all her fellow Christians. The social dimension, for Julian, does not come through representations of those who inflict suffering on Christ but rather involves those who suffer with Christ and who experience divine love. Furthermore, in presenting a crucifixion scene in which she and Christ exist in an intersubjective relationship, and in offering the possibility to others of re-embodying her and Christ's shared experiences (as do the nuns of Cambrai and Paris, as I shall discuss in chapter 2), Julian creates a paradigm of social relations that have significant implications for questions concerned gendered earthly hierarchies that are legitimated and reinforced by positing privileged means of access to the divine.

64. Hodgson and Liegey, *Orcherd of Sion,* 66.

65. Noffke, "Physical in the Mystical," 111.

66. As Karen Scott summarizes, "Raymond stresses that though Catherine received a call to return to the world with a special mission to save souls, from then until her death in 1380 she intensified her life of asceticism and prayer. She continued to fast; she experienced a mystical death, received the stigmata, and had eucharistic visions. . . . Finally, she endured her illnesses and death with great patience, as an offering of prayer to God for the salvation of souls" ("St. Catherine of Siena, Apostola," *Church History* 61.1 [1992]: 35–36).

67. Ibid., 36.

68. See, for example, David Aers's contributions to Aers and Staley, *Powers of the Holy.*

69. Achsah Guibbory indicates that Lanyer "assumes for herself something like the public, priestly power denied to women within the institution of the Christian church. In this assumption of a priestly function, she turns to women's advantage the Protestant emphasis on the priesthood of all believers. But she is also a true descendant of the early Christian women who believed they had the right to preach, and of the medieval holy women who, as Bynum says, 'saw themselves as authorized to teach, counsel, serve, and heal by mysti-

cal experience rather than by office' (*Holy Feast,* p. 235) and thus challenged the exclusive, intimate connection with God enjoyed by the priest" ("The Gospel According to Aemilia," in *Aemilia Lanyer: Gender, Genre, and the Canon,* ed. Marshall Grossman [Lexington: University Press of Kentucky, 1998], 207).

70. Guibbory, suggesting just the sort of continuity that I wish to trace between Lanyer's poem and Catholic devotional traditions, says that "Lanyer's extended attention to" the Virgin Mary "recalls and perhaps revises the devotion to the Virgin Mary that blossomed in medieval Catholicism but withered with Protestantism" ("Gospel According to Amelia," 198). Guibbory further argues, "In what is perhaps a Protestant revision of Catholic mariolatry, the Virgin Mary becomes a pattern for the individual woman's unmediated connection with the divine. Like the Virgin Mary, Lanyer has been 'chosen' to be a vessel for Christ. . . . Thus her poem contains Christ" (206).

71. Susanne Woods, "Vocation and Authorship: Born to Write," in Grossman, *Aemilia Lanyer,* 90.

72. Woods observes that this "*locus amoenus* is most certainly a new place . . . where all the participants are female and where beauty, delight, and harmony are both the natural and artistic consequences. From this place proceeds the countess's psalms, which join art, nature, and the divine harmony, and which also join the attendant ladies with the countess herself" (ibid., 90).

73. Such passages emphasize Lanyer's "unapologetic creation of a community of good women for whom another woman is the spokesperson and commemorator" (Woods, introduction to *Poems of Aemilia Lanyer,* xxxi).

74. Barbara Lewalski, *Writing Women in Jacobean England* (Cambridge, MA: Harvard University Press, 1993), 212 n. 11. For more information on Lanyer's experiences at Cookeham, see the chapter of Lewalski's book entitled "Imagining Female Community: Aemelia Lanyer's Poems."

75. Woods, introduction to *Poems of Aemilia Lanyer,* xxv.

76. Janel Mueller says that these opening lines recount Lanyer's "experience of being called, during her stay there, to a poetic vocation. These enigmatic lines may also intimate that she underwent a conversion; if so, they help to date the onset of the intense religious feeling to which the long title poem of *Salve Deus Rex Judaeorum* bears witness" ("The Feminist Poetics of *Salve Deus Rex Judaeorum,*" in Grossman, *Aemilia Lanyer,* 100).

77. Guibbory argues that "it is far from coincidental that Aemilia Lanyer's poem, with its socially radical interpretation of the Passion as offering a new liberty to women, also implicitly rejects the institution of marriage. Lanyer praises those women whose devotion to Christ has taken the place of earthly, human marriages" ("Gospel According to Amelia," 202).

78. Ibid., 209–10 n. 17.

79. Ibid.

80. As Woods points out, Lanyer's "baroque description of the blood of Christ . . . is not characteristic of Jacobean poetics, but is an early indication of a richly sensuous biblical poetics that we usually associate with that later master of baroque religious imagery, Richard Crashaw" (introduction to *Poems of Aemilia Lanyer,* xxxix).

81. Deborah Shuger, *The Renaissance Bible: Scholarship, Sacrifice, and Subjectivity* (Berkeley: University of California Press, 1994), 115.

82. Guibbory points out that Lanyer "published her version of the Passion, proclaimed her authority as a woman to read and interpret the Bible, and asked for the queen's patronage of her work. Might we not, then, see the *Salve* as in some sense constituting an oppositional alternative to the monumental biblical project of James?" ("Gospel According to Amelia," 193).

83. Shuger, *Renaissance Bible,* 99.

84. In this section, as Guibbory observes, it is not entirely clear who speaks, Pilate's wife or Lanyer. "The confusion of voice is significant, for the poet's identification with Pilate's wife—a woman who also had a dream, whose knowledge came from divine illumination—allows her to speak with and for her. The implication is that both women have not only interpretive power but the right and responsibility to speak publicly" ("Gospel According to Amelia," 199).

85. Naomi Miller, "(M)other Tongues: Maternity and Subjectivity," in Grossman, *Aemilia Lanyer,* 159. See Miller's essay, especially 144–48, for a useful discussion of the place of maternity in *Salve Deus.*

86. Shuger, *Renaissance Bible,* 92.

87. Woods observes that "Christ is . . . very beautiful in Lanyer's vision, as she hold him up to the desiring gaze of women. . . . In both the dedications and the main poem Christ is an object of desire to be admired and consumed by appreciative ladies, with his empowering grace a function of both eucharistic and Petrarchan imagery" ("Vocation and Authorship," 92).

Chapter 2. Medieval Legacies and Female Spiritualities across the "Great Divide"

1. Vera Schwarcz, "Circling the Void: Memory in the Life and Poetry of the Manchu Prince Yihuan (1840–1891)," *History and Memory* 16.2 (2004): 60.

2. On the textual history of Julian's *Showings* in manuscript and print, see Edmund Colledge and James Walsh, *A Book of Showings to the Anchoress Ju-*

lian of Norwich, Part One Introduction and the Short Text (Toronto: Pontifical Institute of Medieval Studies, 1978), 1–18. On a version of Julian's text possibly made by Augustine Baker for the nuns of Cambrai, a version perhaps used by Margaret Gascoigne, see Hywel Wyn Owen and Luke Bell, "The Upholland Anthology: An Augustine Baker Manuscript," *Downside Review* 197, no. 369 (1989): 274–92, especially 280.

3. On the roles of affective and contemplative piety in Julian's spirituality, see Frederick Bauerschmidt, *Julian of Norwich and the Mystical Body Politic of Christ* (Notre Dame: University of Notre Dame Press, 1999), especially 34–36 and 51–57. Bauerschmidt characterizes Julian's spirituality as "neither affective nor contemplative, though containing elements of both" (56).

4. "Records of the Abbey of Our Lady of Consolation at Cambrai, 1620–1793," *Catholic Record Society* 13 (London: Catholic Record Society, 1913), 1.

5. On the history both institutional and intellectual of the Cambrai and Paris nuns, see ibid.; Benedictines of Stanbrook, *In a Great Tradition: Tribute to Dame Laurentia McLachlan, Abbess of Stanbrook* (London: Murray, 1956); and Heather Wolfe, introduction to *Elizabeth Cary, Lady Falkland, Life and Letters*, Medieval and Renaissance Texts and Studies 230 (Tempe, AZ: Center for Medieval and Renaissance Studies, 2001), especially 45–54.

6. The phrase "the way of love" as a description for the Benedictine nuns' distinctive form of spiritual life occurs in Gertrude More's epistle "To the Reader" that precedes *The Spiritual Exercises of the Most Vertuous and Religious D. Gertrude More . . .* (1658, Wing [2nd ed.] M2632), biiii; hereafter cited parenthetically in the text by page number. As will become clear in the course of this chapter, this "unitive" mode of spirituality that Baker fostered among the English Benedictine nuns shares a great deal with the devotional life of the Antwerp Carmelites, similarities that may stem at least in part from a textual connection between the communities. In the mid-1630s "copies of Baker's books were sent to the English Carmelites at Antwerp" (Claire Walker, *Gender and Politics in Early Modern Europe: English Convents in France and the Low Countries* [New York: Palgrave Macmillan, 2003], 145).

7. Benedictines of Stanbrook, *In a Great Tradition*, 12, quote from 13. In fact, the entry in the catalog of the Priory of Our Lady of Good Hope in Paris for the nuns' copy of the Rule of St. Benedict seems to set Baker on a level with St. Benedict himself as an organizing figure for the nuns' mode of monastic life. The entry reads, "The Translation of the Holy Rule of our Holy Father St Benedict Transcribed by the Venerable Father Augustine Baker" (MS Mazarine 4058, 206v). Since the words "Transcribed by the Venerable Father Auguistin Baker" are in red ink, one might even say that Baker is given preeminence over Benedict.

8. Walker, *Gender and Politics,* 134. For a good discussion of the range of approaches to spiritual life that existed in early modern English nunneries, and the tensions surrounding them, see 134–47.

9. Benedictines of Stanbrook, *In a Great Tradition,* 10, 11.

10. Folio numbers for this manuscript are cited parenthetically in the text. See Placid Spearitt, "The Survival of Mediaeval Spirituality among the Exiled English Black Monks," *American Benedictine Review* 25 (1974): 287–309.

11. The commentary on John 21:15 also emphasizes divine love. The biblical text is first given as a heading ("Jesus saith unto Simon Peter, Simon of John Lovest thou Mee more than these? He saith unto Him: yea Lord Thou knowest yt I Love Thee" [65r]), with the following discussion: "[W]hat is there to be Loved but Christ. Certayne it is Love makes like yt wee love" (65r–65v). The passage goes on to treat at some length the transformative nature of love, positing God as the only proper recipient of love because of the love that emanates from God: "God only is to be principally Loved. ffor all other creatures are Either Inferior to us . . . ; or truly Equall with us, haue a created will as wee have. . . . Moreover since Love is a guift and yt a choise and excellent one, it is not to be bestowed but upon one who Recompences Love with Love, and Loves agayne" (65v–66r). In passages from MS Mazarine 1062, italics indicate expanded abbreviations; ampersands have, however, been silently expanded.

12. *Desert* is underlined in the manuscript.

13. Indeed, though Baker frequently expressed opposition to the use of images in prayer for contemplative nuns, a view that constituted part of his strenuous objections to Jesuit forms of devotion, he "urged meditation on the Passion of Christ above all other meditations as the basis for contemplative prayer" (Geoffrey Scott, "The Image of Augustine Baker," in *That Mysterious Man: Essays on Augustine Baker,* ed. Michael Woodward [Abergavenny: Three Peaks, 2001], 113). Geoffrey Scott observes that Baker, "following Blosius, Benet Canfield and Antonio de Rojas, singled out the Passion of Our Lord as the one simple subject fit for 'sensible devotion,' fit to chase away 'seducing images' and a seasonable subject for meditation for 'ignorant and simple persons' as well as 'for the contemplation of the most perfect.' In meditating on the Passion . . . the disciple of Baker was encouraged to adopt the role of Our Lady, Mother of Sorrows" (110). On Baker's views on images, and on his objections to Jesuit techniques of meditation, see especially Scott, "Image of Augustine Baker," 92–94. On Baker and the Jesuits, see also James Gaffney, *Augustine Baker's Inner Light: A Study in English Recusant Spirituality* (Scranton, PA: University of Scranton Press, 1989), especially 147–49. For a useful explanation of

medieval understandings of the operations of affect, and the foundational textual traditions of medieval affective devotion, see ch. 1 of Karma Lochrie, *Margery Kempe and Translations of the Flesh* (Philadelphia: University of Pennsylvania Press, 2001), especially 22–37.

14. Augustine Baker, "Book H," in *Directions for Contemplation (Books F, G,
H)*, Beinecke Rare Books and Manuscript Library, New Haven, Osborn Shelves
b.268, quoted in Heather Wolfe, "Reading Bells and Loose Papers: Reading and
Writing Practices of the English Benedictine Nuns of Cambrai and Paris," in
Early Modern Women's Manuscript Writing, ed. Victoria E. Burke and Jonathan
Gibson (Aldershot: Ashgate, 2004), 139.

15. Ibid., quoted in Wolfe, "Reading Bells," 138. In her *Spiritual Exercises*
Gertrude More also discusses the place of the textual operations of reading and
writing in shaping her spiritual practices. Relating the two textual processes to
each other and to her conception of her identity, she calls herself a "writer
gatherer" (L7r) who writes both to offer her praise to God and to inspire herself to perform her faith in her life (as she says, to "stir up my poor frozen soul"
[L7r]). As Wolfe observes, "This is an instance of the natural progression from
reading to writing back to reading—'I read what I write of thee'—she gathers
matter in order to invent matter, she writes down the matter in order to read it,
she reads it in order to process it and transform it into acts and aspirations that
occur spontaneously and passively (More sig.aixr)" ("Reading Bells," 143).

16. Claire Walker describes the piety of early modern English nuns generally as "an innovative mix of late medieval devotion with the ideas and directives of the post-Reformation Church" (*Gender and Politics*, 133), an assessment
that is quite relevant to the spiritual practices at Cambrai and Paris. She also describes early modern nuns' contemplative piety as a "fusion" of the later medieval and the post-Tridentine (133). That a form of spiritual life strongly rooted
in texts of medieval piety was absolutely fundamental to the nuns' identity and
self-conception is similarly demonstrated by the fact that, in writing the Con-
stitutions for Cambrai's daughter house in Paris, Brigit More (writer of the
French version) and Clementia Cary (writer of the English version) both "carefully stated . . . their desire to continue Dom Augustine's legacy of spiritual
reading and writing" ("Dame Catherine Gascoigne, O.S.B., on Father Augustine Baker's Way of Prayer, from Bibliothèque Mazarine, MS 1202, IV," www
.umilta.net/cath.html, n.d., accessed November 23, 2009). It is also a significant assertion of the place of texts in the spirituality and identity of these nuns
that "many of the manuscripts and printed books that belonged to the Paris
community are inscribed in a seventeenth-century hand: 'This booke belongs

to the English Benedictine nuns of Our Blessed Lady of Good Hope in Paris'"
(Wolfe, "Reading Bells," 136–37).

17. J. T. Rhodes, "Some Writings of a Seventeenth-Century English Benedictine: Dom Augustine Baker, O.S.B.," *Yale University Library Gazette*, April
1993, 111.

18. Quoted in ibid.

19. Though the community of English Benedictine nuns at Brussels from
which nuns were dispatched to train the Cambrai community moved in the direction of the Jesuit approach to spirituality to which Baker and the Cambrai
nuns objected so strenuously, they too had in their library at least some rep-
resentatives of the affective, medieval modes of piety that Baker promoted at
Cambrai. "The 1609 mystical treatise of an English Capuchin friar, William
Fitch (alias Benet Canfield), was dedicated to his cousin Winefrid (Agatha)
Wiseman at Brussels. Canfield's *The Rule of Perfection* combined Franciscan
spirituality with elements of late medieval English mysticism" (Walker, *Gender
and Politics*, 140).

20. The catalog also contains an entry for "Two seuerall Bookes being
Exposition; upon the Booke called the Clowde; vis the first and second parte.
Ye 1st part has ye Epistle depending on ye cloud in it" (MS Mazarine 4058, 60r).
On what the nuns read, see also "Dame Catherine Gascoigne, O.S.B." Baker
seems to have had a strong interest not only in medieval spirituality and devo-
tional texts but also in female authors of devotional texts. See also Elisabeth
Dutton, "Augustine Baker and Two Manuscripts of Julian of Norwich's *Revela-
tion of Love*," *Notes and Queries*, n.s., 52.3 (2005): 329–37.

21. Frances Dolan, "Reading, Work, and Catholic Women's Biographies,"
English Literary Renaissance 33.3 (2003): 328.

22. Christopher Abbott, *Julian of Norwich: Autobiography and Theology*
(Cambridge: D. S. Brewer, 1999), 3.

23. Bauerschmidt, *Julian of Norwich*, x. Lochrie makes a related argument,
stating, "Readers of mystical texts are expected to be able to read the body, not
only the displaced mystical body but the body of Christ. Julian of Norwich's
Showings begins with a trickle of blood from the pierced forehead of Christ.
Her own explications of her visions are themselves readings of the ongoing *in-
signifying* of Christ's body from the first trickle of blood caused by the crown of
thorns to the changing color of Christ's face to the copious bodily bleeding to
the shriveling of the body" (*Margery Kempe*, 75).

24. Augustine Baker, *Five Treatises; The Life and Death of Dame Margaret
Gascoigne, Treatise of Confession*, ed. John P. H. Clark, Analecta Cartusiana 119:23

(Salzburg: Institut für Anglistik und Amerikanistik, 2006), hereafter cited parenthetically in the text from this edition as *Life and Death*. Clark's edition is based on Downside Abbey MS 26598, which he describes as a "seventeenth-century copy in the hand of Dom Leander Prichard" (*Life and Death*, vii). In quotations from this edition, I have retained ampersands as printed; however, in accordance with editorial policy for the series in which this volume appears, I have expanded contractions and indicated expansions with italics.

25. Margaret Gascoigne, *The Devotions of Dame Margaret Gascoigne*, in *Letters and Translations from Thomas à Kempis in the Lille Archives and Elsewhere; The Devotions of Dame Margaret Gascoigne*, ed. John P. H. Clark, Analecta Cartusiana 119:28 (Salzburg: Institut für Anglistik und Amerikanistik, 2007); hereafter cited parenthetically in the text from this edition. In quotations from this edition, I have retained ampersands as printed; however, in accordance with editorial policy for the series in which this volume appears, I have expanded contractions and indicated expansions with italics.

26. Further emphasizing the close relationship between contemplation, the corporeal, and bodily suffering, Baker writes, "And what good the interne liuer doth, besids his interne praier, most commonlie is not a doeng or acting, but a suffering of affliction in some kinds or other, externe or internce [*sic*]" (*Life and Death*, 60).

27. See Stanley Cavell, *The Claim of Reason: Wittgenstein, Skepticism, Morality, and Tragedy* (New York: Oxford University Press, 1999), 368.

28. In interpreting revelations 13 and 14, the longest revelations included in the text, Maud McInerney makes an observation that dovetails with the relationships that I am positing among Christ, Julian, and Margaret Gascoigne. She writes, "The text's distortion is not only quantitative in that some revelations are longer than others, it is temporal, in the complete breakdown of distinction between experience and narrative. . . . Distinction itself is no longer a possibility. The physical or intellectual pain suffered by Saviour, visionary, and reader unites them all in a textual space outside the limitations of time or linear thought" ("'In the Meydens Womb': Julian of Norwich and the Poetics of Enclosure," in *Medieval Mothering*, ed. John Carmi Parsons and Bonnie Wheeler [New York: Garland, 1996], 174).

29. An entry in the Parisian nuns' catalog is highly suggestive that Julian's text was likely not the only medieval work with which the nuns engaged in complex modes of implication. The catalog records "A Treatise of Richard of Hampole touching Temptations transcribed or translated out of old English into newer 2 Bookes ye one of which has bound with it ye Devotions of Dame

Mary Gascoigne" (228v). It seems possible that this copy of Richard Rolle's work bound with Mary Gascoigne's devotions might be something rather like the copy of Julian's text integrated with meditations by Margaret Gascoigne.

30. Nicky Hallett, *Lives of Spirit: English Carmelite Self-Writing in the Early Modern Period* (Aldershot: Ashgate, 2007), 28.

31. Abbott, *Julian of Norwich*, 140, emphasis in original. The sort of constitution of self vis-à-vis others evident in the nuns' writings is very much in harmony with Julian's own understanding of community, since "[i]n terms of Julian's imagining of the social . . . , sociality is fundamentally a matter of the exchange of the self as a gift" (Bauerschmidt, *Julian of Norwich*, 187).

32. Dutton notes that Baker seemed to have just such a model of spirituality organized around processes of sharing religious autobiographies in mind when he provided the nuns with mystical authors to read. Citing Baker's *Secretum,* she states, "In an account of his own spiritual development, Baker emphasizes how he suffered from the lack of such instructive literature when experiencing desolation and, unaware that it was a common spiritual experiences, sinned by despairing. . . . The reading of mystical authors serves to fore-warn and fore-arm those pursuing the mystical way. . . . At moments of crisis, the reader may be guided and consoled by identification of her own spiritual difficulties with those of the author, by patterning her own spiritual development in accord with those about which she has read. Thus texts are very explicitly open to appropriation—an author's words are of interest insofar as they are adaptable to the circumstances of the reader" ("Augustine Baker," 330–31).

33. Cavell, *Claim of Reason,* 348.

34. In his discussion of Wittgenstein's *Philosophical Investigations,* Terry Eagleton writes, "We insist on trying to hide something here, Wittgenstein points out, but the figleaf of language is just concealing the fact that everything is open to view. . . . There can be no private meaning for the unconscious, in the sense of being inherently inaccessible to another, as there can be no private meaning in waking life" ("Self-Writing Subjects," in *Rewriting the Self: Histories from the Renaissance to the Present,* ed. Roy Porter [London: Routledge, 1997], 264–65).

35. On these collections and their use in the monastic community, see Wolfe, "Reading Bells," especially 146–47. There are also entries for "The Spirituall Canticles and Confession of V R Dame Gartrud Mores" (MS Mazarine 4058, 30v) and "The Spirituall Songs of our Verie Reverend and Deare Mother Clementia Carys in three parts" (MS Mazarine 4058, 219v). It is not clear whether these works are purely "original" devotional works or, like many of the others mentioned, a blend of appropriated, "reincarnated," and "new" text.

36. Anna Harrison discusses a similar monastic textual culture in which writing is a communal enterprise, in which nuns write "for the profit of their neighbor and confess belief that their efforts are laden with consequences for their own salvation" in her study of thirteenth-century works associated with Mechtild of Hackeborn and Gertrude of Helfta. See Anna Harrison, "'Oh! What Treasure Is in this Book?' Writing, Reading, and Community at the Monastery of Helfta," *Viator* 39 (2008): 75–106, quote from 86.

37. Wolfe, "Reading Bells," 138.

38. J. T. Rhodes, "Dom Augustine Baker's Reading Lists," *Downside Review* 111 (July 1993): 157. Claire Walker also discusses Baker's uses of "Blosius, John Ruysbroek, John Tauler, Walter Hilton, and Henry Suso" in "Spiritual Property: The English Benedictine Nuns of Cambrai and the Dispute over the Baker Manuscripts," in *Women, Property, and the Letters of the Law in Early Modern England*, ed. Nancy Wright, Margaret W. Ferguson, and A. R. Buck (Toronto: University of Toronto Press, 2004), 243.

39. Wolfe makes a related point, noting the frequency of authorial anonymity in texts by the Cambrai nuns. She observes, "Anonymity was a matter of humility for the nuns, and private ownership of anything, including one's written words, was forbidden" (introduction to *Elizabeth Cary, Lady Falkland*, 46). She continues by stating that attributing individual authorship to particular texts was "largely irrelevant at Cambrai because of the nuns' ideals of monastic humility and corporate identity" (48). Walker characterizes Baker's method of devotion and the texts associated with it as "not solely his creation," saying, "It was the product of collaboration with the nuns" ("Spiritual Property," 244).

40. In his examination of the vernacular and incarnational theology in later medieval English writings, including the *Showings*, Nicholas Watson describes a similar set of phenomena concerning the nature of textuality to the operations I am discussing. He says, "[T]hese texts blur the distinctions between their inner universes and the outside world in which readers birth him [Christ] in their souls, as they blur the distinction between theory (*scientia*) and praxis (*sapientia*). Insisting on the endlessness of the truths to be found within their pages but also on their own incompleteness, they offer themselves as communal focus points for those collective acts of reform, repentance, and informed longing towards Christ they see as necessary to transform the Church into a body fit for his use" (Nicholas Watson, "Conceptions of the Word: The Mother Tongue and the Incarnation of God," *New Medieval Literatures* 1 [1997]: 113–14).

41. Nicholas Watson makes a related argument about *Piers Plowman* in his essay "Conceptions of the Word." He says, "*Piers Plowman* can claim to repeat the incarnation (not merely, as with *Book to a Mother*, to figure it), inasmuch as it

not only holds up to a sinful world a radical understanding of Christ but holds up to Christ an understanding of this world, an understanding notionally not obtainable through the authoritative but abstracted modes of thought Langland associates with Latin and the clergy" (117).

42. The repeated references to Baker as "Venerable" support the idea that the community may have understood texts written by Baker's hand to be relics, since the reference to him as "Venerable" is made "as if the canonisation process was underway" (Walker, *Gender and Politics*, 145). Although the nuns' library was by no means limited to works translated by, transcribed by, or composed by Baker (numerous though all three types are in the catalog), the title page of the catalog suggests Baker's association with every work in it, also in spite of the ambiguous nature of authorship. This feature further indicates the importance of Baker's textual presence to the nuns. The title page reads, "A catalogue of such Bookes as the Verie Reuerend and Ueneable *[sic]* Father Auguisin *[sic]* Baker hath either himselfe originally penned or hath collected out of other Autherus *[sic]* or hath himself Translated out of Latin in to English or els hath only Transcribed according to the writing or penning of some other" (MS Mazarine 4058, 2r). The catalog is organized alphabetically, and each letter is introduced with a statement again emphasizing Baker's role. For instance, the letter E is introduced as follows: "Here folowes the Copies according to the originall of the *Very Reveren*d Unerable Father Auguistin Bakers workes belonging to the Letter E" (59v). Within alphabetic sections the cataloguer repeatedly highlights Baker's textual presence by inserting rubrications indicating, for instance, "[H]eare folowes the vene*rable* Father Augustin Bakers Translation" (228r), or "Translated by the said Auther Venerable Father Auguistin Baker out of the Latine into English" (206r).

43. Harrison also describes the communal value placed on the book as a material object at Helfta. Calling attention as well to reading as an embodied spiritual experience, she indicates, "The very physical presence of the *Book of Special Grace* floods its authors with wondrous feeling" ("'Oh! What Treasure,'" 86). Later, Harrison observes, "The written word appears to have held a place of exceptional value at Helfta. Talk of writing permeates visions. . . . Visions are laced with text. . . . The *Book of Special Grace* insists that it is through his words that God is present to his people, vivifying them" (98).

44. Colwich Abbey MS H9, quoted in Anselm Cramer, "'The Librarie of this Howse': Augustine Baker's Community and Their Books," in *"Stand up to Godwards": Essays in Mystical and Monastic Theology in Honour of the Reverend John Clark on his Sixty-fifth Birthday,* ed. James Hogg, Analecta Cartusiana 204

(Salzburg: Institut für Anglistik und Amerikanistik, Universität Salzburg, 2002), 108. Elisabeth Dutton's essay "The Seventeenth-Century Manuscript Tradition and the Influence of Augustine Baker" (in *A Companion to Julian of Norwich*, ed. Liz Herbert McAvoy [Woodbridge: Boydell and Brewer, 2008], 127–38) includes helpful analysis of the differences between the Paris and Sloane seventeenth-century manuscripts of the *Showings* that has bearing on the methods, as well as on the spiritual significance, of reading and ways of knowing among the nuns under Baker's spiritual direction.

45. I would like to take this opportunity to express thanks to my former colleague Norm Jones, not only for introducing me to Grace Mildmay, but also for many illuminating conversations on early modern religion.

46. Linda Pollock, *With Faith and Physic: The Life of a Tudor Gentlewoman Lady Grace Mildmay, 1552–1620* (New York: St. Martin's, 1995), 69, 87–88; hereafter cited parenthetically in the text for both Grace Mildmay's writings (unless otherwise noted) and Pollock's commentary.

47. All quotations from Julian of Norwich's *Showings* are from Nicholas Watson and Jacqueline Jenkins, eds., *The Writings of Julian of Norwich: A Vision Showed to a Devout Woman and a Revelation of Love* (University Park: Pennsylvania State University Press, 2006), and are cited parenthetically in the text.

48. See, for instance, the famous "hazelnut vision" in chapter 5 of the Long Text (139). On Julian's modes of vision, see Nicholas Watson, "The Trinitarian Hermeneutic in Julian of Norwich's *Revelation of Love*," in *The Medieval Mystical Tradition in England: Exeter Symposium V*, ed. Marion Glasscoe (Cambridge: Brewer, 1992), 79–100, and Hugh Kempster, "Julian of Norwich: The *Westminster Text* of *A Revelation of Love*," *Mystics Quarterly* 22 (1997), especially 190–92. Bauerschmidt argues that Julian's language of bodily sight reveals the significance of "her theology of the humanity of Jesus in overcoming the division between 'affective' and 'contemplative' pieties" (*Julian of Norwich*, 33–34).

49. On mysticism in the Puritan tradition, see Jerald C. Brauer, "Puritan Mysticism and the Development of Liberalism," *Church History* 19.3 (1950): 151–70. Brauer's focus tends more toward the later seventeenth and early eighteenth centuries, but he does discuss earlier seventeenth-century instances of Puritan mysticism as well. His point that the "basic emphasis of the mystical element of Puritanism was on union between man and the Divine" (152) seems apposite for the arguments I am making about Grace Mildmay and the similarities of her practices and texts to those of Julian of Norwich.

50. On the legacies of medieval affective devotion in Foxe's *Acts and Monuments*, see chapter 5.

51. Owen and Bell, "Upholland Anthology," 290 n. 18. The Paris Benedictine nuns' catalog includes listings for "The Booke called the Three Tabernacles (of Thomas de Kempis) yt is to say Pouerty, Humility, and Patience" (MS Mazarine 4058, 228r) and "The Valie of Lillyes of Thomas de Kempis" (238r), as well as a copy of what is likely his *Imitation of Christ,* attributed here, as it is in other texts associated with the exiled English Benedictines that I discuss in this chapter, to Jean Gerson (121r).

52. Alexandra Walsham, *Church Papists: Catholicism, Conformity, and Confessional Polemic in Early Modern England* (Woodbridge: Boydell, 1999), 8.

53. For a discussion of Grace Mildmay in the context of Tudor religious history, in which some material from this chapter appears in considerably shorter form, see Nancy Bradley Warren, "Tudor Religious Cultures in Practice: The Piety and Politics of Grace Mildmay and Her Circle," *Literature Compass* 3.5 (2006): 1011–43.

54. Grace Mildmay calls her maternal grandfather Robert Paget "a religious and good man" (28) and writes, "My grandmother, the mother of my mother, was wife to Farrington of Farrington Hall in Devonshire, also a godly and religious woman. She delighted in the word of God and spent much time therein all her days" (29).

55. The Sharington family seat was Lacock Abbey in Wiltshire. Lacock Abbey had been a house of Augustinian canonesses until it was dissolved. Following its dissolution, Henry Sharington's brother William purchased the property in 1539. William died leaving no children, and Henry inherited the property.

56. See, for instance, the Index of Scriptural Citations in Colledge and Walsh, *Book of Showings,* 779–88. Nicholas Watson also discusses Julian's use of biblical material in "The Composition of Julian of Norwich's Revelation of Love," *Speculum* 68.3 (1993): 637–83; see also Brant Pelphrey, *Love Was His Meaning: The Theology and Mysticism of Julian of Norwich,* Salzburg Studies in English Literature Elizabethan and Renaissance Studies 92.4 (Salzburg: Institut für Anglistik und Amerikanistik, Universität Salzburg, 1982). For further analysis of a medieval Catholic woman and early modern Protestant woman's similar modes of engagement with scripture, see the discussion of scriptural language and biblical lives in the writings of Margery Kempe and Anna Trapnel in chapter 4.

57. Christine Peters, *Patterns of Piety: Women, Gender and Religion in Late Medieval and Reformation England* (Cambridge: Cambridge University Press, 2003). Although my readings of some fundamental aspects of the relationships

of medieval and early modern religion differs from Peters's, as will become clear in the rest of this chapter, there is much in Peters's far-reaching book with which I agree. Her scholarship also provides a welcome model of productively crossing the historical boundary separating the medieval and early modern eras as well as the confessional boundary demarcating pre- and post-Reformation religion.

58. Ibid., 4.

59. Ibid., 347.

60. On this point see Ritamary Bradley's discussion of Julian's understanding of the Incarnation. She says, "[W]hile remaining faithful to the Church's universal teaching on the Incarnation, Julian exactly reverses the reasoning exemplified in Anselm. It is not that Christ by becoming one with humanity and taking on sinful flesh, suffers the wrath of an angry God in our stead—rather, quite the opposite. . . . Precisely through our unity with Christ we are always in God's love. There is no wrath in God because in us he sees his well-beloved son, with whom our flesh is in unity by the Incarnation" ("Julian of Norwich: Everyone's Mystic," in *Mysticism and Spirituality in Medieval England,* ed. William F. Pollard and Robert Boenig [Cambridge: D. S. Brewer, 1997], 152).

61. In clarifying Julian's concepts of substance and sensuality, McInerney succinctly states, "Julian sees soul and body as intrinsically, inseparably linked" ("'In the Meydens Womb,'" 177). On Julian's categories of substance and sensuality, and the ways in which body and soul participate in them, see also Bauerschmidt, *Julian of Norwich,* 146–47, and Nancy Coiner, "The 'Homely' and the Heimliche: The Hidden, Double Self in Julian of Norwich's Showings," *Exemplaria* 5.2 (1993): 305–23.

62. I would add in passing that Julian's text contains almost medically clinical descriptions of the dying Christ's body on the cross (see 181–85). Furthermore, McInerney points out that the Long Text "echoes contemporary scientific knowledge of reproduction" ("'In the Meydens Womb,'" 175).

63. Abbott, *Julian of Norwich,* 135.

64. Ibid., 136.

65. Ibid., 136–37.

66. *Lady Mildmay's Meditations,* microfilm, Northamptonshire Central Library, fols. 63–64. This passage is not included in Pollock's edition.

67. On *ruminatio,* see Jean Leclercq, *The Love of Learning and the Desire for God: A Study of Monastic Culture* (New York: Fordham University Press, 1961). Abbott argues for the importance of *lectio divina* in interpreting Julian's text. He writes, "Brief mention should also be made here of the monastic concept of

lectio divina since it has a particular bearing on the way the interiorization of the scriptures . . . is understood to bring the human subject into personal, existential relation to the mysteries of faith, thus making these mysteries really present in their spiritual meaning and power. This laying open of the self to divine mystery is achieved by reading the Bible in an attitude of faith, by memorizing texts, and by a process of mental rumination in which emotional response (tasting, savouring) is preferred to the more cerebral kinds of analysis" (*Julian of Norwich*, 55). Significantly, as Wolfe points out, "The metaphor of digestion . . . features strongly in Baker's description of spiritual reading" ("Reading Bells," 139). For example, in his advice to the nuns on their library, he says that "good bookes are a necessarie food for your soules; for by them you are (as by the voice of God) incited to devotion, and nourished in it" (Colwich Abbey MS H9, quoted in Cramer, "'Librarie of this Howse,'" 108).

68. The embodied engagement with texts, and especially with scripture, evident in Baker's, the nuns', and Mildmay's writings, itself has scriptural precedents. In his work on early modern Protestant spiritual journals, Tom Webster observes, "Not only did the Decalogue come in written form, it was written upon the hearts of the Israelites as a sign of the Covenant: 'I will put my laws into their minds and write them in their hearts; and I will be to them a God, and they shall be to me a people' (Heb. 8:10)" ("Writing to Redundancy: Approaches to Spiritual Journals and Early Modern Spirituality," *Historical Journal* 39 [1996]: 45). For one example, Webster turns to Thomas Goodwin's 1636 text *Childe of Light*, saying, "This form of writing as validation and authority was taken up, for instance, by Thomas Goodwin, who noted that the Holy Spirit 'writes first all graces in us, and then teaches us to read his handwriting'" (45; the quoted passage is from *Childe of Light*, 116). Webster further notes that such scriptural passages "are important for the godly conception of writing" (45). I would submit, though, that in their commitments to incarnational textual paradigms such texts as Julian's *Showings* and the writings of the nuns of Cambrai and Paris provide evidence that this aspect of godly conceptions of writings shares common ground with both medieval and early modern Catholic understandings of the written word.

69. As Michael Schoenfeldt argues in his analysis of early modern embodiment and interiority, in these passages from Grace Mildmay's writings, "embodiments of emotion" are "not . . . enactments of dead metaphors but rather explorations of the corporeal nature of self" (*Bodies and Selves in Early Modern England: Physiology and Inwardness in Spenser, Shakespeare, Herbert, and Milton* [Cambridge: Cambridge University Press, 1999], 8). For Mildmay, as

for the canonical male Renaissance writers that Schoenfeldt discusses (and in spite of the fact that Schoenfeldt claims not to discern this paradigm in the writings of early modern women), we find "a language of inner emotion whose vehicles were also tenors, whose language of desire was composed of the very stuff of being" (8).

70. The spiritual importance for Grace Mildmay of humility, which is closely related to the moral failures and necessary dependence on divine grace that she acknowledges, appears when she makes such statements as "I have had continued experience all my days of the vanities of this life, in mine own particular, whereby I am taught to turn away my face from beholding them, to put no confidence in them, nor to be led by them or to love them. . . . And only to magnify and praise the goodness of the Lord which hath ever followed me so from time to time, as I am not able to express the least part thereof" (85).

71. The ornamental brackets are added by Pollock to mark a passage that Grace Mildmay deleted in her revision of her journal. Pollock's editorial practice is to exclude passages that Mildmay deleted except when the deletion alters the sense of the entry. In such a case, she encloses the deleted material with ornamental brackets and also includes the emendation. Echoing the *contemptus mundi* theme that strongly informs this dimension of monastic spirituality, Grace Mildmay declares, "Love not this world, neither the things which are in this world. If any man love this world, the love of the father is not in him. For all that is in this world, as the lusts of the flesh, the lusts of the eye and the pride of life, is not of the father but of this world. And this world passeth away, with all the lusts thereof but he that fulfilleth the will of God abideth ever" (78–79).

72. Clark indicates that Baker uses underlining for both biblical quotations and words that are enlarged in the manuscript (*Devotions*, 1).

73. As Bauerschmidt notes, "[R]ather than emphasizing 'feminine' attributes in her various depictions and descriptions of Jesus, Julian has above all a sense of the sheer biological femaleness of his body. . . . [H]is bodiliness itself is portrayed, in a variety of ways, as female" (*Julian of Norwich*, 93).

74. One could make the rather essentialist argument that language of home, maternity, marriage, and family is somehow enduringly feminine. Or, to frame a somewhat similar idea in less essentialist terms, one might also say that in both medieval and early modern culture such language is part of a strongly gendered *habitus* that helped shape women's understandings of themselves and God. I am not inclined to deny some truth to this latter view; indeed, it seems significant that Grace Mildmay writes quite specifically as a mother and grandmother, and that maternal care overlaps strongly with spiritual instruction in her

writings, as it does in the writings of many medieval and early modern women. However, my fundamental argument is that this continuity in medieval and early modern, Catholic and Protestant, cloistered and uncloistered, women's writings has larger implications for the "big picture" of English religious history.

75. On gender and maternity in Julian's writings, see Liz Herbert McAvoy, *Authority and the Female Body in the Writings of Julian of Norwich and Margery Kempe* (Woodbridge: D. S. Brewer, 2004), especially chapter 2. McAvoy argues that "[t]he concept of motherhood as a literal truth, metaphorical tool, textual matrix, religious ideology, and philosophy is central to her [Julian's] work, underpinning both the short and the long texts" (75). On Jesus as Mother in Julian's writings, see also Coiner, "'Homely' and the Heimlich," especially 320–21, and McInerney, "'In the Meydens Womb,'" especially 170–75.

76. For further discussion of nuptial union with Christ in early modern Protestant women's spirituality, see the discussion of Anna Trapnel in chapter 4.

77. Brauer discusses similar elements in the case of Francis Rous, whom he calls the "first Puritan mystic." Rous was a near contemporary of Grace Mildmay, living from 1579 to 1659. As Brauer reports, "Francis Rous stressed the conception of the mystical marriage between Christ and the soul. . . . Rous sought specific union experiences when the Heavenly Bridegroom would visit his soul and overpower him with love" ("Puritan Mysticism," 152).

78. On Julian and the Song of Songs, see McAvoy, *Authority and the Female Body*, especially 83–84 on the famous hazelnut revelation, and 151 on the sexual intimacy of Julian's use of bed imagery.

79. Margaret's religious sister Gertrude More too uses nuptial language echoing the Canticles; see, for instance, *Spiritual Exercises*, 61–62. In her discussion of these passages, Walker also notes, "Several Benedictine obituaries likened the bond between a nun and God to that of the 'spowse in the Canticles'" (*Gender and Politics*, 158).

80. Nicholas Watson's observations about the roles of gender in Julian's texts are relevant to Grace Mildmay's writings as well. He says that "Julian's insistence in the long text on generalizing her experience . . . has the effect of making her experience of Christ—formed within the gendered traditions of bridal mysticism—normative for all Christians, and by extension the world" ("'Yf Wommen Be Double Naturelly': Remaking 'Woman' in Julian of Norwich's *Revelation of Love*," *Exemplaria* 8 [1996]: 23–24). Watson continues, "What Julian does, wittingly or not, in the long text, is thus to render generally applicable to everyone, male and female, a set of assumptions and images that misogynistic discourse applies only to women. Actively accepting the terms of

that discourse, she extends it far beyond its original boundaries, strips it of its gendered particularity and in the process radically alters its meaning" (24). McAvoy too notes the ways in which bodily experiences are at once particularly gendered and shared in Julian's showings. She states, noting the interplay of bodies and texts, "[T]he female-specific experiences of menstruation, gestation, giving birth, breast-feeding are also capable of being transformed into text which is written upon bodies (both male and female, human and divine) and used as a language to validate the equal worth of the feminine" (*Authority and the Female Body*, 15). It is worth noting that Barbara Constable, another of the Benedictines of Cambrai, wrote "A Spiritual Treatise, conteininge some advise for seculars," addressed specifically to "my most deare brother Sir Marmaduke Constable" (*Catholic Record Society Publications* 13 [1913]:10–12; quotes from p. 10). This text highlights the degree to which female monastic experience might have applicability across the lines of gender and beyond the cloister wall.

81. Barry Windeatt points out that Julian's relationship to her audience changes between the Short and Long Texts, noting, for instance, that in the sixteenth revelation she moves from using third-person pronouns in the Short Text to using "we" in the Long Text ("Julian of Norwich and Her Audience," *Review of English Studies*, n.s., 28 [1977]: 5). He also observes that "[t]he allusions to contemplatives [in the Short Text] have become dispensable because they represent a specific, limiting address for the matter of the shewings. That universalism which upon meditation Julian perceives as one of the great themes of her shewings could not be fully expressed if the text continued to be so narrowly directed. . . . [W]ith long reflection Julian comes to see its general significance and application" (7).

82. Terry Eagleton, discussing, like Cavell, Wittgenstein's *Philosophical Investigations*, writes, "Wittgenstein is not out to deny the inner life . . . but to render a different account of how we have access to it, one which entails casting some doubt on the adjective 'inner.' . . . What deconstructs the distinction between inner and outer here, one might say, is the human body itself, whose creativity is a constant passing-over, transgression or transcendence from the one to the other in that perpetual movement we call history" ("Self-Writing Subjects," 265).

83. Colin Richmond, for instance, argues that in the fifteenth century the gentry's focus on reading during the Mass leads to their "insulating themselves against communal religion" ("Religion and the Fifteenth-Century Gentleman," in *The Church, Politics, and Patronage in the Fifteenth Century*, ed. Barrie Dubson

[New York: St. Martin's, 1984), 199). Pamela Graves argues that primers and other similar texts prompted the laity "to muster their own thoughts, rather than construct a communal memory of the passion through the action of the Mass" ("Social Space in the English Medieval Parish Church," *Economy and Society* 18 [1989]: 318). In contrast, Eamon Duffy points to the example of Roger Martin, "our most valuable single commentator on early sixteenth-century parochial religion in East Anglia" (*The Stripping of the Altars: Traditional Religion in England, 1400–1580* [New Haven: Yale University Press, 2005], 122). Duffy writes, "His grandfather seems to have managed Long Melford's summer processional round, and the family's estate chapel was one of the focuses of that round. Roger Martin himself played a leading role in the reconstruction of parochial religion under Mary. Yet the Martin family owned and sat in one such proprietary chantry chapel in their parish church, and Martin's writing about the figure of Christ and his mother reveal *[sic]* a sensibility saturated in the devotional commonplaces which filled the literature being read by the pious. There seems little tension here between the communal and the private. Martin is not unrepresentative. In most communities the gentry and the urban élites chose not to withdraw from communal worship, but to dominate it. To call this process privatization seems unhelpful" (122).

84. Marie Rowlands, "Recusant Women, 1560–1640," in *Women in English Society, 1500–1800*, ed. M. Prior (London: Methuen, 1985), 175. Rowlands goes on to acknowledge that this view of women and the written word likely "belittle[s] the level of participation" of women and "trivialize[s] the issue" (175). On the increased important of the household in the religious sphere and the increased authority of the male head of the household in the seventeenth century, see 174–75.

85. Webster, "Writing to Redundancy," 41.

86. Daniel Rogers, "To the Reader," in *Naaman the Syrian*, quoted in Webster, "Reading to Redundancy," 41.

87. Bauerschmidt observes of the potentially (and in a sense literally) transgressive dimensions of Julian's view of salvation, "Because Julian understands salvation as the union of those who shall be saved within the body of Christ, for her the question of salvation is one of the scope of Christ's body. While Julian will not separate dwelling in Christ from the concrete, institutional boundaries of the church, which includes acceptance of the church as teaching *in persona Christi*, the claim that all shall be well works its way through the body pushing out its boundaries. . . . The body of the saved is one that can be whole only in the transgression of its boundaries by its identification with

the infinite mercy of God displayed in the crucifixion of Jesus" (*Julian of Norwich*, 119). He also observes that in Julian's writings "there is a stubborn refusal to give up . . . tension by claiming certainty, either of the salvation of all or the damnation of some" (171).

88. Bauerschmidt includes a description of Julian's interpretation of predestination (see ibid., especially 156–71). He points out that "[i]n Julian's account of predestination, the human soul of Christ plays a crucial role. When Julian speaks of the 'kynde' (nature) out of which we come, in which we are enclosed, and into which we shall all go, she is speaking not of the divine nature itself, but of the created *human* nature of Christ, which is hypostatically untited with the Logos" (157). He continues, "We are united to God because *Christ* is united to God. Our holiness is *Christ's* holiness. Here we can see the connection between Julian's understanding of the relationship bewteen exemplarity and election, and her putative 'universalism.' Whereas medieval theologians generally stress the difference between Christ's predestination and ours, Julian stresses their similarity—in fact their virtual identity. And in this identification between Christ's election and ours, Julian lays the foundation for her belief in God's promise that 'all shall be well'" (159, emphasis in original).

89. Pollock characterizes Grace Mildmay's position as "applied rather than theoretical Calvinism. It is not what Calvin intended, but it is how Lady Mildmay understood his system" (60).

90. Adiaphora (literally "indifferent matters") were hotly debated during the Protestant Reformation. The 1577 Lutheran Formula of Concord defines adiaphora as church rites neither commanded nor forbidden in the Word of God. In the Calvinist tradition of the Westminster Confession, the circumstances of worship are considered adiaphora, as opposed to the acts and elements of worship. It is worth noting that accommodating attitudes like Grace Mildmay's did have some corollaries in government circles as well, coexisting with official persecutions of recusants. Muriel McClendon rightly observes that Elizabeth's "government never extended anything resembling official toleration to those outside the Church of England" ("Religious Toleration," in *England's Long Reformation, 1500–1800*, ed. Nicholas Tyacke [London: University College of London Press, 1998], 87). Peter Lake and Michael Questier make a persuasive case, though, that even after the 1570 papal bull excommunicating Elizabeth and the concomitant increase in governmental hostility toward papists in England, "Catholics went about their business" with "relative impunity" into the 1590s as a result of the "uneven administration of the recusancy statutes, and indeed the ideological and political disagreements and incoherences which lay behind

both the drafting and enforcing of those laws" ("Agency, Appropriation and Rhetoric under the Gallows: Puritans, Romanists and the State in Early Modern England," *Past and Present* 153 [1996]: 66). Similarly, McClendon, using the example of Norwich, finds that "communal harmony was more important than religious uniformity and that religious unity need not be the most important criterion for the successful conduct of civic life" (108).

91. Interestingly, Brauer notes that among Puritan mystics and spiritualists, "the universal activity of the Divine . . . made imperative a theology of toleration" ("Puritan Mysticism," 154).

92. Bauerschmidt makes a related argument about Julian's understanding of the nature of Christ's body and human sin; see *Julian of Norwich*, 120–21.

93. Hilary Hinds raises some related questions about the nature of Protestant subjectivity, and the relationship between the individual and the community, in *God's Englishwomen: Seventeenth-Century Radical Sectarian Writing and Feminist Criticism* (Manchester: Manchester University Press, 1996); see especially 13–14. I discuss Hinds's work, and the questions she raises, in more detail in chapter 4.

CHAPTER 3.   EMBODYING THE "OLD RELIGION" AND TRANSFORMING THE BODY POLITIC

1. Claire Walker, "Spiritual Property: The English Benedictine Nuns of Cambrai and the Dispute over the Baker Manuscripts," in *Women, Property, and the Letters of the Law in Early Modern England,* ed. Nancy Wright, Margaret Ferguson, and A. R. Buck (Toronto: University of Toronto Press, 2004), 238.

2. Benedictines of Stanbrook, *In a Great Tradition: A Tribute to Dame Laurentia McLachlan* (London: Metheun, 1956), 25.

3. MS Colwich Abbey H9, quoted in Anselm Cramer, "'The Librarie of this Howse': Augustine Baker's Community and Their Books," in *"Stand up to Godwards": Essays in Mystical and Monastic Theology in Honor of the Reverend John Clark on His Sixty-fifth Birthday,* ed. James Hogg (Salzburg: Institut für Anglistik und Amerikanistik, Universität Salzburg, 2002), 109–10.

4. On this dispute, see Placid Spearitt, "The Survival of Medieval Spirituality among the Exiled English Black Monks," in *That Mysterious Man: Essays on Augustine Baker,* ed. Michael Woodward, Analecta Cartusiana 119:15 (Salzburg: Institut für Anglistik und Amerikanistik, Universität Salzburg, 2001), especially 22–24; see also Benedictines of Stanbrook, *In a Great Tradition,* 12–18

and 24–27, and Claire Walker, *Gender and Politics in Early Modern Europe: English Convents in France and the Low Countries* (New York: Palgrave Macmillan, 2003), 143–47, as well as her essay "Spiritual Property."

5. Gertrude More, *The Spiritual Exercises of the Most Vertuous and Religious D. Gertrude More* (Paris: Lewis de la Fosse, 1658), hereafter cited parenthetically. I believe the title of this work is itself a politicized choice. Given the conflict that raged in English female religious communities in exile in the early modern period concerning the place of Jesuit spirituality in the devotional lives of nuns, that Baker would assign a title to Gertrude's text clearly resonant of the Jesuit text par excellence, the *Spiritual Exercises,* stakes a claim for the primacy of his/her form of devotion as the proper one for Benedictine women religious to adopt. In other words, the choice of the title positions Gertrude's spiritual exercises as the *true* spiritual exercises.

6. This chain of associations itself reincarnates what Frederick Bauerschmidt describes as a medieval form of English self-conception. He writes, "[T]he paradigmatic body by which relations among members of the social body were understood was the suffering, generative, eucharistic body of Christ" (Frederick Bauerschmidt, *Julian of Norwich and the Mystical Body Politic of Christ* [Notre Dame: University of Notre Dame Press, 1999], 18). He continues, "The eucharistic body of Christ was the very paradigm not only of the English nation, but of smaller social groupings such as villages or guilds" (18).

7. On the poem and the engraving, see Geoffrey Scott, "The Image of Augustine Baker," in Woodward, *That Mysterious Man*, especially 106–7.

8. On Christ's body as a book in medieval Passion piety, see chapter 5 of Karma Lochrie, *Margery Kempe and Translations of the Flesh* (Philadelphia: University of Pennsylvania Press, 2001).

9. Elizabeth Evasdaughter observes that Julian in fact omits recounting "Christ's actual death" (Elizabeth Evasdaughter, "Julian of Norwich," in *Medieval, Renaissance, and Enlightenment Women Philosophers, AD 500–1600*, vol. 2 of *A History of Women Philosophers*, ed. Mary Ellen Waithe [Dordrecht: Kluwer Academic Publishers, 1989], 217). She also indicates that Julian "noticed, as some of her readers do not, that her visions taken as a whole, spent much more time on Christ's glory than on his suffering, and ended with his glory" (213).

10. Significantly, St. Teresa of Avila features prominently in Augustine Baker's writings. She appears frequently in his *Sancta Sophia,* and excerpts from her *Way of Perfection* and *Life* appear in the Upholland Manuscript (Hywel Owen and Luke Bell, "The Upholland Anthology: An Augustine Baker Manuscript," *Downside Review* 107, no. 369 [1989]: 276–77). In his analysis of a

Middle English verse prayer on Christ's passion, which also portrays the heart as pierced by divine love, Eric Jager observes, "The heart wounded by the arrows of divine love also recalls Augustine's powerful image of his own converted heart wounded by divine 'words like arrows fixed deep in our flesh.' In the *Orison*, the believer's inscribed and wounded heart 'imitates' the penetration of Christ's flesh and thus undergoes an inward conversion through participation in Christ's Passion" (*The Book of the Heart* [Chicago: University of Chicago Press, 2000], 110). Both the possibility of an Augustinian connection and the idea of participation in Christ's passion seem equally applicable to Gertrude More's text.

11. The entries for Margaret Gascoigne and Gertrude More in the "Catalogue of ye names of ye Religious Dames and Sisters professed of this Convent of our Blessed Lady of Consolation in Cambray who are dead" (*Miscelllanea VIII, Catholic Record Society* 13 [London: Catholic Record Society, 1913], 73) both highlight physical suffering and union with Christ. That of Gertrude More, which begins by stating her place in "ye noble family of Sr Thomas ye famous Martyr of happy memory" (74), states: "[S]hee left many examples worthy her blood & vocation, particularly in her last grievous sickness (being indeed very terrible) which shee embraced with much patience & conformity to ye Will of God, showing such an admirable confidence in his mercy yt shee seemed only to be sensible yt shee was so long detain'd from ye union & fruition of his divine Majesty to which she had ever tended, desiring truly to be dissolv'd that she might live in Christ Jesus" (74). That of Margaret Gascoigne ends, "Her exemplary & most comfortable death gives us great hopes yt shee now enjoys yt inseparable union with her Spouse our Saviour which with all her heart shee incessantly sought after" (75). In these quotations I have retained ampersands as printed, but I have expanded contractions and indicated such expansions with italics.

12. David Hillman, "The Inside Story," in *Historicism, Psychoanalysis, and Early Modern Culture*, ed. Carla Mazzio and Douglas Trevor (New York: Routledge, 2000), 310.

13. Claire Walker has commented on the role played by practices embraced by medieval holy women, especially forms of *imitatio Christi*, in the devotional lives of early modern women religious. She argues, "Early modern nuns' piety . . . encompassed an innovative mix of late medieval devotion with the ideals and directives of the post-Reformation Church" (*Gender and Politics*, 133).

14. MS BL 18650; hereafter cited parenthetically in the text. The *Life*'s author is not known, and it cannot be precisely dated. However, Ann Hutchison offers convincing arguments for the text's having been written "very shortly" after Marie's death on April 27, 1580, by someone who was "in all probability a

lay person" living "near London" and who was an eyewitness to Marie's death ("Mary Champney, a Bridgettine Nun under the Rule of Queen Elizabeth," *Bridgettiana* 13 [2002]: 6). She also speculates that the author "might, in fact, be a woman," perhaps "someone like the 'perilous obstynate' Magdalen Heath, if not Mrs Heath herself" (8). The Heaths received Marie's fellow Brigittine nuns Anne Stapleton and Elizabeth Sanders and, according to Hutchison, "must also have allowed their house to be the designated meeting point for some or all of the nuns on their arrival" (8). See also Ann M. Hutchison, "The Life and Good End of Sister Marie," *Bridgettiana* 13 (2002): 33–89.

15. Hereafter cited parenthetically in the text.

16. As Ann Hutchison has indicated, this text is likely "the early version of 'The Wanderings of Syon,'" compiled by Robert Parsons from materials sent by the Brigittine confessor general Seth Foster. Hutchison notes, "Some years later, feeling that the original was 'lacking in completeness' and 'defective in many things,' someone (probably Foster) composed a new version; this may have been sometime in the 1620s" (pers. comm., August 2008). In claiming that the nuns are responsible for the authorship of the *Relacion* (except for the "Preambulo" attributed to Foster), I agree with Hutchison and disagree with Adam Hamilton and J. R. Fletcher. Referring to "The Wanderings of Syon," Hutchison observes, "The authorship is curious, since the voice keeps changing. . . . Hamilton (who edited all but 12 chapters of the enlarged version and published it in *The Poor Souls' Friend*) and Fletcher note the change in voice. Fletcher concluded that the whole thing was composed from dictation by Foster—and I agree with this; he then suggests, as does Hamilton, that one of the brothers wrote it down. Here I disagree; I think one of the Sisters actually compiled it. This helps explain some of the shifts in voice, since at the beginning it certainly seems to have been written by one of the nuns" (pers. comm., August 2008). I am grateful to Professor Hutchison for her cheerful and highly informative responses to my questions concerning Syon's affairs during the sixteenth and seventeenth centuries.

17. See chapter 6 of Nancy Bradley Warren, *Women of God and Arms: Female Spirituality and Political Conflict, 1380–1600* (Philadelphia: University of Pennsylvania Press, 2005).

18. A condensed and differently directed version of my discussion of *The Life and Good End of Sister Marie* and the *Relacion* appears in my essay "Women's Religious Writings and Reformations," in *The History of British Women's Writing, 1500–1610*, ed. Jennifer Summit and Caroline Bicks (New York: Palgrave, 2010). In this essay, I consider briefer selections from the Brigittine texts and Grace Mildmay's *Meditations* in dialogue with an extensive analysis of the writings of

Queen Katherine Parr to elucidate important continuities and hybridities characteristic of Catholic and Protestant women's writings engaged in the work of
religious and cultural reform.

19. As I do in elsewhere in this book, I adopt the term *(auto)biography*
from Douglas Catterall to indicate the blurry boundary between biography and
autobiography and to signal my awareness that "life writing" in the medieval
and early modern periods does not precisely correspond with the genre of autobiography as it is currently understood ("Drawing Lives and Memories from
the Everyday Words of the Early Modern Era," *Sixteenth Century Journal* 36.3
(2005): 651–72.

20. See Jager, *Book of the Heart*, especially chapter 5, entitled "Saints," for
an informative analysis of many examples of this phenomenon in the lives of
saints both male and female. As he notes, "Wounds, signs, and letters on the
heart were reported of saints from the early days of the Church, and by the late
Middle Ages, the legends of the saints, one of the most popular literary genres
of the time, were filled with stories of hearts miraculously inscribed with divine testimonies and opened to be read like books. As bodily scripture, the
saint's inscribed heart transformed the metaphor of the inner book into one of
its most vivid and apparently literal incarnations" (87).

21. Marie's identity as Christ's spouse also features prominently in a section of the *Life* that clearly echoes what Jocelyn Wogan-Browne terms the "virgin's tale" paradigm of the saint's life—an extended account of her interactions
with an English soldier and would-be suitor. This episode recalls the emphasis
placed on the female body, and the conflation of intact virginity with Christian
faith, in the virgin martyrs' lives about which Wogan-Browne writes. See Joce-
lyne Wogan-Browne, "The Virgin's Tale," in *Feminist Readings in Middle English:
The Wife of Bath and All Her Sect*, ed. Ruth Evans and Lesley Johnson (London:
Routledge, 1994), 165–94.

20. Hutchison, "Mary Champney," 23–24.

23. Ibid., 24.

24. The connection between the canonical hour of nones with Christ's suffering and death would have been entirely familiar to a Brigittine nun, since the
Myroure of Oure Ladye makes the link explicit: "At howre of none, oure lorde
Ihesu Crist cryed, & gaue out his soulle by dethe, the same houre a knyght openyd
our lordes syde with a spere, & smote thorugh his herte, where out came water to
our baptym" (John Henry Blunt, ed., *The Myroure of Oure Ladye* [London: EETS,
1873], 13).

25. Colegio San Albano, Valladolid Series II, Legajo 5, no. 12; expansions
are indicated by italics. I am grateful to the rector of the Colegio San Albano

for granting me access to the college's archives and granting me permission to use documents held there in this book. I am also grateful for all the kindness shown to me at the Colegio, particularly by Javier Burrieza Sánchez and Fr. Peter Harris, during the summers of 2004 and 2006.

26. The author of the *Life* suggests something similar, stating that Ann died "also in Englande verie blessedlie, as a witnes for Godes people against the wicked, after manye tempetes of tribulacion in exile susteyned" (5v).

27. Ann Hutchison, pers. comm., August 2008. My thanks to Professor Hutchison for her inquiries to the Lady Abbess on this point, and to the Lady Abbess for her response. Hutchison further notes that the stations of the cross appear "written out in some of the Sisters' own prayer books of a later date."

28. Christopher de Hamel, *Syon Abbey: The Library of the Bridgettine Nuns and their Peregrinations after the Reformation* (London: Roxburghe Club, 1991), 21, English translation 33.

29. This account of Luisa's early life is based on Elizabeth Rhodes, *This Tight Embrace: Luisa de Carvajal y Mendoza (1566–1614)* (Milwaukee: Marquette University Press, 2000), 1–2; hereafter cited parenthetically in the text as *TE* for both its excerpts from Luisa's writings and Rhodes's translations of these excerpts.

30. Interestingly, in the earliest manuscript of her spiritual autobiography, her account breaks off with her first experience with her uncle (*TE*, 65). The details given here come from separate, later confessional documents, likely written "just before her departure for England" (*TE*, 33).

31. Camilo Maria Abad, *Escritos autobiográficos de la Venerable Doña Luisa de Carvajal y Mendoza* (Barcelona: Juan Flors, 1966), 210–11.

32. That Luisa's love for Christ and her desire to imitate the pain he underwent out of love would manifest itself corporeally in this fashion is particularly appropriate, since the cult of the Sacred Heart is one in which devotion focuses centrally on God's love. It is a form of devotion in which the bodily and the spiritual are inseparable; the heart of Jesus is venerated both as his physical, wounded heart and as a symbolic representation of the divine love that led him to suffer and die (see the entry for "Sacred Heart" in the online Catholic Encyclopedia, www.newadvent.org, accessed November 12, 2009). Furthermore, in Luisa's day the Jesuits with whom she is so closely associated were strongly engaged in promoting devotion to the Sacred Heart. Luisa's contemporaries and fellow Spaniards Marina de Escobar and Marina's confessor the Jesuit Luis de la Puente, who had also served as Luisa's spiritual advisor when she was in Valladolid, were known for their devotion to the Sacred Heart (Margaret Rees, *The Writings of Doña Luisa de Carvajal y Mendoza, Catholic Missionary to James I's*

London [Lampeter: Edwin Mellen, 2002], 58); on Luisa's relationships with Marina and Luis, in addition to Rees, see *TE* and especially Javier Burrieza Sánchez, *Los milagros de la Corte: Marina de Escobar y Luisa de Carvajal en la historia de Valladolid* [Valladolid: Real Colegio de los Ingleses, 2002]). In Luisa's poetic writings, her sonnet "De immenso Amor" has particular relevance to the language she uses in the prologue to her vow. In this poem, Luisa (in the figure of Silva, an anagram of her name) enters the wound in Christ's side to repose as a dove in his heart: "De immenso Amor aqueste abrazo estrecho / recibe, Silva, de tu dulce Amado, y por la puerta de este diestro lado / éntrate, palomilla, acá en mi pecho" (lines 1–4, *TE*, 166) [Of immense Love this tight embrace / receive, Silva, from your sweet Beloved, / and through the door of this right side / come in, little dove, here to my breast] (*TE*, 167). On this poem, and on the mystical tradition of the exchange of hearts, see Michael Bradburn-Ruster, "The Beautiful Dove, the Body Divine: Luisa de Carvajal y Mendoza's Mystical Poetics," in *Mystical Gesture*, 159–68.

33. Abad, *Escritos autobiográficos*, 189. Anne Cruz argues that this representation of Luisa's desire for martyrdom as a nearly lifelong one, and its constant association with England, are retrospective constructions inserted into the autobiography that she wrote late in life ("durante los últimos años de su vida") ("Luisa de Carvajal y su conexión jesuita," in *Actos del 11o Congreso de la Asociación Internacional de Hispanistas 24–29 de agosto de 1992, Irvine CA*, ed. Juan Villegas [Irvine: University of California Irvine Press, 1994], 97). She states, "Una lectura cuidadosa de su correspondencia nos comprueba, sin embargo, que en plena contradicción a su relato autobiográfico, sus 'deseos de martirio' no surgieron cuando joven, ni fue Inglaterra su destino inicial" (97) [A careful reading of her correspondence demonstrates, nevertheless, that in contradiction of her autobiography, her "desires for martyrdom" did not surface in her youth, nor was England her initial destination].

34. An association of the Virgin Mary with the English cause was a hallmark of devotion at the Jesuit English College at Valladolid, where Luisa and Robert Parsons had strong ties. The statue of the Virgin Mary known as the "Madonna Vulnerata," an image "removed from one of the city churches in Cadiz in 1596, when English troops under the Earl of Essex destroyed the new Armada," and subsequently publicly desecrated "in the market square," was given to the English College at Valladolid by the Count and Countess of Santa Gadea. It was installed in the chapel so that the "students and professors of Valladolid . . . should make reparation for the insults offered it by their countrymen" (Alison Shell, *Catholicism, Controversy, and the English Literary Imagination, 1558–1660* [Cambridge: Cambridge University Press, 1999], 201). As Shell

notes, "Until very recently a mass and litanies of reparation were regularly offered at the College . . . and it is traditional for seminarians to kneel before the statue . . . and vow to return as priests to England" (201). She further observes, "The Madonna Vulnerata became to expatriate Catholics an emblem of English Catholicism" (201). The English College at Valladolid was not alone among Jesuit colleges in practicing such politically inflected Marian devotion. "There was a tradition at other Jesuit colleges, possibly inspired by Valladolid, of conducting Marian veneration in a manner which referred to the state of England" (205).

35. Camilo Maria Abad, *Una misionera española en la Inglaterra del Siglo XVII Doña Luisa de Carvajal y Mendoza, 1566–1614* (Comillas: Universidad Pontificia, 1966), 164; unless otherwise indicated, translations from this volume are my own.

36. Ibid.

37. Ibid. Luisa had long-standing ties with Parsons. On her way to England, she stopped at St. Omer to visit Robert Parsons's sister Anne: "Un mes estuvo allí en casa de Ana Personio, 'oyendo cada día misa en ella, y como una ermitaña'" (ibid., 177) [She spent a month there in Anne Parsons's house, "hearing Mass there each day, like a female hermit"].

38. Calvin F. Senning, "The Carvajal Affair: Gondomar and James I," *Catholic Historical Review* 56.1 (1970): 45.

39. Ibid.

40. Michael Walpole, *La vida de la ve da Luisa de Carvajal y Mendoza* (Madrid, 1632). Because I have been unable to access an original copy, I quote from pp. 5–6 of a reproduction held in the Colegio San Albano in Valladolid. Translations are my own.

41. The Feast of the Immaculate Conception did not actually originate in England, though it came to England early in its history. It originated in the Byzantine Church and spread to Naples, where it was taken up by the Norman occupiers. The Normans introduced the feast into England in the wake of the Conquest of 1066. See Francis X. Weiser, *Handbook of Christian Feasts and Customs* (New York: Harcourt, Brace, 1958), 292.

42. Abad, *Una misionera española*, 165. I have been unable to determine whether the image of the Virgin Mary with her son in her arms was an image of the Madonna and child or a Pietà. Either one would have significances, albeit different ones, for the incarnational spirituality and epistemological politics that inform Luisa's involvement with the Jesuit English Mission.

43. Ibid.

44. Camilo Maria Abad, ed., *Biblioteca de autores españoles desde la formación del lenguaje hasta nuestros días (continuación)*, vol. 179, *Doña Luisa de*

Carvajal y Mendoza, epistolario y poesias (Madrid: Atlas, 1965), carta [c.] 125, p. 342. Henceforth I quote Luisa's letters from this edition, giving references to the letter number (c.) and page number. Unless otherwise noted, translations are my own.

45. In his analysis of Luisa's poetry, Bradburn-Ruster comments on the centrality of the Eucharist and Passion piety in Luisa's spirituality: "[T]here can be no doubt that the poems reflect the two pillars of her spiritual and mystical life—the Passion and the Eucharist, those two most bodily mysteries" ("Beautiful Dove," 162).

46. Writing once again to Inés de la Asuncion, Luisa similarly describes the case of another executed priest through the lens of Christ's crucifixion narrative. Echoing the account of the conversion of the "good thief" crucified alongside Christ, Luisa indicates that just before this unnamed priest was made a new martyr ("un nuevo mártir"), he reconciled to the Catholic Church "un ladrón de su cárcel" [a thief from his prison] (c. 120, p. 310). This thief was then hanged and "murió con extraordinaria devoción y muestras de verdadero católico" (c. 120, p. 310) [died with extraordinary devotion and the signs of a true Catholic].

47. Luisa's descriptions of scenes involving Roberts and Summer fit comfortably within an English tradition of Jesuit writing. For instance, poems, most likely written by Henry Walpole, on Edmund Campion's death connect his execution with Christ's passion: one entitled "Upon the death of M. Edmund Campion, one of the Societe of the holy name of Jesus," states, for instance, "His hardle drawes us with him to the crosse" (line 169, quoted in Karen Batley, "Martyrdom in Sixteenth Century English Jesuit Verse," *Unisa: English Studies* 26.2 [1988]: 3). Walpole also elevates Campion, along with two other executed priests, to the status of saints. As Batley indicates, "Under Elizabeth's government, Catholics were forbidden to invoke the Saints, but now Walpole, presuming on the elevation of the three priests to that status, propagates the Conciliar 'Decree on the Invocation of Saints'" (3). Walpole writes:

> Rejoyce, be glad, triumph, sing himmes of joye,
> *Campion, Sherwine, Brian* live in blis,
> they sue, they seeke the ease of our annoy,
> they pray, they speake, and al effectuall is,
> not like to men on earth as heretofore,
> But like to saints in heaven, and that is more.
>
> (lines 49–54, quoted in
Batley, "Martyrdom," 3)

48. On the nameless secular priest's identity as Richard Newport, see Rees, *Writings of Doña Luisa*, 43.

49. Luisa also finds spiritual significance in the bodily fates of Protestants. In the same letter in which she describes the Countess of Shrewsbury's conversion, she describes a scene in which a "gran puritano" [great Puritan], whom she calls the principal inventor of the laws against the Catholics ("inventor principal de leyes contra los catolicós") met his end after speaking "muy furiosamente" [very angrily] against the Catholics in Parliament. Repairing to a nearby tavern after his speech, he had a sneezing fit ("estornudando mucho") and, as a result, "cayó de la escalera ye se quebró la cabeza y murió al mesmo punto" [fell down the stairs and broke his head and died immediately] (c. 39, p. 158). She adds, "Y estaba aquella casa señalada a la puerta como mesón, con una cabeza de Papa; y dicen los herejes que están de esto muy contentos los papistas" (c. 39, p. 158) [And this house was marked as an inn by a sign at the door with the pope's head, and the heretics said that the papists were very happy with this].

50. Luisa indicates, "Apercibimos entre nosotras una procesión, cada una con dos cendelas en las manos, que fueron doce; y todo el camino de abajo arriba adornado de muchas flores y ramos" (c. 151, p. 369) [We prepared a procession amongst ourselves, each one with two candles in her hands, which made twelve, and the entire way from the top to the bottom was adorned with many flowers and branches].

51. The other occasion of sweetness that she reports is when she fights the errors of the English people effectively with her arguments; see c. 164, p. 389. In her verbal rhetorical skills, Luisa resembles both Margery Kempe and Anna Trapnel (see discussion of these latter figures in chapter 4).

52. Jager makes a related point in his discussion of Vincent of Beauvais's version of the legend of St. Ignatius of Antioch. During his martyrdom, St. Ignatius claims to have the name of Jesus Christ written on his heart. After his death, his heart is removed and examined, and the inscription found in it prompts the witnesses to it to convert to Christianity. In the *Speculum historiale,* "[T]he saint's heart was not simply cut open to be read, but also divided up to provide individually legible relics. According to Vincent, when the saint's heart 'had been divided into small pieces, the name of the Lord Jesus Christ was found written in golden letters, so that it might be read, on each part.' The division of the inscribed heart suggests the fragmentation of the consecrated Host in the Mass. It also resembles the scribal reproduction of a text, although here the process of textual multiplication is a divine miracle . . . that attends the communal effort to multiply, share, and incorporate the bodily scripture of the saint's heart" (*Book of the Heart*, 93).

53. See Caroline Walker Bynum, *Holy Feast and Holy Fast: The Religious Significance of Food to Medieval Women* (Berkeley: University of California Press, 1988), and Caroline Walker Bynum, *Fragmentation and Redemption: Essays on Gender and the Human Body in Medieval Religion* (New York: Zone Books, 1992).

54. As Rhodes points out, "[T]he host symbolized not only Christ's presence, but the Catholics' as well" (*TE*, 243 n. 9).

55. As Rhodes observes, "There is no doubt but that Carvajal was sensitive to the political importance of Catholics' bodily presence in England. . . . Catholic presence in England signified the equation of Rome and holiness" (*TE*, 23). Luisa further emphasizes the importance of the Spanish embassy as a locus of holiness in a letter to her brother, who was, at the time she wrote the letter, being considered as a future ambassador. Describing England as "una corte de infierno junto" [a close corner of hell], she says that the "casa del embajador de España" [the Spanish ambassador's house] must be ("debe estar") "como clara lumbrera en noche tenebrosa" [like light in the dark night] (c. 161, p. 384).

56. Doreen Massey, *Space, Place, and Gender* (Minneapolis: University of Minnesota Press, 1994), 269.

57. I quote David Wallace's chapter "Holy Amazon: Mary Ward of Yorkshire," from his book *Strong Women: Life, Text, and Territory, 1347–1645*, forthcoming from Oxford University Press. My thanks to David for sharing the manuscript of this chapter and, even more importantly, for many stimulating exchanges on medieval and early modern women, religion, and questions of historical periodization.

58. This dimension of Jesuit spirituality may well have been familiar to the Brigittines in the later sixteenth century, since there were close ties between the Company of Jesus and Syon. In fact, Seth Foster's "Preambulo" to the *Relacion*, a text originally written for the Jesuit Robert Parsons and translated by a Jesuit of the English College in Valladolid, highlights the importance of sacred geography in its account of Syon and Sheen being founded "para perpetuar mas en Inglaterra la memoria dela tierra santa" (2v) [more greatly to perpetuate in England the memory of the Holy Land]. Further reinforcing its Jesuit dimensions, the *Relacion* also bears an introductory "Aprobacion" from the Jesuit Pedro de Ribadeneyra.

59. The quotation comes from Ex. 47 in Michael Ivens's translation of the *Spiritual Exercises* (Leominster: Gracewing, 2004), included in Nicholas Standaert, "The Composition of Place: Creating Space for an Encounter," *The Way* 46.1 (2007): 7.

60. Standaert, "Composition of Place," 7, 17.

61. Ibid., 16.

62. Quoted in Batley, "Martyrdom," 5.

63. Alain Boureau, "The Letter-Writing Norm, a Mediaeval Invention," in *Correspondence: Models of Letter-Writing from the Middle Ages to the Nineteenth Century,* ed. Roger Chartier, Alain Boureau, and Cécile Dauphin, trans. Christopher Woodall (Princeton: Princeton University Press, 1997), 28.

64. Grant Boswell, "Letter Writing among the Jesuits: Antonio Possevino's Advice in the *Bibliotheca Selecta* (1593)," *Huntington Library Quarterly* 66.3–4 (2003): 255.

65. Boswell, "Letter Writing," 256.

66. Rhodes points out, "In 1599, the *Historia particular de la persecución en Inglaterra* was published [*Detailed History of the Persecution in England*], an account written largely by Creswell but published in Diego de Yepez's name. This book was extremely popular at the Spanish court, and it contained two long accounts by Elizabeth Sanders of the harried adventures of some English nuns, formerly at Syon Abbey, before they settled in Portugal. These texts surely inspired Carvajal, who later opened her house in Valladolid to recusant women seeking shelter on their way to convents of their choice" (*TE,* 12).

67. I take this phrase from M. García-Verdugo, who says in discussing Luisa's poetry, "Las fuentes de esta estética del dolor fueron los martirologios . . . y los escritos de San Ignacio de Loyola" ("Luisa de Carvajal: Aventurera y escritora," *Espéculo: Revista de estudios literarios,* 2004, www.ucm.es /info /especulo / numero26 /carvajal.html) [The sources of this aesthetic of suffering were the martyrologies . . . and the writings of St. Ignatius Loyola].

68. On the ways in which this passage functions to authorize Luisa's bold stance in providing political advice to the Spanish monarchy, see Elena Levy-Navarro, "The Religious Warrior: Luisa de Carvajal y Mendoza's Correspondence with Rodrigo de Calderón," in *Women's Letters across Europe, 1400–1700: Form and Persuasion,* ed. Jane Couchman and Ann Crabb (Burlington, VT: Ashgate, 2004), 268.

69. García-Verdugo, in "Luisa de Carvajal," observes that in Luisa's writings we find "un intento de representación de un Jesucristo en mujer y de la transfiguración de una mujer en Crist" [an intention to represent Christ in a woman and the transfiguration of a woman into Christ].

70. The blurring of the boundaries between Luisa's suffering, that of the Catholic Church, and that of a national body politic echoes not only the similar set of alignments found in the writings of the English Benedictines in exile but

also those found in English Jesuit poetry. As Karen Batley says of an untitled poem most likely written by Henry Walpole, "The speaker wants martyrdom, and to this end Calvary and the events of the Crucifixion are transposed into the setting of the English persecutions" ("Martyrdom," 5).

71. Luisa's Society included English women from a range of social backgrounds. It is somewhat difficult to determine the precise membership, since Luisa carefully refers to the women only by first names, to protect their identities (*TE*, 25). At the beginning, Luisa had two women who lived with her and formed the core of the Society, and by November 5, 1608, "the number had risen to five, with another two expected" (Rees, *Writings of Doña Luisa*, 25). We know that Henry Garnet's cousin Anne was a longtime member of the Society, and evidence from the process of beatification held for Carvajal suggests that Mary Ward's aunt was also a member (Abad, *Escritos autobiográficos*, 106).

72. Remarking on this passage, Levy-Navarro observes, "We can also sense in these letters a degree of disdain for those women who choose . . . a traditional life of monastic retreat and contemplation. . . . The language she uses juxtaposes the 'weak' piety of the cloistered convent with the 'strong' piety that is required in the existing warlike situation facing the Church" ("Religious Warrior," 272). Abad, in his introduction to Luisa's *Escritos autobiográficos*, underlines the fact that, in spite of Luisa's objections to traditional female monasticism, what she, like her contemporary Mary Ward, sought to found was a new religious order: "No es posible dudar . . . que Doña Luisa trató de fundar en Inglaterra una verdadera Congregación religiosa, a la que dio el nombre de '*Compañia de la soberana Virgen María Nuestra Señora*' con algún rasgo tan ignaciano como el del cuarto voto de obediencia al Romano Pontífice" (105) [It is impossible to doubt . . . that Doña Luisa tried to found a true religious congregation in England, to which she gave the name "Company of the Sovereign Virgin Mary, Our Lady," with a certain Jesuit characteristic such as the fourth vow of obedience to the Roman Pontificate].

73. In a letter to the Duke of Lerma, Luisa similarly indicates, "De dos delitos me ha acusado de la mesa del Consejo de Estado, delante de don Diego, el falso arzobispo de Cantorbery . . . : el uno, que he fundado monasterios de monjas, y el otro que he reducido con mi persuasión [a] muchos protestantes a mi religión" (*TE*, 294) [In the session of the Council of State, according to Don Diego, the false archbishop of Canterbury has accused me of two crimes . . . : one, that I have founded monasteries for nuns, and the other that I have brought many Protestants to my religion by means of persuasion] (*TE*, 295).

74. Quoted in Senning, "Carvajal Affair," 55.

75. Quoted in ibid., 52. Senning indicates that the description of Luisa as a "Jesuitess" may suggest that Abbot "suspected her community to be either identical with or closely connected with a similar community which Mary Ward, foundress of the Institute of the Blessed Virgin Mary, had recently established in Louvain. . . . The first filiation of the congregation in England . . . had apparently been set up in the very neighborhood of Dona Luisa's house, about the same time that she and her companions had moved into the area" (52).

76. Quoted in ibid., 57.

77. Rees, *Writings of Doña Luisa*, 28.

78. This description harmonizes with Loyola's emphasis on the importance of unity and love; as Grant Boswell observes, "Loyola had stressed unity as the supreme virtue. . . . Loyola's goal . . . was to establish an 'apostolic community of love'" ("Letter Writing," 275).

79. I quote from the facsimile edition of James Hogg, ed., *The Rewyll of Seynt Sauioure and Other Middle English Brigittine Legislative Texts*, vol. 2, Salzburger Studien zur Anglistik und Amerikanistik 6 (Salzburg: Institut für Englische Sprache und Literatur, Universität Salzburg, 1978), 56r–56v.

80. See Warren, *Women of God and Arms*, 139–49.

81. Similarly, in writing to her cousin the Marquesa de Caracena in 1612, Luisa says that the women of her Society strive "en cause gloriosa y felicísima" [in a glorious, happy cause] and that none of them has any fear for their own sakes ("ninguna dellas hay que tema cosa alguna por sí misma"). She goes on to say that they would happily suffer prison and chains ("alegremente sufrirán cadenas y cárceles") if they could free the priests from the wolves and wild beasts by doing so ("y como puedan librar los pastores destos lobos y fieras bestias") (c. 152, p. 317).

82. Levy-Navarro notes that in Luisa's Orders for the Society, the plight of the women of the Society under the English persecutions "becomes a metaphor for the condition of the Catholic Church generally" ("Religious Warrior," 271).

83. Glyn Redworth, *The She-Apostle: The Extraordinary Life and Death of Luisa de Carvajal* (Oxford: Oxford University Press, 2008), 223.

84. Quoted in ibid., 224.

85. Ibid., 223, 224.

86. Ibid., 223.

87. Ibid., 224.

88. Walker, *Gender and Politics*, 124.

89. On the Infanta's support for English nunneries, see Paul Arblaster, "The Infanta and the English Benedictine Nuns: Mary Percy's Memories in 1634," *Recusant History* 23.4 (1997): 508–27.

90. Caroline Bowden, "The Abbess and Mrs. Brown: Lady Mary Knatchbull and Royalist Politics in Flanders in the Late 1650s," *Recusant History* 24.3 (1999): 294.

91. Ibid., 289, 294.

92. Quoted in ibid., 294.

93. See ibid.; Caroline Bowden, "The Role of Mary Knatchbull in the English Benedictine Foundations of the Seventeenth Century," *Magistra* 8.1 (2002): 26–52; Claire Walker, "Prayer, Patronage, and Political Conspiracy: English Nuns and the Restoration," *Historical Journal* 43.1 (2000): 1–23; and Walker, *Gender and Politics.*

94. Bowden, "Abbess and Mrs. Brown," 297.

95. Walker, *Gender and Politics,* 127.

96. Bowden, "Abbess and Mrs. Brown," 293.

97. Anne Neville, "Abbess Neville's Annals of Five Communities of English Benedictine Nuns in Flanders, 1598–1687," in *Catholic Record Society Miscellanea,* ed. M. J. Rumsey, Catholic Record Society 6 (London: Catholic Record Society, 1909), 36. In accordance with editorial policy, I have expanded contractions in quotations from the "Annals" (though I retain ampersands as printed); expansions are indicated with italics.

98. Ibid., 36.

99. Ibid. Other convent records from the period also indicate the perception that there might well be a link between embodied spiritual virtues and a community's temporal success. In discussing convents' choices of monastic superiors, Claire Walker notes, "There were more practical reasons for choosing a saintly superior. One so close to God would secure heavenly assistance in her task, and this might prove crucial to houses in economic difficulties. After Margaret Mostyn's rise to power, the Lierre Carmelites attributed their improved fortunes to God's providence, secured in part by their admirable prioress" (*Gender and Politics,* 156).

100. Ibid., 117.

101. Ibid., 118.

102. As Walker observes, "It is this seemingly modest aim which best illuminates her overtly political ambitions" ("Prayer, Patronage," 12).

103. All quotations here are from ibid., 18. On the foundation at Dunkirk, and the difficulties Mary Knatchbull encountered, see ibid.; St. Scholastica's Abbey, *A History of the English Benedictine Nuns of Dunkirk Now at St. Scholastica's Abbey, Teignnmouth, Devon* (London, 1958); and Anne Neville, "Abbess Neville's Annals," pp. 40–41.

104. Similarly, "The Rouen Poor Clare convent was founded in 1644 partly on the understanding of its benefactors that it would pray for their homeland's conversion. To that end the nuns recited the Litany of the Saints each night. Their devotions became more explicitly subversive in 1657 when Abbess Mary (Mary Francis) Taylor ordered prayers and penance for the preservation of Dunkirk from Oliver Cromwell's besieging forces" (Walker, *Gender and Politics*, 119).

105. St. Scholastica's Abbey, *History*, 11.

106. Ibid. Shell points out that, similarly, "[t]he pious Catholic conception of England as Mary's dowry had especial resonance at Valladolid. In *The Running Register*, Lewis Owen reports on a picture at the College: Mary spreading out her mantle, with her hand over kneeling Jesuits who are presenting her a scroll, upon which is written *sub umbra alarum tuarum manebimus, donec transeat iniquitas* (we will remain under the shade of your wings till the wickedness passes). The superscription was *Anglia dos Mariae* (England: Mary's dowry: p. 54)" (*Catholicism, Controversy*, 206).

107. St. Scholastica's Abbey, *History*, 9.

108. Walker states, "The regular royal intercourse of the 1650s inspired confidence in the princes' return to the Roman faith, and prayers for the conversion of England became synonymous with petitions for Charles's and James's salvation" (*Gender and Politics*, 128).

109. Ibid., 125.

110. Ibid., 126.

CHAPTER 4. WOMEN'S LIFE WRITING, WOMEN'S BODIES, AND THE GENDERED POLITICS OF FAITH

1. On Wynkyn de Worde's version of Margery's text, see chapter 6 of Karma Lochrie, *Margery Kempe and Translations of the Flesh* (Philadelphia: University of Pennsylvania Press, 1999).

2. Sanford B. Meech and Hope Emily Allen, eds., *The Book of Margery Kempe*, by Margery Kempe, EETS, o.s., 212 (London: EETS, 1940), 359. All quotations from *The Book of Margery Kempe* are taken from this edition (hereafter cited as *Book*) and are cited parenthetically in the text.

3. See ibid., Appendix III, 362–68, for records concerning John Kempe.

4. For a concise overview of Elizabeth Cary's life and literary career, see Stephanie Hodgson-Wright, "Cary, Elizabeth, Viscountess Falkland (1585–1639)," in *Oxford Dictionary of National Biography*, ed. H. C. G. Matthew

and Brian Harrison (Oxford: Oxford University Press, 2004), www.oxforddnb
.com/view/article/4835 (accessed June 29, 2009).

5. See Nicholas Watson, "The Composition of Julian of Norwich's Revelation of Love," *Speculum* 68.3 (1993): 637–83.

6. See Nancy Bradley Warren, *Spiritual Economies: Female Monasticism in
Later Medieval England* (Philadelphia: University of Pennsylvania Press, 2001),
92–108.

7. Though *The Life of Lady Falkland* does not directly state the identity of
the daughter who wrote it, Heather Wolfe makes a persuasive case for Lucy (in
religion Dame Magdalena) as the most likely candidate. See Heather Wolfe's
introduction to *Elizabeth Cary, Lady Falkland: Life and Letters,* ed. Heather Wolfe,
Renaissance Texts from Manuscript 4 (Tempe: Arizona Center for Medieval and
Renaissance Studies, 2001).

8. Ibid., 89.

9. Nigel Smith, *Perfection Proclaimed: Language and Literature in English
Radical Religion, 1640–1660* (Oxford: Clarendon Press, 1989), 17.

10. Ibid., 13. Anna Trapnel provides evidence for her literacy. In *The Cry of
a Stone* (London, 1654; Wing (2nd ed.) T2031; hereafter cited parenthetically in
the text), the very next sentence that follows Anna's account of her mother's
dying words that catalyzed her prophetic gifts is "I was trained up to my book
and writing" (3). Anna Trapnel thus begins by emphasizing not only her divine
inspiration but also her possession of the literacy skills that enable her textual
production. With this juxtaposition, Trapnel sets the stage for the ambiguous
and paradoxical attitude toward authorship that permeates her texts; she simultaneously adopts passive and active roles in the process of textual production.
She repeatedly states that the voice that speaks her prophecies is not hers but
God's, that she is simply a channel or conduit, yet she also adopts an authoritative position within textual culture. As Kate Chedzgoy argues, "Anna Trapnel
constantly insists on her own insignificance and passivity, representing herself
as merely the transmitter of God's message; yet she is also empowered by the
social status that being a prophet gives her" ("Female Prophecy in the Seventeenth Century: The Instance of Anna Trapnel," in *Writing the English Renaissance,* ed. William Zunder and Suzanne Trill [London: Longman, 1996], 250).
In her discussion of Trapnel's prophecies recorded in an untitled volume in the
Bodleian Library, Chedzgoy notes that Trapnel discounts her own voice as foul
and insignificant, yet with "curious irony . . . it is her own poetic voice which
encloses and oscillates between statements both of her own supposed degrada-
tion and of the 'royal grace' of her divine master" (250).

11. In her analysis of early modern Catholic women's biographies, Frances Dolan points to these texts' strong ties to the bodily. She discusses the frequent occurrence of nursing the sick as something of great spiritual significance in these texts, arguing that the accounts "share an intense corporeality that corresponds to the 'real presence' of the body in Catholicism" ("Reading, Work, and Catholic Women's Biographies," *English Literary Renaissance* 33.3 [2003]: 343). She then explicitly distinguishes such aspects of Catholic texts from Protestant ones, saying, "These texts dwell on the details of bodily failure, the assault of the diseased on the caretaker's senses, in a way that is not typical of Protestant women's biographies and autobiographies" (343). The bodily is certainly very much present in the Catholic texts upon which Dolan focuses, as well as in the somewhat different group of Catholic texts upon which I concentrate in this and in earlier chapters. I also agree that there is a strong alliance between the bodily dimensions of Catholic texts and the Catholic belief in the "real presence," as my analysis of incarnational textuality suggests—though, as we have already seen in the writings of Grace Mildmay, in which the body has important spiritual dimensions and vice versa, this quality is not confined to Catholic texts alone. Indeed, the overlap of the linguistic registers in Mildmay's spiritual and medical writings shares much with the writings of the Antwerp Carmelite nuns, in which, as Nicky Hallett points out, "the closeness of medicinal, clerical, and miraculous discourses . . . indicates how interconnected these systems were" (*Lives of Spirit: English Carmelite Self-Writing of the Early Modern Period* [Aldershot: Ashgate, 2007], 23).

12. Katharine Gillespie comments on the generic complexity of Anna Trapnel's texts, saying, "Anna Trapnel . . . published several major versions of her prophecies in generically 'hybrid' blends of autobiography, songs, prayers, letters, factual narrative, and politically-visionary poetry throughout the protectorate years of the 1650s" ("Anna Trapnel's Window on the Word: The Domestic Sphere of Public Dissent in Seventeenth-Century Nonconformity," *Bunyan Studies* 7 [1997]: 50).

13. For Margery Kempe especially, the role of the scribe has been the subject of much critical debate. In *Margery Kempe's Dissenting Fictions* (University Park: Pennsylvania State University Press, 1994), Lynn Staley strongly argues for the literariness of *The Book of Margery Kempe*. She distinguishes between "Kempe" the author and "Margery" the character and examines the function of the scribe's presence as a trope. Diana Uhlman, in "The Comfort of Voice, the Solace of Script: Orality and Literacy in *The Book of Margery Kempe*" (*Studies in Philology* 91 [1994]: 50–69), too considers the scribe as a trope. In an early

essay on Margery Kempe ("Author and Scribe in *The Book of Margery Kempe*," *Medium Aevum* 44 [1975]: 145–50), John Hirsch suggests that Margery's second scribe coauthors the *Book*. In contrast, Nicholas Watson asserts that "Kempe herself, not her scribe, was primarily responsible for the *Book*'s structure, arguments, and most of its language" ("The Making of *The Book of Margery Kempe*," in *Voices in Dialogue: Reading Women in the Middle Ages*, ed. Linda Olson and Kathryn Kerby-Fulton [Notre Dame: University of Notre Dame Press, 2005], 397), an argument with which Felicity Riddy takes issue in her essay "Text and Self in *The Book of Margery Kempe*," in Olson and Kerby-Fulton, *Voices in Dialogue*, 435–53. Like Watson, I attribute significant agency to Margery Kempe in the production of the *Book*, an agency I also attribute to Anna Trapnel in the production of her texts. In a related argument, Lochrie explores the textual influences evident in *The Book of Margery Kempe* and revisits the question of Margery's purported illiteracy, arguing that we should not be so quick to attribute the literate, and even Latinate, elements of the *Book* simply to the scribe. Pointing to a passage in which Christ refers to Margery's both reading and hearing texts read (*Book*, 281), Lochrie argues, "Christ here recognizes both her reading and her hearing works read. The distinction itself points to her ability to read, although neither her editors nor modern scholars have commented on this puzzling evidence. It is interesting that her scribe does not dispute it either. . . . If Kempe could read after all, it is time her late twentieth-century readers realized it" (*Margery Kempe*, 126–27).

14. On Anna Trapnel's use of the third person, see Susannah Mintz, "The Specular Self of *Anna Trapnel's Report and Plea*," *Pacific Coast Philology* 35.1 (2000): 1–16, and Maria Magro, "Spiritual Autobiography and Radical Sectarian Discourse: Anna Trapnel and the Bad Girls of the English Revolution," *Journal of Medieval and Early Modern Studies* 34.2 (2004): 405–73, especially 417.

15. Elspeth Graham et al., *Her Own Life: Autobiographical Writings by Seventeenth-Century Englishwomen* [London: Routledge, 1989], 17. Sarah Beckwith lucidly sets out the problems inherent in many critical attempts to read *The Book of Margery Kempe* as autobiography, assessments that are quite apposite to Anna Trapnel's writings as well. Beckwith notes that such readings tend to focus not on "the soul reflecting God" but rather on "the personality of Margery Kempe herself" ("Problems of Authority in Late Medieval English Mysticism: Language, Agency, and Authority in *The Book of Margery Kempe*," *Exemplaria* 4 [1992]: 176). She indicates that the difficulty in such readings is not with finding "something autobiographical about her book" but with "models of thinking the relation of self and world" that "vitiate any dynamic and historical account of the way self

and world are imbricated in her book" as well as with "a static and moralistic essentialism" that "pervades the critical encounter with her text" (197).

16. In the introduction to *Her Own Life* (a collection of early modern women's autobiographical writings), the editors point out, "It is clear from the shared features of many of the texts included in this collection that a motivation for the women who wrote them was to make the truth about themselves known. And repeatedly we find the texts have been entitled (whether by the women themselves or by their original editors) a 'true relation,' 'a vindication,' a 'plea,' or a 'record,' all of which suggest factuality or a demand to be believed. With different degrees of explicitness, these women wrote and were perceived by their contemporaries as writing, with the intention of speaking themselves in order to make that self heard and known. This intention coincides with a modern sense of what autobiography is. . . . But although it may be clear that autobiography takes its form from an articulation of the self, definitions of autobiography are, in fact, notoriously hard to draw up" (Graham et al., *Her Own Life*, 16–17). The editors also observe, "The question of 'truth,' so vigorously asserted by many of the women . . . can be problematic to the modern reader" (17). For a useful survey of critical approaches to and problems surrounding women's autobiographical writing, see Susan Stanford Friedman, "Women's Autobiographical Selves: Theory and Practice," in *The Private Self: Theory and Practice of Women's Autobiographical Writing,* ed. Shari Benstock (Chapel Hill: University of North Carolina Press, 1988), 34–62.

17. Staley, *Margery Kempe's Dissenting Fictions,* xii.

18. Mintz in fact argues of *Anna Trapnel's Report and Plea,* "Trapnel's self-presentation accords with recent theories of autobiography, which suggest that self-writing is less a straightforward record of being than an imposition of narrative shape on the events of a life, a process of 'becoming' that creates rather than communicates 'self'" ("Specular Self," 6). My position is similar to that of Nicholas Watson, who says of *The Book of Margery Kempe,* "[M]y discussion thus deliberately blurs the roles of author, narrator, and protagonist literary criticism often separates" ("Making of *The Book*," 397). He continues, "At the same time, my reading of the *Book* takes it seriously as argument as well as narration: an argument that uses Kempe's life to explore ideas about the inscrutability of the divine will, about the relation between embodiment, worldly living, and holiness, and about suffering prayer as a path to divine mercy, while also using those ideas to reflect on the puzzling *miraculum* that was her life" (397). Felicity Riddy, responding to Watson's essay, says, "Treating the text as autobiography does not mean treating it as historically true, however, as Watson seems to do"

("Text and Self," 443). While I am not sure I agree that Watson does treat the text as "historically true" in precisely the way Riddy claims he does, I certainly agree with her view of autobiography. Historical truth, however, may well mean something different than Riddy intends by her use of the concept when human history and salvation history overlap in the way that they do in the *Book*. Magro's remarks on *Anna Trapnel's Report and Plea* are also apposite. She says, "What is apparent in the *Report and Plea* . . . is not a dissolution of self, but a representation of the self as a product of diverse enunciative acts, memory, and writing. . . . Significantly, Trapnel refers to her narration as a book even before it is written . . . , blurring the boundaries between speech and writing. What is left is a multivalent model of textuality in which memory, writing, and identity are represented as contingent and mutually constructing. Truth and self are not set in opposition. Rather, Trapnel's narration suggests the textuality and intersection of both concepts" ("Spiritual Autobiography," 417).

19. In my consideration of Margery's embodied piety, my reading of the *Book* diverges from that of Lynn Staley, who argues that Margery Kempe does not "provide the detailed account of physical sensation or of spiritual insight that we find in other works of devotion. Where such descriptions are integral to the *Incendium Amoris*, they are incidental to the *Book*" (*Margery Kempe's Dissenting Fictions*, 98). She elaborates: "If the *Book* can sometimes seem punctilious about the details of late medieval female sanctity, it is because Kempe, like Chaucer, knew that writers must evolve ways of speaking that at once drew upon and transformed traditional images and modes. The overarching fiction of the *Book* as recorded sound and the references to Margery's religious impulses and experience are designed to serve as 'generic stimuli' in a reader. However, as I have reiterated, the *Book* is finally not 'about' that religious experience; instead, it uses Margery to examine what were some extremely provocative issues. One of these is the issue of spiritual authority" (102). I do not wish to downplay the ways in which the *Book* is a literary text that draws upon and transforms traditional images and modes. However, I do not believe that necessarily precludes the text's being about religious experience. As I have already suggested, part of my interest is precisely in the ways in which religious experience is itself textually inflected. Nor do I see it as impossible for the *Book* both to be about an individual's religious experience and at the same time to engage in social critique as it explores "extremely provocative issues," including spiritual authority. Nicholas Watson's discussion of the physical in *The Book of Margery Kempe* is relevant to my discussion of Kempe's, and of Trapnel's, embodied piety. Watson argues, "Just as, in the logic of simile, a concrete object is a more comprehensible point of comparison for an abstraction than is another abstraction, so in the *Book*

the physical is in many ways actually closer to the infinite than the spiritual" ("Making of *The Book,*" 421).

20. In this chapter, Jesus also describes his relationship with Margery Kempe using the paradigms of mother (Kempe) and son (Christ) as well as father (Christ) and daughter (Kempe), a fact that enhances the argument I make in the first chapter that nuptial unions with the divine are not the only ones in which gender plays a significant role. On the multiplication of familial roles here and elsewhere in *The Book of Margery Kempe,* see Sarah Beckwith, "A Very Material Mysticism: The Medieval Mysticism of Margery Kempe," in *Medieval Literature: Criticism, Ideology, and History,* ed. David Aers (Brighton: Harvester, 1986); and Liz Herbert McAvoy, *Authority and the Female Body in the Writings of Julian of Norwich and Margery Kempe* (Cambridge: D. S. Brewer, 2004).

21. Lochrie, *Margery Kempe,* 14. See also Lochrie's discussion of Richard Rolle's use of sensual language. She notes, "Rolle's description of mystical experience in terms of the three-fold way of fire, sweetness, and song has recently been defended by scholars as metaphorical language. Therefore, Rolle is not guilty of corporeal mystical experience or of being seduced by the carnal pleasures of language. This defense is a response to earlier criticism of Rolle's failure to ascend to the higher reaches of contemplation. Insistence on the metaphoricity of Rolle's language is used, in turn, to criticize Kempe and all who use sensual language too literally as *misreaders* of Rolle" (5–6). Lochrie further argues that scholars who attribute metaphorical status to Rolle's language might rather be the ones guilty of misreading; see her discussion of a fifteenth-century annotator of the *Book*'s references to Rolle in relation to Margery's practices (121).

22. Such complex interplay is also a feature of Anna Trapnel's writing. Discussing *Cry of a Stone,* Hilary Hinds points out, "Trapnel's writing . . . reads her prophecies from the text of the capital, and then writes them through the recitation and reinvocation of the godly signs that have, as it were, risen, materially, before her eyes. Her literal capacity to see—consciously to register material data through one of the five senses whose existence and persistence confirm her as a sentient and bodily being—is here merged with her spiritual capacity to see (in these sense of 'understand'). Her visions elide with her vision" ("Sectarian Spaces: The Politics of Space and Gender in Seventeenth-Century Prophetic Writing," *Literature and History* 13.2 [2004]: 17). Magro additionally observes that in sectarian women's spiritual autobiographies, "The workings of the soul . . . acquire a tangibility that for many sectarians was as tangible as that of the body" ("Spiritual Autobiography," 412).

23. James Holstun, *Ehud's Dagger: Class Struggle in the English Revolution* (London: Verso, 2000), 282.

24. Holstun's claim is troublingly reminiscent of early modern Protestant writings about nunneries, which tended toward either pity or prurient satire. Similar sets of attitudes are still all too commonly visible in scholarship focusing on Protestant female spirituality of the early modern period, which is set in contrast to its medieval "other." As the cases of the exiled English Carmelites, Benedictines, and Brigittines discussed previously make clear, most women who joined these communities were not forced to do so. Rather, like most medieval English women who entered nunneries, they "freely chose" their professed status, a choice realized, in the case of the post-Dissolution early modern English nuns, through no small amount of hardship and trouble. Erica Longfellow specifically references the writings of Gertrude More to argue that "early modern English Catholic women approached mystical marriage as key to their cloistered virginity in a way that would have seemed foreign and superstitious to . . . Protestant women" (*Women and Religious Writing in Early Modern England* [Cambridge: Cambridge University Press, 2004], 14–15). She thus seems to draw a fairly firm distinction between Catholic and Protestant manifestations of this form of spiritual identity. She then notes, however, quite rightly in my view, "[Y]et, of course, these traditions are connected, not only by a common scriptural basis but also by an interpretative heritage. Despite the virtual disappearance of many medieval manuscript works from the reading of early modern individuals, a multitude of traces of the Catholic past remains in the culture: St Bernard of Clairvaux and before him Origen of Alexandria defined the basic allegorical approach to mystical marriage texts that continued to influence Protestant thinkers, and George Scheper has argued that in fact Protestant commentaries are fundamentally similar to their medieval counterparts in their conservative use of allegory. Similarly, the Puritan forms of meditation that underlie much mystical marriage writing can be traced directly to Ignatian models. The cultural influences of the Catholic past—and present—allowed for greater commonalities between medieval and early modern Catholic holy women and their English Protestant counterparts than many of those Englishwomen would have acknowledged" (15).

25. Smith's observation about the nature of Independent religion is relevant: "[T]he Independents were noted for their vocabulary of 'in-comings, out-lettings, and in-dwellings.' It was a form of mysticism which lay at the very heart of Puritan experience" (*Perfection Proclaimed*, 15).

26. Longfellow observes that Anna Trapnel uses her "identity as the bride of Christ to justify . . . politically and socially subversive speech" (*Women and Religious Writing*, 4).

27. Anna Trapnel, *A Legacy for Saints* (London, 1654), Wing (2nd ed.) T2032; hereafter cited parenthetically in the text.

28. On Anna Trapnel's negotiations of the categories of public and private through her identity as bride of Christ, see chapter 5, "Anna Trapnel Sings of Her Love," in Longfellow, *Women and Religious Writing*, especially 166 ff. Centrally, Longfellow argues, "Trapnel's spiritual autobiography *A legacy for saints* uses images of marriage to Christ to define her experience of conversion. Her account employs the conventions of the genre to underline that her calling is both personally felt and outwardly confirmed, and thus crosses the divide between public and private" (167).

29. Anna also says that God subsequently upbraids her for not having proclaimed her identity even more assertively: "[T]he Lord spoke to me, and said, I have made thee as sure of salvation, as I am God in heaven; why didst thou say hopest, and didst not rather tell that thy God had assured thee that Christ was thine . . . ?" (*Legacy*, 10).

30. Anna Trapnel, *Anna Trapnel's Report and Plea, or, A narrative of her journey into Cornwal* (London, 1654), 14; Wing (2nd ed.) T2033; hereafter cited parenthetically in the text.

31. On Anna's mobilization of language from the Canticles in the spiritual songs recorded in the untitled Bodleian volume, see Matthew Prineas, "The Discourse of Love and the Rhetoric of Apocalypse in Anna Trapnel's Folio Songs," *Comitatus* 28 (1997): 90–110. Holstun points out the importance of the Song of Songs in Anna's adoption of the identity of "the Spouse" or Christ's "Rose of Sharon" in exhorting her companions (*Ehud's Dagger*, 298).

32. In her essay "Soul-Ravishing and Sin-Subduing: Anna Trapnel and the Gendered Politics of Free Grace," Hilary Hinds makes a related argument. She says of *Legacy*, "Citing . . . the Song of Songs (1:2, 2:6, 4:10, 12, 8:3) to characterize the relationship of the saint with the savior in a state of grace, Trapnel taps into long-established readings of this book of the Bible, whose erotics had been variously understood within the Christian tradition as an allegory of the individual soul's union with Christ, of Christ's love for his Church, and of the apocalypse. Drawing on this common stock of associations, as had many women visionaries before her, Trapnel's use of the image underwrites the figuring of the joy of the saint's union with Christ through grace as erotic, and specifically endorses the bodiliness of the pleasures that follow from this" (Hilary Hinds, "Soul-Ravishing and Sin Subduing: Anna Trapnel and the Gendered Politics of Free Grace," *Renaissance and Reformation/Renaissance et Réforme* 25.4 [2001]: 127). She further argues, "[I]t is the conjunction of the discourse of free grace

with the spiritualized erotics of the Song of Songs that provides Trapnel with a dynamic language for rewriting and reclaiming the prophetic body. Thereby the body is empowered, transformed from object to subject, instrument to agent, as the fears of the body under Law are replaced by the desires of the body under Grace" (127–28).

33. Diane Purkiss, "Producing the Voice, Consuming the Body: Women Prophets of the Seventeenth Century," in *Women, Writing, History, 1640–1740*, ed. Isobel Grundy and Susan Wiseman (Athens: University of Georgia Press, 1992), 144. See also Hinds, "Sectarian Spaces," and Sue Wiseman, "Margaret Cavendish among the Prophets: Performance Ideologies and Gender in and after the English Civil War," in *Women's Writing: The Elizabethan to Victorian Period* 6.1 (1999): 95–111, especially 101–2 on Anna Trapnel. Maria Magro also discusses Anna Trapnel's body and the production of authentic, authorized meaning, saying, "Trapnel's textual practice, for example, positions the author's body as the locus of meaning *and* that which produces an endless deferral of meaning. As a mystic prophet, Trapnel's ecstatic fits (her transcendence of body) legitimate her utterances. Her ecstasies, which are fashioned by Trapnel as moments during which she has no control over her physical person, provide the mark of authenticity of the visionary prophet. Put simply, people pay attention to Trapnel, they give heed to her utterance, precisely because she makes a spectacle of her body. . . . At the same time as it provides the mark of truth-value, Trapnel's body is an opaque text which, precisely because it produces an excessive fund of often contradictory meanings (witch, lunatic, whore, prophet, traitor), eludes any essential, stable signification. . . . Language and body work together to convince the spectator that Trapnel is the 'real thing'" ("Spiritual Autobiography," 415).

34. Hilary Hinds, *God's Englishwomen: Seventeenth-Century Radical Sectarian Writing and Feminist Criticism* (Manchester: Manchester University Press, 1996), 93.

35. These medieval women's suffering and divinely assisted endurance also serve the sort of authorizing, authenticating function that Purkiss ("Producing the Voice") describes, helping guarantee the orthodoxy of their lives and their texts.

36. As Watson indicates, Margery's "contemplative recreations of the Passion bridge past and present . . . as she travels back in time in her body as well as soul" ("Making of *The Book*," 420).

37. Margery Kempe, as we have seen, understands some of her suffering to result from divine punishment. And as Christ makes clear when he refuses to take away Margery's public cries, her attendant suffering that accompanies her

cries (the great pain she feels in her heart in addition to the pain of being excluded from church as a result of her cries) will aid in her salvation, since it will prevent her from suffering as and after she departs from this world. Anna Trapnel too finds a corrective, redemptive dimension to her suffering of imprisonment (though not, presumably, the form of correction that those who imprisoned her intended!). She writes: "I said not, O when will there be an end of this or the other affliction, but I often said and desired a purging out of my corruption, before a removall of sufferings, that so I might come out more holy and more humble, and more selfe-denying and selfe-debasing . . . : That so I might all my dayes be willing to take up the Crosse of Christ, and follow him, whether so ever he would have me, either to do or suffer" (*Report and Plea,* 45).

38. See also chapter 26, where Margery Kempe tells of being reproved by her fellow pilgrims for her fasting, weeping, and conversation.

39. There are numerous other instances of Margery Kempe's being accused of hypocrisy or fakery by clerics and orthodox religious (see, for instance, chapter 50, where she is rebuked by an anchoress, and chapter 63, where people believe she is a hypocrite because of a friar's preaching against her. However, there are also plenty of examples of clerics and other religious expressing approval for and embracing Kempe's piety, including the anchoress Julian of Norwich (see *Book,* 42–43) and the Franciscan nuns of Denny (see *Book,* 202–3). Anna Trapnel too recounts both positive and negative responses to her piety and prophecy by figures of ecclesiastical authority; that authority is, of course, in Trapnel's time even more fragmented and subject to competing claims than in Kempe's era.

40. Margery Kempe faces a similar accusation while she is on pilgrimage, when a priest states, "Now wote I wel þat þu has a deuyl wyth-inne þe, for I her hym spekyn in þe to me" (85).

41. See, for instance, Christ's promise to Margery Kempe that he will grant her grace to answer any cleric, and Anna Trapnel's description of the Lord's teaching her to speak (*Report and Plea,* 15), as well as the divine reassurance she is given about her ability to respond adequately during her interrogation (*Report and Plea,* 19).

42. Meech and Allen posit that "hymyr" is an error for "hyndyr," but Lynn Staley points out that "*hymyr* appears plainly in the manuscript." She adds, "I am inclined to accept it and to think that *hymyr* is a variation of *himmere,* a word whose roots the editors of the *Middle English Dictionary* question, but conjecture as meaning inglorious or miserable" (*Margery Kempe's Dissenting Fictions,* 9 n. 19).

43. Staley too observes the connection between the hostile reactions Margery Kempe encounters and *imitatio Christi*. She argues, "In a literary fiction where Margery's life seems a reenactment of the Passion of Christ or of the persecution of the early martyrs, her neighbors play the part of the hostile, crucifying, tormenting crowd that sought to destroy Christ and his church" (*Margery Kempe's Dissenting Fictions*, 65–66).

44. Esther Gilman Richey also discusses Anna Trapnel's understanding of her experience as a reiteration of Christ's; see the chapter entitled "Re-covering Paul: The True Church and the Prophecies of Mary Cary, Anna Trapnel, and Margaret Fell," in her book *The Politics of Revelation in the English Renaissance* (Columbia: University of Missouri Press, 1998), especially 204–5.

45. Margery Kempe illustrates such valuation of slander and rejection when she tells a group of hostile monks a story about a man who, as a penance, pays to be reproved and laughs when he receives chiding for free, comparing his situation to her own (28).

46. See especially Lochrie, *Margery Kempe*, and McAvoy, *Authority*.

47. Holstun, *Ehud's Dagger*, 280.

48. Ibid., 298–99.

49. See Bodleian S 1. 42 Th. 725, "723" (i.e., 732), 757, 827, 867.

50. Purkiss, "Producing the Voice," 150.

51. Purkiss observes, "In these maternal metaphors, there is an underlying linkage between female reproduction and the production of the Word of God. . . . The polyvalence of the metaphor of Christ as Word allows [the female prophet] to represent herself both as a conduit for the Word of God and as the bearer of God, the producer of ultimate meaning" (ibid., 153). See also Warren, *Spiritual Economies*, for my analysis of a similar alignment of textual production and the reproductive work of the Virgin Mary in the Incarnation in medieval Brigittine texts (53–54).

52. Prineas, "Discourse of Love," 103.

53. Tamsin Spargo claims, "The signs of Trapnel's possession of the *logos* were to be read on her body, in her trances, strange movements as she lay in bed prophesying in fragments of verse and song. Physicality lurks at the edges of Trapnel's narrative like the repressed threatening to return" ("The Father's Seduction: Improper Relations of Desire in Seventeenth-Century Nonconformist Communities," *Tulsa Studies in Women's Literature* 17.2 [1998]: 261). While I agree that the signs of Trapnel's possession of the *logos* manifest themselves corporeally, I find physicality at the center of, rather than on the margins of, Trapnel's narrative.

54. Watson's assessment of *The Book of Margery Kempe* intersects with my argument here. He says that "it rewards readers' fidelity with an understanding of Christ as she and her *Book* reveal him, and with the promise of salvation, if they can become, like her, 'qwyk and gredy to hy contemplacyon in God' (253). At least in this respect, the *Book* is more like *Piers Plowman*, in its attempt to absorb the reader into its inner processes by breaking down the distinction between reading and living, than any other Middle English religious work I know" ("Making of *The Book*," 424).

55. Hinds observes that Anna Trapnel "turn[s] to the only language that is *not* subject to . . . carnal fallibility: that is, the undisputed word of God himself, as found in the Bible. This is precisely what happens in this text [i.e., *Report and Plea*], through a process of what we might call 'self-inscripturation': the writing-in of herself, her text and her life to the scriptures. The most straightforward way in which she does this is by applying passages from the scriptures to the circumstances she finds herself in—a well-established and uncontroversial Puritan practice. . . . Secondly, Trapnel makes direct comparisons between herself and her situation with figures and events from the Bible. . . . These comparisons extend even to Christ himself" (Hilary Hinds, "Anna Trapnel, *Anna Trapnel's Report and Plea*," in *A Companion to Early Modern Women's Writing*, ed. Arturo Pacheco and Anita Pacheco [Oxford: Blackwell, 2002], 185–86).

56. For an in-depth consideration of the importance of Mary Magdalene for Margery Kempe, see Catherine Sanok, *Her Life Historical: Exemplarity and Female Saints' Lives in Late Medieval England* (Philadelphia: University of Pennsylvania Press, 2007), 116–44. It is worth noting that Kempe's relationship with Mary Magdalene is complex, including (as does her relationship with St. Birgitta) a sort of competitive aggressiveness as well as identification.

57. Anna Trapnel also connects her experiences to those of—among others—Moses (*Report and Plea*, 2), and Joseph (*Report and Plea*, 27). Prineas observes that Trapnel "cast[s] her persecution as the reenactment of scriptural drama and herself as an unjustly maligned prophet" ("Discourse of Love," 99). Mintz too connects Trapnel's spirituality with drama and performance. She says that Anna Trapnel "consistently figures herself a character in a drama of her own devising. . . . Trapnel consistently joins in the looking at herself, and she also *looks back*; at court, for instance, Trapnel stares at those who gaze on her. . . . In the most fascinating instance of Trapnel's staging of herself, she begins suddenly to construct the courtroom scene as a literal play" ("Specular Self," 5). Wiseman similarly explores Anna Trapnel's relationship to performance and theatricality, saying, "Though clearly elaborately 'theatrical,' Trapnel's visions

and trances are not, of course, subject to discussion within those terms" ("Margaret Cavendish," 102). Speaking of seventeenth-century prophetic texts more generally, Smith argues too for the understanding of prophecy as "dramatic experience" (*Perfection Proclaimed*, 53) in an explicitly theatrical sense. He says, "[T]he idea of visions as dramas which took place on the stage of the prophet's mind is expanded so that the prophet plays a symbolic role in his waking life" (31). Interestingly, as Gail McMurray Gibson has persuasively argued, Margery Kempe's spirituality also has strong connections with the drama of her day (see *The Theater of Devotion: East Anglian Drama and Society in the Late Middle Ages* [Chicago: University of Chicago Press, 1989]).

58. Richey, in "Re-covering Paul," presents extensive evidence from both *Legacy for Saints* and *Anna Trapnel's Report and Plea* for Anna's affiliation with Paul. She says that throughout these texts "Trapnel continues to trace the various details of her life as they are illuminated by Paul's visions, afflictions, incarcerations, miraculously broken fetters, storms at sea, and shipwrecks. In events at once intertextual and highly personal, she recapitulates the narrative of the persecuted church in Acts 16:27 as she experiences it under the oppressive 'Lord Protector' Cromwell. One of the most obvious intertextual parallels occurs when Trapnel refashions Acts 16:24 in her *Report and Plea*. In the biblical account, Paul and Silas are thrown into the 'inner prison,' their 'feet fast in the stocks.' Even when an earthquake occurs and their chains are broken, Paul remains to convert the jailer. The two are legally freed the next morning, but Paul refuses to leave until the authorities who have placed him in prison apologize for violating his rights. Trapnel recapitulates the same series of events as she too is thrown into prison" (205). Richey does not, however, devote attention to Anna's public religious speech being authorized through association with Paul's mandate as a preacher.

59. On Anna Trapnel's justification of "female public speech as it was practiced under the auspices of the house-bound private conventicle" in her exchanges with Justice Lobb, see Gillespie, "Anna Trapnel's Window," 57–58. Prineas claims, "That Trapnel is able in part to circumvent the many obstacles to women's preaching owes much to good timing. . . . Yet I would argue that it is precisely her response to the continuing and even increasing resistance to women's preaching which drives Trapnel's more interesting rhetorical efforts and encourages the development of a distinctive prophetic idiom. For the boundaries between preaching and prophesying were never entirely clear" ("Discourse of Love," 96).

60. On this passage, and on Margery Kempe and the issue of preaching, see Lochrie, *Margery Kempe*, 104–14; see also Carolyn Dinshaw and David Wal-

lace's introduction to the *Cambridge Companion to Medieval Women's Writing*, ed. Carolyn Dinshaw and David Wallace (Cambridge: Cambridge University Press, 2003).

61. Magro makes an observation that illuminates the similarity between Anna's strategic maneuverings and Margery's denial of preaching for lack of a pulpit. She notes, "The status of Trapnel's prophetic spectacles falls into the interstitial territory between public and private. Trapnel's interrogation upon her arrest in Cornwall makes clear that the lack of a strict boundary between public and private in Trapnel's performances is something of a scandal. Justice Lobb accuses Trapnel of knowingly leaving her bedroom door and window open so that she will have an audience for her prophecy. Trapnel replies, she had instructed the maid to keep both locked" ("Spiritual Autobiography," 420).

62. Lochrie, *Margery Kempe*, 113.

63. Smith points out that radical Protestant writings frequently take "the form of prophetic epistles after Paul" (*Perfection Proclaimed*, 53). Prineas observes that in *Anna Trapnel's Report and Plea* Anna's appropriation of language from the Song of Songs and Revelations mobilizes "the biblical discourse of love not only to ground her visions in scriptural authority but also to deflect charges of 'carnal boldness'" ("Discourse of Love," 101).

64. As Sarah Beckwith observes, this sort of complexity is also a feature of Margery Kempe's *Book*, which does not clearly distinguish God's voice and Kempe's in the ways in which mystical texts were expected to do in order to be safely orthodox. She says, "For the mystic voice to underwrite authoritative discourse, the separation and hierarchy of voices has to remain intact; the boundary between her voice and God's must remain solid, hard and clearly delineated. It is this line, this separation of voices which is so confused in the *Book of Margery Kempe*" ("Problems of Authority," 191).

65. Hinds says of this passage, "The word of God is . . . more than just a transparent medium, for it is also seen to render Christ concrete to the reader . . . representing him as material rather than spiritual, and hence able to be internalised and consumed by the reader. . . . Experiencing the truth through the written word means ingesting that truth, incorporating it into the bodily self. . . . [T]he ingestion of Christ through the written word of God will be transformative of the consuming body, and will mark it as sacred rather than profane" (*God's Englishwomen*, 124). Though Hinds does not comment on the Eucharistic dimensions of the passage, her assessment here fits well with my understanding of the transubstantiative, sacramental elements of incarnational textuality. However, Hinds follows the passage quoted above with a statement from Michel de Certeau that (somewhat bizarrely) draws a distinction between corporeal

language like Trapnel's and medieval "spiritual" language: "The life of the body becomes in effect the allegory (the theatre) of spiritual life. . . . A language written in terms of sicknesses, levitations, visions, odors, etc., in other words in corporeal terms, replaces the 'spiritual' vocabulary forged by the medieval tradition" (Michel de Certeau, *The Writing of History*, trans. Tom Conley [New York: Columbia University Press, 1988], 145 n. 34, quoted in Hinds, *God's Englishwomen*, 124). This points to a central difference in my reading of Anna's texts and that of Hinds (not to mention a central difference in my interpretation and Certeau's of what constitutes the vocabulary of "medieval" spiritual language). The "body language" in Anna Trapnel's writing, and the nature of the relationships between bodies and texts, have deep roots in medieval female piety. For medieval women and early modern women alike, the "life of the body" *is* the "theatre of spiritual life," not allegorically but quite materially, in that the life of the body is precisely where spirituality is enacted, is performed. Furthermore, the language in which Anna Trapnel and Margery Kempe both represent their experiences is precisely that of "sicknesses, levitations, visions, odors, etc."

66. Though he is speaking more generally of Puritan thought rather than specifically addressing Anna's writings, Smith's claim that "Church and believer could be identified as different elements of one perfected body" (*Perfection Proclaimed*, 15) seems quite relevant to this dimension of Anna's spirituality.

67. Staley, *Margery Kempe's Dissenting Fictions*, 39.

68. It is worth calling attention to Louise Stewart and Helen Wilcox's observation that the "blend of the personal and political, often considered to be characteristic of feminism, is also fundamental to autobiographical writing, which gives public meaning to that which is primarily held to be a private concern" ("'Why hath this Lady writ her own Life?': Studying Early Female Autobiography," in *Teaching Women: Feminism and English Studies*, ed. Ann Thompson and Helen Wilcox [Manchester: Manchester University Press, 1989], 1).

69. Smith provides an illuminating description of the dissolution of boundaries in seventeenth-century radical Protestantism. He says, "Versions of self were created which moved increasingly towards the merging of the individual with the Godhead, the ultimate claim for perfection. As experience gave way to prophecy, so the distinction between expression and behaviour disappeared. . . . Undoubtedly the language of radical religion was founded upon irrationality in theory and in practice as the difference between the internal and the external, the literal and the figurative, disappeared. Self, church, and Godhead became one" (*Perfection Proclaimed*, 18).

70. Quoted in Beckwith, "Problems of Authority," 192.

71. Beckwith argues that *The Book of Margery Kempe* is persistently dialogic and double voiced; its "riven" subject matter is "both God and herself" (ibid., 180).

72. Staley, *Margery Kempe's Dissenting Fictions*, xii.

73. Richey, "Re-covering Paul," 204.

74. My understanding of the nature of Anna Trapnel's embodied experience, the nature of her subjectivity, and the sociopolitical implications of that subjectivity, differs from Hinds's interpretation. Hinds states that seventeenth-century sectarian writings, including Anna's, "suggest neither the disembodied Cartesian 'individual,' nor the re-embodied 'subject' of recent cultural theory. Instead, the sectarian discursive project turns on the establishment of an *unselved body*—a body commandeered by God, emptied of subjectivity and thus of social meaning, and marked out instead for its capacity to signify spiritually" ("Sectarian Spaces" 102, emphasis in original). Hinds elsewhere makes a similar point in somewhat different language, saying that Trapnel's "insistence on her own readings of her body argues for both the significance and the power to signify of the prophetic body. . . . [T]he transparency of self that Trapnel seeks to secure is not that of a disembodied subject, but, on the contrary, that of an unselved body, commandeered by God, emptied of *social* meaning and marked out instead for *spiritual* meaning" ("Anna Trapnel," 183–84, emphasis in original). While I agree that neither the Cartesian model of the individual nor the model of the self embraced by recent cultural theory adequately describes Anna Trapnel's notion of selfhood, I do not see her body as unselved, emptied of social meaning. Instead, I would contend that for Trapnel social meaning and spiritual meaning cannot readily be separated. I would say her body is filled with social meaning predicated on the openness of her body to the divine and on the availability of her bodily experiences to others. My interpretation of the nature of Anna's selfhood also departs from that of Sue Wiseman. In discussing why humanist feminist scholars have focused more often on Royalist rather than on prophetic women writers, she states, "[T]he prophetic voice is never an 'I,' a unified subject, and therefore is never directly addressing the symbolic order from a marginal (feminine) position . . . ; there is no obvious *woman* standing behind the text to guarantee it as 'woman's writing'" (Sue Wiseman, "Unsilent Instruments and the Devil's Cushions: Authority in Seventeenth-Century Women's Prophetic Discourse," in *New Feminist Discourses: Critical Essays on Theories and Texts*, ed. Isobel Armstrong [London: Routledge, 1992], 189).

75. Ruth Nisse Shklar argues that Margery Kempe's "version of dissent . . . relies . . . on the spiritual gap between the Church and Kempe herself as a literal

embodiment of a devotional ideal. The discrepancies her *Book* accentuates are between an institutional body in chaos and her own body as a site of intercession and grace" ("Cobham's Daughter: *The Book of Margery Kempe* and the Power of Heterodox Thinking," *Modern Language Quarterly* 56.3 [1995]: 279–80). Though she does not make the comparison to the political anxieties spawned by Lollardy in the Lancastrian era, Gillespie's discussion of Henry Jacob's 1605 petition to King James raises issues that sound very similar. Jacob petitioned "for permission to 'assemble together somewhere publicly to the service and worship of God, to use and enjoy peaceably among ourselves alone the whole exercise of Gods worship and of church government.' Jacob petitioned the king again in exile in 1609 for toleration of 'some churches to be gathered by your majesty's special grace in some parts of this kingdom' free from episcopal oversight but subject to 'your subordinate civil magistrates.' However, this 'limited and temporary' notion of the gathered church was soon replaced by a notion of the non-parochial gathered church as 'a true visible church in its own right' when Jacob's congregational theory began to stress the 'kingly office of Christ as the immediate head of each individual congregation.' When the 'kingly office' of Christ was labeled the 'immediate head,' all sorts of traditionally-placed heads in English social hierarchies were bypassed by implication, including that of the king himself although the Separatists denied that they were against the monarchy" ("Anna Trapnel's Window," 53–54). Additionally, in seventeenth-century controversies concerning separatists, as in medieval debates about Lollardy, vernacular translation of the Bible and the potential threat it posed to gender hierarchies were at issue: "Reformers had issued translations of the Bible into vernaculars and encouraged individuals to read and interpret the Bible for themselves rather than to rely on the authority of ecclesiastical interpreters such as priests. Sectarian women oftentimes enjoyed equal access with men through prayer and extended Scriptural literacy to the Bible because many sects considered all of its members to be spiritually 'equal' to one another" (54–55).

76. Gillespie discusses the political anxieties provoked by a wide range of religious dissenters and the connection of these anxieties to fears about threats to gendered power relations. "Church 'independency,'" wrote the author of *Tub-preachers Overturn'd*, was to be 'abandon'd and abhor'd as destructive to the Majesty and Ministry, of the Church and Common-wealth of England' because it brought into existence a whole new group of 'lay illiterate men and women' who 'usurp the Ministry, and Audaciously vent their own hereticall opinions, in their house—(alias Tub)—Preachings.' Decrying the fact that, in the wake of the

Reformation, large numbers of lower- and middle-class men and (even more shockingly) women had begun to separate themselves both on the Continent and in England from official churches, to form alternative 'private conventicles' within such 'secret' spaces as their own home, and themselves to become ministers of the Bible, the author tries to neutralize this subversive new phenomenon" ("Anna Trapnel's Window," 52–53). Such critique sounds very like that made by opponents of Lollardy in the fifteenth century. One famous example appears in Thomas Hoccleve's poem "To Sir John Oldcastle," in which he writes:

> Some wommen eeke, thogh hir wit be thynne,
> Wele argumentes make in holy writ!
> Llewde calates! Sitteth down and spynne,
> And kakele of sumwhat elles, for your wit
> Is al to feeble to despite of it!
> To Clerkes grete apparteneth þat aart
> The knowleche of þat, god hath fro yow shut;
> Stynte and leue of for right sclendre is your paart.
>
> 145–52

Hoccleve's Works, vol. 1, *The Minor Poems,* ed. Frederick J. Furnivall, EETS, e.s., 61 [London: Oxford University Press, 1892], 13.

77. Watson says of Margery Kempe, "[T]he very fact of her arrest in Leicester—once her white clothing and passionate crying before a crucifix had identified her to the authorities in a town she may never have visited before—suggests that this middle-aged mother of fourteen was considered a force to be reckoned with by some of the most powerful people of her day. . . . In these closing months of 1417, and in a society increasingly nervous about dissent . . . Margery Kempe was everywhere treated as a miracle, a scandal, a *cause celèbre*" ("Making of *The Book,*" 396).

78. Margery was not simply suspected of treasonous behavior through her purported involvements with Oldcastle and Lollardy, though. Her embodied piety and her body language also entailed what Paul Strohm calls "treason in the household," a treason that ultimately might have been the more troubling variety of the two (see ch. 6, entitled "Treason in the Household," of his book *Hochon's Arrow: The Social Imagination of Fourteenth-Century Texts* [Princeton: Princeton University Press, 1992], 121–44). Margery's travels without her husband, and the autonomy she obtained when she got her husband's consent to a vow of chastity reveal, as David Aers has shown, her departure from the social ideologies that set the norms of female behavior ("Making of Margery Kempe:

Individual and Community," in David Aers, *Community, Gender, and Individual Identity* [London: Routledge, 1988], 101–2). Such departures constituted a form of rebellion on the microcosmic level with larger, macrocosmic ramifications, ramifications that help illustrate the degree to which the personal or autobiographical is not just a screen for larger social issues but rather the very stuff of social negotiations and power struggles. As Aers argues, Margery "subverts the dominant powers' official version of correct sexual, religious, and social order, a threat to major and interlocking areas of control" (100).

79. Hilary Hinds, introduction to *The Cry of a Stone*, by Anna Trapnel, ed. Hilary Hinds (Tempe: Arizona Center for Medieval and Renaissance Studies, 2000), xvii.

80. Marchamont Needham to the Protector, February 7, 1654, in *Calendar of State Papers: Domestic*, quoted in Hinds, introduction to *Cry of a Stone*, xvii–xviii.

81. Shklar, "Cobham's Daughter," 297. Aers points out that Lollardy essentially serves as a catch-all term for transgressions both social and sexual in nature ("Making of Margery Kempe," 97). Of this interrogation scene, he states, "The extraordinary, violent aggression in this conclusion displays as deep an anxiety about female commitment to the marital household as that shown by the Mayor of Leicester. And a friar had more intimate and general knowledge than most men of the grounds for such anxiety through his confessorial role" (102). Similarly, in the seventeenth century, religious idiosyncrasy and sexual transgression also tend to get lumped together. Magro points out, "Though the Puritan movement was ideologically fractured, there is a good deal of evidence to suggest that the more radical branches it spawned (Quakers, Fifth Monarchists, Baptists, Ranters) were coded as feminine, and, hence, as sexually suspect. This feminine encoding stemmed probably from the large numbers of women actually associated with sectarian activity, but the symbolic power of sexual difference was also recruited by Royalist and republican alike to ridicule what were seen as the excesses of radical Puritans" ("Spiritual Autobiography," 408–9).

82. Longfellow, *Women and Religious Writing*, 166.

83. Magro says of this incident, "Even among many of the more radical elements that were agitating for ecclesiastical, legal, and parliamentary reform, *Ranter* was a byword for sexual promiscuity, gross immorality, bad manners, and, in particular, sexual self-determination for women. The matron's pithy epithet draws together a network of meanings that fix Trapnel's political, class, and sexual identity. . . . The semantic and ideological confusion driving the ma-

tron's designation of Trapnel as a 'Ranting slut' . . . is symptomatic of a more general seventeenth-century anxiety about an alterior feminized Puritan discursivity. In contrast to the masculine authority underpinning the Independents' rational Protestantism (Milton, Cromwell, Ireton), sectarian groups including the Fifth Monarchists and radical cultural collectivities like the Ranters defined themselves through antirationalist practices of prophecy and embodied communicative performance that functioned in opposition to a ratiocinating, masculine Protestantism" ("Spiritual Autobiography," 405).

84. Magro makes a related argument, saying, "The extent to which Trapnel's radical performative politics were taken seriously by Cromwell's government can be judged by its swift and brutal reaction. . . . In order to dilute the potency of Trapnel's political critique, her adversaries recoded and redeployed the political content of her performance as sexual licentiousness. This strategy figured the female religious zealot as a prostitute sprawled on her back" (ibid., 421–22).

85. On Margery's fasting, see, for instance, the way in which Jesus's directives to fast and then not to fast feature in Margery's negotiations with her husband to gain his consent to a vow of chastity. On the ways in which the role of food in Margery's religious practices differs from that of many medieval holy women, see Staley, *Margery Kempe's Dissenting Fictions*, 50–52.

86. On Bessie Poulter's conversion and her profession at the Antwerp Carmel, see *Life*, 133 and 133 n. 91.

87. *The Life of Lady Falkland*, in Wolfe, *Elizabeth Cary*, 133. All subsequent citations to the *Life* are to this edition and are cited parenthetically in the text.

88. The reality of Cary's situation may have been somewhat different from its textual representation in *The Life of Lady Falkland*, since, as Heather Wolfe notes, "Welstead informs HF [Henry Falkland] that 'my Lady keepes a plentifull Table att hir Lodginges in drury Lane' (letter 34)" (133 n. 92).

89. Wolfe, introduction to *Elizabeth Cary*, 74.

90. Dolan, "Reading, Work," 348, 350.

91. Ibid., 350.

92. The way in which the biographer writes about her sister's monastic vocation is revealing. She reports that Elizabeth Cary believed that vocations were "the worke of God," and that consequently "she never went about to incline that daughter to it (whom she had offred to our Blessed Lady, with a promisse to further her being a Nunne" (*Life*, 217). Nevertheless, the daughter biographer perceives the importance of her mother's role in her sister Mary's vocation. She writes, "[B]ut, as it may be our Ladyes accepting her vowe . . . might haue

obtained her daughter the grace of Vocation, so it was certaine that vowe did much in inclining her to consent to it, which, att that time, she would ells have had difficulty enough to haue bene brought to" (217–18).

93. See *Life*, 149–52, especially 151 on Elizabeth Cary's translation of Perron.

94. Wolfe points out that the "House History of the Our Lady of Good Hope, Paris (a monastery founded by Lady Falkland's daughter Anne in November 1651) described Lady Falkland's 'Extraordinary Capacity & Piety' in successfully converting six of her nine surviving children. Her daughter Lucy's death-notice gratefully observed that Lady Falkland 'never ceas'd to implore Heaven for the conversion of her children, being a woman of an extraordinary piety' (letter 125) and Anne's death-notice said of Lady Falkland's conversion, 'how reeal a conuersion it was the effectes sufficiently proue' (letter 137)" (introduction to *Elizabeth Cary*, 7–8).

95. Ibid., 33. For examples of this signature, see letters 78, 89, and 90 in Wolfe, *Elizabeth Cary*.

96. Indeed, it would be fairly surprising if we did, since the Benedictine culture in which Elizabeth's daughter biographer wrote explicitly understood such forms of union to evolve from the distinctive mode of contemplative devotion that they practiced.

97. Wolfe, *Elizabeth Cary*, 294, letter 24, emphasis added. On Elizabeth Cary's conversion to Catholicism as marital infidelity, see Wolfe, introduction to *Elizabeth Cary*, 18–20.

98. Wolfe, introduction to *Elizabeth Cary*, 2.

99. Quoted in ibid., 7.

Chapter 5. The Embodied Presence of the Past

1. Paul Strohm, writing about Edward IV's return to England in 1471 to reclaim the throne from the recently reinstated Henry VI, describes a dynamic similar to the one upon which I focus, pointing out the inseparability of desired and undesirable effects that result from mobilizing history for political ends. Strohm notes that the account of Edward's return in the *Historie of the Arrivall of Edward IV* deliberately connects Edward's landing in England with the return to England of Henry IV after his banishment by Richard; he then observes, "Representational, and ultimately political, capital is to be had from invocation of so influential a precedent. . . . But an adherence to pattern also carries a downside

risk for an imitator who wants to capitalize upon some, but not all, of a pattern's previous implications. Here, the risk for Edward involves the difficulty of establishing a difference between his own reassertion of legitimate sovereign claims and the stark fact of Henry's original usurpation" (*Politique: Language of Statecraft between Chaucer and Shakespeare* [Notre Dame: University of Notre Dame Press, 2005], 24). Strohm continues, "[T]he problem with a recognized pattern, and precedent, rests in the difficulty of using it for some things and not for others. In this case the affirmative and negative elements of Henry's previous pattern will finally turn out to be inextricable" (25).

2. John N. King, *Tudor Royal Iconography: Literature and Art in an Age of Religious Crisis* (Princeton: Princeton University Press, 1989), 216.

3. Polydore Vergil, *Anglica historia* (London: Nichols, 1846), 193; hereafter cited parenthetically in the text.

4. The Yorkist claim through Lionel, Duke of Clarence—an elder son of Edward III than the Lancastrian progenitor John of Gaunt, Duke of Lancaster—depended at two points on succession through women: Lionel's daughter Philippa and his great-granddaughter Anne Mortimer. On these Lancastrian representational strategy, see chapter 5 of Nancy Bradley Warren, *Spiritual Economies: Female Monasticism in Later Medieval England* (Philadelphia: University of Pennsylvania Press, 2001). Henry Tudor's Lancastrian connection came through his mother, Margaret Beaufort, a descendant of John of Gaunt and his third wife, Katherine Swinford. The Tudor claim to Lancastrian descent was further complicated by the fact that Margaret descended from one of John and Katherine's children born prior to their marriage but later made legitimate.

5. Sigmund Freud, *Introductory Lectures on Psycho-Analysis*, ed. and trans. James Strachey (New York: Norton, 1933), 364.

6. *STC* (2nd ed.) 7593, p. A3v; hereafter cited parenthetically in the text. This text, although printed in 1604, is based on one printed only nine days after the events in question entitled *The Quenes maiesties Passage through the Citie of London to Westminster the Day before her coronacion*.

7. For an example of such genealogical propaganda, see the elaborate frontispiece illumination in London, MS BL Royal 15 E VI, depicting Henry VI's claims to the thrones of England and France.

8. Richard Grafton, *Graftons Abridgement of the Chronicles of Englande*, 1570, *STC* (2nd. ed.) 12151, 178v. I include a briefer discussion of the precoronation pageants in chapter 6 of Nancy Bradley Warren, *Women of God and Arms: Female Spirituality and Political Conflict, 1380–1620* (Philadelphia: University of Pennsylvania Press, 2005).

9. Grafton, *Graftons Abridgement,* 178v.

10. On Elizabeth's engagement with medieval female spirituality, especially the cult of the Virgin Mary, see Helen Hackett, *Virgin Mother, Maiden Queen: Elizabeth I and the Cult of the Virgin Mary* (New York: St. Martin's, 1995), and Frances Yates, *Astraea: The Imperial Theme in the Sixteenth Century* (London: Routledge, 1975); see also chapter 6 of Warren, *Women of God and Arms.*

11. R. Doleman (Robert Parsons), *A Conference about the Next Succession to the Crowne of Inglond, 1594,* TEE 481 (Amsterdam: Theatrum Orbis Terrarum; New York: Da Capo, 1972); hereafter cited parenthetically in the text as *Conference,* with all page numbers in citations referring to pt. 2 of this edition (pts. 1 and 2 are numbered separately). Leo Hicks believes Parsons was a contributor to the *Conference* but not its sole author or even its main contributor; see his "Father Robert Persons S.J. and *The Book of Succession,*" *Recusant History* 3 (1957): 126–28. I tend to agree with Victor Houliston's perspective that "although Allen and Englefield, and possibly others, provided material for the book, Parsons compiled and wrote the final version" (Victor Houliston, "The Hare and the Drum: Robert Persons's Writings on the English Succession, 1593–6," *Renaissance Studies* 14.2 [2000]: 237). In addition to the evidence Houliston marshals, Parsons's rehearsal of virtually the same argument about the Lancastrian line as he presents in the *Conference* in his history of Syon, which was produced at the same time as the *Conference,* gives further weight to the case for his authorship. On Parsons's history of Syon and the Lancastrian line, see below.

12. Hicks, "Father Robert Persons," 105; for a detailed description and summary, see 104–6.

13. Parsons declares that "in this king Henry the 6 and his sonne prince Edward, ended all the blood royal male of the house of Lancaster, by Blanch the first wife of Iohn of Gaunt" (44).

14. On Parsons's possible involvement in a plot to kill Elizabeth, see John Bossy, "The Heart of Robert Parsons," in *The Reckoned Expense: Edmund Campion and the Early English Jesuits,* ed. Thomas M. McCoog (Woodbridge: Boydell, 1996), especially 144–50.

15. Quoted in John Nichols, *The Progresses and Public Processions of Queen Elizabeth,* 2nd ed. (London, 1823), 3:232.

16. Ronald Corthell, "Robert Persons and the Writer's Mission," in *Catholicism and Anti-Catholicism in Early Modern English Texts,* ed. Arthur F. Marotti (New York: St. Martin's, 1999), 46.

17. For accounts of Elizabeth's reaction to the work, and Essex's response, see Hicks, "Father Robert Persons," 123. Hicks notes that it may have been

Lord Burghley or his son Sir Robert Cecil who showed a copy of the *Conference* to the queen; as relations between Essex and the Cecils were at this time "very strained," they may have given Elizabeth the book "for the very purpose of causing a rift in the Earl's relations with the Queen" (123).

18. Paul Strohm, *Theory and the Premodern Text* (Minneapolis: University of Minnesota Press, 2000), xii–xiii. Stowe's *Annales* were printed several more times after Elizabeth's reign, but beginning with the first edition after her death, that of 1605, the title page was changed and no longer contained a genealogical component.

19. Parsons writes, "[S]o by this marriage of lady Phillip, to the first king Iohn, these princes of the house of Portugal that liue at this day, do pretende that the inheritance of Lancaster is only in them, by this lady Phillip, for that the succession of her elder brother king Henry the fourth, is expired long ago" (*Conference*, 161).

20. Houliston writes, "The treatise can be said to promote, not simply one candidature, but a certain frame of mind in the reader" ("Hare and the Drum," 242). Drawing on Annabel Patterson's work on Holinshed, he suggests that an application of her version of the concept of "indifference" can be made to Parsons's text. He says that Patterson "argues that indifference is central to the entire Holinshed project: what appears to be shapeless or incoherent in the *Chronicles* derives from a deliberate attempt to allow the reader to confront the past indifferently in all its multivocal diversity and self-contradiction. In an obvious sense this applies to Part Two of the *Book of Succession*, where each claim is allowed to speak for itself" (243).

21. Jean-Christophe Mayer, "'This Papist and His Poet': Shakespeare's Lancastrian Kings and Robert Parsons's *Conference about the Next Succession*," in *Theatre and Religion: Lancastrian Shakespeare*, ed. Richard Dutton, Alison Findlay, and Richard Wilson (Manchester: Manchester University Press, 2003), 123.

22. Philip II ruled Spain from 1556 to 1598; he was ruler of Portugal (as Philip I) from 1580 to 1598. His son succeeded him upon his death, ruling Spain and Portugal (the latter as Philip II) from 1598 to 1621.

23. Cardinal William Allen's interpretation of the *Conference*, outlined in "The opinion and iudgment of C. A. before his deathe concernyng the late printed Booke of the succession of England, and certayne poyntes therunto apperteyning," bolsters the assertion that Parsons's text has a clear pro-Infanta message. It also suggests that this position was not an idiosyncratic one confined to Parsons. The author, Roger Baines (Allen's secretary), who signs himself "Yors euer to command B.S." (Colegio San Albano, Valladolid, Serie II, legajo 12,

document 9, version 3, fol. 10v), declares that "[t]owching . . . the Ladye Infanta of Spaine, the opinion of C. A. was that . . . all thinges consydered . . . he did see no other person in the worlde so fytt to accommodate all matters and to end all controuersyes to breake all difficulties and to avoyde all dangers on euery syde, as yf this Ladye should be agreed on of all handes to haue hir tytle preferred & established" (5r–5v). On the authorship of this text, see Hicks, "Father Robert Persons," 128, and Houliston, "Hare and the Drum," 237, 237 n. 9.

24. In asserting Lancastrian superiority to the Yorkists, Parsons says, "Moreouer it is alleaged for Henry that his title came by a man, and the others by a woman, which is not so much fauoured either by nature law or reason" (*Conference,* 75). However, as he notes in an earlier passage, upon the death of Henry VI and Prince Edward, "[T]he inheritance of the said lady Blanch returned by right of succession . . . vnto the heyres of lady Phillip her eldest daughter, married into Portugal, whose nephew named Alfonsus the fift kinge of Portugal liued at that day when king Henry the 6 and his heyre were made away" (44). To accomplish the necessary but daunting representational tasks before him in legitimating a female successor whose claim depends on descent through the female line, Parsons spends some time explaining that the French prohibition of succession through the female line does not apply in England, where Salic Law has never been in force. Cardinal William Allen reinforces this point regarding Salic Law. In "The opinion and iudgment," Baines reports that, in Allen's view, "England . . . regardeth no law Salique as all the worlde knoweth" (5r). But given Parsons's denigration of the English Yorkist claim as a lesser one since it relies on the female line, this argument about Salic Law is not entirely persuasive.

25. See, for instance, the elaborate genealogical frontispiece in MS Royal 15 EVI; for an insightful discussion of this image, see Michel-André Bossy, "Arms and the Bride: Christine de Pizan's Military Treatise as a Wedding Gift for Margaret of Anjou," in *Christine de Pizan and the Categories of Difference,* ed. Marilynn Desmond (Minneapolis: University of Minnesota Press, 1998), 236–56.

26. For Birgitta's revelation regarding England's right to rule France, see *Liber celestis,* book 4, chapters 104–5 (*The Liber celestis of St. Bridget of Sweden,* ed. Roger Ellis, EETS, o.s., 291 [Oxford: Oxford University Press, 1987]). See also André Vauchez, "St. Birgitta's Revelations in France at the End of the Middle Ages," in *Santa Brigida profeta dei tempi nuove / Saint Bridget Prophetess of New Ages* (Rome: Casa Generalizia Suore Santa Brigida, 1991), 180–81. I discuss St. Birgitta's importance for Lancastrian political strategies at greater length in chapter 5 of Warren, *Spiritual Economies.* For instances of the importance of Mary's maternal transmission of salvation in Brigittine divine service,

see John Henry Blunt, *The Myroure of Our Ladye,* EETS, e.s., 19 (London: Kegan Paul, 1873), 104, 141, 194.

27. See Robert Parsons's "Preface to the History of the Wanderings of Syon," excerpts of which are included in *The Story of the English Bridgettines of Syon Abbey,* ed. John Rory Fletcher (Devon: Syon Abbey, 1933).

28. Quoted in Adam Hamilton, *The Angel of Syon: The Life and Martyrdom of Blessed Richard Reynolds, Martyred at Tyburn, May 4, 1535* (Edinburgh: Sands, 1905), 97–98.

29. Quoted in ibid., 111.

30. The description of Edward IV as Syon's "second founder" comes from Arthur Jeffries Collins, *The Bridgetting Breviary of Syon Abbey, from the ms. with English Rubrics F.4.11 at Magdalene College, Cambridge* (London: Hendy Bradshaw Society, 1969), iv n. 5.

31. Hamilton, *Angel of Syon,* 111.

32. David Loades, introduction to *John Foxe and the English Reformation,* ed. David Loades (Aldershot: Scolar Press, 1997), 1–2.

33. As Loades observes, "In 1563 the tone had been optimistic, even triumphalist. The forces of Antichrist, represented in England by Mary, Pole, and Gardiner, had been routed. The Church had endured a fiery purgation, and emerged with its vocation tested and its credentials established for the task with which God now confronted it. The purpose was immediate: to cast as much discredit as possible upon the preceding regime, and to persuade the queen to press on with the godly labour which she had undertaken. By 1570 the agenda was different. The triumphalism had disappeared, to be replaced by a gnawing anxiety that the Roman enemy had not been finally defeated, after all. . . . There seemed to be a real possibility that the Reformation might be defeated. . . . By 1583 these anxieties had receded again to some extent" (ibid., 4–5).

34. As John King has argued, the material composition of the edition makes it possible to see Foxe's response to current political developments. King points out that "[m]any disruptions in collation" of the 1570 edition "demonstrate that Foxe continued to work under pressure and to provide unstable copy to which he frequently added new material, thus forcing pressmen to insert unplanned signatures" (*Foxe's Book of Martyrs and Early Modern Print Culture* [Cambridge: Cambridge University Press, 2006], 117).

35. Ibid., 113.

36. Ibid., 113–14.

37. Ibid., 217.

38. Ibid., 115.

39. Ibid., 223.

40. Unless otherwise noted, all quotations from the *Acts and Monuments* are from the online version of the 1570 edition at www.hrionline.ac.uk/johnfoxe/ and are hereafter cited parenthetically in the text; I give page numbers according to the corrected pagination in the online edition.

41. King, *Foxe's Book of Martyrs*, 250.

42. Ibid., 251.

43. Translation quoted from ibid., 248.

44. The quoted phrase is King's, *Foxe's Book of Martyrs*, 257.

45. Ibid., 117.

46. Margaret Aston and Elizabeth Ingram, "The Iconography of the *Acts and Monuments*," in Loades, *John Foxe*, 100.

47. "Documents Relating to Nuño da Silva's Trial by the Inquisition," in *New Light on Drake: A Collection of Documents Relating to His Voyage of Circumnavigation 1577–1580*, ed. and trans. Zelia Nuttall, Works Issued by the Hakluyt Society, n.s., 34 (London: Hakluyt Society, 1914), 352–53.

48. Ibid., 354.

49. Ibid., 356–57.

50. Ibid., 357.

51. The deposition includes the following as a preface to Rengifo's report of Drake's speech about Elizabeth: "Conjecturing from what the witness understood and from his tone and mein, it seemed to him that Francis Drake did not think rightly about all this" (ibid.).

52. King, *Foxe's Book of Martyrs*, 116.

53. Ibid.

54. "Petition a La Altissima Señora Prinçesa de Walia," in *Syon Abbey: The Library of the Bridgettine Nuns and Their Peregrinations after the Reformation*, ed. John Martin Robinson and Christopher de Hamel (London: Roxburghe Club, 1991); hereafter cited parenthetically in the text. I quote both the Spanish text and the English translation from this edition. I discuss the "Petition," including the passages mentioned here, in greater detail in chapter 6 of Warren, *Women of God and Arms*.

55. The abbess and nuns also invoke the biblical lives of Esther and Mordecai. Calling the Infanta their Queen Esther ("nuestra Reyna Hester" ["Petition," 13]), they say that "mas que todas otras religiosas Inglezas podemos con el devoto Mardocheo dizir (quien sabe) porque nuestro caso siendo singular, y no solamenta começado con los primeros desterrados por nuestra sancta fee catholica Sino Tambien estando nosotras solas de todas las ordenes y monasterios de Religiosas ynglezas que continuaron, y perseveraron en este dicho

durissimo destierro desde su primero comensamiento hasta aora" ("Petition," 13) [more than all other English religious Sisters we are able to say with the devout Mordecai *who knoweth*, because our case is unique, since not only were we the first exiles for our Holy Catholic Faith, but also the only ones, of all the orders and convents of English nuns, who have continued and persevered in this very hard exile from its first inception until now] ("Petition," 25).

56. Cristina Malcolmson, "'As Tame as the Ladies': Politics and Gender in *The Changeling*," *English Literary Renaissance* 20.2 (1990): 333.

57. Ibid., 333–34.

58. Thomas Robinson, *The Anatomie of the English nunnery at Lisbon in Portugall Dissected and laid open by one that was sometime a younger brother of the conuent* (London, 1622), *STC* (2nd ed.) 21124; hereafter cited parenthetically in the text. A much briefer discussion of *The Anatomie* and the Spanish Marriage appears in chapter 6 of Warren, *Women of God and Arms*.

59 The petition dates "to the early 1620s, probably to the year 1623" (John Martin Robinson, introduction to J. Robinson and Hamel, *Syon Abbey*, 3).

60. Thomas Robinson asserts that he "did chance to make a hole in a hollow place in a wall . . . out of which hole I pulled sundry bones of some dead children, and left many more remaining behind" (27; italics indicate expansion).

61. Margery Kempe, *The Book of Margery Kempe*, ed. Sanford B. Meech and Hope Emily Allen, EETS, o.s., 212 (London: EETS, 1940), 112.

62 Quoted in Malcolmson, "'As Tame as the Ladies,'" 334, emphasis in original.

63. Thomas Goad, *The Friers Chronicle, or the Trve Legend of Priests and Monkes Lives* (London, 1623), *STC* (2nd ed.) 11510, B1v; hereafter cited parenthetically in the text.

64. The *Oxford English Dictionary* explains that *legend* derives from the Latin *legenda*, meaning "what is read." The earliest sense given for *legend* is "the story of the life of a saint," a meaning first used in 1375. The sense of a legend as "a story, history, or account" emerges in 1385, and that of "a book of readings or 'lessons' for use at divine service, containing passages from Scriptures and the lives of the saints" appears in 1440. The sense of "an inauthentic or nonhistorical story" was current, though recent, when Goad wrote his text; it first appeared in 1613 (http://dictionary.oed.com, accessed November 30, 2009).

65. Victor Slater, "Cavendish, Christian, Countess of Devonshire (1595–1675)," in *The Oxford Dictionary of National Biography*, ed. H. C. G. Matthey and Brian Harrison (Oxford: Oxford University Press, 2004), www.oxforddnb.com/view/article/4929.

66. The anonymous broadside is entitled "An Elegy on the Truly Honourable, and Most Virtuous, Charitable, and Pious Lady, Countesse of Devonshire, Who lately Departed this Life, being a hundred and odd Years of Age, whose Corps now Lies in Deserved State in *Holbourn*" (London, 1675).

67. John Fielde, *A Caueat for Parsons Howlet . . .* (London, 1581), *STC* (2nd ed.) 10844, 20.

68. William Guild, *Anti-Christ pointed and painted out . . .* (Aberdeen, 1655), Wing (2nd ed.) G2203, 162, . Walter Pope, "The Catholick Ballad: or an Invitation to Popery on Considerable Grounds and Reasons" (London, 1674), Wing (2nd ed.) P2906.

69. John Oldham, *The Works of Mr. John Oldham, together with his Remains* (London, 1684), Wing (2nd ed.) O225.

70. Edward Fowler, *A Friendly Conference between a Minister and a Parishioner of his, Inclining to Quakerism* (London, 1676), 103, Wing (2nd ed.) F1706.

71. Thomas Pomfret, *The Life of the Right Honourable and Religious Lady Christian Late Countess Dowager of Devonshire* (London, 1685), Wing (2nd ed.) P2799, 62; hereafter cited parenthetically in the text.

72. Christopher Hibbert, *Cavaliers and Roundheads: The English Civil War, 1642–1649* (New York: Scribners, 1993), 11.

73. Marguerite Tjader Harris, ed., and Albert Ryle Kezel, trans., *Birgitta of Sweden: Life and Selected Revelations* (New York: Paulist Press, 1990), 72.

74. Ibid., 73–74.

75. In 1678, Titus Oates swore under oath that there was a French, Catholic plot to kill Charles II and his Protestant allies in order to install a Catholic government. This purported plot, unlike some in Elizabeth I's day, was a fabrication, but it resulted in a new wave of arrests and persecutions of Catholics and in the promulgation of a second Test Act, requiring members of the House of Commons to swear an oath of allegiance recognizing the monarch as Head of the Church of England and to receive Protestant communion. Under this act, unlike the first Test Act, however, James, Duke of York, was exempted.

76. Mayer, "'This Papist and His Poet,'" 127.

77. Robert Parsons, *Severall Speeches Delivered at a Conference concerning the Power of Parliament, to proceed against their King for Misgovernment* (London, 1648), *STC* (2nd ed.) P573, 20.

Index

Syon Abbey, 22, 25–28, 63, 117, 127,
135, 136, 143, 151, 188, 194, 213,
233, 245n.1, 246n.8, 251n.34,
290n.58, 318n.11; in exile, 14,
102–15, 119, 130, 139–40,
210–11, 221–30, 283n.16,
291n.66, 322n.55. *See also*
Champney, Marie; *Orcherd of
Syon, The*; Parsons, Robert:
history of Syon; *Relacion*;
Robinson, Thomas: *Anatomie
of the English Nunnery at Lisbon
in Portugal*; *Rewyll of Seynt
Sauioure*; Sanders, Elizabeth;
Stapleton, Ann

Teresa of Avila, St., 2, 3, 4, 14, 42,
101, 242n.16, 281n.10
Thomas, St., 110, 255n.47
Trapnel, Anna, 10, 15–16, 147–83,
185, 186, 187, 188, 189, 191–92,
193, 216, 225, 289n.51, 296n.10,
297nn.12–13, 298n.15,
300n.19, 302n.26, 303n.31,
304n.33, 305n.39, 306n.53,
307n.57, 308nn.58–59,
309n.61, 309n.65, 310n.66,
311n.74, 314n.83, 315n.84;
Bodleian S1.42. Th., 158, 168,
171–72, 176, 296n.10, 297n.13,
297n.15; *Cry of a Stone*, 16, 150,
161, 162, 168–71, 176–77, 180,
296n.10, 301n.22; *A Legacy
for Saints*, 150, 157, 161–62,
303n.28, 303n.32; *Report and
Plea*, 16, 150, 157–58, 161–66,
173–75, 176, 181–83, 299n.18,
304n.37, 305n.41, 307n.55,
307n.57, 308n.58, 309n.63

treason. *See* sedition
Tree of Jesse, 199, 205
Trinity, 35–36, 73, 88, 149, 155–56,
249n.23, 250n.31
Tudor, Henry. *See* Henry VII (king of
England)
Tudor, Mary. *See* Mary I (queen of
England)

Uhlman, Diana, 297n.13

Valladolid, 285n.32, 286n.34,
290n.58, 291n.66, 295n.106
Vergil, Polydore, 195–97, 204
Virgin Mary, 7, 27, 28, 30–31, 32,
52, 103, 105, 108, 119–22, 128,
135–36, 143–45, 174, 188–89,
201, 223–24, 229–30, 248n.20,
277n.83, 286n.34, 287n.42,
315n.92; Annunciation, 25, 40,
252n.39; Assumption of, 144,
232; compassion of, 36, 38–39,
57, 112, 167–69, 248n.20,
249n.23, 264n.13; dowry of, 121,
144, 232, 295n.106; Immaculate
Conception of, 232, 287n.41;
maternal labor of, 25–26, 47,
56–57, 136, 159, 167–69, 171,
210, 248nn.21–22, 261n.70
vita Christi, 43, 67, 70, 84, 105, 111,
112–14, 127–29, 158–69, 172,
179–80, 183, 255n.48

Wake, Margaret. *See* Mary Margaret
of the Angels
Waldegrave, Edward, 134
Walker, Claire, 64, 141, 142, 265n.16,
276n.79, 282n.13, 294n.99,
294n.102, 295n.106

Nancy Bradley Warren

is professor of English at Florida State University. She is the author
of *Women of God and Arms: Female Spirituality and Political Conflict,
1380–1600* and *Spiritual Economies: Female Monasticism in Later
Medieval England.*